Doral Publishing's

HANDS-ON DOG CARE

The complete book of canine first aid

By Sue M. Copeland and
John A. Hamil, DVM

How-to photography by Kevin McGowan
Cover photo by Gloria Kerr

· At-A-Glance Phone Numbers ·

Veterinarian _____

Back-up Veterinarian _____

Closest Emergency Center _____

_____

ASPCA National Animal Poison Control Center:

(900) 680-0000; (888) 426-4435

Copyright © 2000 Doral Publishing, Inc.
10451 Palmeras Dr., Suite 225 West
Sun City, Arizona 85373
800-633-5385

Printed in the U.S.A.

Authors: Sue M. Copeland and John A. Hamil, DVM
Editor: Noreen Cartwright
Art Director: Lauryl Suire Eddlemon
Photographers: How-to photography, Kevin McGowan; cover photo, Gloria Kerr

Distributed by National Book Network

Printed on American paper by Patterson Printing

ISBN: 0-944-875-68-8

Library of Congress Cataloging-in-Publication Data
(Provided by Quality Books, Inc.)

Copeland, Sue M.
    Hands-on dog care : the complete book of canine first aid /
Sue M. Copeland and John Hamil , illustrator Lauryl Eddlemon. -- 1st ed.
    p. cm
    Includes bibliographical references and index.
    LCCN: 00-100196
    ISBN: 0-944-875-68-8

    1. Dogs--Wounds and injuries--Treatment.
2. Dogs--Diseases--Treatment. 3. Veterinary emergencies.
4. First aid for animals.
I. Hamil, John.   II. Eddlemon, Lauryl.   III. Title.

SF991.C67 2000   636.7'08960252
            QB100-238

To my dogs, Jasmine, MacGilla, and Boomer, the
hands-on stewardship of whom provided the inspiration
for this book. And to my husband, Rick, for
his endless support and patience.

—Sue M. Copeland

Acknowledgements

A special thanks to Karen E.N. Hayes, DVM, MS, author of our sister
publication, HORSE & RIDER'S HANDS-ON HORSE CARE (created and
edited by Sue M. Copeland). Portions of this book were adapted from that one.

To obtain a copy of HANDS-ON HORSE CARE (1997, Horse & Rider, Inc.,
400 pages, $29.95), call 1-800-952-5813 (order #ZB28)
or visit your local book retailer.

THANKS ALSO TO:
• Julie Beaulieu, for her invaluable help in coordinating the direct marketing of this book
through the PRIMEDIA Special Interest Publications *Horse & Rider, Practical Horseman,*
EQUUS, and Dressage Today.
• Lauryl Suire Eddlemon, art director of this book and its sister publication, *HORSE &*
RIDER'S HANDS-ON HORSE CARE, for her talent, speed, and professionalism.
• Kevin McGowan, master photographer, for being so generous with his time, studio, and talent. The book wouldn't look the same without him.
• Susan Hamil, wife of Dr. John A. Hamil, for her patience with this project.
• Chris George, and her Corgis Lucky and Daisy; and Marcia Long and her Briard Chance,
and Cairn Terriers Fiona and Doogie, for spending the day in the photography studio. We
couldn't have asked for better canine models than those Chris and Marcia provided.
• Betsey Strohl, of Zia Golden Retrievers, for her "you've got to do this!"
support, and for introducing us to Gloria Kerr, photographer of our dynamic cover photo.
• Jasmine, 14-year-old Rottie and model in many of the how-to photos, for her endless
patience and cooperation, and unique ability to portray an injured/ill dog.
• Mitsuko Williams, veterinary medicine librarian and associate professor of library administration, the University of Illinois, for digging into her slide collection and providing the toxic
plant photo on page 349.
• Dennis Paulson, of the Slater Museum of Natural History, University of Puget Sound,
Washington, for the menacing Western Rattlesnake photo on page 343.

Table of Contents

SECTION II: HANDS-ON DOGKEEPING SKILLS

SECTION III: REFERENCE INFORMATION

NOTICE TO READERS
This book provides useful instructions, but we can't anticipate all of your working conditions or the characteristics of your dog, or his injury/illness. For safety, you should use caution, care, and good judgment when following the procedures described in this book. Consider your own skill level and the instructions and safety precautions provided. Neither the authors nor the publisher can assume responsibility for any injury to persons or dogs as a result of misuse of the information provided. Consult your veterinarian whenever you have a question about the care of your dog.

Foreward

You love your dog and want to provide him with the best possible care. *Hands-On Dog Care* was crafted to help you reach that goal. It's specifically designed to provide you with knowledge and information that can help you quickly identify a problem in your dog so you can work closely with your veterinarian to resolve it. Your ability to do so not only will benefit your pet, but also will benefit you and your veterinarian. Potentially dangerous signs you spot will get prompt and proper attention, giving your pet his best chance at a quick, seamless recovery.

Recognizing and understanding what's normal for your dog is a key part of being able to identify abnormal situations. This book will help you get a basic understanding of normal canine physiology and behavior, so you can clearly communicate with your vet should something appear to be amiss. Preventive care is also key. You'll find tips for maximizing your dog's health and wellbeing to help keep potential problems at bay. The payoff? You'll not only be doing right by your canine buddy, but could also save money on vet bills.

So think of *Hands-On Dog Care* as a valuable tool with which you can help craft a long, healthy life for your dog. After all, as dog lovers, we all share that common goal.

Sue M. Copeland and John A. Hamil, DVM

Sue M. Copeland

An award-winning journalist in the equine field, Sue is a life-long dog owner who turned her attention to canine care after the success of HANDS-ON DOG CARE'S sister publication, HORSE & RIDER'S HANDS-ON HORSE CARE. "All of my horse friends are also dog people," Sue explains. "They said to me, 'We need a dog care book like this!'" The horse care book, which she created and edited, won the American Horse Publication's Best Equine-Related Book honors in 1998. Sue was editor of *Horse & Rider* Magazine, a PRIMEDIA publication, for 11 years. There, she garnered numerous writing and editing awards, including the AHP's coveted General Excellence award. In 1999, Sue stepped back from the editorship to pursue book projects. She remains a contributing editor to the magazine, and shows hunter/jumpers in her spare time. Sue plans to someday try her hand in the canine obedience ring. She and her husband, Rick, share their Richmond, Texas farm with three Rottweilers, three cats, and five horses.

John A. Hamil, DVM

A graduate of Oklahoma State University's veterinary school, Dr. Hamil tends to his popular small-animal practice at Canyon Animal Hospital in Laguna Beach, California, while remaining active in animal welfare concerns. These include the American Veterinary Medical Association's Animal Welfare Committee, the California Counsel of Companion Animal Advocates, and the National Council on Pet Population Study and Policy. Dr. Hamil is a past president of the California Veterinary Medical Association. His commitment to his practice and to animal welfare in general earned him the 1999 AAHA's Practitioner of the Year honors for the Western region. His wife, Susan, is a top breeder of Bloodhounds, with numerous national titles to her credit. Their dogs have also appeared in national television shows and commercials, including a Pedigree dog food ad featuring Dr. Hamil. The couple has three sons.

How To Use This Book

Hands-On Dog Care is like having a veterinarian on call in your home—someone who can ask you the right questions and give you an action plan based on your answers. Having that kind of help at your fingertips provides a three-fold benefit: Your dog will get the best care possible; you'll save on worry and expense; and your vet can provide your dog with the prompt, proper treatment he deserves (and will have fewer after-hour calls!).

This book is organized into three sections:

1 In **ACTION PLANS**, you'll find most of the signs of illness or injury that your dog might exhibit in his adult life. Each is listed as you'd describe it: If your dog has a bloody nose, simply look up *Bloody Nose* in the Table of Contents. (All signs are also listed in our Index.) Turn to the appropriate page, and you'll be asked a series of yes-and-no questions, each pointing to an action plan. You'll be told whether to call your veterinarian, when, and any first aid you'll need to administer before leaving for the clinic. If veterinary attention isn't needed, you'll be given clear, concise instructions for at-home treatment.

2 Use **HANDS-ON DOGKEEPING SKILLS** as a step-by-step, photographic guide to the treatments recommended in Section 1. Do you need to rinse your dog's eye, clean his ears, trim his toenails, or bandage a foot? You'll find the how-to instructions here. You'll also find valuable preventive tips in this section, such as diet guidelines, vaccination information, a guide to toxic substances in your home, and a chart outlining normal dog behavior, so you'll know immediately if something is amiss.

3 The **GLOSSARY** section is your personal, quick-reference guide to veterinary terms you might hear at your vet's, or see in this book. You'll see any Glossary terms in our text marked (G) accordingly. When you see that notation, simply turn to this section for a clear definition of the condition or procedure.

Note: Each section is cross-referenced in the other two sections, using page numbers or the Glossary (G) notation to provide you with flip-to-it-ease.

SECTION I

FIRST-AID
ACTION PLANS

CHAPTER 1

Problems of

THE SKIN AND HAIRCOAT

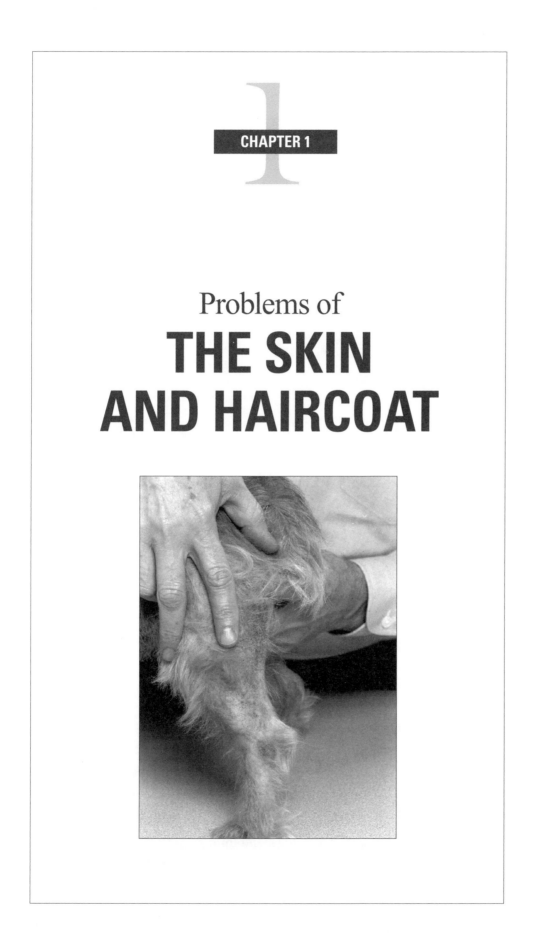

Dull, dry
HAIRCOAT

What you see: Your dog's coat looks dull and dry, despite your grooming efforts.

What this might mean: It can be a signpost of a serious underlying problem.

ACTION PLAN:

Is your dog overweight, inactive, sensitive to cold temperatures, and/or is the skin on his abdomen darker than normal?

 YES Call your veterinarian *TODAY* if you answered yes to any of these queries—your dog might be hypothyroid[G].

NO

Is your dog thin, pot-bellied, and/or does he have diarrhea?

 YES Call your veterinarian *TODAY* if you answered yes to any of these queries—it could be malnutrition due to a dietary imbalance or internal parasites.

NO

Is your dog lethargic and less hungry than usual? Is he feverish?

 YES Call your veterinarian *TODAY* if you answered yes to either query—it could be due to a systemic problem, such as cancer[G], or an infectious condition.

NO

Is your dog's coat thin? Is his skin red and itchy?

 YES It could be external parasites and/or an allergy. Go to **page 19**.

NO

Call your veterinarian for an appointment.

Fast Fact...

If your dog has a dull haircoat, but is otherwise healthy, consider adding fatty acids to his ration to add luster to his coat. Essential fatty acids are necessary for normal oil-gland function, which can improve the health and appearance of the skin and hair. Commercial products such as Lipiderm, Linatone, and others are available at pet stores, through pet-supply catalogs, and through your veterinarian. Consult your vet about what he or she might recommend for your dog.

What you see: Hair is missing from your dog's coat, in a single location, in broad patches, or in a symmetrical pattern. On closer inspection, individual hairs may or may not be broken off, and the skin in the hairless area may or may not appear irritated.

What this might mean: A cosmetic problem, at the least. It also can indicate a serious underlying problem.

LOSS OF HAIR

ACTION PLAN:

Is your dog suddenly scratching or chewing at his skin to the point of injuring it? **YES** Go to **page 19**.

NO

Is the loss on a front or rear leg, associated with chronic chewing? **YES** Go to **page 19**.

NO

Is the hair loss in an area where his skin has been damaged previously, such as over a healed flesh wound? **YES** It's likely to be a permanent scar-related hair loss called cicatricial alopecia^G. Call your veterinarian for advice.

NO

Is the hairless area flaky or scaly? **YES** Go to **page 17**.

NO

Does your dog have a thin, dull, dry coat? **YES** Go to **page 14**.

NO

Is his hair coming out in tufts, with a crust or scab at the base of each tuft? Is it coming out in circular spots of various sizes? Do the hairs appear to be broken? **YES** Go to **page 17**.

NO

Is your dog losing hair equally on both sides of his body? **YES** Call your veterinarian *TODAY*—it could be a hormonal problem such as Cushing's disease^G, Sertoli cell tumor^G, or an ovarian imbalance.

NO

Is he a young dog with patchy hair loss on his face and/or front legs? **YES** Call your veterinarian *TODAY*—it could be demodectic mange^G.

NO

➤

YOUR VET MAY NEED TO:

- **Submit skin scrapings or a biopsy to a laboratory for definitive diagnosis.**
- **Get fungal or bacterial cultures.**
- **Perform blood-work to check for hormonal conditions.**

ACTION PLAN (CONTINUED):

Is your dog a dilute color mutation, such as the blue fawn typically found in Dobermans and Great Danes?

 YES Call your veterinarian *TODAY*—it could be a genetic mutation that will require a lifetime of management.

 NO

Is your dog a Dachshund? Does he have increased pigmentation in his flanks and "armpits"?

 YES Call your veterinarian *TODAY*—it could be acanthosis nigricans[G], a disease specific to this breed.

 NO

Does your Dachshund have hair loss on his ears?

 YES Call your veterinarian *TODAY*—it could be a breed-specific problem, such as ear-margin seborrhea[G].

FACTOID

If portions of your dog's formerly dark skin begin to develop pink spots (vitiligo[G]), it could mean a loss of pigmentation following deep injury, such as a wound or burn, or a surgical procedure such as cryosurgery[G]. Loss of pigment on the nose has been associated with plastic food and water dishes, and is known as plastic-dish dermatitis[G], a form of contact dermatitis[G].

What you feel/see: When you touch your dog's skin, you feel scabs and crust. When you brush his coat, dandruff emerges.

What this might mean: It can indicate a minor skin condition, or it could be a sign of a serious underlying problem.

Flaky, crusty, or
SCALY SKIN

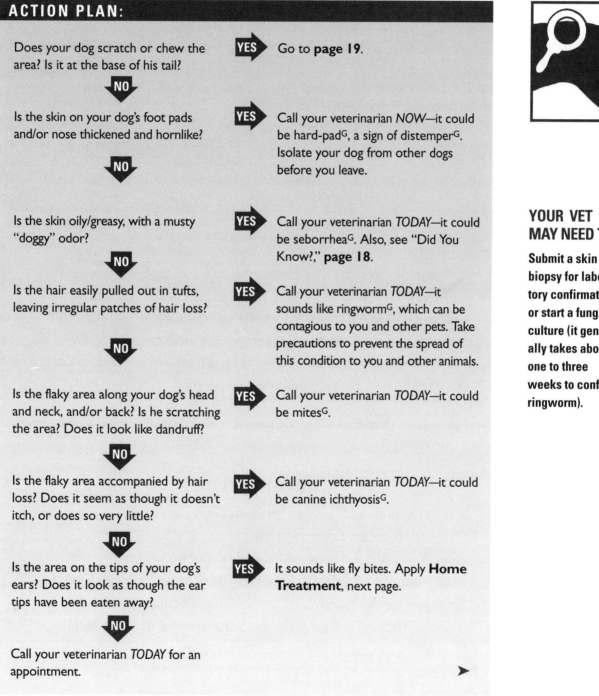

ACTION PLAN:

Does your dog scratch or chew the area? Is it at the base of his tail? **YES** → Go to **page 19**.

NO ↓

Is the skin on your dog's foot pads and/or nose thickened and hornlike? **YES** → Call your veterinarian *NOW*—it could be hard-pad^G, a sign of distemper^G. Isolate your dog from other dogs before you leave.

NO ↓

Is the skin oily/greasy, with a musty "doggy" odor? **YES** → Call your veterinarian *TODAY*—it could be seborrhea^G. Also, see "Did You Know?," **page 18**.

NO ↓

Is the hair easily pulled out in tufts, leaving irregular patches of hair loss? **YES** → Call your veterinarian *TODAY*—it sounds like ringworm^G, which can be contagious to you and other pets. Take precautions to prevent the spread of this condition to you and other animals.

NO ↓

Is the flaky area along your dog's head and neck, and/or back? Is he scratching the area? Does it look like dandruff? **YES** → Call your veterinarian *TODAY*—it could be mites^G.

NO ↓

Is the flaky area accompanied by hair loss? Does it seem as though it doesn't itch, or does so very little? **YES** → Call your veterinarian *TODAY*—it could be canine ichthyosis^G.

NO ↓

Is the area on the tips of your dog's ears? Does it look as though the ear tips have been eaten away? **YES** → It sounds like fly bites. Apply **Home Treatment**, next page.

NO ↓

Call your veterinarian *TODAY* for an appointment. ➤

YOUR VET MAY NEED TO:

Submit a skin biopsy for laboratory confirmation, or start a fungal culture (it generally takes about one to three weeks to confirm ringworm).

HOME TREATMENT:

*(See **Action Plan** to determine whether home treatment is appropriate for your dog's skin condition. If at any time during home treatment, your answers on the action plan change for the worse, call your vet.)*

Step 1. *Soften and loosen scabs.* Apply a medicated scab softener (see page 306) generously to your dog's ear tips. Leave on for an hour, or until scabs are easily removed.

Step 2. *Clean the area.* Use a square gauze pad and homemade saline solution (see page 306) to remove softened scabs and grunge from ear tips.

Step 3. *Apply fly-repelling wound ointment.* Generously apply a layer of a wound ointment that repels flies, such as Onex (by Happy Jack), Flys-Off (by Farnam), or Swat (an equine fly-repellent wound ointment). These products are available through pet stores, feed stores, or through pet-supply catalogs.

Step 4. *Keep it up.* Repeat Steps 1 through 3 daily for seven days, or until lesions are healed. Continue with Step 3 until biting insect season ends in your region.

Step 5. *Control the environment.* Clean your yard frequently, secure trash-can lids, and use dog- and people-safe fly baits to control fly populations. See "Caution," below.

CAUTION

Some fly baits, such as Golden Malrin, can be toxic to pets. If you use such baits, be sure to keep them out of the reach of pets and children. Or, opt for a safer option, such as bag-type fly traps (available in commercial forms such as Trap 'n Toss, Big Stinky, and Fly Terminator). These are effective fly killers, yet can be placed out of the reach of pets and people.

Did You Know...

...seborrhea^G should be taken seriously. This skin condition normally is secondary to an underlying problem, such as mites^G, allergies, hormonal conditions, or ringworm^G.
If your dog is suffering from seborrhea, bathe him with a tar shampoo such as Sebalyt, T-Lux tar/sulfur shampoo, or Sebolux, to remove irritating sebum^G and soothe inflamed skin. After bathing, apply a topical anti-seborrheac product such as LyTar Spray.

What you see: Your dog is repeatedly chewing and scratching.

What this might mean: Although unlikely to be a life-threatening problem, the itch can be intense, and in an effort to relieve it your dog can damage his hair-coat, skin, and structures near the itchy spots (eyes, for example, or joints). If the itchiness is a sign of a contagious skin problem, there's a danger the condition will spread to other pets—or to people.

SCRATCHING/ CHEWING SKIN

ACTION PLAN:

Are there distinct, smooth bumps that look like hives or welts, with unbroken skin, particularly following a vaccination or bee sting? Is your dog acting anxious, breathing rapidly, or wheezing? **YES** 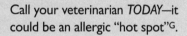 Call your veterinarian *NOW* if you answered yes to either query—it could be a severe allergic reaction called anaphylaxis^G. Go to **page 25**.

 NO

Does he have sudden-onset chewing/ itching, to the point of injuring his skin? **YES** Call your veterinarian *TODAY*—it could be an allergic "hot spot"^G.

 NO

Is your dog chewing or rubbing primarily at the base of his tail? Do you see fleas? **YES** Call your veterinarian *TODAY*—it could be a flea-bite dermatitis^G or an anal sac infection^G. For fleas, also see **Home Treatment Steps 1** and **2**.

 NO

Is he rubbing his face or chewing at his flanks and feet? **YES** Call your veterinarian *TODAY*—it could be atopic allergy^G.

 NO

Is your male dog chewing his scrotum? Is the skin there red, weepy, and raw? **YES** Call your veterinarian *TODAY*—it could be scrotal dermatitis^G.

 NO

Is there patchy hair loss, with hot, red skin and intense itching? **YES** Call your veterinarian *TODAY*—it could be sarcoptic mange^G, which is transmissible to people.

 NO

Do you see a localized area on a front or rear leg that your dog chews chronically, when stressed or bored? **YES** Call your veterinarian *TODAY*—it could be an acral lick granuloma lesion^G, which is similar to obsessive/compulsive disorder^G in humans.

 NO

➤

YOUR VET MAY NEED TO:

Identify skin parasites under the microscope.

19

ACTION PLAN (CONTINUED):

Is the itchy skin crusty, scaly, or flaky?

 NO

 YES It could be ringworm[G] or seborrhea[G]. Go to **page 17**. For seborrhea, also see **Home Treatment Steps 4** and **5**.

Is the season too cool for biting insects? Do you see dandruff when you examine his skin with a magnifying glass?

YES It could be lice[G] or mites[G]. Apply **Home Treatment Step 3**.

NO

Call your veterinarian for an appointment.

HOME TREATMENT:

*(See **Action Plan** to determine whether home treatment is appropriate for your dog's itchy skin. If at any time during home treatment, your answers on the action plan change for the worse, call your vet.)*

> Never use the "if a little is good, more is better" theory when using canine pest repellents or insecticides. Higher concentrations and/or more frequent use can result in toxic amounts for your pet. You could truly end up doing more harm than good. Also, take precautions when using such products. Protect yourself from inhalation of and contact with the bug blaster.

Step 1. *Minimize biting insects in your dog's environment.* If fleas and ticks are a problem, choose one or more of the following:

• Use an in-house treatment specifically targeted toward fleas, such as Flea Busters, or one of the many home foggers on the market.

• Vacuum weekly to pick up immature fleas. Try vacuuming up some flea powder to kill any fleas that get sucked into the vacuum bag. Dispose of the bag outside immediately, so fleas trapped inside won't hatch and reinfest your home.

• Use flea-specific premise insecticides in your yard to decrease pest insect populations. Mow the lawn and rake up leaves, brush, or clippings. Then spray the yard, concentrating on your pet's favorite spots. **Caution: Do not allow people or ani-** mals into yard unless it's completely dry. Otherwise, you risk a toxic encounter.

Step 2. *Minimize biting insects on your dog's body.*

• Consult your vet about a prescription flea-control medication. Multi-purpose products are available (such as Sentinel) that control not only fleas, but also heartworms, hookworms, whipworms, and roundworms.

• Consider applying a topical, monthly flea, tick, and mosquito insecticide, such as Advantage, Revolution, or Frontline, which are a new generation of safer insecticides. A few drops applied at your dog's shoulder blades and the base of his tail can prove effective against flea infestations for up to 30 to 90 days.

• If you opt out of the monthly topical insecticides, use commercial flea/tick shampoos, sprays, and dips—as directed—to combat biting insects. (**Caveat:** Do not mix canine insecticide and/or repellent products without thoroughly reading manufacturers' warnings/instructions. And if your dog wears a flea collar, avoid applying additional flea treatments. Doing so could cause poisoning.)

• If flies bother your dog, bring him indoors during the day, and put him out at night, when biting flies are less prevalent. See page 23 for tips on fly control.

Step 3. *Eliminate skin parasites from the affected area.* If mites and lice are a problem, use canine insecticides (such as Hilo Dip for lice and LymDyp, Revolution, or Paramite Dip for mites). Follow label instructions exactly.

Step 4. *Soothe irritated skin.*
• If your dog is suffering from seborrhea[G], bathe him with a tar shampoo such as Sebalyt, T-Lux tar/sulfur shampoo, or Sebolux, to remove irritating sebum[G] and soothe inflamed skin. After bathing, apply a topical anti-seborrheac product such as LyTar Spray.
• If your dog has itchy, dry irritated skin, bathe him with a soothing moisturizing shampoo, such as Epi-Soothe Emolient Oatmeal Shampoo. After bathing, apply a topical anti-itch, anti-sting preparation to the area, such as colloidal oatmeal (Aveeno®, 1 tablespoon per gallon of water), witch hazel (alone or in commercial preparations such as Allerderm®), calamine lotion, or zinc oxide paste. If your dog's skin is dry and flaky, top that layer with an emollient product such as a solution of Avon Skin-So-Soft® (diluted 1-to-3 in water, and spritzed from a spray bottle).

Step 5. *Remove scale and scurf.* For crusty, scaly, flaky skin conditions, clip hair from the affected areas, extending well into healthy skin around the lesion's perimeter. This will help eliminate bacteria residing in the hair, prevent the accumulation of serum or crust, which would attract more bacteria (and insects) and allow you to apply medication directly to the area, which could accelerate healing.

A Couple of Clip Tips...

Keep these safety precautions in mind when using electric clippers on your dog:

• Clip only dry hair. When clipping a wet area, the risk of electric shock to you and/or your dog is great. If you've already gotten the area wet, towel it off, and allow it to air-dry completely before clipping.
• Use a properly installed and grounded GFI (ground fault interrupt) outlet. That way, if a mishap occurs, the outlet's circuit will be interrupted and power to the clippers will be cut off.
• Stand on a dry surface while you're clipping, to reduce the risk of shock.

What you see: Your dog has one or more lumps in or under his skin. The lump might be smaller than a pea, or as large as your hand.

LUMP, BUMP OR WART
On skin or ears

What this might mean: At the least, it's a cosmetic problem. It could indicate an infection or previous injury in that location, or it could be a sign of a cyst[G] or tumor[G] (possibly even a malignancy[G]).

YOUR VET MAY NEED TO:

Perform an aspiration biopsy[G] in order to make a diagnosis.

ACTION PLAN:

Are there several, distinct, smooth bumps that look like hives or welts, covered by unbroken skin? Is your dog acting anxious, breathing rapidly, or wheezing?

 YES Call your veterinarian *NOW* if you answered yes to either query—it could be hives or a severe, allergic-type reaction called anaphylaxis[G]. Before you leave, go to **page 25**.

NO

Are there dark masses in the skin?

 YES Call your veterinarian *TODAY*—it could be melanoma[G].

NO

Is the lump where an injection was given within the past 3 days?

 YES Call your veterinarian *TODAY*—it could be a local inflammation or infection that requires treatment.

NO

Does the lump feel warmer than surrounding tissues? Does your dog flinch when you touch it?

 YES Call your veterinarian *TODAY*—it could be a deep bruise or abscess[G].

NO

Are there red, raised pustular lesions in the skin, with or without itching or hair loss?

 YES Call your veterinarian *TODAY* if you answered yes to any of these queries—it could be impetigo[G], pyoderma[G], or folliculitis[G]. It could require a medicated shampoo and/or an antibiotic.

NO

Is it (or are they) located around his anus? Are the lump(s) smooth and non-painful?

 YES Call your veterinarian *TODAY*—it could be a perianal adenoma[G].

NO

Does your dog's ear flap appear to be swollen and filled with fluid?

 YES Call your veterinarian *TODAY*—it may be an aural hematoma[G], and might require surgical treatment.

NO

ACTION PLAN (CONTINUED):

Is the lump ulcerated, raw, and/or draining fluid?

 YES Call your veterinarian *TODAY*—it could be an abscess^G, draining cyst^G, or a malignant^G or benign^G tumor.

NO

Is it a wart-like mass that's pink or grey in color?

 YES Call your veterinarian *TODAY*—it may be a sebaceous cyst^G, papilloma^G, or other skin tumor.

NO

Is there one or more soft, moveable masses under the skin? Is your dog middle-aged or older?

 YES Call your veterinarian *TODAY* if you answered yes to one or more of these queries—it could be a fatty lipoma^G or a more serious tumor.

NO

Is it a pea-sized or smaller bump, with a hard, red, crusty center?

 YES It could be a tick bite, with the head buried inside the bite site. See page 248 for how to remove a tick head.

NO

Call your veterinarian for an appointment.

Keep Bugs at Bay...

To help control biting insects, try these tips:

• Consult your vet about prescription flea-control medication. Sentinel, a multi-purpose product, also controls heartworms, hookworms, whipworms, and roundworms.

• Consider applying an adult flea killer. Repeated monthly, such products as Advantage, Frontline, and Revolution have proven effective against fleas.

• Use an in-house treatment, such as Flea Busters, an in-house premise spray, or flea-specific foggers, to control in-house infestations.

• To keep flying insects at bay, spritz your dog as needed with a mixture of 1 part Avon's Skin-So-Soft® bath oil to 3 parts water. (Spray him at least once a day—this mixture's not toxic.)

• Provide a shady, breezy place for your dog when flies are bad. (Many biting flies are active mainly where it's hot and sunny.)

• Keep him indoors during the day, and put him out at night, when flies are less of a problem.

• Apply a medicated fly repellent, such as Onex (by Happy Jack) or Flys-Off (by Farnam) to your dog's ear tips to prevent/treat fly bites.

• Keep your yard clean; be sure trash cans are securely closed, and use fly traps— out of the reach of people and pets. (See "Caution," page 18.)

YELLOW-TINTED EYES, GUMS & SKIN

What you see: The white's of your dog's eyes and/or gums appear yellowish, and/or there's a yellowish tint to the skin of his inside ear or flank, or wherever his coat is thin.

What this might mean: What you're seeing could be jaundice^G, which could indicate liver disease.

ACTION PLAN:

Is your dog not eating, depressed, or feverish? — **YES** → Call your veterinarian *NOW*—it could be a serious problem such as liver disease, poisoning^G, anemia^G, or internal bleeding. Go to **Before You Leave,** below.

NO ↓

Do his skin and/or the whites of his eyes and/or his gums appear yellow-tinged? — **YES** → Go to **page 66**.

NO ↓

Is the skin in the affected area oozing and/or crusty? — **YES** → Go to **page 17**.

NO ↓

If you wipe your dog's skin with a damp, white cloth, does the cloth turn yellow? — **YES** → It's pollen. You can stop worrying.

NO ↓

Call your veterinarian for an appointment.

BEFORE YOU LEAVE:

1. *Isolate your dog from other dogs in case it's contagious.* To prevent spread of possible infectious disease, confine your dog to an area apart from other dogs. Wash your hands and disinfect your shoes (see page 374) after handling your dog and before handling other dogs.

What you see: A forest of smooth, BB- to pea-sized bumps under your dog's skin, making his hair appear to stick up in little patches. They usually start on his face; his eyelids and lips may swell. In female dogs, the vulva may swell too. As the hives spread, they can coalesce into large, doughy areas of swelling. Press on their centers, and your fingertip will leave a temporary depression. Your dog may scratch violently.

What this might mean: hives, a sign of an allergic reaction. It could be something he's eaten, something that's bitten him, something he's inhaled, or a medication you or your veterinarian gave him. Whether you realize it or not, it's something he's been exposed to before. What makes hives potentially dangerous is that they tell you that your dog has become *sensitized* to the allergen, and at some point his body might react to further exposure by throwing a sort of allergic tantrum—an often fatal, body-wide reaction called anaphylaxis^G. A dog having an anaphylactic reaction can die within hours.

1-G
RASH/HIVES

ACTION PLAN:

Has your dog suffered a sudden swelling and thickening of the skin on his face, eyelids, and/or lips? Is he scratching violently? If she's a female, is her vulva swollen?

YES ▶ Call your veterinarian *NOW*—if you answered "yes" to one or more of these queries. It could be an early sign of hypersensitivity, which could lead to an anaphylactic reaction. Go to **Before You Leave,** next page.

NO ⬇

Is your dog wheezing or panting?

YES ▶ Call your veterinarian *NOW*—it could be an anaphylactic reaction. Go to **Before You Leave**.

NO ⬇

Is your dog behaving anxiously, for no apparent reason?

YES ▶ Call your veterinarian *NOW*—it could be an anaphylactic reaction. Go to **Before You Leave**.

NO ⬇

Would you like to figure out what it is he's reacting to?

YES ▶ Call your veterinarian *TODAY*—skin tests and/or detective work might identify the allergen. A prescription (antihistamines and/or corticosteroids) might hasten shrinkage of hives.

NO ⬇

Does your dog have a rashlike lesion on his feet or abdomen?

YES ▶ Call your veterinarian *TODAY*—it could be a contact allergy, such as to grass, chemicals, carpet fiber, etc.

NO ⬇

Try to minimize allergens in your dog's environment. Go to **Home Treatment,** next page.

▶

BEFORE YOU LEAVE:

1. *Protect yourself.* If your dog is displaying anxious behavior—pacing, whining, eyes open wide, panting—his judgment is impaired and he might inadvertently hurt you. Be especially cautious.

2. *Improve ventilation.* If your dog is having difficulty breathing, make fresh air available. Much of the anxiety displayed in dogs with anaphylaxis is the result of panic due to difficulty breathing.

3. *Recall all potential allergens.* Think back: can you think of anything that might have brought on this allergic response? A change in feed sources? A change to a different type of topical flea/tick insecticide? Any medications, vaccinations, or vitamin products given? Any topical cosmetic or therapeutic substances applied to his skin? Any biting or stinging bugs noticed? Be sure to report all suspicions to your veterinarian.

HOME TREATMENT:

*(See **Action Plan** to determine whether home treatment is appropriate for your dog's hives. If at any time during home treatment, your answers on the action plan change for the worse, call your veterinarian.)*

Step 1. *Work with your vet to develop a hypoallergenic diet for your dog, to determine if his diet is contributing to his allergy problem.* Protein sources in such a diet could include mutton, cottage cheese, tofu, or white fish. Rice and potatoes can supply carbohydrate needs, and corn oil can be added as a

> **FYI...**
>
> Allergy testing can be useful for helping you help your dog battle the allergens that torment him. In fact, you have a 60- to 70-percent chance of helping to control that itch.
>
> To make the most of allergy testing, ask your vet to recommend a canine allergy specialist.
>
> Once you get the results, ask the vet if it's possible for you to give allergy shots at home (if they're prescribed), to help save money. If so (and if you're willing), ask him or her to show you how to properly administer the shots.

source of fat. The key is to feed a ration that doesn't contain ingredients your dog had been eating previously. (There's nothing truly "hypoallergenic" about the ingredients mentioned above except that they're simply not part of the usual canine diet.) If your dog's skin allergy improves on a hypoallergenic diet, then deteriorates when he's returned to his regular diet, he may have a food allergy. Your vet can help you develop a long-term diet and management plan to control the allergy.

Step 2. *Reduce potential allergens in your dog's environment.* For example:

• Limit his exposure to grass and weeds, especially in the spring and fall, when pollen is a problem.

• Limit his contact with carpet, if his allergy outbreaks seem to coincide with carpet contact. (Wool is a common allergen for both dogs *and* humans.)

• Clean you dog's environment of fleas/ticks, spider webs, wasp/hornet nests, and other biting/stinging insects. (For more information on flea/tick control, see page 241.)

• Eliminate, minimize, or switch chemical exposure (insecticides, grooming sprays, etc.).

• Vacuum your home frequently to reduce flea-larvae populations, and to minimize other possible allergens that could reside in carpet fibers. Dust frequently, too, to reduce that potential allergy trigger.

Itch Fighters

You have many options for helping your dog battle that drive-him-batty itch. Work with your vet to choose the right arsenal from:

- Medicated baths and dips

- Clipping the affected area

- Topical medications, including:
    - antibiotics
    - corticosteroids
    - antihistamines
    - emollients
    - moisturizers
    - insecticides

- Oral medications, including:
    - fat-soluble vitamins and fatty acids
    - antihistamines
    - antibiotics
    - antiprostaglandins
    - corticosteroids

- Injectable medications, including:
    - corticosteroids and antibiotics

Did You Know...

...there are two types of allergic reaction in dogs. The "immediate" type happens within moments of exposure to an allergen (such as food, an insect bite, or a drug such as penicillin—which is used as a preservative in some vaccines). It often produces hives and itching. A "delayed reaction" produces itching hours or days after exposure. Anaphylactic shock[G] is an example of the immediate type.

LOSS OF SKIN PIGMENT
(Vitiligo^G)

What you see: Portions of your dog's formerly dark skin have begun to develop pink spots, which are most noticeable when he's wet.

What this might mean: Loss of pigmentation can be serious, or it can be as simple as a problem associated with plastic food and water dishes.

ACTION PLAN:

Is there a "butterfly-shaped" area of irritation, hair loss, or depigmentation on the face between his eyes and nose? **YES** Call your veterinarian *TODAY*—it could be a sign of discoid lupus^G.

 NO

Is the loss of pigmentation around your dog's eyes? **YES** Call your veterinarian *TODAY*—it could be an autoimmune^G problem such as pemphigus foliaceus^G.

 NO

Is the loss of pigmentation on top of your dog's nose? **YES** Call your veterinarian *THIS WEEK*—it could be nasal-solar dermatitis^G, which can become progressively worse. See "Sun Beater Tips", below.

 NO

Is there depigmentation on his nose and lips? **YES** Call your veterinarian *THIS WEEK*—it could be contact dermatitis^G from plastic food dishes or other such sources of irritation. See **page 16**.

 NO

Are there previously pigmented areas that have lost pigment? **YES** Call your veterinarian *THIS WEEK*—it could be secondary to trauma, burns, infection, surgery, or sunlight.

NO

Call your veterinarian *THIS WEEK* for advice.

Sun-Beater Tips

Does your dog's skin rebel at sun exposure? Use these tips to help:

• Limit his exposure to sunlight, by keeping him in during the day, and putting him out at night. If you can't control his exposure to sunlight, apply a light coat of an SPF 15 or higher sunscreen to his nose, to help block ultraviolet rays.
• Talk to your vet about tattooing your dog's nose and any pink skin on his face with black ink, to permanently protect it from sun exposure.

What you see/feel: You're rubbing your male or female dog's stomach when you feel something. It's one or more hard or soft lumps beneath one of his/her nipples. The dog may ignore your manipulation of the bump, or react by flinching or yelping.

What it might mean: Lumps in the mammary gland area can signal an infection, cyst^G, or tumor^G.

LUMPS/BUMPS ON BELLY

ACTION PLAN:

Are your female dog's mammary glands hot and painful? Has she recently been in heat or had a litter of puppies? Is her milk an abnormal color (such as gray, yellow, or reddish brown)?

YES ▶ Call your veterinarian *NOW*—it could be mastitis^G associated with a false pregnancy^G or nursing, or a mammary abscess.

NO ▼

Does your female dog have solitary or multiple firm lumps in one or more of her mammary glands?

YES ▶ Call your veterinarian *TODAY*—it could be a mammary cyst^G or tumor^G.

NO ▼

Has your female dog recently been in heat? Does she have marked mammary development?

YES ▶ Call your veterinarian *THIS WEEK*— the dog could be pregnant, or going through a false pregnancy^G.

NO ▼

Is your female dog in heat? Are her mammary glands slightly enlarged and/or tender?

YES ▶ Don't worry. These are normal changes associated with being in season.

NO ▼

Does your male dog have enlarged mammary glands (nipples)? Does he have a thin hair coat? Pendulous penis? Is he attractive to male dogs? Are his testicles unequal in size?

YES ▶ Call your veterinarian *TODAY*—it could be a Sertoli cell^G or other type of testicular tumor^G.

NO ▼

Have you seen or felt a firm mass in the area of your male dog's nipples?

YES ▶ That may be normal for the nipples on your male dog, or in rare instances, he may have a mammary tumor^G or cyst^G. Call your veterinarian for advice.

NO ▼

Call your veterinarian for an appointment.

YOUR VET MAY NEED TO:

Sedate your dog to take a biopsy, to determine whether the mass is cancerous.

29

NOTES

CHAPTER 2

Problems of
THE NOSE

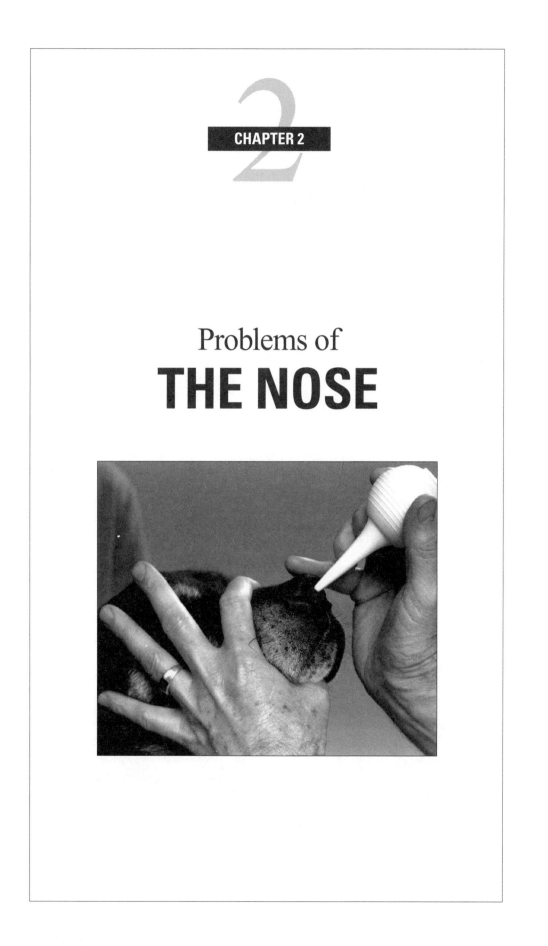

NASAL DISCHARGE

Wet or crusty

What you see: Your dog has a crusty or runny nose. The discharge is watery, pus-like, mucoid, or may be blood-tinged. It may even contain bits of food.

What this might mean: It could signal the beginning of a localized fungal or bacterial infection. Or it could be due to a growth, trauma, or a small, lodged foreign body such as a plant seed. It also can indicate that there's an infected tooth.

YOUR VET MAY NEED TO:

Sedate your dog in order to facilitate a thorough and safe examination of his nose and teeth. Your vet may also need to pass a scope into the nasal cavity in order to identify the problem, and/or take tissue samples for further testing.

ACTION PLAN:

Does the discharge contain water or food particles? — **YES** → Call your veterinarian *NOW*—it could be an oro-nasal fistula^G.

NO ↓

Does your dog have a fever? Weepy eyes? Is he lethargic? Not eating? — **YES** → Call your veterinarian *NOW* if you answered yes to any of these queries—it could be an infectious disease, such as distemper^G. Go to **Before You Leave, #1,** opposite page.

NO ↓

Is your dog sneezing? Is he scratching or pawing at his nose? — **YES** → Call your veterinarian NOW if you answered yes to either query—there could be a foreign body lodged in your dog's nasal cavity, which could lead to infection. See **Before You Leave #2**, opposite page.

NO ↓

Is the crust or discharge pus-like? — **YES** → Call your veterinarian *NOW*—it could be an infection due to a foreign body, fungus, or bad tooth.

NO ↓

Does the discharge look like undiluted blood? — **YES** → Go to **page 34.**

NO ↓

Is the discharge blood-tinged? — **YES** → Call your veterinarian *TODAY*—it could be an infection associated with an ulcerated tumor, trauma, or a foreign body in the nasal cavity, or a dental infection.

NO ↓

ACTION PLAN (CONTINUED):

Is the discharge clear, but foamy? Is your dog snorting and sniffling? Do his nostrils appear constricted? Is he a short-nosed breed, such as a Pug, Bulldog, Boxer, Mastiff, or Pekinese? **YES** Call your veterinarian *TODAY*—it could be collapsed nostrils^G, a condition specific to short-nosed breeds. Surgical repair could ultimately be needed.

NO

Does your dog show any other signs, such as lethargy, or lack of appetite? **YES** Call your veterinarian *TODAY* for an appointment.

NO

Was your dog outside? Is the discharge clear and watery? **YES** It's possibly a minor nasal irritation from pollen/seeds. It should resolve itself. But moniter it closely. If your dog changes for the worse, call your vet.

NO

Call your veterinarian for an appointment.

BEFORE YOU LEAVE #1

1. *Isolate your dog from other dogs in case it's contagious.* To prevent possible spread of infectious disease, confine your dog to a warm, dry area with a separate water supply, one that's apart from your other dogs. Wash your hands and disinfect your shoes (and later, the area, if the diagnosis is infectious disease) after handling your dog and before handling others. (For how to properly disinfect your shoes and a sick-bay, see page 373.)

BEFORE YOU LEAVE #2

1. *Keep your dog still.* If you suspect a foreign body, keep your dog as quiet as possible. Any movement on his part can cause the object to migrate farther up his nasal cavity.

Did You Know...

...foreign bodies can be life-threatening in some instances. Undetected (or untreated), they can result in an infection that can erode the barrier between your dog's nasal cavity and his brain, resulting in encephalitis^G. Or, he could aspirate the foreign body into his lungs, causing pneumonia^G or an abscess^G.

...dog's don't catch colds the way humans do. Nervous and excited dogs may secrete a clear, watery discharge that stops once they calm down. But if your dog has a runny nose, globs of mucous coming from his eyes, a cough, and a fever, it could indicate a serious problem, such as distemper^G. Call your vet immediately.

BLOODY NOSE

What you see: Dried blood in your dog's nostril, watery-looking blood dripping from one or both nostrils, or bright-red blood flowing out at an alarming rate.

What this might mean: It could be a sign of a serious underlying problem.

YOUR VET MAY NEED TO:

Examine your dog's nose and/or lungs with X-rays or endoscopy^G, either of which may require sedation for safety and to facilitate a more thorough exam.

ACTION PLAN:

Is your dog bleeding from any other areas, such as his mouth or rectum? Does he have blood in his urine or stool, or skin bruising? Does he have access to rodent bait such as D-Con®?

 NO

YES Call your veterinarian *NOW* if you answered yes to any of these queries—it could be a form of hemophilia^G, or poisoning with a blood thinner present in some rodent poisons.

Is the blood flowing profusely?

 NO

YES Call your veterinarian *NOW*—it could be due to trauma to the head. Go to **Before You Leave,** opposite page.

Is your dog sneezing? Does he intermittently have a snotty or runny nose?

 NO

YES Call your veterinarian *NOW* if you answered yes to either of these queries—it could be a foreign body, tumor, nasal mites^G, a serious infection, or an abscessed tooth.

Does your dog bleed excessively from wounds? Bruise easily? Is he intermittently lame?

 NO

YES Call your veterinarian *NOW* if you answered yes to any of these queries—it could be von Willebrand's Disease^G, or another form of hemophilia^G.

Call your veterinarian for an appointment—the blood could be due to trauma, or an abnormality inside the nostril(s).

Timing is Everything...

If your dog is bleeding profusely from the nose, you'll need to act quickly. A significant amount of blood can be lost in a short amount of time, putting his life at risk. Don't hesitate—dial up your vet and reach for ice to stem the bleeding.

BEFORE YOU LEAVE:

1. *Calm your dog.* If he's excited, his heart will pump harder, meaning that his blood will run faster.

2. *Apply ice.* Select a flexible ice pack (see page 311) such as a bag of frozen peas, and lay it over the top of your dog's face, below his eyes. Hold it there without applying pressure. Ice on: 5 minutes. Ice off: 15 minutes. This will help slow the bleeding, if it's originating within the nasal cavity, without risk of displacing possible facial bone fracture fragments. Be sure to avoid covering your dog's nostrils with the ice pack. This would inadvertently impair his ability to breathe, causing him to panic and fight your efforts.

If you use poison to control mice, rat, and other rodent populations, NEVER place it in a site that can be accessed by pets—or children. Most such poisons use a blood-thinning ingredient that causes fatal hemorrhage in rodents. Accidental ingestion can cause the same result in loved ones. Because of the increased effectiveness of poisons on the market today, ingestion is now more difficult to treat than in years past. Be poison smart—keep such products out of the reach of children and pets.

3. If possible, have someone drive you to the vet clinic while you continue to ice your dog's nose.

Some Breeds Commonly Affected by
Von Willebrand's Disease

- Chesapeake Bay Retrievers
- Doberman Pinschers
- German Shepherds
- German Shorthaired Pointers
- Golden Retrievers
- Standard Poodles
- Shetland Sheepdogs
- Scottish Terriers

Did you Know...

...dogs can also get poisoned from ingesting poisoned rodents, which are easier to catch than their healthy cousins. Never allow your dog to eat rodents, *especially* after you've put out rodent poison.

2-C

What you hear: An abnormal noise when your dog breathes during exercise, at rest, or all the time.

NASAL NOISE
(Sneezing or snorting)

What this might mean: Something is partially obstructing his nasal cavity, such as a nasal irritant, foreign body, allergic swelling, or even a collapsed nostril.

YOUR VET MAY NEED TO:

Examine the tissues deep within your dog's nasal passages and throat, using X-ray and/or endoscopy[G]. Either of these may require sedation for safety and to facilitate a thorough exam.

ACTION PLAN:

Is your dog collapsed, overheated, or in obvious respiratory distress? **YES** ▶ Call your veterinarian *NOW*—your dog's in immediate danger due to a nasal obstruction or heat stroke[G].

NO

Does your dog have a discharge coming from his nose? Is the sneezing violent? Is he pawing or scratching at his nose? **YES** ▶ Go to **page 32.** It could be a foreign body, dust, or other nasal irritant.

 NO

Is his nose bleeding? **YES** ▶ Go to **page 34.**

 NO

Is he sneezing, with no evidence of a discharge? **YES** ▶ Call your veterinarian *TODAY*—your dog may have gotten a foreign body up his nose, or may be suffering from a nasal allergy.

NO

Does his breathing sound labored? Is he snorting and sniffling? Are his nostrils constricted? Does he have a clear, foamy nasal discharge? Is he a short-nosed breed, such as a Pug, Boxer, Pekinese, Mastiff, or Bulldog? **YES** ▶ Call your veterinarian *TODAY* if you answered yes to two or more of these queries—it could be a collapsed nostril[G], a problem specific to short-nosed breeds. It could ultimately require surgery for repair.

 NO

Does it sound like a violent, repeated snorting or snoring sound? As though your dog is trying to forcefully inhale air through his nose? **YES** ▶ Call your veterinarian *TODAY*—it sounds like reverse sneezing[G]. While these episodes generally go away on their own, surgical treatment may occasionally be required to solve the underlying problem.

 NO

Is he snorting after having been digging in the dirt? **YES** ▶ He's likely irritated his nasal passages. See **Home Treatment**, opposite page.

HOME TREATMENT:

*(See **Action Plan** to determine whether home treatment is appropriate for your dog's irritated nasal passages. If at any time during home treatment, your answers on the action plan change for the worse, call your vet.)*

Step 1. Gently use a bulb syringe and a gentle stream of warm water to irrigate your dog's nose to remove the irritant. (You'll likely need a helper to hold your dog as you do so, and may need to apply a muzzle to avoid a reactive bite. For how to flush your dog's nose and apply a muzzle, see pages 270 and 328.)

Step 2. Repeat until irrigation water runs clear, and/or your dog quits snorting.

Step 3. Watch him closely for signs of nasal irritation (sneezing or snorting) and/or discharge. If you see one or both of these signs, call your veterinarian.

Did You Know...

...although your dog can suffer from a nasal allergy, it's rare. So when you hear him sneezing and sniffling, it's most likely a sign of some other type of problem. While people commonly fall prey to such sneezing/sniffing allergies as hay fever, those in dogs tend to present themselves in different ways. One common sign of a canine allergic condition is a skin problem.

...your short-nosed dog has more risk of suffering from heat-related problems than his long-nosed cousins. That's because dogs cool off via panting, and the compact nose and mouth design of such short-nosed breeds as Bulldogs, Boxers, Pugs, and Pekinese makes their cooling mechanisms less efficient. So make sure your short-nosed dog can stay cool even when summer heats up. This is especially true if he's aged and/or has a debilitating condition, such as heart disease. Here's how:

• Provide a constant supply of fresh water. A bowl under a lightly dripping faucet works well.
• If you leave him outside, make sure he has easy access to plenty of shade, so he can escape the sun's punishing rays.
• Be sure that shade is in an area that catches the prevailing breeze, so your dog can take advantage of nature's air conditioner.

What you see: Your dog's normally dark nose now has irregular pink or light areas.

2 - D

LOSS OF PIGMENTATION

What this might mean: It could mean that the skin on your dog's nose is irritated, which could be the result of any number of different causes. Some could be benign—others could be serious.

YOUR VET MAY NEED TO:

Sedate your dog, in order to thoroughly check his nasal cavities either manually or with the aid of a scope.

ACTION PLAN:

Does your dog have a nasal discharge?

 YES Go to **page 32**.

 NO

Is the skin on your dog's foot pads and/or nose thickened and hornlike?

 YES Call your veterinarian *NOW*—it could be hard-pad[G], a sign of distemper[G]. Isolate your dog from other dogs before you leave.

 NO

Is there crusting at the nostril?

 YES That indicates there's a discharge. See **page 32.**

 NO

Is there a raw area on the skin of his nose?

 YES Call your veterinarian *TODAY*—it could be due to trauma, sun exposure, or squamous cell carcinoma[G].

 NO

Is the skin between his nose and eye inflamed, with redness, scales, and ulcerations? Is it "butterfly-shaped?"

YES Call your veterinarian *TODAY*—it could be discoid lupus[G], an autoimmune problem. See **page 28.**

 NO

Is there weeping and crusting on the nose skin itself? Is it red and/or inflamed? Do you live in a warm, sunny climate such as Florida? Or in a high-elevation area such as Denver?

 YES Call your veterinarian *TODAY*—it sounds like nasal-solar dermatitis (collie nose)[G], which can get progressively worse. Also see **Home Treatment**, opposite page.

 NO

Is your dog's black pigment gradually fading to chocolate brown?

YES Sounds like vitiligo[G]. There's no known cure, and your dog may recover on his own.

 NO

Is your dog white-coated? Does his black nose lighten during the winter, then darken as summer approaches?

YES It could be snow nose[G], a cosmetic problem. See **Home Treatment, Step 2**, opposite page.

NO

ACTION PLAN (CONTINUED):

Does your dog eat and/or drink from a plastic dish?

 YES

Sounds like plastic-dish dermatitis^G, a form of contact dermatitis^G. Simply retire that plastic wear and switch to glass, ceramic or stainless-steel dishes.

NO

Has your dog experienced a recent trauma to his nose, such as a scrape or scratch?

 YES

When the area heals, dark pigment will gradually migrate back to the site. See **Home Treatment, Step 1.**

NO

Call your veterinarian for an appointment.

HOME TREATMENT:

*(See **Action Plan** to determine whether home treatment is appropriate for your dog. If at any time during home treatment, your answers on the action plan change for the worse, call your vet.)*

Never feed your dog (or yourself or your family) out of ceramic dishes made in a foreign country, unless you know for certain the dishes are lead-free. Picking up traces of lead from such dishes can lead to poisoning. When in doubt, use glass and stainless steel dishes for your dog.

STOP

Step 1. If the skin is broken, clean the area by dabbing it with hydrogen peroxide. Then apply a thin layer of povidone iodine cream.

Step 2. Limit your dog's exposure to sunlight, by keeping him in during the day, and putting him out at night. If you can't, apply a light coat of an SPF 15 or higher sunscreen to his nose, to help block ultraviolet rays.

Step 3. Talk to your vet about tattooing your dog's nose with black ink, to permanently protect it from sun exposure.

Did You Know...

...discoid lupus^G is most often found in breeds of Collie, German Sheperd, Siberian Husky, and Shetland Sheepdog heritage. It's the second most common autoimmune problem in dogs. The first is pemphigus foliaceus^G.

NOTES

CHAPTER 3

Problems of
THE MOUTH

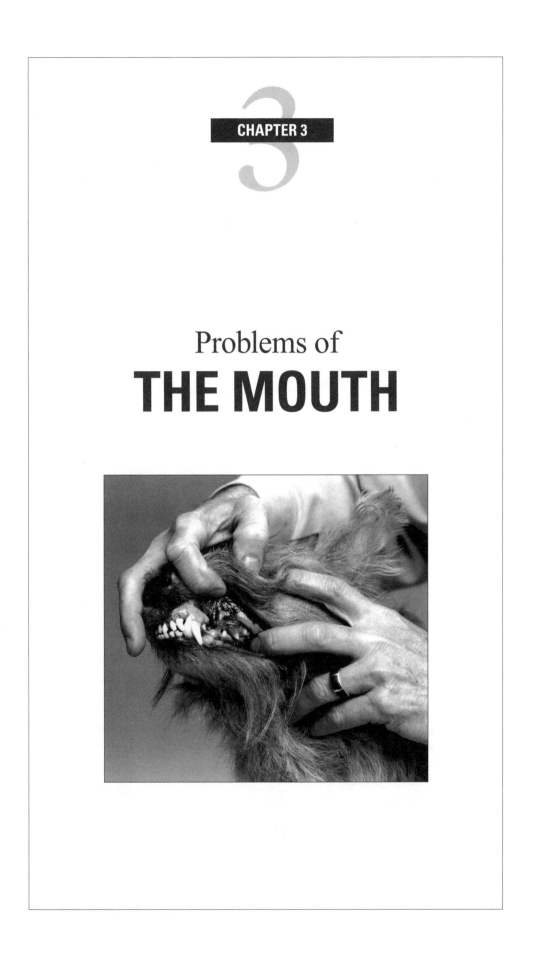

What you see: Your dog's gums are a noticeably abnormal color, such as yellow, very pale pink, dark red, or chocolate brown.

3-A

Abnormal
GUM COLOR

What this might mean: There may be a simple explanation, or it could indicate a serious underlying problem, such as anemia[G] or hepatitis[G].

ACTION PLAN:

Are his gums deep red or bright pink? Is your dog breathing rapidly or acting as though he's having trouble breathing? Is he acting anxious or weak?

 NO

 YES Call your veterinarian *NOW* if you answered yes to any of these queries—unless your dog has just been very physically active, intensely pink gums can be a sign of endotoxic shock[G] or carbon monoxide poisoning[G].

Are his gums a dark maroon or muddy color? Is your dog unusually quiet, not eating, or weak?

 NO

 YES Call your veterinarian *NOW* if you answered yes to any query—it could be blood poisoning (endotoxemia[G]).

Is there a blue line on his gums, just around the rims of his teeth? Does your dog seem weak?

 NO

YES Call your veterinarian *NOW* if you answered yes to any of these queries—it could be lead poisoning[G].

Are his gums chocolate brown in color?

 NO

YES Call your veterinarian *NOW*—it could be due to nitrate poisoning (such as from eating fertilizer), or from eating acetaminophen (Tylenol).

Are his gums white, or so pale that they're just barely pink?

 NO

 YES Call your veterinarian *TODAY*—it could be anemia[G] or poor blood pressure due to shock[G].

Are his gums red/inflamed at the gum-line (where they meet your dog's teeth)? Are his teeth yellow or brown? Can you see plaque on the teeth?

 NO

 YES Call your veterinarian *TODAY*—it could be dental disease (periodontal disease[G]).

Are his gums yellowish or orange?

 NO

Call your veterinarian for an appointment.

YES Yellowish gums are usually accompanied by yellow whites of the eyes. He may have hemolytic anemia[G] or hepatitis[G]. Go to **page 66**.

Tooth Trivia

One cubic millimeter of doggie dental plaque contains over 300 million bacteria. As bacteria invade your dog's gums and teeth, they can also enter his bloodstream, causing infection in such critical areas as his kidneys and heart. Save yourself some future vet bills by investing in regular dental exams for your dog, and brushing his teeth weekly at home. (See page 273.)

What's normal for your dog?

Many normal dogs have grey, dark brown, or black mouth pigment on their gums, and even tongues, rather than the typical pink. In order to identify a problem, you'll first need to familiarize yourself with what's normal for your dog. Take a moment to study his mouth before he has a problem, so you can spot any abnormalities early. (For how to safely examine your dog's mouth, see page 273.)

What you smell: A strong, persistant unpleasant odor, reminiscent of rotting flesh or amonia.

3 - B

BAD BREATH

What this might mean: Bad breath, known as halitosis[G]. It could be serious, because bad odor can indicate the presence of infection in the teeth or gums. Or, it could be a sign of kidney failure.

YOUR VET MAY NEED TO:

• Sedate your dog in order to facilitate a thorough and safe examination of the dog's teeth and mouth.

• X-ray your dog's jaw or skull if a fractured tooth root or abscess is suspected.

• Draw blood and urine for analysis.

ACTION PLAN:

Does your dog's mouth seem sore? Is he approaching food/water, but not eating/drinking? Or, is he allowing food to fall out of his mouth?

YES → Call your veterinarian *TODAY*—it could be pain due to infection, a foreign body, or an injury inside your dog's mouth.

NO ↓

Is your dog not eating, dull, or feverish?

YES → Call your veterinarian *TODAY*—it could be pain and/or infection that may or may not have anything to do with your dog's mouth, such as that associated with systemic disease.

NO ↓

Has your dog lost weight? Is his coat dull? Is he drinking/urinating more than normal? Does his breath have an amonia odor?

YES → Call your veterinarian *TODAY*—it could be kidney disease.

NO ↓

Does your dog pull back abruptly when you touch his face or mouth? Is he drooling or slobbering excessively?

YES → Call your veterinarian *TODAY* if you answered yes to any of these queries—it could be a dental problem.

NO ↓

Is there a swelling or drainage below your dog's eye? Or a crust on a non-healing wound there? Does his face seem asymmetrical?

YES → Call your veterinarian *TODAY* if you answered yes to any of these queries—it could be an abscessed tooth.

NO ↓

Call your veterinarian for an appointment. It could be early periodontal disease[G] or gaseous odors from his stomach. For the latter, try giving your dog chlorophyll or activated charcoal (available at pharmacies), per manufacturer's instructions.

What you see: Saliva dripping from your dog's mouth, or strings of saliva hanging from his mouth.

What this might mean: Drooling can indicate either an overproduction of saliva, or the inability to swallow. It can be a sign of a serious underlying problem, and it can cause significant losses of fluid within a day or two, particularly if your dog is feeling sick and not eating to replace those losses. It can also be a sign of poisoning. And, although it's rare, drooling also can be a sign of rabies^G.

3 - C

DROOLING
Or slobbering

ACTION PLAN:

Is your dog feverish? Has his behavior been unusually dull, or overly excitable and/or aggressive? Is his gait abnormal? Does he seem incoordinated, weak, or "drunk"?

 YES → Call your veterinarian *NOW*—it could be an injury or disease of your dog's nervous system (including rabies^G; see **Caution**, next page).

NO ↓

Is your dog having trouble eating?

 YES → Call your veterinarian *NOW*—it could be pain in your dog's mouth, jaw, or throat; or poisoning or disease of his nervous system.

NO ↓

Are your dog's pupils abnormal? Is he unusually excitable? Suffering from muscle tremors? Has he been exposed to insecticides?

YES → Call your veterinarian *NOW* if you answered yes to any query— it could be poisoning.

 NO ↓

Does your dog seem normal aside from white, foamy saliva bubbling around his mouth? Has he had contact with any toads?

 YES → Call your veterinarian *NOW*—your dog could have bitten a poisonous toad.

 NO ↓

Does your dog have foul-smelling breath?

YES → Call your veterinarian *TODAY*—it could be a dental problem, a lodged foreign body in the mouth, or disease.

 NO ↓

Call your veterinarian for an appointment.

➤

45

CAUTION

Among the possible causes of drooling, an inability to swallow, mental changes, and/or gait abnormalities is a rare but notorious one: **Rabies**[G]. If rabies is a consideration in your dog's case, don't take chances—take precautions.

1. **Call for help!** This is a veterinary 9-1-1. Call your veterinarian and/or animal control. Such professionals can advise you of how to impound the dog. Rabies is always fatal in dogs—your goal now will be to minimize exposure to yourself, your family, and other pets/animals.

2. **Isolate!** Immediately isolate the dog from all other animals and humans in your household. A rabid dog's saliva is teaming with rabies virus, which is highly contagious to humans/animals. Avoid any contact with the dog. If you must handle him, don intact, water-repellant gloves (such as household rubber gloves), and protect all other body parts (especially broken skin) from contact with his saliva. Shower immediately after exposure to the dog.

3. **Be alert** for unexpected behavior. Rabies can cause aggression and/or a lack of coordination. Stay out of harm's way.

4. **If you or anyone in your family is bitten** or licked by a suspected rabies carrier, immediately wash the area with warm, soapy water—and call your doctor for advice.

5. **Clean up!** Ask your vet and/or animal control official how to properly disinfect any areas the dog has been.

6. **Think back.** Has your dog had any contact/exposure with wildlife, such as skunks, bats, racoons, or foxes? Familiarize yourself with those animals that are known rabies carriers in your area, and protect your pets—and children—from them.

7. **Alert animal control** officials if you see an odd-behaving critter in your area. (For instance, if you see a nocturnal animal such as a skunk or racoon moseying around during daylight, that's a red-alert.)

8. **Save it.** If your dog kills a wild animal, use the above clothing precautions, then bag the carcass and call your vet or the health department. They can test the animal for the rabies virus, so you'll know whether your dog—and family—have been exposed.

What you see: Your dog acts hungry. He's interested in eating, but shortly after lowering his mouth to feed, he turns away.

What this might mean: An inability to pick up, chew, and/or swallow feed could be a sign of a serious problem. Your dog literally can starve if someone fails to notice his problem soon enough. Certain neurological problems that affect the nerves of his lips and tongue also can affect other nerves, and can threaten your dog's recovery—even his life.

DIFFICULTY EATING

ACTION PLAN:

Is food and/or water coming from your dog's nostril(s)?

  YES Call your veterinarian *NOW*—it could be an oral-nasal fistula^G or nerve damage that's preventing normal swallowing.

Does your dog beg, watch intently, and/or otherwise act interested when you prepare his food?

   NO Call your veterinarian *NOW*—loss of appetite can mean general illness.

YES

Is your dog's gait abnormal? Does he seem drunk, weak, or dizzy? Does he have access to insecticides?

  YES Call your veterinarian *NOW* if you answered yes to any of these queries—it could be poisoning or a disease of the central nervous system. (See **Caution**, page 46.)

NO

Does one or more features of your dog's face droop or sag? Does his tongue loll outside his mouth?

 YES Call your veterinarian *NOW* if you answered yes to any of these queries—it could be damage to the nerve(s) of your dog's head from injury or disease.

NO

Is your dog dropping food from his mouth? Does he pull back abruptly from a water source when drinking? Does he tilt his head to one side when eating?

 YES Call your veterinarian *TODAY* if you answered yes to any of these queries—it could be a painful dental or jaw problem, a growth in your dog's mouth, or a foreign body.

NO

Call your veterinarian for an appointment.

YOUR VET MAY NEED TO:

X-ray your dog's head if fractured or infected teeth, or a fractured skull or jaw are suspected.

Dropping or SPITTING OUT FOOD

What you see: Wads of partially chewed food on the ground or in your dog's feed container.

What this might mean: One of two things—difficulty chewing, or difficulty swallowing, either of which could be a sign of a serious underlying problem.

ACTION PLAN:

Is your dog's appetite depressed? Does he have a fever? Is he showing any abnormal behavior, such as circling, pressing his head against surfaces, dullness, or aggression?

NO ↓

YES ▶ Call your veterinarian *NOW* if you answered yes to any of these queries—it could be illness of the central nervous system, including rabies[G]. (See **Caution**, opposite page.)

Is either of his ears or eyes drooping? Is his muzzle pulled to one side? Is he drooling?

NO ↓

YES ▶ Call your veterinarian *TODAY* if you answered yes to any of these queries—it could be damage to one or more facial nerves.

Does your dog have bad breath?

NO ↓

YES ▶ Go to **page 44**.

Has your dog lost weight?

NO ↓

YES ▶ Call your veterinarian *TODAY*—it could be a severe dental problem.

Call your veterinarian *TODAY* for an appointment—it could be a dental problem.

CAUTION

Among the possible causes of drooling, an inability to swallow, mental changes, and/or gait abnormalities is a rare but notorious one: **Rabies**^G. If rabies is a consideration in your dog's case, don't take chances—take precautions.

1. **Call for help!** This is a veterinary 9-1-1. Call your veterinarian and/or animal control. Such professionals can advise you of how to impound the dog. Rabies is always fatal in dogs—your goal now will be to minimize exposure to yourself, your family, and other pets/animals.

2. **Isolate!** Immediately isolate the dog from all other animals and humans in your household. A rabid dog's saliva is teaming with rabies virus, which is highly contagious to humans/animals. Avoid any contact with the dog. If you must handle him, don intact, water-repellant gloves (such as household rubber gloves), and protect all other body parts (especially broken skin) from contact with his saliva. Shower immediately after exposure to the dog.

3. **Be alert** for unexpected behavior. Rabies can cause aggression and/or a lack of coordination. Stay out of harm's way.

4. **If you or anyone in your family is bitten** or licked by a suspected rabies carrier, immediately wash the area with warm, soapy water—and call your doctor for advice.

5. **Clean up!** Ask your vet and/or animal control official how to properly disinfect any areas the dog has been.

6. **Think back.** Has your dog had any contact/exposure with wildlife, such as skunks, bats, raccoons, or foxes? Familiarize yourself with those animals that are known rabies carriers in your area, and protect your pets—and children—from them.

7. **Alert animal control** officials if you see an odd-behaving critter in your area. (For instance, if you see a nocturnal animal such as a skunk or racoon moseying around during daylight, that's a red-alert.)

8. **Save it.** If your dog kills a wild animal, use the above clothing precautions, then bag the carcass and call your vet or the health department. They can test the animal for the rabies virus, so you'll know whether your dog—and family—have been exposed.

What you see: Bright red blood dripping from your dog's mouth, and/or on his tongue and gums. Or, you may see dried blood on the fur around his mouth and/or front legs/feet.

3-F

BLOOD IN MOUTH

What this might mean: He could have suffered an injury to his mouth or teeth. Or, he could have been exposed to an anticoagulant, such as that found in some rodent poisons, or have an autoimmune disease^G that decreases his blood's ability to clot. Whatever the cause, it's a serious sign that's not to be ignored.

YOUR VET MAY NEED TO:

• Perform extensive lab work in order to get a diagnosis.
• X-ray your dog's mouth, jaw, and/or head, to rule out breaks/fractures
• Hospitalize your dog to provide intense supportive therapy.
• Give him blood transfusions and/or intravenous fluids.

ACTION PLAN:

Is there bright red blood dripping from or visible in your dog's mouth? Do you see blood coming from his nose or anus, or in his urine or stool? Is there bruising visible on his skin?

YES ▶ Call your veterinarian *NOW*—it could be a life-threatening condition caused by poison or an autoimmune disease^G.

 NO

Are there visible breaks in the skin around his mouth, gums, or tongue? Can you see any broken or loose teeth?

YES ▶ Call your veterinarian *NOW*—there may be other injuries of which you're not aware, or the injury could require surgical repair.

 NO

Can you see yellow or brown teeth? Are your dog's gums dark red, purplish, or inflamed-looking where they meet his teeth?

YES ▶ Call your veterinarian this week for an appointment. It sounds like dental (periodontal) disease.

NO

Call your veterinarian for an appointment.

What you see: You dog is pawing at his mouth, rubbing his face, gagging, or having trouble swallowing.

What this might mean: It could mean lots of things, but a lodged foreign body in his mouth is your most immediate concern.

PAWING AT THE MOUTH

ACTION PLAN:

Is your dog gagging or having trouble swallowing?

YES → Call your veterinarian *NOW*—your dog may have an obstruction due to a foreign body, so needs immediate help. See **Before You Leave #1**, page 159.

NO ↓

Is he pawing at his mouth? Yawning? Rubbing his face? Drooling? Does he have bad breath?

YES → Call your veterinarian *TODAY*—it could be a foreign body, allergy, and/or an infection.

NO ↓

Call your veterinarian for an appointment.

Common Foreign Bodies

Sometimes dogs ingest—or try to ingest—the strangest things, in the name of hunger, boredom (chewing), or play. When a dog regularly eats objects despite a healthy diet, it could mean a condition called PICA^G. Here's a list of common foreign bodies that vets run across:

- Chunks of wood
- Pieces of plastic
- Chunks/shards of bone (poultry and pork bones are common offenders)
- Sewing needles
- Straight pins
- Grass seeds
- Awns
- Sticks/twigs
- Small balls
- Splintered cow-hoof chews

3-H

Loose, Broken, or
MISSING TEETH

What you see: You notice that one or more of your dog's teeth is broken, fractured, or cracked. Or you spot other loose or missing teeth.

What this might mean: At the very least, your dog needs dental care. At the worst, mouth pain resulting from the problem could make him reluctant to eat and drink.

**YOUR VET
MAY NEED TO:**

• X-ray your dog's head if fractured or infected teeth, or a fractured skull or jaw are suspected.

• Refer you to a canine dental specialist, in the event your dog's damaged tooth requires a root canal, capping, or other such specialized treatment.

ACTION PLAN:

Is part of the tooth missing? Do you see exposed pulp in the tooth stump?

YES → Call your veterinarian *NOW*—immediate medical attention is necessary if the tooth is to be saved.

NO ↓

Do you see blood dripping from or in your dog's mouth?

YES → Go to **page 50**.

NO ↓

Does your dog have bad breath?

YES → Call your veterinarian *TODAY*—it could be periodontal[G] disease.

NO ↓

Is your dog drooling or slobbering?

YES → Go to **page 45**.

NO ↓

Does your dog's mouth seem sore? Is he approaching food/water, but not eating/drinking? Or, is he allowing food to fall out of his mouth?

YES → Call your veterinarian *TODAY*—it could be pain due to infection and/or an abscess resulting from the damaged tooth.

NO ↓

Can you see a crack or an obviously loose tooth?

YES → Call your veterinarian *TODAY*—the crack could be a sign of a deeper injury, and/or could ultimately result in a fracture. Tooth laxity could indicate advanced periodontal[G] disease, tumor, or such metabolic diseases as hyperparathyroidism[G].

NO ↓

Is the involved tooth pink, grey, beige, or brown?

YES → Call your veterinarian *TODAY*—the tooth's pulp could be dead or dying as a result of trauma, a condition known as pulpitis[G].

NO ↓

Are all of your dog's teeth yellow or brown? Are his gums red/inflamed where they meet his teeth?

YES → Call your veterinarian *TODAY*—it could be advanced periodontal disease[G].

Tooth Check

Have you checked your dog's teeth lately? Familiarizing yourself with what's normal for him will help you identify a problem, should it occur. As bacteria from dental disease invade your dog's gums and teeth, they can also enter his bloodstream, causing infection in such critical areas as his heart and kidneys. Save yourself some future vet bills by investing in regular dental exams for your dog, and brushing his teeth weekly at home. (See page 273.)

Fast Fact:

Periodontal disease[G] is the most common cause of tooth loss in adult dogs. And, it can be easily prevented with diligent dental care.

ABNORMAL GROWTH
In Mouth

What you see: A pink, dark-colored, and/or ulcerated lump or bump in your dog's mouth. It could be on his gum, cheeks, the roof of his mouth, or under his tongue.

What this might mean: It could be a number of things, from a benign epulis^G to a malignant melanoma^G (cancer) that could spread to other parts of his body. Any growth in your dog's mouth is cause for concern.

YOUR VET MAY NEED TO:

- **Sedate your dog, in order to thoroughly examine his mouth.**
- **Biopsy the growth and send it to a lab, to determine whether it's malignant.**
- **X-ray your dog's mouth, head, and chest, to determine whether a malignancy has spread to other parts of his body.**

ACTION PLAN:

Is the growth related to an embedded foreign body? (For instance, is the tissue around an embedded seed, twig, or awn angry, swollen, and inflamed?)

 YES Call your veterinarian *NOW*—immediate attention is needed to prevent further damage, and/or infection.

 NO

Does the lump/bump have an uneven surface? Is it bleeding? Does your dog have bad breath? Trouble eating?

 YES Call your veterinarian *TODAY* if you answered yes to any of these queries. It could be a benign^G tumor—or a malignant^G one, such as fibrosarcoma^G, melanoma^G or squamous cell carcinoma^G.

 NO

Does it appear to be a firm enlargement on the gum near the base of a tooth? Is your dog's breath foul?

YES Call your veterinarian *TODAY* if you answered yes to either one of these queries. It could be a benign oral tumor originating from your dog's gums, known as an epulis^G, or an abscessed tooth.

NO

Call your veterinarian for an appointment.

Cancer Facts

- Most mouth cancers occur in older dogs, with descendents of Cocker Spaniels and German Shepherds having the highest incidence.
- 95 percent of mouth growths are cancerous.
- Mouth cancers can be among the most aggressive forms of the disease.
- Surgery, chemotherapy, and radiation therapy are treatment options in some forms of cancer.

Oral Cancer Warning Signs

- Bleeding or discharge from the mouth or nose
- Abnormal swellings or growths that continue to grow
- Difficulty eating and/or swallowing
- Bad breath
- Difficulty breathing
- Lack of interest in food
- Dull, depressed attitude
- Weight loss

NOTES

CHAPTER 4

Problems of
THE EYE

What you see: Your dog is holding an eye partially or tightly closed, or is acting sensitive to light.

4-A

SQUINTING

What this might mean: His eye hurts. Depending on the cause of pain, the eye itself might be in jeopardy. Even a minor eye problem can be very painful. The discomfort will tempt your dog to rub or scratch his eye, which could result in further damage.

YOUR VET MAY NEED TO:

• Sedate your dog, and/or numb and immobilize the eye with medicated drops, in order to safely and thoroughly examine and treat it.

• Use a topical dye to check for corneal injury.

ACTION PLAN:

Does the cornea^G appear blue or very hazy? Is your dog lethargic, not eating, or vomiting? Are the whites of his eyes yellow?

 NO

YES → Call your veterinarian *NOW* if you answered yes to any query—it could be hepatitis blue eye^G. Isolate your dog from other pets until you head for the vet hospital.

Do you see any redness in or around your dog's eye and/or in his tears? Are the eyelids or skin around his eye swollen and/or abraded? Does he seem sensitive to light?

 NO

YES → Call your veterinarian *NOW* if you answered yes to any query—it could be injury, infection, or a foreign body in contact with your dog's eye, inflammation and/or infection of the tissues around the eye, or an eye condition called uveitis^G.

Is his eye cloudy or "steamy" looking?

 NO

YES → Call your veterinarian *NOW*—it could be trauma due to keratitis^G, corneal injury^G, uveitis^G, or glaucoma^G.

Do you see a foreign body?

 NO

YES → Call your veterinarian *NOW*—immediate medical treatment will be necessary to avoid further damage. See warning, opposite page.

Is the eye weeping? Are your dog's eyelids stuck together by a glue-like mucous discharge?

 NO

YES → Call your veterinarian *TODAY*—your dog may not be producing enough tears. See **page 60**.

Will your dog allow you to open the eyelid and treat his eye? Is any long hair around his eye stained or discolored by tears?

 NO

YES → It may be an irritant, such as hair, dirt, or dust. Apply **Home Treatment**, opposite page.

Call your veterinarian *NOW*—prompt treatment might be needed to prevent further eye injury.

HOME TREATMENT:

*(See **Action Plan** to determine whether home treatment is appropriate for your dog's squinting eye. If at any time during home treatment, your answers on the action plan change for the worse, call your vet.)*

Step 1. *Ice the eye.* Slip an ice pack (see page 311) between layers of a soft, clean, folded cloth. Using the technique outlined on page 310, chill the inflamed tissues around your dog's eye to reduce inflammation, discomfort, and swelling, and to relax the muscles around it. Hold the ice pack on for 5 minutes.

Step 2. *Wash the eye.* Warm a bottle of sterile saline irrigating eye wash (see page 300) by holding it under a stream of hot tap water until the saline is warm enough to feel barely perceptible when drizzled onto your wrist (about 98° F). Using the eye-rinsing technique out-lined on page 264, irrigate your dog's eye.

Step 3. *Lubricate the eye.* Using the technique for applying ophthalmic ointment outlined on page 265, apply a thin film of boric acid or Lacri-lube™ ophthalmic ointment to soothe and lubricate your dog's eye.

Step 4. *Clip the area.* Carefully clip or snip any offending hairs, to prevent further irritation.

Step 5. *Re-evaluate.* Five minutes after completing treatment, look at your dog's eye without approaching or touching his face. (If you were to do so, you might cause him to squint in anticipation.) Is the eye wide open, in its normal position? If so, the problem may have been due to irritation from dust or other loose debris, which you've washed out. If not, call your veterinarian NOW.

AVOID PULLING FOREIGN BODIES!

If you pull foreign matter (such as long hairs or grass stems) that are protruding from beneath your dog's eyelids, it could damage the cornea[G]. Instead, bandage the eye (see page 61) and call your veterinarian. He or she can sedate your dog if necessary, block his blink reflex if necessary, and safely lift any foreign matter off the cornea.

What you see: Your dog's eye has fluid coming from it, such as watery tears, a thick, pus-like discharge, or blood. It's collecting on his face, where a crust is forming.

4 - B

DISCHARGE FROM EYE

What this might mean: Eye irritation, possibly due to serious problems, including a foreign body, trauma, or infection. Even if it's a minor external problem (such as dust in the eye), the discomfort might tempt him to rub or scratch the eye, which could result in serious damage.

YOUR VET MAY NEED TO:

Sedate your dog, and/or numb and immobilize the eye using medicated drops, in order to facilitate a thorough and safe exam and treatment.

ACTION PLAN:

Is blood coming from the eye? Or is blood visible on the white of the eye, in/on the eye's surface, or anywhere else?

 YES ▶ Call your veterinarian *NOW* if you answered yes to any of these queries—it could be a bleeding disorder (see page 50), or eye trauma or internal eye disease. Fast action might be required to minimize damage. Go to **Before You Leave,** opposite page.

NO

Is the discharge cloudy, watery, or pus-like? Is the eye squinting or closed, even when you're making no motions to approach it?

 YES ▶ Call your veterinarian *NOW*—it could be a serious problem. Unprovoked squinting is a sign that eye pain is severe, making self-trauma likely and treatment difficult. Go to **Before You Leave.**

NO

Is the discharge cloudy, pus-like, or watery, but your dog is holding open his eye, and there's no cloudiness or redness in the eye itself?

 YES ▶ Call your veterinarian *TODAY*—it could be a less serious problem, such as conjunctivitis^G, that could worsen over time.

NO

Do you see a heavy, thick discharge that can sometimes "glue" the eye shut? Does the eye surface have a dull, dry, or pigmented appearance?

 YES ▶ Call your veterinarian *TODAY*—your dog may have dry eye^G, meaning he's not producing adequate tears, causing damage to his cornea^G.

NO

Will your dog allow you to open the eyelid and treat his eye?

 YES ▶ Apply **Home Treatment** (opposite page) if you answered yes to both queries—it could be irritation from dust.

NO

Call your veterinarian for an appointment. It could be a blocked nasolacrimal duct^G.

BEFORE YOU LEAVE:

1. *Keep your dog quiet.* Activity could cause further damage to the eye.

2. *Bring your dog indoors; stop him if he rubs.* Confine your dog to a dark room or otherwise protect him from wind, dust, and bright light that can further irritate his eye. Assign someone to watch and stop him if he rubs or scratches.

3. *Bandage the eye.* If your dog has been squinting and/or attempting to rub his eye, apply a padded eye bandage, such as a stack of gauze pads or a sanitary napkin. Secure it in place with an Ace bandage. *Be sure to apply no pressure to the eye as you do so, which could cause a fragile orb to rupture.* A bandage will help keep his eyelid closed. (When open, its frequent blinking and squinting can add more irritation to an already irritated eye). The bandage also will protect the eye from self-trauma.

HOME TREATMENT:

*See **Action Plan** to determine whether home treatment is appropriate for*

> **AVOID PULLING FOREIGN BODIES!**
> If you pull foreign matter (such as long hairs or grass stems) that are protruding from beneath your dog's eyelids, it could damage the cornea^G. Instead, bandage the eye and call your veterinarian. He or she can sedate your dog if necessary, block his blink reflex if necessary, and safely lift any foreign matter off the cornea.

> **AVOID FORCING AN EYE OPEN!**
> Some eye injuries are so severe that the eyeball is at risk of rupturing, either because of direct damage from the injury or because the injured eye's layers are weakened from infection. Your dog's defense against further eye injury—his blink reflex—is too powerful to overwhelm if it's fully activated. If you were to persist, your efforts could cause a fragile eye to rupture.

your dog's weeping eye. If at any time during your home treatment, your answers on the action plan change for the worse, call your vet.)

Step 1. *Clean dried discharge from around eye.* Wet a clean gauze sponge with room-temperature saline solution (see page 306) until saturated but not dripping. Lay the gauze over the trail of discharge. Hold for several seconds or as needed to soften, then wipe clean. This will prevent skin irritation from developing beneath the crust, and eliminate the risk of it attracting insects, which can further irritate the eyes.

Step 2. *Soothe and protect the eye and surrounding tissues.* Using the technique for applying ophthalmic ointment outlined on page 265, apply a thin film of boric acid or Lacri-lube™ ophthalmic ointment to soothe and lubricate your dog's eye.

Step 3. *Re-evaluate.* Five minutes after completing treatment, look at the eye: Is it still weeping? If so, call your vet NOW.

TIP:

To get an unenhanced look at your dog's uncomfortable eye without touching it or otherwise activating his blink reflex, stand 3 feet away, just in front of the bad eye's side. Make a sound that'll arouse his interest (whistle or kiss). Unless the eye pain is extreme, he'll widen his eye to see what you're doing.

BULGY-EYED BREEDS

If you own a bulgy-eyed breed such as a Pug, Pekinese, Bulldog, Boston Terrier, or Boxer, you may notice a chronic, small amount of discharge at the corner of your dog's eye. Bring it to your vet's attention, so he can check the dog for pigmentary keratitis^G, an inflammation of the cornea. (To be safe, have your dog checked even if he doesn't have a discharge.) The condition is so common in such breeds that it's considered almost "normal." However, it can be associated with such problems as dry eye^G, and if allowed to progress, could require a correction. Early detection may enable you to control the problem before it causes major damage.

4-C

What you see: Instead of a normal, clear appearance, your dog's eye looks cloudy—either there's a white spot, or the whole eye looks foggy or "steamy".

CLOUDY EYE

What this might mean: A potentially serious problem within or on the surface of the eyeball that threatens to impair your dog's vision.

ACTION PLAN:

Is your dog's eye reddened or squinting?

 YES ➤ Call your veterinarian *NOW*—redness or squinting can indicate eye pain, which in conjunction with cloudiness suggests a serious eye condition (e.g., corneal ulcer^G, keratitis^G, corneal wound, uveitis^G, trauma, or glaucoma^G).

NO ⬇

Does the cornea appear blue or very hazy? Is your dog lethargic, not eating, or vomiting? Are the whites of his eyes yellow?

 YES ➤ Call your veterinarian *NOW* if you answered yes to any query—it could be hepatitis blue eye^G. Isolate your dog from other pets until you head for the vet hospital.

NO ⬇

Is it a grayish, veil-like haze with blood vessels gradually creeping across the cornea^G, from temple to nose side? Is your dog of German Shepherd descent?

 YES ➤ Call your veterinarian *TODAY*—it could be pannus^G, a progressive condition.

NO ⬇

Do you see red vein-like structures extending onto the eyeball from its outer margins?

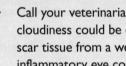 **YES** ➤ Call your veterinarian *TODAY*—the cloudiness could be due to edema or scar tissue from a well-established inflammatory eye condition.

NO ⬇

Does the cloudiness seem to be inside his pupil?

 YES ➤ Call your veterinarian *TODAY*—the cloudiness could indicate a cataract^G or lenticular sclerosis^G.

NO ⬇

ACTION PLAN (CONTINUED):

Do you see a free-moving, floating brown sphere, or "balloon" poking out from behind the iris, into the pupil?

 YES Sounds like an iris cyst^G. No treatment is necessary, but call your vet immediately if you notice a change for the worse.

 NO

Call your veterinarian for an appointment.

Are your old dog's eyes clouding up?

You may have noticed a blue/grey coloration within the pupil of your older dog's eye. Most dogs over the age of 6 or 7 will have this condition to some degree. It's called lenticular (or nuclear) sclerosis^G, and fortunately it doesn't greatly affect your dog's vision. However, if you see a general cloudiness or chrystalline look to one or both pupils, accompanied by any of the symptoms outlined in the Action Plan, call your vet immediately.

It could be a cataract or a serious eye condition.

EYE LOOKS RED

What you see: The inside of the eyelid or the white part of your dog's eye appears red.

What this might mean: The eye is inflamed. This could be a serious problem, or a simple one, depending on the underlying cause.

ACTION PLAN:

Is the red resulting from blood in or on the eye? **YES** Go to **page 60**.

 NO

Is the redness in the white part of your dog's eye? Does the eye appear to be cloudy or sore? **YES** Call your veterinarian *NOW* if you answered yes to either query—it could be a serious problem, such as trauma, glaucoma^G, or uveitis^G. See **Before You Leave**, opposite page.

 NO

Are the eyelids red and/or swollen? **YES** Call your veterinarian *NOW* if you answered yes to either query—it could be a serious allergic response.

 NO

Can you see a foreign body in the eye? **YES** Call your veterinarian *NOW*—immediate professional attention is necessary to remove the object, and thus help prevent further damage to your dog's eye. See **Before You Leave**.

 NO

Is the lid's inside lining red? **YES** Call your veterinarian *TODAY*—it could be conjunctivitis^G.

NO

Call your veterinarian for an appointment.

YOUR VET MAY NEED TO:

• Sedate your dog, and/or numb and immobilize the eye with medicated drops, in order to safely and thoroughly examine and treat it.

• Use a topical dye to check for corneal injury.

BEFORE YOU LEAVE:

1. *Keep your dog quiet.* Activity could cause further damage to the eye.

2. *Bring your dog indoors; stop him if he rubs.* Confine your dog to a dark room or otherwise protect him from wind, dust, and bright light that can further irritate his eye. Assign someone to watch him and stop him if he rubs or scratches.

3. *Bandage the eye.* If your dog has been squinting and/or attempting to rub his eye, apply a padded eye bandage, using a stack of gauze pads or a sanitary napkin. Secure it in place with an Ace bandage. *Be sure to apply no pressure to the eye as you do so, which could cause a fragile orb to rupture.* A bandage will help keep his eyelid closed. (When closed, the eyelid provides warmth, moisture, and form-fitting support to his eyeball; when open, its frequent blinking and squinting can add more irritation to an already irritated eye). The bandage also will protect the eye from self trauma.

AVOID PULLING FOREIGN BODIES!
If you pull foreign matter (such as long hairs or grass stems) that are protruding from beneath your dog's eyelids, it could damage the cornea[G]. Instead, bandage the eye and call your veterinarian, who can sedate your dog if necessary, block his blink reflex if necessary, and safely lift any foreign matter off the cornea.

AVOID FORCING AN EYE OPEN!
Some eye injuries are so severe that the eyeball is at risk of rupturing, either because of direct damage from the injury or because the injured eye's layers are weakened from infection. Your dog's defense against further eye injury—his blink reflex—is too powerful to overwhelm if it's fully activated. If you were to persist, your efforts could cause a fragile eye to rupture.

The whites of
EYES ARE YELLOW

What you see: The whites of your dog's eyes are yellow- or orange-tinged, a condition called icterus^G or jaundice^G. You also may notice a yellowish cast to his gums.

What this might mean: A blood disorder or liver disease.

ACTION PLAN:

Is your dog not eating, depressed, or feverish? Are his corneas^G blue or hazy?

 YES → Call your veterinarian *NOW*. Jaundice plus any of these signs could indicate acute^G liver disease. Go to **Before You Leave,** below.

 NO

Are your dog's lips and gums also pale or yellowish? Is his urine dark or tea-colored?

 YES → Call your veterinarian *NOW*—it could be a blood disorder called hemolytic anemia^G.

NO

Is your dog displaying abnormal behavior? Is he drooling? Weak/uncoordinated? Bleeding from the mouth or other openings? Does he have bruising evident on his skin?

YES → Call your veterinarian *NOW* if you answered yes to any of these queries—it could be a condition affecting your dog's central nervous system, such as poisoning, or toxins from liver disease.

 NO

Do your dog's limbs appear swollen? Is his abdomen bloated? Is he having trouble breathing?

 YES → Call your veterinarian *TODAY*—it could be a liver tumor, either benign^G or malignant^G.

NO

Call your veterinarian *TODAY* for an appointment.

YOUR VET MAY NEED TO:

• **Pull blood or urine samples for analysis.**
• **Provide intravenous fluid and/or blood transfusions.**

BEFORE YOU LEAVE:

1. *Isolate your dog from other pets in case it's contagious.* To prevent spread of possible infectious disease, confine your dog away from other pets. Wash your hands/disinfect your shoes (see page 374) after handling him and before handling other dogs.

TIP...

Regardless of the cause of your dog's jaundice, the yellow pigment in his skin can make him super-sensitive to ultraviolet rays of the sun, particularly if he's a light-colored dog with light or pink skin. As long as your dog's jaundice persists, protect him from the sun by keeping him indoors during the day, and/or applying non-chemical sunblock to exposed, light-colored skin.

Did You Know...

...autoimmune hemolytic anemia[G] can occur in any breed, and at any age. Both sexes are affected, but there is a greater incidence in middle-aged female dogs.

What you see: Your dog appears to be having difficulty seeing. He's reluctant to leave your side, stepping on things he'd usually avoid, colliding with obstacles, lifting his legs higher than usual, or stepping extra cautiously. (*Note:* The **Action Plan** that follows might mislead you if what you think is vision impairment turns out to be something else, such as dizziness or a mental disorder. If possible, confirm your suspicions with the **Quick Vision Test** that follows on the next page. If your dog's vision is not impaired, turn to the chapter that better describes his symptoms.)

What this could mean: Brain injury or illness, or injury or disease within the eye itself. It also may make your dog fearful. Be alert, and give him plenty of notice when you approach.

4-F

IMPAIRED VISION

ACTION PLAN:

Is the affected eye squinting, weeping, or cloudy looking?

 YES Go to **pages 58, 60, and 62,** respectively.

NO

Did your dog recently suffer a blow to the head? (See **The Nitty Gritty,** opposite.)

 YES Call your veterinarian *NOW*—it could be an injury to your dog's brain and/or optic nerve.

NO

Has your dog been dull, not eating, feverish, or diagnosed with an illness within the past week?

YES Call your veterinarian *NOW*—several diseases, including distemper[G], can cause blindness. Prompt treatment might restore your dog's vision.

NO

Does he seem blind only in diminished light? Is he of Retriever, Pointer, or Spaniel descent?

 YES Call your veterinarian for an appointment if you answered yes to any query—it could be progressive retinal atrophy[G].

NO

Are his pupils dilated? Do you notice a chrystalline white tint to his pupils?

 YES Call your veterinarian *TODAY*—it could be cataracts[G].

NO

Call your veterinarian for an appointment.

QUICK VISION TEST

USE THIS TEST TO HELP YOU DECIDE WHETHER YOUR DOG IS TRULY VISION-IMPAIRED, AND WHETHER THE PROBLEM HAS AFFECTED ONE OR BOTH EYES.

1. Blindfold one eye by laying a thick pad, such as a stack of gauze squares, across the eye. Hold the pad in place with an Ace bandage.

2. Wear clothing that doesn't "swish." In a well-lit area with minimal distractions, have a helper loosely hold your dog. Stand 3 feet away, in front of the uncovered eye, and lob 3 cotton balls toward him, one after the other, so they bounce gently off the top of his face between his eye and nose. Did he flinch when the first one approached, before it touched him? Did he try to catch the second? Did he watch the third one? If your answers are no, no, and no, he probably can't see. Repeat with the other eye.

3. If you're still unsure, in a well-lit area and with one of his eyes covered, lead your dog on a loose leash toward a low obstacle, such as a stick or small log (depending on your dog's size) set 10 feet ahead. Walk purposefully—don't go so slowly that he has time to lower his head and smell it. Does he try to avoid hitting the obstacle? If not, he probably can't see it. Cover the other eye, and repeat.

Adapted from "Horse & Rider's Hands-On Horse Care"

The Nitty Gritty
Here are some things that may cause blindness in your dog

THE CAUSE	THE SOURCE
General illness	• Rabies • Parvovirus • Distemper • Rocky Mountain spotted fever • Encephalitis • Influenza • Liver disease • Meningitis • Staphylococcus • Streptococcus • E-Coli • Pseudomonas • Systemic fungi
Cancer	• Malignant lymphoma • Multiple myeloma • Tumors of brain or eye
Eye conditions	• Uveitis • Pannus • Cataracts • Corneal degeneration • Retinal degeneration • Retinal detachment • Lens luxation • Glaucoma • Infection
Injury	• Direct trauma to eye • Imbedded foreign body • Head/brain trauma
	(See Glossary for detailed descriptions.)

What you see: Growths and/or ulcerated sores around your dog's eye, which are smooth or rough in texture, or raw and angry-looking. They can involve only the lids, or they can invade the eyeball itself.

4-G

EYE GROWTHS
Or sores

What this might mean: The presence of an invasive local condition, such as squamus cell carcinoma^G or some other form of tumor, which could grow aggressively and impair your dog's vision and/or threaten his appearance. Some types of eye cancer can spread to other parts of the body.

YOUR VET MAY NEED TO:

Obtain a sample of the growth to send to a laboratory for identification. This might require sedation or anesthesia.

ACTION PLAN:

Is the growth a red, ulcerated lesion on white or pink skin around your dog's eye? → **YES** → Call your veterinarian *TODAY*—it could be an erosive skin condition such as pemphigus^G, photosensitization^G, or squamous cell carcinoma^G. Go to **Before You Leave**, below.

NO

Is the growth on the pink membrane on the inside corner of your dog's eye? → **YES** → Go to **page 73**.

NO

Is it a dark, hair-covered growth on the eyelid, white part of the eye, or over the cornea^G? → **YES** → Call your veterinarian *TODAY*—it might be a dermoid^G.

NO

Does the growth extend to or into the eyeball itself? → **YES** → Call your veterinarian *TODAY*—it could be cancer.

NO

Is the involved eye squinting, weeping, or cloudy? → **YES** → Go to **pages 58, 60, and 62**, respectively.

NO

Is the growth at the edge of your dog's eyelid? Is it wart-like, or round and smooth? → **YES** → Call your veterinarian *TODAY*—it could be a cyst^G, tumor^G, or infection.

NO

Call your vet for an appointment.

BEFORE YOU LEAVE:

Protect against UV exposure. If you have a lightly pigmented dog and live in the sunbelt, or a high-altitude area and until a veterinary exam rules out sun-sensitive lesions, such as photosensitization^G or certain kinds of skin cancer^G, bring your dog indoors. Otherwise, apply a UV-blocking sunscreen, and/or talk to your vet about tatooing the light areas black, to provide permanent sun protection.

What you see: Your dog's upper eyelid seems to droop on one side, draping across his eye and giving him a sad look.

What this might mean: A problem in part of the nerve supply to his head. It's the underlying problem, rather than the eyelid droop itself, that poses a threat.

DROOPING EYELID

ACTION PLAN:

Is your dog showing signs of loss of appetite, fever, dullness, weight loss, weakness, dizziness, or lack of coordination?

 NO

Is his ear drooping on the same side as the droopy eyelid? Are his lips and/or muzzle drawn over to one side?

 NO

Is there a pale pink "curtain" (the third eyelidᴳ) drawn up over the inner corner of his eyeball(s)? And/or is the pupil constricted on the same side?

 NO

Call your veterinarian for an appointment.

YES ▶ Call your veterinarian *NOW*—it could be a general illness affecting your dog's nervous system, possibly including rabiesᴳ. (See **Caution**, next page.)

YES ▶ Call your veterinarian *TODAY* if you answered yes to either query—it could be a paralyzed facial nerve (see **The Nitty Gritty**, next page). Go to **Before You Leave,** below.

 YES ▶ Call your veterinarian *TODAY* if you answered yes to either query—it could be Horner's syndromeᴳ.

YOUR VET MAY NEED TO:

• X-ray your dog's head and/or neck if injury in either area is suspected to have damaged the nerves there.

• Perform lab work, to help confirm a diagnosis.

BEFORE YOU LEAVE:

1. *Protect the affected eye.* Facial nerve injury can cause decreased tear production and make it difficult for your dog to close his eyelids completely. If rabies is *not* a possibility, use the technique for applying ophthalmic ointment outlined on page 265. Apply a thin film of boric acid or Lacri-lube® ophthalmic ointment to keep your dog's eye moist. ➤

The Nitty Gritty

Here are some possible causes of facial nerve paralysis in your dog, and possible causes of damage to the nerves that supply his head.

- *Blunt trauma to the side of your dog's face.* Sample scenario: He was hit by a car.
- *Infection in the brain or spinal cord.*
- *Injury to his neck.*
- *IV injection.* Sample scenario: Injected medication leaked outside the vein and into adjacent tissues that house nerve fibers.
- *Injury, abscess, or tumor in the brain, spinal cord, or chest.*

CAUTION

Among the possible causes of facial paralysis, an inability to swallow, mental changes, and/or gait abnormalities is a rare but notorious one: **Rabies**G. If rabies is a consideration in your dog's case, don't take chances—take precautions.

1. **Call for help!** This is a veterinary 9-1-1. Call your veterinarian and/or animal control. Such professionals can advise you of how to impound the dog. Rabies is always fatal in dogs—your goal now will be to minimize exposure to yourself, your family, and other pets/animals.

2. **Isolate!** Immediately isolate the dog from all other animals and humans in your household. A rabid dog's saliva is teaming with rabies virus, which is highly contagious to humans/animals. Avoid any contact with the dog. If you must handle him, don intact, water-repellant gloves (such as household rubber gloves), and protect all other body parts from contact with his saliva. Shower immediately after exposure to the dog.

3. **Be alert** for unexpected behavior. Rabies can cause aggression and/or a lack of coordination. Stay out of harm's way.

4. **If you or anyone in your family is bitten** or licked by a suspected rabies carrier, immediately wash the area with warm, soapy water—and call your doctor for advice.

5. **Clean up!** Ask your vet and/or animal control official how to properly disinfect any areas the dog has been.

6. **Think back.** Has your dog had any contact/exposure with wildlife, such as skunks, bats, racoons, or foxes? Familiarize yourself with those animals that are known rabies carriers in your area, and protect your pets—and children—from them.

7. **Alert animal control** officials if you see an odd-behaving critter in your area. (For instance, if you see a nocturnal animal such as a skunk or racoon moseying around during daylight, that's a red-alert.)

8. **Save it.** If your dog kills a wild animal, use the above clothing precautions, then bag the carcass and call your vet or the health department. They can test the animal for the rabies virus, so you'll know whether your dog—and family—have been exposed.

What you see: A pink curtainlike membrane or red mass is covering the inner corner of your dog's eyeball, as much as one-third of it. It extends across the eyeball at an angle.

What this might mean: What you're seeing is a normal structure called the third eyelid^G. Usually it's hidden, tucked into the inner corner of your dog's eye where the upper and lower lids meet. A variety of problems can make the third eyelid come out of hiding: Some are mild and temporary, such as superficial pain from dust; others can be severe and permanent, such as brain damage.

THIRD EYELID
Or Red Mass Is evident

ACTION PLAN:

Is your dog showing other signs of illness, such as lethargy, no appetite, lack of water consumption, fever, and/or diarrhea?

YES → Call your veterinarian NOW if you answered yes to any of these queries—it could be a serious systemic disease. Go to **Before You Leave #1**, next page.

NO ↓

Does his upper lid droop? Is the pupil on the same side constricted?

YES → Call your veterinarian NOW if you answered yes to either query—it could be a neurological injury resulting in facial paralysis, or Horner's syndrome^G. See **Before You Leave #2**.

NO ↓

Do you see a red mass on the inside corner of his eye?

YES → Call your veterinarian TODAY—it could be hypertrophy^G of the gland on his third eyelid, commonly called "cherry eye^G."

NO ↓

Does the affected eye squint?

YES → Go to **page 58**.

NO ↓

Call your veterinarian today for an appointment.

➤

YOUR VET MAY NEED TO:

X-ray your dog's head and/or neck if injury in either area is suspected to have damaged the nerves there.

BEFORE YOU LEAVE #1:

1. *Isolate your dog from other dogs in case it's contagious.* To prevent spread of possible infectious disease, confine your dog with a separate water supply, apart from other dogs by at least 20 feet. Wash your hands and disinfect your shoes (see page 374) after handling your dog and before handling other dogs.

2. *Protect yourself.* A dog with neurological problems may increasingly have trouble controlling his muscles and might move in spastic or unexpected ways. Be alert, and avoid putting yourself in harm's way.

3. *Keep him quiet.* Protect your dog against noises and excitement. A neurological problem could cause him to over-react, putting him—and you—at risk for injury.

BEFORE YOU LEAVE #2:

1. *Protect the affected eye.* Facial nerve injury can cause decreased tear production and make it difficult for your dog to close his eyelids completely. This leaves the eyeballs at risk of drying. Using the technique for applying ophthalmic ointment outlined on page 265, apply a thin film of boric acid or Lacri-lube™ ophthalmic ointment.

Eye Out of it's Socket—A True Emergency

If your dog is of a type that has large, bulging eyes and a short, flat face (such as a Pug, Pekinese, Boston Terrier, or a mixed breed of that type), you could face an emergency in which his eye pops out of its socket, a problem not uncommon with such dogs. Known as proptosis[G], it's generally caused by trauma. If it happens to your dog:

- Immediately call your vet. Describe the problem and tell him/her that you're on your way. The faster you can get your dog to medical help, the better his chance for a full recovery. (Swelling behind the eye, which begins shortly after the eye leaves its socket, can make replacing it more difficult as time passes.)
- Unless otherwise instructed by your vet, do not attempt to replace the eye. If you were to do so, you could inadvertently cause additional trauma and swelling to the area.
- Gently cover the eye with a moistened stack of gauze pads and an Ace bandage, applying just enough pressure to hold the bandage in place, but not so much as to press the orb, which could damage it.
- Head to your vet's—STAT! He or she will replace the eye in its socket. If much swelling has occurred, your vet may need to suture the eyelids closed, to hold the eye in place until swelling has subsided.

What you see: A cut on your dog's upper or lower eyelid.

What this might mean: If not properly repaired, it could leave the eyeball unprotected and/or allow it to heal out of position (and cause trauma to your dog's eye).

CUT EYELID

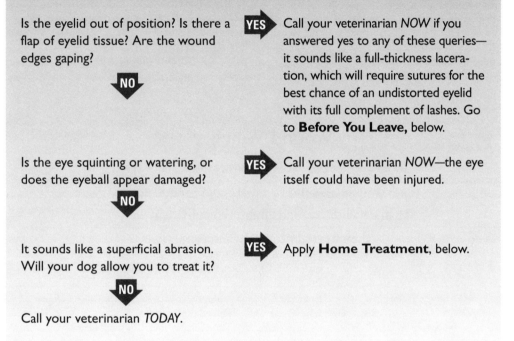

ACTION PLAN:

Is the eyelid out of position? Is there a flap of eyelid tissue? Are the wound edges gaping?

NO ↓

YES ▶ Call your veterinarian *NOW* if you answered yes to any of these queries—it sounds like a full-thickness laceration, which will require sutures for the best chance of an undistorted eyelid with its full complement of lashes. Go to **Before You Leave,** below.

Is the eye squinting or watering, or does the eyeball appear damaged?

NO ↓

YES ▶ Call your veterinarian *NOW*—the eye itself could have been injured.

It sounds like a superficial abrasion. Will your dog allow you to treat it?

NO ↓

YES ▶ Apply **Home Treatment**, below.

Call your veterinarian *TODAY*.

YOUR VET MAY NEED TO:

Sedate your dog, and/or numb and immobilize the eye using medicated drops, in order to facilitate a thorough and safe exam and treatment.

BEFORE YOU LEAVE:

1. *Ice the eye.* To reduce inflammation, discomfort, and swelling, and to relax the muscles around the eye, slip an ice pack (see page 311) between layers of a soft, clean, folded cloth. Lay the covered pack over your dog's eye, making sure there are no large clumps in the bag that might cause discomfort. Keep the ice on for 5 minutes, then off for 15. Repeat.

HOME TREATMENT

*(See **Action Plan** to determine whether home treatment is appropriate for your dog's eyelid laceration. If at any time during home treatment, your answers on the action plan*

AVOID FORCING AN EYE OPEN!
Some eye injuries are so severe that the eyeball is at risk of rupturing, either because of direct damage from the injury or because the injured eye's layers are weakened from infection. Your dog's defense against further eye injury—his blink reflex—is too powerful to overwhelm if it's fully activated. If you were to persist, your efforts could cause a fragile eye to rupture.

change for the worse, call your veterinarian.)

Step 1. *Ice the wound.* Slip an ice pack ▶

(see page 311) between layers of clean cloth. Lay the covered pack over the wound, making sure there are no large clumps in the bag that might cause discomfort. Hold it in place for 5 minutes.

Step 2. *Clean the wound.* Wet a stack of gauze sponges or a clean, folded washcloth in homemade saline solution (see page 306). Dab it gently over the wound until it appears visibly clean, replacing the gauze or cloth when it becomes soiled.

Step 3. *Dress the wound.* Apply a thin layer of an emollient such as Lacri-Lube™ (see page 265) to keep the wound edges moist and to act as a barrier to dust and insects.

Step 4. *Keep it up.* Repeat Steps 2 and 3 once or twice daily, depending on how dirty and/or crusty the wound becomes. Begin by cleaning it twice daily; reduce to once daily if it becomes only slightly crusty. Continue until the wound remains clean and uncrusted between cleanings (about 3 to 4 days).

Wound Watch...

Your dog's eyelid laceration may look nasty, but
don't despair. Thanks to an excellent blood supply
to his eyelids, wounds there typically heal well
when treated promptly and properly.

What you see: Your dog's pupils are both widely dilated in normal light, or are unequal in size.

What this might mean: The reason could be as benign as a recent fright or excitement, or your dog's pupil irregularity could indicate problems involving his brain, nervous system, or the eye itself.

ABNORMAL PUPILS

ACTION PLAN:

Is there any evidence/history of head trauma, such as wounds, scrapes, bruising, or swelling? **YES** ➤ Call your veterinarian *NOW*—it could be a serious brain injury.

 NO

Is your dog unconscious or having seizures? Is he poorly responsive, uncoordinated, and/or drooling? Is he exhibiting any other abnormal behavior? **YES** ➤ Call your veterinarian *NOW*—it could be rabies^G, encephalitis^G, concussive head injury, or other serious neurological problem. See **Caution**, page 72, and **Before You Leave**, next page.

 NO

Does one eye have a smaller pupil than the other? Is there redness or cloudiness in the small-pupil eye? **YES** ➤ Call your veterinarian *NOW*—it could be an eye injury or other cause of ocular^G inflammation.

 NO

Is one pupil dilated (large)? Is the eye inflamed, larger, and more tense than the other eye? Is the cornea^G cloudy? **YES** ➤ Call your veterinarian *NOW*—it could be glaucoma^G.

 NO

Are both pupils dilated and unresponsive to bright light? Does your dog seem blind in normal light? Do his pupils appear to be gray or white instead of black? **YES** ➤ Call your veterinarian *NOW*—it could be cataracts^G, or retinal, optic nerve, or brain injury/disease.

 NO

Are both pupils dilated? Are they sluggishly responsive to bright light? Does your dog seem blind in reduced light but able to see in bright light? **YES** ➤ Call your veterinarian *TODAY*—it could be progressive retinal atrophy^G.

 NO ➤

YOUR VET MAY NEED TO:

- **Sedate your dog in order to do a thorough neurological work up, which could include X-raying the affected area.**
- **Refer you to a specialist, who could perform such neurological tests as a CAT scan^G, MRI^G, or myelogram^G.**

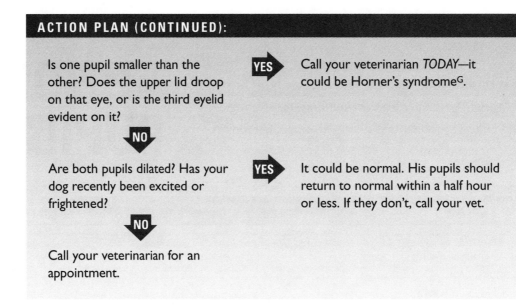

ACTION PLAN (CONTINUED):

Is one pupil smaller than the other? Does the upper lid droop on that eye, or is the third eyelid evident on it? — **YES** → Call your veterinarian *TODAY*—it could be Horner's syndrome[G].

NO ↓

Are both pupils dilated? Has your dog recently been excited or frightened? — **YES** → It could be normal. His pupils should return to normal within a half hour or less. If they don't, call your vet.

NO ↓

Call your veterinarian for an appointment.

BEFORE YOU LEAVE #1:

1. *Isolate your dog from other dogs in case it's contagious.* To prevent the spread of possible infectious disease, confine your dog away from other dogs. Wash your hands and disinfect your shoes (see page 374) after handling your dog and before handling other dogs.

2. *Remove loose objects.* To prevent inadvertent injury, remove any loose/sharp objects with which your dog could intersect.

Breeds Prone to Inherited Cataracts[G]

- Afghan Hounds
- American Cocker Spaniels
- Boston Terriers
- Chesapeake Bay Retrievers
- German Shepherds
- Golden Retrievers
- Labrador Retrievers
- Miniature Schnauzers
- Old English Sheepdogs
- Siberian Huskies
- Staffordshire Bull Terriers
- Standard Poodles
- Welsh Springer Spaniels
- West Highland White Terriers

Breeds Prone to Inherited Progressive Retinal Atrophy (PRA)[G]

- Akitas
- American Cocker Spaniels
- Belgian Sheepdogs
- Border Collies
- Briards
- Collies
- English Cocker Spaniels
- Irish Setters
- Labrador Retrievers
- Longhaired Dachshunds
- Miniature Schnauzers
- Miniature Poodles
- Norwegian Elkhounds
- Samoyeds
- Shetland Sheepdogs
- Tibetan Terriers
- Toy Poodles

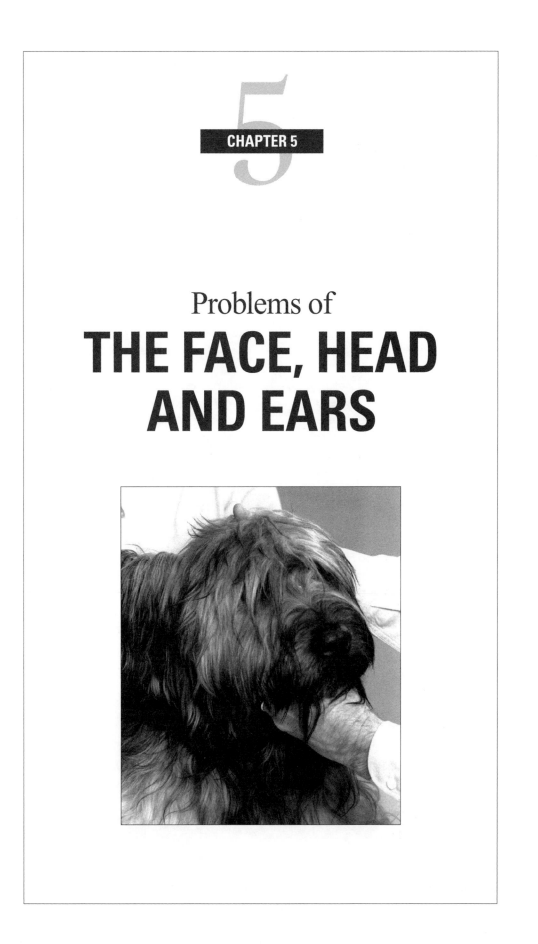

CHAPTER 5

Problems of
THE FACE, HEAD
AND EARS

What you see: Your dog suddenly and almost violently starts shaking his head and/or tilting it. He may also scratch at his ear.

5-A

HEAD SHAKING/TILT

What this might mean: Head-shaking can be a sign of a injury to his ear flap, infection of the ear canal, or a foreign body in his ear canal.

ACTION PLAN:

Is your dog tilting his head? Does he appear dizzy? Is he stumbling or circling in one direction? Does he appear to have lost his hearing in the ear?

 YES Call your veterinarian *NOW* if you answered yes to two or more of these queries—it could be an inner-ear infection, tumor, or an infectious disease such as distemper[G] or encephalitis[G]. See **Before You Leave**, opposite.

 NO

Is your dog shaking his head violently? Is there a visible wound, drainage, or bleeding from the ear? Do you see a dry, reddish-brown or black wax, or coffee-ground like specs in the ear canal? Does he act painful when you touch him around the ear(s)?

 YES Call your veterinarian *NOW* if you answered yes to any of these queries— it could be a foreign body in the ear canal, ear mites[G] (the "coffee grounds" you see are dried blood), a tick infestation, and/or your dog could cause further damage by shaking or scratching at his ear. (See page 323 for how to protect the ear until you leave.)

 NO

YOUR VET MAY NEED TO:

Sedate your dog to thoroughly examine the ear and canal, collect a sample for culture or cytology[G], and remove a foreign body, if necessary.

Does your dog's face droop on the affected side, with his ear hanging lower than normal? Is there a foul-smelling discharge present in the ear canal? Does he exhibit pain when he opens his mouth?

 YES Call your veterinarian *NOW* if you answered yes to any of these queries— it could be a middle-ear infection and/or a ruptured ear drum.

 NO

Is the ear flap swollen or fluid-filled?

 YES Call your veterinarian *NOW*—it could be an allergic response or a hematoma[G].

 NO

Is there intermittent head shaking? Does he stand with his head cocked to one side? Is your dog scratching at his ear? Is the inner ear red, with no discharge?

 YES Call your veterinarian *TODAY*—it could be a foreign body, allergy, or infection in the external ear canal.

 NO

Call your vet for an appointment.

BEFORE YOU LEAVE:

1. *Avoid triggers.* If you've identified a possible trigger for the head-shaking (such as insects), help your dog avoid it until you get him to a veterinarian.

2. *Minimize stress.* If your dog is showing any other signs of abnormal nerve function (abnormal gait, dizziness, staggering, circling, body or tail bent to one side), minimize his stress and isolate him. This is both for his protection and to limit spread of a possible contagious condition. Wash your hands and disinfect your shoes (see page 374) after handling your dog and before handling others.

Did You Know...

...your aging canine's deafness is considered a normal condition and is seen in at least 50 percent of all geriatric dogs. As the eardrum and nerves associated with hearing deteriorate, loss of hearing can occur. Fortunately, the hearing loss generally is a gradual one, and rarely affects your dog's well-being. There is currently no treatment, nor is there a way to predict the full extent of the deafness.

What you see: Your dog's face is drooping, due to one or more of the following: One eyelid, ear, or lip is sagging; or his muzzle is pulled over to one side.

DROOPY FACE
(Deviated muzzle, sagging eye, slanted ear)

What this might mean: At the very least, it means a facial nerve is paralyzed, and there's no way of knowing right now whether it's permanent. What's more important is what caused the paralysis, and whether any other nerves, and/or the brain itself, are involved.

ACTION PLAN:

Is your dog ill, confused, agressive, incoordinated or feverish?

 NO

 YES Call your veterinarian *NOW*—it could be a disease involving the brain, including rabies^G. See **Caution**, and go to **Before You Leave,** next page.

Does his upper eyelid or lip droop on the same side? Does he have a history of ear infections or trauma?

 NO

 YES Call your veterinarian *NOW* if you answered yes to any of these queries—it could be a possible facial nerve injury.

Is your dog's head tilted? Does his ear droop? Does he stagger, or appear dizzy?

 NO

 YES Call your veterinarian *NOW*—it could be a an external-, middle-, or inner-ear infection.

Do your dog's jaws appear to be paralyzed? Is he having trouble eating/drinking, and/or is he unable to close his mouth?

 NO

 YES Call your veterinarian *NOW*—it could be Horner's syndrome,^G or trigeminal neuritis^G.

Is his droopy face the only symptom?

 NO

 YES Call your veterinarian *TODAY*—it could be a facial nerve injury.

Call your veterinarian *NOW*.

BEFORE YOU LEAVE:

1. *Isolate your dog from other dogs in case it's contagious.* To prevent spread of possible infectious disease, confine your dog to an area with a separate water supply, apart from other dogs. Wash your hands and disinfect your shoes (see page 374) after handling your dog and before handling other dogs.

2. *Protect your dog from further injury.* Remove protruding objects from his area, and keep noise to a minimum.

3. *Protect his affected eyes, if necessary.* Facial nerve injury can cause decreased tear production and make it difficult for your dog to close his eyelids completely. This leaves the eyeball at risk of drying. Using the technique for applying ophthalmic ointment outlined on page 265, apply a thin film of boric acid or Lacri-lube™ ophthalmic ointment to keep your dog's eye(s) moist.

CAUTION

Among the possible causes of drooling, facial paralysis, mental changes, and/or gait abnormalities is a rare but notorious one: **Rabies**[G]. If rabies is a consideration in your dog's case, don't take chances—take precautions.

1. Call for help! This is a veterinary 9-1-1. Call your veterinarian and/or animal control. Such professionals can advise you of how to impound the dog. Rabies is always fatal in dogs—your goal now will be to minimize exposure to yourself, your family, and other pets/animals.

2. Isolate! Immediately isolate the dog from all other animals and humans in your household. A rabid dog's saliva is teaming with rabies virus, which is highly contagious to humans/animals. Avoid any contact with the dog. If you must handle him, don intact, water-repellant gloves (such as household rubber gloves), and protect all other body parts from contact with his saliva. Shower immediately after exposure to the dog.

3. Be alert for unexpected behavior. Rabies can cause aggression and/or a lack of coordination. Stay out of harm's way.

4. If you or anyone in your family is bitten or licked by a suspected rabies carrier, immediately wash the area with warm, soapy water—and call your doctor for advice.

5. Clean up! Ask your vet and/or animal control official how to properly disinfect any areas the dog has been.

6. Think back. Has your dog had any contact/exposure with wildlife, such as skunks, bats, racoons, or foxes? Familiarize yourself with those animals that are known rabies carriers in your area, and protect your pets—and children—from them.

7. Alert animal control officials if you see an odd-behaving critter in your area. (For instance, if you see a nocturnal animal such as a skunk or racoon moseying around during daylight, that's a red-alert.)

8. Save it. If your dog kills a wild animal, use the above clothing precautions, then bag the carcass and call your vet or the health department. They can test the animal for the rabies virus, so you'll know whether your dog—and family—have been exposed.

5-C

EAR HELD TO ONE SIDE

What you see: Your dog's normally erect ear is being held to one side.

What this might mean: A mild, simple problem such as irritation of the upright portion of his ear, or a severe problem such as a brain injury.

ACTION PLAN:

Is your dog not eating, depressed, and/or feverish?

YES → Call your veterinarian *NOW*—it could be distemper[G] or encephalitis[G]. Go to **Before You Leave,** opposite page.

 NO

Does your dog stagger or act drunk when walking? Is his head held at a tilt?

YES → Call your veterinarian *NOW* if you answered yes to either of these queries—it could be a brain injury, encephalitis[G], or a deep infection in the inner ear.

 NO

Has he been shaking his head? Is he scratching at his ear/face?

YES → Go to **page 80**.

 NO

Does your dog have a droopy eyelid? Is his muzzle pulled over to one side?

YES → Go to **page 71** and **page 82**, respectively.

 NO

Do you see a large, fluid-filled lump on your dog's ear flap?

YES → Call your veterinarian *NOW*—it could be an aural hematoma[G].

 NO

Is there a reddish/brownish wax on the inside of the upright portion of his ear?

YES → Call your veterinarian *TODAY*—it could be ear mites[G].

 NO

Do the tips of your dog's ears appear to be raw, crusty and "eaten away"?

YES → Sounds like fly bites. See **Home Treatment**, opposite page.

 NO

Call your veterinarian for an appointment.

BEFORE YOU LEAVE:

1. *Isolate your dog from other dogs in case it's contagious.* To prevent the spread of possible infectious disease, confine your dog to an area with a separate water supply, apart from other dogs. Wash your hands and disinfect your shoes (see page 374) after handling your dog and before handling other dogs.

2. *Protect your dog from further injury.* Remove protruding objects from his area, and keep noise to a minimum to avoid startling him.

HOME TREATMENT

(See Action Plan to determine whether home treatment is appropriate for your dog's case of ear drooping. If at any time during home treatment, your answers on the action plan change for the worse, call your veterinarian.)

Step 1. *Soften and loosen scabs.* Apply a medicated scab softener (see page 306) generously to your dog's ear tips. Leave on for an hour, or until scabs are easily removed.

Step 2. *Clean the area.* Use a square gauze pad and homemade saline solution (see page 306) to remove softened scabs and grunge from ear tips.

Step 3. *Apply fly-repelling wound ointment.* Generously apply a layer of a wound ointment that repels flies, such as Onex (by Happy Jack), Flys-Off (by Farnam), or Swat (an equine fly-repellent wound ointment). These products are available through pet stores, feed stores, or through pet-supply catalogs.

Step 4. *Keep it up.* Repeat Steps 1 through 3 daily for seven days, or until lesions are healed. Continue with Step 3 until biting insect season ends in your region.

Step 5. *Control the environment.* Clean your yard frequently, secure trash-can lids, and use dog- and people-safe fly baits to control fly populations. (See "Caution," page 18.)

What you see: The flap of your dog's ear has a fluid-filled bulge in it.

SWOLLEN EAR FLAP

What this might mean: This condition is called an aural hematoma[G], and is the result of trauma to his ear flap. As it heals, it's common for an untreated ear flap to become misshapen from shrinkage of damaged cartilage.

ACTION PLAN:

Is the swollen ear warm? Is your dog shaking his head often? Does he resent having the ear touched?

NO

YES Call your veterinarian *NOW*—it might be ear mites[G] or infection in the ear canal, with self-trauma to the ear as a result. (See page 323 for how to protect the ear until you leave.)

Is the entrance to the ear canal swollen?

NO

YES Call your veterinarian *NOW*—the ear canal should be cleaned out to prevent or treat infection.

Call your veterinarian for an appointment.

Keep Bugs at Bay...

To keep flying insects from pestering your dog's ears without using chemical insecticides, try these tips:

• Put him out at night and bring him inside during the day, when biting flies are a problem.
• Or, apply a thin coat of petroleum jelly on the inner and outer surface of the upright portion of his ear, which will discourage bugs from landing.

What you see: There's a draining wound on your dog's face, which you discovered after cleaning off a scab or wad of crust.

What this might mean: It could be a sign of a tooth abscess, or the result of a bite wound that's gotten infected. Whatever the cause, your dog could suffer permanent damage without proper treatment.

DRAINING WOUND
On the face

ACTION PLAN:

Is the drainage coming from under your dog's lower jaw?

 YES Call your veterinarian *TODAY*—it might be an injury or an abscessed lower tooth.

 NO

Is the opening below his eye or on the side of his muzzle? Is the drainage pus-like?

YES Call your veterinarian *TODAY* if you answered yes to both queries—it might be an infected injury or an abscessed upper tooth.

 NO

Is the opening on or near the bony ridge that forms the front of your dog's face? Is there a swelling, or a dent, in or near that location?

YES Call your veterinarian *TODAY*—it might be a previous injury, possibly a facial bone fracture.

 NO

Call your veterinarian for an appointment.

YOUR VET MAY NEED TO:

Sedate your dog in order to facilitate a thorough and safe examination and/or treatment of the dog's teeth and mouth, if a dental problem is suspected.

Fast Fact:
Periodontal disease is the most common cause of tooth loss in adult dogs. And, it can be easily prevented with diligent dental care.

FLESH WOUND
On the ear

What you see: Your dog's ear flap has been cut, mangled, or the tip's missing.

What this might mean: The ear could become permanently misshapen.

ACTION PLAN:

Has the ear been lacerated? **NO**

YES Call your veterinarian *NOW*—it might need stitches to prevent or minimize curling or puckering.

Has the ear been mangled or bitten? **NO**

YES Call your veterinarian *NOW*—it might need surgical reconstruction for a cosmetically improved result.

Has the ear tip become blunted after a sub-zero cold spell? **NO**

YES Call your veterinarian *TODAY*—it's probably frostbite. Frostbitten ears can be re-shaped surgically to look more normal.

Call your veterinarian *TODAY* for an appointment.

Ear-Flap Fact...

Your dog's ear flap injury needs immediate veterinary attention in order to obtain the best possible cosmetic result. Here's why: The ear flap is built with one layer of cartilage sandwiched between two layers of skin. When injured, the space between cartilage and skin can fill with blood, which can distort the tissues and lead to puckering. With surgical help, this can generally be minimized—or even eliminated.

What you see: Your dog holds his head cocked to one side.

What this might mean: It could mean there's been an injury or an irritating condition in his inner ear or brain.

HEAD TILT

ACTION PLAN:

Is your dog not eating, depressed or feverish?

 YES Call your veterinarian *NOW* if you answered yes to any of these queries—it could be a brain disease, including rabies^G. See **Caution** below, and go to **Before You Leave,** below.

 NO

Is your dog shaking his head and/or scratching at it?

 YES Go to **page 80**.

NO

Call your veterinarian *TODAY* for diagnosis and treatment of the underlying cause. Go to **Before You Leave,** below.

BEFORE YOU LEAVE:

1. *Isolate your dog from other dogs in case it's contagious.* To prevent spread of possible infectious disease, confine your dog to an area with a separate water supply, apart from other dogs. Wash your hands and disinfect your shoes (see page 374) after handling your dog and before handling other dogs.

2. *Protect your dog from accidents.* If your dog is having trouble with his equilibrium, remove protruding objects from his area and keep noises to a minimum, to avoid startling him.

> **CAUTION**
> Among the possible causes of nervous system disease causing nerve dysfunction is a rare but notorious one: Rabies. Don't take chances—take precautions. See page 83.

What you see: Your dog's face or head is obviously swollen or misshapen. The swelling may be hard (as though it's part of his bone structure), or soft, like swollen soft tissue. It could feel cool or warm to the touch.

SWOLLEN
Or misshapen
FACE OR HEAD

What this might mean: Several potentially serious problems can cause facial distortion, ranging from an abscessed tooth to a snakebite.

YOUR VET MAY NEED TO:

Sedate your dog in order to facilitate a thorough and safe examination of his teeth and mouth, if a dental problem is suspected.

ACTION PLAN:

Is the swelling around your dog's nose and lips? Do you see two small puncture wounds? Is the area purple or painful?

 YES Call your veterinarian *NOW* if you answered yes to any query—it could be due to a snakebite^G (see page 343), an insect sting or bite, or secondary to a vaccine, medication, or other acute allergy. Go to **Snakebite Do's and Dont's,** opposite page.

 NO

Is the swelling over a bony area? Is it painful? Is there a crackly feeling when you touch the area? Is it abnormally warm?

 YES Call your veterinarian *NOW* if you answered yes to any of these queries—it could be secondary to trauma, and there could be a fractured facial bone.

 NO

Is there a draining wound on or near the swelling, on the side of his muzzle or below an eye?

 YES Call your veterinarian *TODAY*—it could be an abscessed tooth.

 NO

Is the swollen area hard, not painful, and on one side of the face, below his ear?

 YES Call your veterinarian *TODAY* if you answered yes to any of these queries—it could be a salivary duct stone^G or obstruction, or a jaw tumor.

 NO

Is the swelling below his jaw? Does it feel fluid-filled, sort of like a water-balloon?

YES Call your veterinarian *TODAY* if you answered yes to either query—it could be a salivary cyst^G.

 NO

Call your veterinarian for an appointment.

SNAKEBITE DO'S AND DON'TS:

• **DO** call your vet to find out if he routinely stocks antivenin before you have a snakebite emergency. That way, you won't waste precious time in a snakebite emergency driving from clinic to clinic in search of one that has antivenin. If your vet doesn't keep it on hand (and many vets don't, due to the drug's high cost and short shelf life), ask him or her to tell you the nearest vet or emergency clinic that does.

• **DON'T** apply a tourniquet above the bite site. Doing so could cause more problems than it solves by restricting circulation to the affected area, exacerbating the toxin's affect.

• **DON'T** cut incisions above the fang marks and attempt to suck out the venom. First, such incisions don't dispel enough venom to make a difference, and thus merely increase the degree of injury to your dog. Second, you could absorb venom through a sore in your mouth, putting yourself at risk of a toxic reaction.

• **DON'T** apply ice or other such cooling agent to the bite site. Doing so could impair circulation already compromised by the venom.

• **DO** stay cool and calm, and get your dog to help–*NOW!*

Tooth-Care Trivia...

It's a common mistake to think that if your dog is young, he shouldn't need to have his teeth checked. But periodontal disease[G], which can cause bad breath and lead to premature tooth loss, is common in youngsters at the time their permanent teeth appear. Start early when caring for your dog's teeth— you can save on vet bills in the long run. For how to perform at-home dental care, see page 273.

5-1

HAIR LOSS
On face or head

What you see: Thinning of hair or patchy hair loss on your dog's face or head, with or without itching or redness.

What this might mean: It could mean anything from an allergy to mange.

YOUR VET MAY NEED TO:

Biopsy the area, perform blood work, culture a skin sample for fungus, or take a skin scraping to check for mites (mange).

ACTION PLAN:

Is the hair loss associated with redness, scratching, or other self-trauma? **YES** → Call your veterinarian *NOW*—it could be an acute allergic response.

 NO

Is there patchy or circular hair loss on your dog's face or around his eyes? **YES** → Call your veterinarian *TODAY*—it could be demodectic mange^G or ringworm^G.

 NO

Is the hair loss or crusting on your dog's ears? **YES** → Call your veterinarian *TODAY*—it could be seborrhea^G or hypothyroidism^G.

 NO

Is the hair loss on the lips or side of your dog's face? Is he rubbing or scratching the area? **YES** → Call your veterinarian *TODAY*—it could be an allergy, lip-fold dermatitis^G, or a dental infection.

 NO

Is it a short-nosed dog, with the irritated skin, discharge, or odor between the folds of the nose and eye? **YES** → Call your veterinarian *TODAY*—it could be nasal-fold dermatitis^G.

 NO

Is there a butterfly-shaped area of redness, hair loss, and/or irritation on his face between his eyes and nose? **YES** → Call your veterinarian *TODAY*—it could be a form of lupus^G.

 NO

Is there hair loss or redness along the top of your dog's nose? **YES** → It could be nasal-solar dermatitis^G. See **page 28** for "Sun Beater Tips."

 NO

Is the hair loss associated with an injury or wound? **YES** → Call your veterinarian *TODAY*—it could require cleaning, and/or repair and antibiotics.

 NO

Call your veterinarian *TODAY* for an appointment.

What you see/smell: Your dog's external ear opening is red, dirty, and smelly. He may shake his head and/or scratch at the affected ear.

What this might mean: It could be an infection with or without a foreign body, a tumor, or a tick in the ear canal.

EAR SCRATCHING/
Red, painful, dirty, or swollen flap

ACTION PLAN:

Is your dog shaking his head violently, scratching at his ear, or obviously in pain? Is there blood or wax in his ear?

 NO

YES → Call your veterinarian *NOW* if you answered yes to any query—it could be an infection, foreign body, tumor, or tick infestation. Your dog needs to be seen before causing further injury to his ear. (See page 343 for how to protect the ear until you leave.)

Is there a head tilt, circling, or lack of coordination?

 NO

YES → Call your veterinarian *NOW*—it could be a neurological disease, including rabies^G, or a middle- or inner-ear problem. See **Caution** and **Before You Leave**, next page.

Is the ear flap swollen or fluid filled?

 NO

YES → Call your veterinarian *NOW*—it could be an allergic response or an aural hematoma^G. (See page 343.)

Is his head shaking/scratching intermittent?

 NO

YES → Call your veterinarian *TODAY*—it could be an infection or foreign body. (See page 343.)

Is the ear red and irritated, with a black/brown waxy discharge?

 NO

YES → Call your veterinarian *TODAY*—it could be ear mites^G or a yeast infection^G.

Call your veterinarian today for an appointment.

➤

YOUR VET MAY NEED TO:

• Sedate your dog, to thoroughly examine and clean the ear, and/or to remove a foreign body.
• Perform surgery, if a hematoma is involved.
• Collect samples for culture or other diagnostic tests.

BEFORE YOU LEAVE:

1. *Isolate your dog from other dogs in case it's contagious.* To prevent spread of possible infectious disease, confine your dog to an area with a separate water supply, apart from other dogs. Wash your hands and disinfect your shoes (see page 374) after handling your dog and before handling other dogs.

CAUTION

Among the possible causes of nervous system disease causing nerve dysfunction is a rare but notorious one: Rabies. Don't take chances—take precautions. See page 83.

2. *Protect your dog from accidents.* If your dog is having trouble with his equilibrium, remove protruding objects from his area and keep noises to a minimum, to avoid startling him.

Did You Know...

...your dog's red, irritated, dirty ear—especially when it's driving him to scratch it—could result from a yeast or bacterial infection, mites, a foreign body, or a tumor. Take prompt action to help prevent further injury from self-trauma. See page 343.

Did You Also Know...

...contrary to what you might think, foreign bodies are more common in dogs with flap ears than in those with pointed ears. That's because grass awns and seeds can get caught under the flap, then migrate into your dog's inner ear.

EAR-FLAP HEMATOMAS

A hematoma on your dog's ear-flap, known as an aural hematoma[G] is no minor matter. When head shaking, ear scratching, or other such trauma cause damage to the ear-flap's tissues, blood vessels will break. But, because the ear flap is comprised of a layer of cartilage sandwiched between two layers of skin, there's no place for the blood to go. The result? The hematoma gets bigger and bigger, especially if your dog continues his head shaking/scratching behavior. Surgery will be needed to alleviate the "blood blister," provide your dog with relief, and achieve a cosmetically appealing result. To help prevent ear-flap trauma, keep those ear-biting insects at bay. (See page 23.) Any irritation to the ear flap can lead to ear scratching/shaking, which in turn can lead to a hematoma.

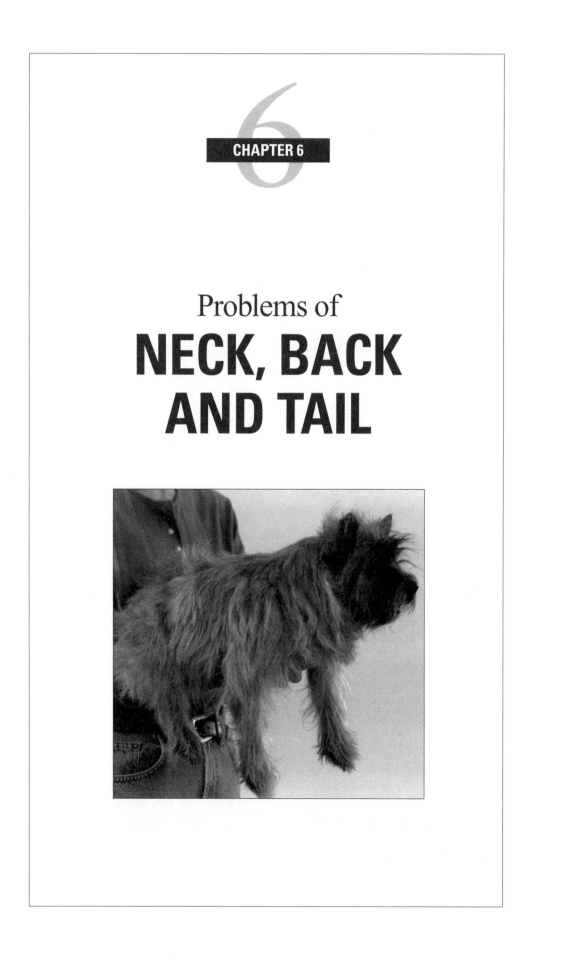

CHAPTER 6

Problems of

NECK, BACK AND TAIL

STIFF/SORE NECK

What you see: Your dog is showing signs of neck pain. He may be reluctant to raise, lower, or turn his neck to the side. He may move stiffly, "robot-like", or have difficulty lowering his head to eat or drink. He may cry with sudden neck/head movement, when patted on top of his head, or when you take him out on leash and apply pressure to his neck via the collar.

What this might mean: Your dog is suffering pain and stiffness in his neck, which could be the result of illness, injury, spinal misalignment, or vertebral disk problems.

YOUR VET MAY NEED TO:

• **Sedate your dog in order to do a thorough neurological work up, which could include X-raying the affected area.**
• **Refer you to a specialist, who could perform such neurological tests as a CAT scanG, MRIG, or myelogramG.**

ACTION PLAN:

Does your dog seem depressed, lethargic, uncoordinated, or does he have a head tilt? Is he squinting or acting as though he has a headache?

 NO

 YES Call your veterinarian *NOW* if you answered yes to any of these queries—it could be an infectious disease such as encephalitisG or meningitisG, or even rabiesG. See **Caution**, opposite page; go to **Before You Leave #1**, opposite page.

Is your dog not eating? Is he lethargic or feverish?

 NO

 YES Call your veterinarian *NOW* if you answered yes to either query—it could be a systemic illness. Go to **Before You Leave #1**, opposite page.

Is your dog in a lot of pain? Is he unable to lower his head to eat? Is he favoring a front leg? Uncoordinated or weak in his hind end?

 NO

 YES Call your veterinarian *NOW* if you answered yes to any query—it could be a ruptured cervical diskG or cervical spinal instabilityG. See **Before You Leave #2**.

Are there any signs of abrasions, wounds, and/or swelling on his head/neck? Is there any history of recent rough physical activity with animals or people? Could he have been hit by a car?

 NO

 YES Call your veterinarian *NOW* if you answered yes to any query—it could be a muscle, bone, or nerve injury. See **Before You Leave #2**.

Has your dog been injected with any medications or vaccines in the last several days? Is there a warm or painful swelling at the base of his neck or shoulders?

 NO

YES Call your veterinarian *TODAY*—it could be an injection site reaction. See **Before You Leave #3**.

Call your veterinarian *TODAY* for an appointment.

BEFORE YOU LEAVE #1:

1. *Isolate your dog from other dogs in case it's contagious.* To prevent spread of possible infectious disease, confine your dog to a warm, dry area with a separate water supply away from other dogs. Wash your hands and disinfect your shoes (see page 374) after handling your dog and before handling other dogs.

2. *Protect your dog.* Remove anything in the area that could result in collisions or spills, and keep stress and noise to a minimum to avoid exciting him.

BEFORE YOU LEAVE #2:

1. *Keep him quiet.* Place him in a quiet, confined place (such as a crate or box) until you leave, to minimize movement and thus help prevent him from causing further damage. Minimize stress and noise to avoid exciting him.

2. *Take care in transport.* If your dog is small enough to carry, do so in such a way as to keep his spine straight from head to tail. One method is to insert your forearm lengthwise between his hind and front legs, then lift, supporting his chest with your hand. (His legs will straddle your forearm, both left legs on one side, both right legs on the other.) For a medium to large dog, squat with your chest opposite your dog's rib cage. Place one arm under his chest, just behind his front legs; place the other under his abdomen, just in front of his hind legs. Slowly stand to lift him, concentrating on keeping his back perfectly straight as you do so. (For more information on safe emergency transport, see page 335.)

3. *Use car sense.* If he's a small dog, place him/his box on the car floor, so he won't inadvertently fall off the car seat, causing further damage. If he's a medium-sized or larger dog who won't fit on the floor, transport him in a crate or box that can be secured on the seat. If you can, have a helper drive with you to be sure the carrier doesn't move around.

BEFORE YOU LEAVE #3:

1. *Help him eat and drink.* Stiffness and soreness at a vaccination site can make it painful for your dog to lower his head to eat and drink. Elevate his feed and water so he can reach them without hurting himself. Stacked phone books work well to raise feed and water bowls. (**Note:** If after doing so your dog remains uninterested in eating, go back to the beginning of the action plan and reassess your responses.)

2. *Apply cold packs.* Grab a small bag of frozen peas or other such vegetables, or place several handfuls of ice cubes in a plastic bag. Hold the cold pack on the site for 5 minutes, then take it off for 15 minutes. Repeat the cycle 3 times, or until you leave for the veterinarian's office. ➤

CAUTION

If your dog is showing any signs that could point to the rare—but dangerous—disease rabies, don't take chances, take precautions. See page 83.

STOP

Before you rush out the door in an emergency situation, stop and call ahead to your veterinarian. Be sure to describe the emergency in detail and estimate how long it will take to get your dog to the clinic. That way, your vet can prepare for your arrival, ensuring the best—and fastest—possible care for your dog.

Some Breeds Susceptible to Disk and Spinal Instability

Note: Purebred dogs are not the only susceptible ones. If you have a mutt that physically resembles any breed listed, he, too, could carry that breed's predisposition for problems. Also, many large- and giant-breed dogs are susceptible by virtue of their size, as well as are some toy breeds.

- Afghan Hounds
- Beagles
- Boston Terriers
- Boxers
- Brittany Spaniels
- Bulldogs
- Cocker Spaniels
- Dachshunds
- Doberman Pinschers
- English Pointers
- French Bulldogs
- German Shepherds
- Great Danes
- Jack Russell Terriers
- Miniature Poodles
- Pekinese
- Sheepdogs (and other tail-less or naturally short-tailed breeds)
- Swedish Laplands
- Weimaraners

What you see: Your dog's back is arched, and/or he may flinch, move away, or cry out when you pat him on his back or pelvis. You also may notice rear-leg pain/weakness or lack of coordination

What this might mean: Your dog is suffering from back and/or pelvic pain, which could be due to systemic illness, injury, spinal-disk disorder, or lumbo-sacral instability[G].

Arched Back and/or
BACK/PELVIC PAIN

ACTION PLAN:

Is your dog lethargic or feverish? Does he have reduced appetite or a change in water consumption? Has there been a change in volume or frequency of urination, and/or a change in urine color?

YES → Call your veterinarian *NOW* if you answered yes to any query—it could be a systemic illness such as kidney disease (nephritis[G]).

 NO

Is your dog suddenly less active than normal? Is he reluctant to jump? Does he have difficulty going up/down stairs or getting in/out of your car?

YES → Call your veterinarian *NOW* if you answered yes to any query—it could be spinal disk disease. See **Before You Leave**, next page.

 NO

Does your dog have rear leg pain, weakness, or incoordination? Does he have difficulty posturing to urinate or defecate? Does he strain or take an unusually long time to defecate?

YES → Call your veterinarian *NOW* if you answered yes to any query—it could be spinal or lumbosacral[G] arthritis, with or without lumbosacral instability[G]. See **Before You Leave**, next page.

 NO

Is there any sign of bruising, abrasion, or skin breaks? Has he been playing rough with people or other pets? Could he have been hit by a car?

YES → Call your veterinarian *NOW*—it could be muscle, bone, or nerve injury. See **Before You Leave**, next page.

 NO

Call your veterinarian for an appointment.

➤

YOUR VET MAY NEED TO:

• **Sedate your dog in order to do a thorough neurological work up, which could include X-raying the affected area.**
• **Refer you to a specialist, who could perform such neurological tests as a CAT scan[G], MRI[G], or myelogram[G].**

BEFORE YOU LEAVE:

1. *Keep him quiet.* Place him in a quiet, confined place (such as a crate or box) until you leave, to minimize movement and thus help prevent him from causing further damage. Also minimize stress and noise.

2. *Take care in transport.* If your dog is small enough to carry, do so in such a way as to keep his spine straight from head to tail. One method is to insert your forearm lengthwise between his hind and front legs, then lift, supporting his chest with your hand. (His legs will straddle your forearm, both left legs on one side, both right legs on the other.) For a medium to large dog, squat with your chest opposite your dog's rib cage. Place one arm under his chest, just behind his front legs; place the other under his abdomen, just in front of his hind legs. Slowly stand to lift him, concentrating on keeping his back perfectly straight as you do so. (For more information on safe emergency transport, see page 335.)

3. *Use car sense.* If he's a small dog, place him/his box on the car floor, so he won't inadvertently fall off the car seat, causing further damage. If he's a medium-sized or larger dog who won't fit on the floor, transport him in a crate or box that can be secured on the seat. If you can, have a helper drive with you to be sure the carrier doesn't move around.

> Before you rush out the door in an emergency situation, stop and call ahead to your veterinarian. Be sure to describe the emergency in detail and estimate how long it will take to get your dog to the clinic. That way, your vet can prepare for your arrival, ensuring the best—and fastest—possible care for your dog.

What you see: Your dog's front and/or hind legs are weak. He may stagger as though he's drunk, he may drag or shuffle his hind feet as though weak, or move his hind legs in a spastic, jerky way. He may or may not exhibit signs of pain.

What this might mean: It could be a neurological problem due to injury or illness, a cervical spinal disk disorder, or lumbo-sacral instability^G.

UNCOORDINATED/ WEAK LEGS
Front or Hind

ACTION PLAN:

Is your dog lethargic and not eating? Is he feverish? Is he uncoordinated on all four legs?

 NO

YES Call your veterinarian *NOW*—it could be an inflammatory brain disease such as rabies^G (see **Caution**, next page), or enchephalitis^G, or it could be a brain tumor.

Was the uncoordination rapid-onset in all four legs? Is your dog vomiting? Does he have diarrhea?

 NO

YES Call your veterinarian *NOW*—it could be poison. Try to determine the toxin if possible. See **page 352**.

Is your dog less active than normal? Is he reluctant to jump? Does he have difficulty going up/down stairs or getting in/out of your car?

 NO

YES Call your veterinarian *NOW* if you answered yes to any query—it could be a spinal cord tumor^G, degenerative spinal cord disease, spinal disk disease, or cervical spinal instability^G. See **Before You Leave**, next page.

Does he have difficulty posturing to urinate or defecate? Does he strain or take an unusually long time to defecate?

 NO

YES Call your veterinarian *NOW* if you answered yes to any query—it could be spinal or lumbosacral^G arthritis, with or without lumbosacral instability^G. See **Before You Leave**, next page.

Is there any sign of bruising, abrasion, or skin breaks? Has he been playing rough with people or other pets? Could he have been hit by a car?

 NO

YES Call your veterinarian *NOW*—it could be muscle, bone, or nerve injury. See **Before You Leave**, next page.

➤

YOUR VET MAY NEED TO:

• Sedate your dog in order to do a thorough neurological work up, which could include X-raying the affected area.

• Refer you to a specialist, who could perform such neurological tests as a CAT scan^G, MRI^G, or myelogram^G.

ACTION PLAN (CONTINUED):

Has his hind-end weakness been gradual in onset? Is your dog less active than normal? Does he have difficulty getting up or lying down? Going up and down stairs, and getting in and out of your car? Can you see atrophy[G] in his hind leg muscles?

 YES ► Call your veterinarian *TODAY*—it could be hip dysplasia[G]

 NO

Is your dog of a small breed? Does he seem to hop or skip occasionally with one or both rear legs?

 YES ► Call your veterinarian *TODAY*—it could be a luxating patella[G].

NO

Call your veterinarian for an appointment.

BEFORE YOU LEAVE:

1. *Keep him quiet.* Place him in a quiet, confined place (such as a crate or box) until you leave, to minimize movement and thus help prevent him from causing further damage. Also minimize stress and noise.

2. *Take care in transport.* If your dog is small enough to carry, do so in such a way as to keep his spine straight from head to tail. One method is to insert your forearm lengthwise between his hind and front legs, then lift, supporting his chest with your hand. (His legs will straddle your forearm, both left legs on one side, both right legs on the other.) For a medium to large dog, squat with your chest opposite your dog's rib cage.

> **If your dog is showing any signs that could point to the rare—but dangerous—disease rabies, don't take chances, take precautions. See page 83.**

Place one arm under his chest, just behind his front legs; place the other under his abdomen, just in front of his hind legs. Slowly stand to lift him, concentrating on keeping his back perfectly straight as you do so. (For more information on safe emergency transport, see page 335.)

3. *Use car sense.* If he's a small dog, place him/his box on the car floor, so he won't inadvertently fall off the car seat, causing further damage. If he's a medium-sized or larger dog who won't fit on the floor, transport him in a crate or box that can be secured on the seat. If you can, have a helper drive with you to be sure the carrier doesn't move around.

Prominent
SPINE/PELVIC BONES

What you see/feel: Bumps or bony protrusions along the top of your dog's back and over his pelvis.

What this might mean: It could be normal for your dog's breed/body type, or it could be evidence of illness and or weight loss.

ACTION PLAN:

Are any of the protrusions hot and/or painful?

YES ▸ Call your veterinarian *NOW*—it could be an injury or infection.

 NO

Are only a few areas prominent? Are they non-painful?

YES ▸ Call your veterinarian *TODAY*—it could be cysts[G] or tumors[G].

 NO

Is your dog's entire backbone prominent? Are his pelvic bones protruding? Does he seem thinner than normal?

YES ▸ Call your veterinarian *TODAY*—it could be systemic illness or malnutrition.

 NO

Does your dog exhibit normal appetite and activity? Is he old? Does he have a short hair coat? Is he of the sight-hound body type (e.g., Greyhound or Whippet)?

YES ▸ This may be normal for your dog. But call your veterinarian if he exhibits any additional signs, such as loss of appetite or lethargy.

 NO

Call your veterinarian for an appointment.

YOUR VET MAY NEED TO:

• **Sedate your dog in order to do a thorough neurological work up, which could include X-raying the affected area.**
• **Refer you to a specialist, who could perform such neurological tests as a CAT scan[G], MRI[G], or myelogram[G].**

Did You Know...

…certain breeds are naturally prone to prominent ribs, spines, and hip bones. This is due to their lithe body types and activity levels. Particularly prone to the lean look are sight hounds, so called because the vision of these dogs is so acute that the slightest movement draws their attention, even from great distances. They can often outrun their prey once they sight it, due to their inherent speed, physical endurance, and lithe, streamlined bodies. The following fall into the sight hound category:

Afghan Hounds • Borzoi • Greyhounds • Ibizan Hounds • Irish Wolfhounds
Pharaoh Hounds • Salukis • Scottish Deerhounds • Whippets

6-E

LIMP OR SORE TAIL

What you see: Your dog's tail is limp or just hanging loosely. He's unwilling or unable to raise or wag it, and may or may not show signs of pain (such as yelping), particularly when he moves or you raise the tail. You might notice an obvious misalignment of his tail.

What this might mean: Your dog may have injured or fractured his tail, or may be showing signs of lumbo-sacral instability[G].

YOUR VET MAY NEED TO:

• Sedate your dog in order to do a thorough neurological work up, which could include X-raying the affected area.
• Refer you to a specialist, who could perform such neurological tests as a CAT scan[G], MRI[G], or myelogram[G].
• If the injury is a chronic one, he or she may ultimately have to dock the tail.

ACTION PLAN:

Can you see abrasions, bruising, or breaks in the tail skin? Is the tail misaligned? **YES** Call your veterinarian *NOW*—it could be a muscle, nerve, or bone injury.

 NO

Is the tail raw or bleeding? **YES** Go to **page 105**.

 NO

Is the tail limp, and/or does your dog show signs of pain when he moves the tail or you lift it? **YES** Call your veterinarian *TODAY*—it could be an injury to the tail base, or lumbosacral instability[G].

 NO

Call your veterinarian today for an appointment.

Breeds Susceptible to Tail Damage

Those breeds (or mixed breeds) that have long, thin tails with little hair are more susceptible than other breeds to tail-tip trauma. Dogs with thicker hair on their tails (Such as Labs and Golden Retrievers) seem to be able to better get away with damage-free wagging. Here's a sampling of breeds that can suffer self-inflicted tail troubles.

- Dachshunds
- Dalmations
- Great Danes
- Greyhounds
- Pointers
- Whippets

What you see: The tip of your dog's tail is raw and/or bleeding.

What this might mean: He's chewed his tail tip, or has otherwise injured it by hitting it against walls/furniture, having it shut in a door, being stepped on, etc.

RAW/BLEEDING TAIL TIP

ACTION PLAN:

Is the tail bleeding?
NO ↓

YES ▶ Call your veterinarian *NOW*—it could require vet attention to minimize damage. See **Before You Leave**, below.

Is your dog chewing his tail?
NO ↓

YES ▶ Call your veterinarian *NOW*—it could be an allergy or neurological injury.

Is the tail limp or misaligned?
NO ↓

YES ▶ Go to **page 104**.

Does your dog have a "happy tail," meaning he wags it hard and often? Does he frequently bang it against walls and furniture?
NO ↓

YES ▶ Call your veterinarian *TODAY*—he or she can help you with management care and advice.

Call your veterinarian today for an appointment.

YOUR VET MAY NEED TO:

Sedate your dog in order to thoroughly examine, clean, bandage, and/or suture the wound. If it's a chronic problem, he or she may ultimately need to dock the tail.

BEFORE YOU LEAVE:

1. *Apply cold packs.* Grab a small bag of frozen peas or other such vegetables, or place several handfuls of ice cubes in a plastic bag. Place the cold pack between the fold of a clean hand towel. Hold the cold pack on the site for 5 minutes, then take it off for 15 minutes. Repeat the cycle 3 times, or until you apply a pressure bandage.

2. *Apply a pressure bandage.* See page 315 for how to apply a pressure bandage. To keep it on the tail end, cover the wound with a Telfa-type pad. Hold that in place with a wrap of roll cotton, covering an area from the tail tip to a point about one-third of the way up the tail. Secure that with gauze wrap. Hold the bandage in place with masking tape, wrapping it up and down the entire tail in a barber-pole pattern. Be sure not to tape so tightly that you could constrict circulation.

3. *Keep him still and quiet.* Confine your dog to a crate or box to keep him still and quiet, which will help minimize bleeding and reduce the risk of further damage to his tail. Keep noise and distractions to a minimum, to keep him from getting excited.

What you see: Your dog appears to be paralyzed on a single leg, is down and unable to move both front and rear legs, or can't move his rear legs. If you see the latter, you may see your dog trying to pull himself around with his front legs. He may seem agitated or distressed. He may or not be in severe pain, and may or may not seem to have feeling in his hind feet or tail.

6-G

PARALYSIS

What this might mean: He may have a tumor, or an acute spinal injury, which could include a ruptured intervertebral disk[G] or other problem.

YOUR VET MAY NEED TO:
- **Sedate your dog in order to do a thorough neurological work up, which could include X-raying the affected area.**
- **Refer you to a specialist, who could perform such neurological tests as a CAT scan[G], MRI[G], or myelogram[G].**

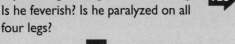
ACTION PLAN:

Is your dog lethargic and not eating? Is he feverish? Is he paralyzed on all four legs?

YES → Call your veterinarian *NOW* if you answered yes to any query—it could be an inflammatory brain disease such as rabies[G] (see **Caution**, opposite page), or enchephalitis[G], or it could be a brain tumor. See **Before You Leave #1**, opposite page.

NO ↓

Has your dog been a victim of recent trauma, such as being hit by a car or falling a long distance? Does he have neck pain/stiffness (reluctance to turn his head, and/or lower it to eat/drink)? Is he paralyzed on all four legs and his tail?

YES → Call your veterinarian *NOW* if you answered yes to any query—it could be a fracture or other serious injury to your dog's cervical spine (neck). See **Before You Leave #2**.

NO ↓

Was the paralysis rapid-onset in all four legs? Is your dog vomiting? Does he have diarrhea?

YES → Call your veterinarian *NOW*—it could be poison. Try to determine the toxin if possible. For more information, call the ASPCA National Poison Control Center, at (800) 548-2423.

NO ↓

Is your dog paralyzed in his hindquarters, attempting to drag himself around with his front legs? Was the paralysis rapid-onset?

YES → Call your veterinarian *NOW*—it could be a ruptured intervertebral disk[G]. See **Before You Leave #2**.

NO ↓

Was the paralysis gradual in onset? Is your dog of German Shepherd descent?

YES → Call your veterinarian *NOW*—it could be degenerative myelopathy[G].

NO ↓

Call your veterinarian *NOW*.

BEFORE YOU LEAVE #1:

1. *Isolate your dog from other dogs in case it's contagious.* To prevent the spread of possible infectious disease, confine your dog to an area with a separate water supply, apart from other dogs. Wash your hands and disinfect your shoes (see page 374) after handling your dog and before handling other dogs.

If your dog is showing any signs that could point to the rare—but dangerous—disease rabies, don't take chances, take precautions. See page 83.

2. *Protect your dog from further injury.* Remove protruding objects from his area, and keep noise to a minimum to avoid startling him.

BEFORE YOU LEAVE #2:

1. *Keep him quiet.* Place him in a quiet, confined place (such as a crate or box) until you leave, to minimize movement and thus help prevent him from causing further damage. Minimize stress and noise to avoid exciting him.

2. *Take care in transport.* If your dog is small enough to carry, do so in such a way as to keep his spine straight from head to tail. One method is to insert your forearm lengthwise between his hind and front legs, then lift, supporting his chest with your hand. (His legs will straddle your forearm, both left legs on one side, both right legs on the other.) For a medium to large dog, squat with your chest opposite your dog's rib cage. Place one arm under his chest, just behind his front legs; place the other under his abdomen, just in front of his hind legs. Slowly stand to lift him, concentrating on keeping his back perfectly straight as you do so. (For more information on safe emergency transport, see page 335.)

Before you rush out the door in an emergency situation, stop and call ahead to your veterinarian. Be sure to describe the emergency in detail and estimate how long it will take to get your dog to the clinic. That way, your vet can prepare for your arrival, ensuring the best—and fastest—possible care for your dog.

3. *Use car sense.* If he's a small dog, place him/his box on the car floor, so he won't inadvertently fall off the car seat, causing further damage. If he's a medium-sized or larger dog who won't fit on the floor, transport him in a crate or box that can be secured on the seat. If you can, have a helper drive with you to be sure the carrier doesn't move around.

NOTES

7

Problems of
THE LEGS

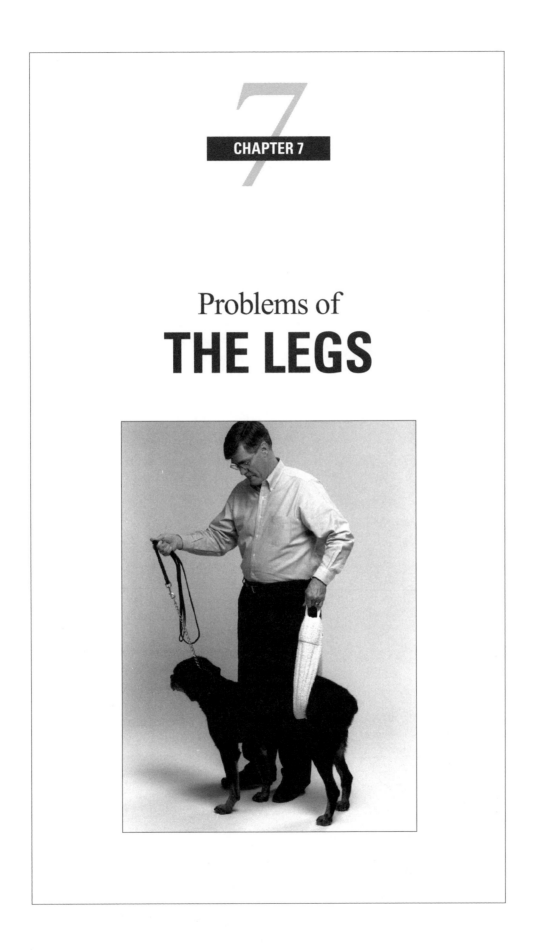

What you see: Your dog appears to be limping on one or more legs. At the very least, you see a mild head bob or shortening of his stride. At worst, he won't bear any weight on the affected leg.

LAME ON ONE OR MORE LEGS

What this might mean: It could range from something as simple as blistered foot pads, to a foreign body in the foot, joint arthritis, a fracture, or a ruptured spinal disk^G.

YOUR VET MAY NEED TO:

• **X-ray the area to help determine the source of the lameness**

• **Prescribe anti-inflammatory medications.**

ACTION PLAN:

Did the lameness appear suddenly? Is there evidence of trauma and/or bleeding? Is your dog in severe pain? Is he disoriented, profoundly weak, unresponsive, and/or having difficulty breathing? Are his gums pale pink or white?

 NO

YES Call your veterinarian *NOW* if you answered yes to two or more queries—your dog may have been struck by a car, or suffered other trauma that requires immediate vet attention. He also may be in shock^G. See **Before You Leave #1**, opposite.

Is your dog lame on all four legs? Reluctant to walk? Feverish? Are his joints swollen?

 NO

YES Call your veterinarian *NOW* if you answered yes to any query—it could be a condition such as Lyme disease^G, arthritis^G, myositis^G, hypertrophic osteodystrophy^G, or polyarthrophathy^G. See **Before You Leave #2**.

Is your dog unwilling to bear weight on the affected limb(s)?

 NO

YES Call your veterinarian *NOW*—it could be a fracture or other serious problem, including cervical or spinal lesions caused by a disk rupture or disease, tumor, or trauma. See **Before You Leave #2**.

Is your dog severely lame after physical activity?

 NO

YES Call your veterinarian *TODAY*—it could be a bone injury, or ligament or other soft-tissue problem.

Was the lameness progressive in onset? Is your dog lame/stiff/sore after sleeping or resting, but improves with moderate activity?

 NO

YES Call your veterinarian *TODAY*—it could be a soft-tissue injury or arthritis.

ACTION PLAN (CONTINUED):

Is your dog a large, older one? Is he getting progressively more lame/stiff in both hind limbs? Does he have trouble getting up and down, going up and down stairs, and getting in and out of your car? Call your veterinarian *TODAY*—it could be hip dysplasia^G.

Is your dog of a small breed? Does he seem to hop or skip occasionally with one or both rear legs? Call your veterinarian *TODAY*—it could be a luxating patella^G.

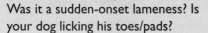

Was it a sudden-onset lameness? Is your dog licking his toes/pads? YES Call your veterinarian *TODAY*—it could be a broken toe, cut or torn nail, or cut/blistered pad.

Is this a young, rapidly growing, large-breed dog? YES Call your veterinarian *TODAY*—it could be any one of many growth-related problems (i.e., OCD^G, elbow dysplasia^G, hip dysplasia^G) affecting dogs of this type.

Does the lameness seem to shift from one leg to another in your growing dog? Call your veterinarian *TODAY*—it could be panosteitis^G

Is your dog favoring the leg but bearing weight? Did the lameness occur after physical activity? Are you unable to locate an area of acute discomfort by palpating the foot and leg? YES It sounds like a mild bruise, strain, or sprain. Apply **Home Treatment,** next page.

Call your veterinarian for an appointment if your dog has not improved in 24 to 48 hours.

BEFORE YOU LEAVE #1:

1. *Apply first-aid for shock.* Keep your dog warm and quiet; if he's unconscious, slightly elevate his hindquarters using a stack of folded towels. If the dog is small enough to transport in a box, place him in one immediately, taking care not to cause further damage to the limb(s). If he's a medium- to large-breed dog, use a blanket sling to carefully move him. (See page 335.) Whatever you do—do it fast. Time is of the essence. He needs veterinary care STAT!

2. *Stop any bleeding.* Apply direct pressure to the bleeding site. Forget about whether the blood's coming from an artery or a vein—the treatment's the same. (Your frightened dog may snap out in pain and confusion. For how to apply a temporary ➤

muzzle, see page 328.) Apply pressure over the site with a clean pad of sufficient size to cover the wound and its margins. A folded hand towel, disposable diaper, or 1-inch thick stack of gauze sponges will make a suitable pad. If an ice pack is immediately available, sandwich it between the pad's layers to further stem bleeding. Use the same amount of pressure you'd use to feel the contours of your thigh bone.

3. *Apply a pressure bandage.* After 5 to 10 minutes of pressure, apply a pressure bandage. For how to do so, see page 315.

Never administer human medicines to your dog without first consulting your vet. Routinely used human meds such as aspirin, ibuprofen (Advil), and acetaminophen (Tylenol) can cause problems in dogs. Aspirin and ibuprofen can cause gastrointestinal irritation, vomiting, diarrhea, intestinal bleeding, ulceration, and peritonitis[G]; acetaminophen can be toxic.

4. *Use car sense.* If he's a small dog, place him/his box on the car floor, so he won't inadvertently fall off the car seat, causing further damage. If he's a medium-sized or larger dog who won't fit on the floor, transport him in a crate or box that can be secured on the seat. If you can, have a helper drive with you to be sure the carrier doesn't move around.

BEFORE YOU LEAVE #2:

1. *Confine your dog.* Movement might make things worse. Confine him to a crate, portable pen, or other small area. Keep noise and commotion to a minimum, to keep him from getting excited.

2. *Use car sense.* If he's a small dog, place him/his box on the car floor, so he won't inadvertently fall off the car seat, causing further damage. If he's a medium-sized or larger dog who won't fit on the floor, transport him in a crate or box that can be secured on the seat. If you can, have a helper drive with you to be sure the carrier doesn't move around.

HOME TREATMENT:

*(See **Action Plan** to determine whether home treatment is appropriate for your dog's mild lameness. If lameness is still present after 3 days of home treatment, or if your answers on the action plan change for the worse at any time, call your vet.)*

Step 1. *Limit activity.* To prevent further damage to the affected limb, keep your dog confined and quiet. Avoid allowing unruly play with other pets or family members. Walk him on leash for 5 minutes, several times a day to help satisfy his urge to move without risk of him over-exerting the injured leg. Maintain this limited activity until your dog stays sound for several consecutive days. Gradually return him to his normal routine. Call your vet if, at any time during the rehab period, your dog's lameness increases.

Don't apply a splint without your vet's advice and without hands-on experience in applying such a device. Even though a splint can help to minimize further injury by helping to immobilize an unstable leg, in some cases it makes things much worse. If you know how to apply one skillfully, and your vet recommends it after you've described, in detail, your dog's specific injury, then it's your call.

Step 2. *Ice the site.* If you can easily determine where the pain is, ice the site. Select an ice pack (see page 311). Slip it between layers of a clean cloth, center it over the area, and hold it there. Ice on: 5 minutes. Ice off: 15 minutes. Repeat this cycle 4 more times. Continue twice daily for 3 days.

Step 3. *Massage the leg.* Gently massage the muscles and soft tissues on the affected leg, to increase circulation to the area, which will accelerate healing. (If your dog objects, chances are you're pressing too hard.) Massage the leg for 10 minutes, 3 times a day.

Don't Mask Pain Without Permission

Pain is Nature's way of telling you—and your dog—that something's wrong. It will help prevent your dog from causing further damage to the leg, by restricting his use of it. If you were to administer aspirin or other pain relievers without talking to your vet, you could mask that pain. Your dog would feel better, and thus could injure himself further. For the sake of your dog, never administer pain relievers without first calling your vet. (*See "Stop!" box, page 112.*)

What you see: Your dog is moving with a strange gait. He may seem uncoordinated or weak in his front or rear end, staggering or moving as though he's drunk. Or, he may move stiffly, with a rigid neck and/or arched back.

7-B

STIFF/WEAK UNCOORDINATED
Front or Rear Legs

What this might mean: Your dog may have been injured, he could have spinal disk disease or cervical or lumbar spinal instability, or he may have arthritis in his elbows or hips.

YOUR VET MAY NEED TO:

- Sedate your dog in order to do a thorough neurological work up, which could include X-raying the affected area.
- Refer you to a specialist, who could perform such neurological tests as a CAT scan[G], MRI[G], or myelogram[G].

ACTION PLAN:

Is your dog lethargic and not eating? Is he feverish? Is he uncoordinated on all four legs? **YES** → Call your veterinarian *NOW*—it could be an inflammatory brain disease such as rabies[G] (see **Caution**, next page), or enchephalitis[G], or it could be a brain tumor. See **Before You Leave #1**, opposite page.

 NO

Was the uncoordination rapid-onset in all four legs? Is your dog vomiting? Does he have diarrhea? **YES** → Call your veterinarian *NOW*—it could be poison. Try to determine the toxin if possible. See **page 352**.

 NO

Does your dog appear to be paralyzed? **YES** → Call your veterinarian *NOW*—it could be a ruptured disk[G]. See **Before You Leave #2**, next page.

 NO

Does your dog have front- or rear-leg lameness or uncoordination, with or without pain in his neck or over his pelvis? **YES** → Call your veterinarian *NOW*—it could be cervical or lumbosacral instability[G]. See **Before You Leave #2**.

 NO

Is there evidence of trauma? Are there open wounds, bruising, or abrasions on his head, limbs, or body? **YES** → Call your veterinarian *NOW*—it could be due to serious muscle, bone, or nerve injury. See **Before You Leave #2**.

 NO

Do one or more legs tremor or jerk uncontrollably? **YES** → Call your veterinarian *NOW*—it could be due to poison (such as insecticides) or secondary to systemic illness such distemper[G], or due to nerve injury.

 NO

ACTION PLAN (CONTINUED):

Is he reluctant to jump up, or having trouble climbing stairs?

 YES Call your veterinarian *NOW*—it could be spinal disk disease. See **Before You Leave #2**.

 NO

Is your dog less active than normal? Does he have difficulty going up or down stairs, or getting in and out of your car? Is he having trouble getting up and down? Have you noticed any atrophyG in his hind leg muscles?

 YES Call your veterinarian *TODAY*—it could be elbow or hip dysplasiaG.

NO

Is your dog of a small breed? Does he seem to hop or skip occasionally with one or both rear legs?

 YES Call your veterinarian *TODAY*—it could be a luxating patellaG.

NO

Call your vet today for an appointment.

BEFORE YOU LEAVE #1:

1. *Isolate your dog from other dogs in case it's contagious.* To prevent the spread of possible infectious disease, confine your dog to an area with a separate water supply, apart from other dogs. Wash your hands and disinfect your shoes (see page 374) after handling your dog and before handling other dogs.

2. *Protect your dog from further injury.* Remove protruding objects from his area, and keep noise to a minimum to avoid startling him.

BEFORE YOU LEAVE #2:

1. *Keep him quiet.* Place him in a quiet, confined place (such as a crate or box) until you leave, to minimize movement and thus help prevent him from causing further damage. Minimize stress and noise to avoid exciting him.

2. *Take care in transport.* If your dog is small enough to carry, do so in such a way as to keep his spine straight from head to tail. One method is to insert your forearm lengthwise between his hind and front legs, then lift, supporting his chest with your hand. (His legs will straddle your forearm, both left legs on one side, both right legs on the other.) For a medium to large dog, squat with your chest opposite your dog's rib cage. Place one arm under his chest, just behind his front legs; place the other under his abdomen, just in front of his hind legs. Slowly stand to lift him, concentrating on keeping his back perfectly straight as you do so. (For more information on safe emergency transport, see page 335.)

3. *Use car sense.* If he's a small dog, place him/his box on the car floor, so he won't inadvertently fall off the car seat, causing further damage. If he's a medium-sized or larger dog who won't fit on the floor, transport him in a crate or box that can be secured on the seat. If you can, have a helper drive with you to be sure the carrier doesn't move around.

> If your dog is showing any signs that could point to the rare—but dangerous—disease rabies, don't take chances, take precautions. See page 83.
>
> CAUTION

7-C

DRAGGING FEET

Or Knuckling Over

What you see: Your dog is not advancing one or more front or rear feet properly. His nails may be worn to the quick from dragging his feet forward, and he may have sores on the tops of his toes from dragging his feet. He also may stand seemingly unaware that his toes/feet are folded over.

What this might mean: Your dog is exhibiting symptoms of neurological dysfunction. This could be due to a problem in his spinal cord or peripheral nerves[G].

ACTION PLAN:

Is it happening on more than one leg? Is your dog dull, lethargic, and feverish? Is he uncoordinated? Is his third eyelid[G] evident?

 NO

 YES Call your veterinarian *NOW*—it could be a systemic illness such as rabies[G], or a brain inflammation. See **Caution**, opposite, and go to **Before You Leave #1**, opposite.

Is your dog paralyzed in his hind end?

 NO

 YES Call your veterinarian *NOW*—it could be a ruptured disk[G]. See **Before You Leave #2**.

Did the symptoms appear suddenly? Is there any evidence/history of trauma, such as wounds, bruises, or abrasions?

 NO

YES Call your veterinarian *NOW*—it could be an injury to your dog's spine or to the nerves supplying his legs. See **Before You Leave #2**.

Are there signs of weakness or incoordination of his front/rear legs? Is there a sign of neck stiffness? Is he arching his back? Was the problem sudden-onset?

 NO

YES Call your veterinarian *NOW*—it could be a ruptured disk[G], or cervical or lumbosacral instability[G]. See **Before You Leave #2**.

Have symptoms been present for a long time, or have they gradually worsened?

 NO

 YES Call your veterinarian *TODAY*—it could be due to spinal disk deterioration, or worsening cervical instability or arthritis secondary to lumbosacral instability[G].

Call your veterinarian for an appointment.

BEFORE YOU LEAVE #1:

1. *Isolate your dog from other dogs in case it's contagious.* To prevent the spread of possible infectious disease, confine your dog to an area with a separate water supply, apart from other dogs. Wash your hands and disinfect your shoes (see page 374) after handling your dog and before handling other dogs.

> **CAUTION**
> If your dog is showing any signs that could point to the rare—but dangerous—disease rabies, don't take chances, take precautions. See page 83.

2. *Protect your dog from further injury.* Remove protruding objects from his area, and keep noise to a minimum to avoid startling him.

BEFORE YOU LEAVE #2:

1. *Keep him quiet.* Place him in a quiet, confined place (such as a crate or box) until you leave, to minimize movement and thus help prevent him from causing further damage. Minimize stress and noise to avoid exciting him.

> **STOP**
> Before you rush out the door in an emergency situation, stop and call ahead to your veterinarian. Be sure to describe the emergency in detail and estimate how long it will take to get your dog to the clinic. That way, your vet can prepare for your arrival, ensuring the best—and fastest—possible care for your dog.

2. *Take care in transport.* If your dog is small enough to carry, do so in such a way as to keep his spine straight from head to tail. One method is to insert your forearm lengthwise between his hind and front legs, then lift, supporting his chest with your hand. (His legs will straddle your forearm, both left legs on one side, both right legs on the other.) For a medium to large dog, squat with your chest opposite your dog's rib cage. Place one arm under his chest, just behind his front legs; place the other under his abdomen, just in front of his hind legs. Slowly stand to lift him, concentrating on keeping his back perfectly straight as you do so. (For more information on safe emergency transport, see page 335.)

3. *Use car sense.* If he's a small dog, place him/his box on the car floor, so he won't inadvertently fall off the car seat, causing further damage. If he's a medium-sized or larger dog who won't fit on the floor, transport him in a crate or box that can be secured on the seat. If you can, have a helper drive with you to be sure the carrier doesn't move around.

REAR LEG PARALYSIS

What You See: Your dog is down in his rear end, pulling himself around with his front legs. He may seem agitated or distressed. He may or may not be acutely painful, and may or may not seem to have feeling in his hind feet or tail when you touch them.

What this might mean: A spinal injury, including a ruptured disk.

ACTION PLAN:

Did the symptoms appear suddenly? Is there any sign of bruising, abrasion, or skin breaks? Has your dog been playing rough with people or other pets? Could he have been hit by a car?

 YES ▶ Call your veterinarian *NOW* if you answered yes to any query—it could be spinal or nerve injury. See **Before You Leave**, below.

NO ▼

Is the paralysis of rapid progression or sudden onset, without any outward signs of trauma?

YES ▶ Call your veterinarian *NOW*—it could be due to a herniated disk^G, infection of the spinal cord, congenital malformation of the spine, or degeneration of the spinal cord. See **Before You Leave.**

NO ▼

Is the paralysis a result of a gradually worsening condition?

YES ▶ Call your veterinarian *TODAY*—it may be due to spinal cord pressure from a disk protrusion of tumor, or due to degenerative myelopathy. See **Before You Leave**, below.

 NO ▼

Call your vet *NOW* for an appointment.

BEFORE YOU LEAVE:

1. *Keep him quiet.* Place your dog in a quiet, confined place (such as a crate or box) until you leave, to minimize movement and thus help prevent him from causing further damage. Minimize stress and noise to avoid exciting him.

2. *Take care in transport.* If your dog is small enough to carry, do so in such a way as to keep his spine straight from head to tail. One method is to insert your forearm lengthwise between his hind and front legs, then lift, supporting his chest with your hand. (His legs will straddle your forearm, both left legs on one side, both right legs on the other.) For a medium to large dog, squat with your chest opposite your dog's rib cage. Place one arm under his chest, just behind his front legs; place the other under his abdomen, just in front of his hind legs. Slowly stand to lift him, concentrating on keeping his back perfectly straight as you do so. (For more information on safe emergency transport, see page 335.)

3. *Use car sense.* If he's a small dog, place him/his box on the car floor, so he won't inadvertently fall off the car seat, causing further damage. If he's a medium-sized or larger dog who won't fit on the floor, transport him in a crate or box that can be

Before you rush out the door in an emergency situation, stop and call ahead to your veterinarian. Be sure to describe the emergency in detail and estimate how long it will take to get your dog to the clinic. That way, your vet can prepare for your arrival, ensuring the best—and fastest—possible care for your dog.

secured on the seat. If you can, have a helper drive with you to be sure the carrier doesn't move around.

Some Breeds Susceptible to Disk and Spinal Instability

Note: Purebred dogs are not the only susceptible ones. If you have a mutt that physically resembles any breed listed, he, too, could carry that breed's predisposition for problems. Also, many large- and giant-breed dogs are susceptible by virtue of their size, as well as are some toy breeds.

- Afghan Hounds
- Beagles
- Boston Terriers
- Boxers
- Brittany Spaniels
- Bulldogs
- Cocker Spaniels
- Dachshunds
- Doberman Pinschers
- English Pointers
- French Bulldogs
- German Shepherds
- Great Danes
- Jack Russell Terriers
- Miniature Poodles
- Pekinese
- Sheepdogs (and other tail-less or naturally short-tailed breeds)
- Swedish Laplands
- Weimaraners

SWOLLEN/ LUMPY LEGS

What you see/feel: Your dog's leg or legs is/are swollen. The swelling may be cool or warm, and hard, soft, or fluid-filled. Your dog may flinch or pull away when you touch it.

What it might mean: Your dog may have suffered a blow to his leg, he may have a soft-tissue, bone, or joint injury, or he may have an infection, cyst[G]—or tumor[G].

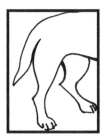

YOUR VET MAY NEED TO:

Sedate your dog, in order to X-ray the leg or legs, biopsy or culture the site, and perform other lab work. Surgery may be required in some cases.

ACTION PLAN:

Is your dog lame on all four legs? Reluctant to walk? Feverish? Are his joints swollen?

 YES Call your veterinarian *NOW* if you answered yes to any query—it could be a condition such as Lyme disease[G], arthritis[G], myositis[G], hypertrophic osteodystrophy[G], or polyarthrophathy[G]. See **Before You Leave**, opposite page.

 NO

Are there wounds or any other evidence of trauma? Is the area bleeding? Is your dog in pain?

 YES Call your veterinarian *NOW*—it could be a bone or soft-tissue injury needing immediate care. If there's a bleeding wound, go to **Before You Leave #1,** page 111.

 NO

Is the swelling hot and/or painful? Is there a draining wound evident? Does it feel fluid-filled?

 YES Call your veterinarian *NOW* if you answered yes to any query—it could be an infection.

 NO

Is the lump/swelling on or near a joint? Is there lameness and/or pain associated with it? Do the joints seem fluid-filled?

 YES Call your veterinarian *NOW* if you answered yes to any query—it could be an injury involving joints, ligaments, or cartilage or may be a joint infection or rheumatoid arthritis. See **Before You Leave**.

 NO

Is the lump/swelling firm or hard? Cool and not painful? Or, is it warm and painful? Is it over a bony portion of the leg?

 YES Call your veterinarian *NOW* if you answered yes to any query—it could be a fracture, dislocation, infection, or bone tumor. **See Before You Leave.**

 NO

ACTION PLAN (CONTINUED):

Is the swelling spread over a wide area? Is it hot/painful, and located over a soft-tissue portion of the leg?

 YES → Call your veterinarian *TODAY*—it could be a cyst^G, tumor^G, or other muscle or soft-tissue abnormality.

NO ↓

Call your veterinarian today for an appointment.

BEFORE YOU LEAVE:

1. *Confine your dog.* Movement might make things worse. Confine him to a crate, portable pen, or other small area. Keep noise and commotion to a minimum, to keep him from getting excited.

2. *Use car sense.* If he's a small dog, place him/his box on the car floor, so he won't in-advertently fall off the car seat, causing further damage. If he's a medium-sized or larger dog who won't fit on the floor, transport him in a crate or box that can be secured on the seat. If you can, have a helper drive you. His or her job will be to hold onto the carrier so it doesn't move around.

> **CAUTION**
> If your dog is in pain, he may snap at you out of fear. To be safe, muzzle him when you examine and transport him. (For how to apply a makeshift or regular muzzle, see page 328.) However, if he's having difficulty breathing or acts as though he's going to vomit, remove the muzzle immediately.

NOTES

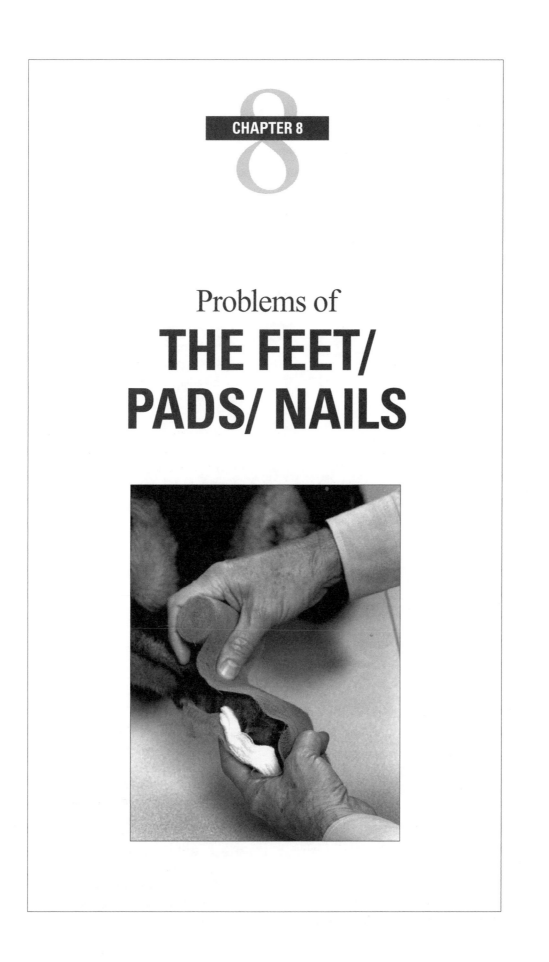

CHAPTER 8

8

Problems of
THE FEET/
PADS/ NAILS

DRAINING WOUND

Between Toes/Pads

What you see: When you check between your dog's foot pads, you find one or more wounds draining blood, serum^G, or pus^G. He may lick and/or chew the affected foot, and may favor it when standing or moving.

What this might mean: These signs could mean that the wound has penetrated deep into the tissues, that it's becoming infected (which can delay healing, increase risk of scarring, and possibly spread to other locations in your dog's body), or that your dog has a foreign body embedded in his foot.

YOUR VET MAY NEED TO:

Sedate or anesthetize your dog and/or numb the tissues, in order to fully determine the depth and extent of the injury, extract a foreign body, and help facilitate the best possible treatment.

ACTION PLAN:

Is there profuse bleeding and/or severe pain?

 NO

YES ➤ Call your veterinarian *NOW*—it could be a bone or soft-tissue injury requiring immediate care. For profuse bleeding, see **Before You Leave #1**, below.

Do you see a foreign body embedded in the tissues of your dog's foot?

 NO

YES ➤ Call your veterinarian *NOW*—to prevent further damage and/or infection, the object will need to be removed by your vet. See **Before You Leave #2**.

Is there a wound that's draining serum or pus?

 NO

YES ➤ Call your veterinarian *TODAY*—it could be an infection and/or imbedded (and not visible) foreign body. See **Before You Leave #2**.

Call your veterinarian for an appointment.

BEFORE YOU LEAVE #1:

1. *Calm your dog.* If he's excited, his heart will pump harder and his blood will run faster than if he's calm. If possible, have a helper hold and soothe him as you work. **Caution:** If your dog is in pain, he may snap out of fear. Take precautions, and see page 329 for how to apply a homemade muzzle.

2. *Apply direct pressure.* Forget about whether the blood's coming from an artery

Never try to remove an imbedded foreign body unless directed to do so by your veterinarian. There's always a risk that you could cause additional damage in your efforts to remove it, or that a portion of the object could break off in your dog's tissues, resulting in infection and/or abscess. With the object in place, your vet can determine depth, direction, and vital structures in its path, then can remove it with minimal damage.

or a vein—the treatment's the same. Apply pressure over the site with a clean pad of sufficient size to cover the wound and its margins. A folded hand towel, disposable diaper, or 1-inch thick stack of gauze sponges will make a suitable pad. If an ice pack is immediately available, sandwich it between the pad's layers to further stem bleeding. Use the same amount of pressure you'd use to feel the contours of your thigh bone.

3. *Apply a pressure bandage.* After 5 to 10 minutes of pressure, apply a pressure bandage. For how to do so, see page 315.

BEFORE YOU LEAVE #2:

1. *Confine your dog.* Crate or otherwise contain your dog, to minimize movement. Pressure applied to his foot through standing, walking, etc., could cause a foreign body to migrate further into tissues, complicating his treatment and recovery.

DRUG-WISE TIP

Avoid using antibiotic powders, sprays, or ointments without consulting your veterinarian. Indiscriminate use of antibiotics in any form can favor the growth of tougher, antibiotic-resistant bacteria.

FOOT PAIN/ SENSITIVITY

What you see: Your dog is refusing to bear weight on his foot, favors it when standing or moving, and/or is sensitive when you apply pressure to the area.

What this might mean: He may have a bone or soft-tissue injury or infection.

YOUR VET MAY NEED TO:

• Sedate your dog, to allow a thorough examination of the foot.
• X-ray the foot, to confirm a tentative diagnosis.
• Prescribe antibiotics, to fight infection.

ACTION PLAN:

Is your dog's foot severely painful? Can you see wounds or other evidence of trauma?

 Call your veterinarian *NOW*—it could be a serious bone or soft-tissue problem. See **Before You Leave**, opposite page.

NO

Is your dog refusing to bear weight on his foot, or touching it down but not bearing full weight on it? Can you see a misalignment of his foot or toes?

 Call your veterinarian *NOW*—it could be a fracture or joint injury. See **Before You Leave**.

NO

Is your dog chewing or licking his foot? Is there moisture and/or redness between his toes or pads?

 Call your veterinarian *NOW*—it could be a skin injury due to an allergic or chemical reaction, or other condition.

NO

Can you see drainage from a wound between your dog's toes and pads?

 Call your veterinarian *NOW*—it could be a foreign body or infection. Go to **page 124**.

NO

Is there a broken, bleeding, or misaligned nail?

Call your veterinarian *TODAY*—it could be a fractured nail, or infection or tumor of the nail bed.

NO

Are the pads blistered and raw?

See **page 128**.

NO

Is there matted hair between your dog's toes and pads? Can you see a foreign body that hasn't penetrated your dog's skin?

Carefully comb or cut out the matted hair, and/or remove the foreign body. If your dog continues to limp, call your veterinarian for an appointment.

NO

ACTION PLAN (CONTINUED):

Is there snow on the ground? Can you see ice balls between your dog's toes? **YES** See **Home Treatment**, below.

NO

Call your veterinarian for an appointment.

BEFORE YOU LEAVE:

1. *Confine your dog.* Crate or otherwise contain your dog, to minimize movement. Pressure applied to his foot through standing, walking, etc., could cause a foreign body to migrate further into tissues, complicating his treatment and recovery.

HOME TREATMENT:

*(See **Action Plan** to determine whether home treatment is appropriate for your dog's feet.*

If at any time during home treatment your answers on the action plan change for the worse, call your veterinarian.)

Step 1: *Melt the ice.* Use a hair dryer to melt the ice balls. Using the lowest possible "warm" setting to avoid burning your dog's feet, hold the dryer about 6 inches away from his paws. Keep it moving until the ice has melted.

CAUTION

If your dog is in pain, he may snap at you out of fear. To be safe, muzzle him when you examine and transport him. (For how to apply a makeshift or regular muzzle, see page 328.) However, if he's having difficulty breathing or acts as though he's going to vomit, remove the muzzle immediately.

Did You Know...

...your dog's toe nails grow constantly, just like yours do. When he doesn't naturally wear them down by activity on hard or rough ground, you'll need to clip them regularly to prevent excessive length from leading to problems. Failure to do so can lead to such problems as in-grown nails, as well as painful nail breakage or even loss. For how to properly trim his nails, see page 279.

What you see: Your dog's pad is cut, blistered, or cracked, exposing pink, possibly bleeding tissue. He may refuse to bear weight on the foot, and may lick and/or chew at it.

8-C

PADS CUT
Or Blistered/Cracked

What this could mean: He stepped on something sharp, ran over rough ground and abraded his pads, injured them digging, or perhaps burned them by walking on a hot surface, such as a sidewalk during the heat of summer.

**YOUR VET
MAY NEED TO:**

• **Sedate your dog,** to allow a thorough examination of the pad.
• **Suture and/or bandage the site.**
• **Prescribe antibiotics,** to fight infection.

ACTION PLAN:

Are his pads bleeding or severely painful (meaning your dog won't walk on the foot)? Is he licking/chewing his foot to the point of causing further injury?

YES ▶ Call your veterinarian *NOW*—your dog may need his pad(s) sutured and/or bandaged. See **Before You Leave**, opposite page.

 NO

Is the skin on your dog's foot pads and/or nose thickened and hornlike?

YES ▶ Call your veterinarian *NOW*—it could be hard-pad^G, a sign of distemper^G. Isolate your dog from other dogs before you leave.

 NO

Is your dog's foot mildly to moderately painful (meaning he's favoring the affected foot but bearing weight on it)?

YES ▶ Call your veterinarian *TODAY*—the injury may need cleaning, antibiotics, and/or bandaging. See **Before You Leave**.

 NO

Are his pads blistered or raw?

YES ▶ Call your veterinarian *TODAY*—see **Before You Leave**.

 NO

Are his pads worn smooth? Are they tender, but with unbroken skin?

YES ▶ See **Home Treatment**, **Steps 1** and **3**.

 NO

Are his pads cracked, but not bleeding?

YES ▶ See **Home Treatment**, **Steps 2** and **3**.

 NO

Call your veterinarian for an appointment.

BEFORE YOU LEAVE:

1. *Control any bleeding.* If your dog's pad is bleeding, apply direct pressure to the bleeding site. Forget about whether the blood's coming from an artery or a vein—the treatment's the same. (Your frightened dog may snap out in pain and confusion. For how to apply a homemade muzzle, see page 329.)

Apply pressure over the site with a clean pad of sufficient size to cover the wound and its margins. A folded hand towel, disposable diaper, or 1-inch thick stack of gauze sponges will make a suitable pad. If an ice pack is immediately available, sandwich it between the pad's layers to further stem bleeding. Use the same amount of pressure you'd use to feel the contours of your thigh bone.

2. *Apply a pressure bandage.* After 5 to 10 minutes of pressure, apply a pressure bandage to his foot. For how to do so, see page 315.

3. *Even if there's no bleeding, protect the foot from further damage.* Wrap the foot (see pages 315), or slip a sock or golf wedge cover over it, to prevent further contact damage, or that from licking/chewing. Hold the sock/cover in place with duct or electrical tape. (See page 321.)

4. *Confine your dog.* Crate or otherwise contain your dog, to minimize movement. Pressure applied to his foot through standing, walking, etc., could cause further damage to tissues, complicating his treatment and recovery.

HOME TREATMENT:

*(See **Action Plan** to determine whether home treatment is appropriate for your dog's pads. If at any time during home treatment your answers on the action plan change for the worse, call your veterinarian.)*

Step 1. *Toughen the pads.* Apply a skin-thickening agent, such as Tough Skin (a human product available at drug and grocery stores), the canine products Pad Tuf, Tuf-Foot, or Pad-Tough, or the equine hoof product Kopertox (available through feed and tack stores, and via vet-supply catalogs) to the pad, per manufacturer's directions. Repeat until your dog's sensitivity passes or for 3 days, whichever comes first.

Step 2: *Moisturize the pads.* Apply a canine moisturizing agent, such as Protecta-Pad, Pad Protection Plus, or Musher's Secret to your dog's pads, per manufacturer's instructions.

Step 3: *Limit your dog's activity.* Limit your dog's exercise to short walk sessions on leash (and on soft surfaces, such as lush, green grass) until he shows no further foot sensitivity. Carefully monitor his movement. If you're unable to make him comfortable after 3 days of treatment, consult your veterinarian.

8-D

CHEWING/ LICKING

At Feet or Toes

What you see: Your dog is worrying something in his foot/feet. He relentlessly licks and/or chews at it/them, or between his toes or pads.

What this might mean: He could be experiencing pain somewhere in his foot or feet, or perhaps itching, due to an allergy. Or he could be demonstrating a behavioral disorder.

ACTION PLAN:

Is your dog licking or chewing his foot to the point of injuring his skin? Can you see a wound with profuse bleeding? Is your dog in severe pain?

 YES Call your veterinarian *NOW*—it could be an acute allergic or chemical reaction, or other injury requiring immediate care. Go to **page 128**.

NO

Can you see a draining wound between his toes or pads?

YES Call your veterinarian *TODAY*—it could be a foreign body or infection. Go to **page 124**.

NO

Can you see a foreign body imbedded in his foot tissues?

YES Call your veterinarian *NOW* and go to **page 124**.

NO

Is there moisture at the nail bed^G? Is the nail-bed area wet, sticky, bloody, or pus-filled? Does it smell bad? Is there a misalignment of a nail, or pain when you manipulate a nail?

YES Call your veterinarian *TODAY* if you answered yes to any query—it could be a fractured nail, a nail-bed^G infection, or a tumor^G.

NO

Is your dog licking the area, with or without any visible injury to his foot or toes?

YES Call your veterinarian *TODAY*—it could be a behavioral problem such as obsessive/compulsive disorder^G, resulting in a lick granuloma^G. See box, opposite page.

NO

Can you see visible matting of the hair between your dog's toes, or a foreign body lodged between the toes or pads that's not breaking the skin?

YES Carefully comb or cut matted the hair and/or remove the foreign body. Call your veterinarian if your dog continues to lick/chew.

NO

Call your veterinarian for an appointment.

Obsessive/Compulsive Disorder in Dogs

Can your dog feel anxiety? Concern? Boredom? You bet.
And he may reveal those emotions in the form of an obsessive/compulsive disorder[G], meaning he's psychologically driven to repeat the same behavior—over, and over, and over. (Such repetition of a single behavior is known as "stereotypical behavior.")

Chronic licking is a typical sign of such a disorder in dogs. You'll notice that your canine buddy is constantly licking at a specific spot on his body, usually on his lower leg or foot. While that type of licking can indicate a problem, or even "phantom pain" from a past injury, if your vet has ruled those out, chances are your dog is revealing a neurosis of some kind. The sores that result from such licking (known as lick granulomas[G]) are often called "boredom sores," as boredom is thought to be a common trigger for the condition.

The syndrome is most often seen in large, active breeds that require constant attention, such as Labrador Retrievers, German Shepherds, Doberman Pinschers, Great Danes, Boxers, and Irish Setters. But it can occur in any breed. It typically appears after the age of 3 and frequently appears in middle-aged dogs that have become less active, especially bird dogs.

What can you do? Here are some tips:
• Work with your vet to try to break the itch-lick cycle (though this can be tough; some cases are never cured).
• Spend more time playing with your dog, to provide needed attention and exercise.
• Get him a canine or feline companion to help alleviate his boredom.
• Avoid keeping him in "solitary confinement". Dogs are social animals by nature, so crave companionship.
• Talk to your vet about a referral to a qualified animal behaviorist, and/or about the possible use of antidepressants and other anti-anxiety medications (such as Clomicalin® and Prozac®), which can help some dogs, particularly during times of stress.

NAILS LONG/ BROKEN

Or Bleeding/Draining

What you see: One or more of your dog's nails are long, cracked, misaligned, bleeding, or draining at the nail bed[G].

What this could mean: It could be as simple as your dog needing a nail trim, or as severe as a fracture or tumor of his nail bed[G].

ACTION PLAN:

Is your dog favoring or chewing at his affected foot? Can you see blood or pus at the nail bed[G]? Is there misalignment of a nail(s)?

YES Call your veterinarian *NOW*—it could be a fractured nail, or a nail-bed[G] infection or tumor.

NO

Is there bleeding from the nail end? Has your dog been digging or running on hard surfaces?

YES See **Home Treatment**, below.

NO

Are your dog's nails extending below his pads? Do his nails make a clicking sound when he walks on hard surfaces?

YES Trim his nails at home (see **page 279**) or have your groomer or vet do so.

HOME TREATMENT:

*(See **Action Plan** to determine whether home treatment is appropriate for your dog's bleeding nails. If at any time during home treatment your answers on the action plan change for the worse, call your veterinarian.)*

Step 1: *Stop the bleeding.* Apply direct pressure to the bleeding nail, using a cotton ball. Resist the urge to check the bleeding for 5 minutes. If, after that time, the blood hasn't clotted, use a styptic pencil (a human shaving product available at drug and grocery stores) or a canine product such as Kwik-Stop (available through feed and pet stores, or through pet supply catalogs). Apply per manufacturer's instructions. (For more information see page 281.) Call your vet if the bleeding fails to stop after pressure and product application.

CHAPTER 9

GASTRO-INTESTINAL

(Digestive Problems)

What you see: Your dog is gagging and/or retching without vomiting (also known as "dry heaves").

GAGGING/ RETCHING

What this could mean: Such signs can be associated with a non-productive cough, sore throat, or vomiting on an empty stomach. Or they could signal a serious systemic disease or gastrointestinal problem.

YOUR VET MAY NEED TO:

• X-ray your dog, and perform lab work to confirm a tentative diagnosis.

• Perform surgery, if bloat^G is diagnosed.

ACTION PLAN:

Is your dog lethargic, feverish, or lacking appetite? Is he unable to keep down food/water? Do you see a marked abdominal distension?

YES Call your veterinarian *NOW*—it could be a serious systemic disease, such as parvovirus^G, or it could be secondary to kidney disease or bloat^G See **Before You Leave**, below. Go to **page 139** for emergency information on bloat.

NO

Has he been vomiting repeatedly, and now is bringing up nothing or small amounts of yellow fluid or blood?

YES Call your veterinarian *NOW*—it could be gastritis^G due to infection, poison, foreign body, or a tumor.

NO

Does your dog have a harsh, dry cough followed by gagging and/or retching?

YES Call your veterinarian *NOW*—it could be kennel cough^G, a foreign body lodged in his throat, or other serious problem. See **Before You Leave**.

NO

Is your dog pawing at his mouth? Is he drooling, having difficulty swallowing, or does he have bad breath? Does he lick carpet or other rough surfaces? Does he chew grass, sticks, or other foreign materials?

YES Call your veterinarian *NOW* if you answered yes to any query—it could be a foreign body lodged in the back of your dog's throat, or he may have tonsillitis^G or pharyngitis^G.

NO

Call your veterinarian for an appointment.

BEFORE YOU LEAVE:

Isolate your dog from other dogs in case it's contagious. To prevent spread of possible infectious disease, confine your dog to a warm, dry area with a separate water supply, apart from other dogs. Wash your hands and disinfect your shoes (see page 374) after handling your dog and before handling other dogs.

Kennel Cough Caution

If your dog is diagnosed with kennel cough, please be a responsible owner. While most cases are mild, this is a highly contagious disease that requires forward thinking on your part to prevent inadvertent spread to other dogs:

• **Isolate your dog from other dogs.** Keep him in a warm, dry area with a separate water supply. Wash your hands and disinfect your shoes (see page 374) after you handle him and before handling other dogs. Disinfect his "sick bay" once he's given a clean bill of health. Don't walk him off your property. To avoid spreading the disease, keep your dog at home, providing moderate, on-leash exercise there, as instructed by your veterinarian.

• **Avoid taking him to public places.** For the sake of other dogs, keep him home from the groomers until he's declared disease-free. If you absolutely must board him, alert the boarding facility as to his condition. Do the same when you take him to your veterinary clinic.

9-B

What you see: Your dog is vomiting food, or water, bile, or blood. He may vomit once and seem fine, or he may vomit repeatedly.

VOMITING

What this might mean: It could be due to problems ranging from gastric irritation from "dietary indescretions," to gastric tumors^G, or a serious systemic disease.

**YOUR VET
MAY NEED TO:**

- Take X-rays.
- Perform
lab work.
- Perform an
endoscopy^G to
check for such
problems as
ulcers, tumors, or
foreign bodies.
- Perform a
biopsy if a mass
is detected.

ACTION PLAN:

Is your dog making repeated, unsuccessful attempts to vomit? Is his abdomen distended/bloated?

 NO

YES ▶ Call your veterinarian *NOW*—it could be gastric-dilatation volvulus^G (bloat). Go to **page 139**.

Is your dog lethargic? Feverish? Does he have a poor appetite or diarrhea? Is he unable to keep down food or water? When you palpate his abdomen, does it seem tense or painful? Is he standing with his front end lowered and his hind end in the air (the "praying" position)?

NO

YES ▶ Call your veterinarian *NOW* if you answered yes to any query—it could be a serious systemic disease, such as parvovirus^G, pancreatitis^G, kidney failure, or a foreign body, intestinal obstruction, Addison's disease^G, or a tumor^G. See **Before You Leave #1**, opposite page.

Is your dog vomiting bright red blood or dark fluid containing flecks that look like coffee grounds (which are actually blood)?

 NO

YES ▶ Call your veterinarian *NOW*—it could be gastric bleeding secondary to ulceration due to infection or tumor. See **Before You Leave #1**.

Has your dog recently eaten anything unusual or gotten into garbage? Have you fed him table scraps? Does he chew bones, sticks, rocks, plastic, etc?

 NO

YES ▶ Call your veterinarian *NOW* if you answered yes to any query—it could be food or chemical poisoning, or a foreign body. See **Before You Leave #1**.

Has your dog vomited up spaghetti-like worms? Does he have a dull, dry hair coat and a pot belly?

YES ▶ Call your veterinarian *TODAY* if you answered yes to either query—it could be intestinal parasites, such as ascarids^G (roundworms). See **Before You Leave #2**.

ACTION PLAN (CONTINUED):

Is your dog vomiting, but otherwise normal? He's bright, active, alert, with no fever, and is interested in eating and drinking? Have you recently changed dog food or fed fresh table scraps? **YES** It sounds as though he may have simple gastritis^G. See **Home Treatment #1**.

NO

Does your puppy or adult dog vomit shortly after eating? Is he otherwise normal? **YES** It may be due to eating too rapidly, or overeating. See **Home Treatment #2**.

 NO

Call your veterinarian for an appointment.

BEFORE YOU LEAVE #1:

1. *Isolate your dog from other dogs in case it's contagious.* To prevent spread of possible infectious disease, confine your dog to a warm, dry area, apart from other dogs. Wash your hands and disinfect your shoes (see page 374) after handling your dog and before handling other dogs.

2. *Pick up food and water.* Ingestion of solids or liquids could further exacerbate your dog's digestive upset. If he acts thirsty, allow him to lick an ice cube. Ask your veterinarian for specific post-appointment feeding/watering instructions.

BEFORE YOU LEAVE #2:

1. *Take in a fresh stool sample to your vet.* Use a tongue depressor or plastic spoon to get a tablespoon-sized sample of a fresh stool pile (one that's less than an hour old). Put the sample in a plastic baggie or clean margarine container. (If you can't leave right away, store the sample in your refrigerator until you do, to preserve parasite eggs.) Your vet can then test the sample for parasites, and treat your dog if the test is positive.

HOME TREATMENT #1:

*(See **Action Plan** to determine whether home treatment is appropriate for your dog's vomiting. If at any time during home treatment your answers on the action plan change for the worse, call your veterinarian.)*

Step 1: *Withhold food and water.* Pick up food and water sources for 24 hours to give your dog's gastrointestinal system a chance to "rest." (If he acts thirsty, offer him an occasional ice cube.)

Step 2: *Give him a stomach-soothing product.* Give your dog a liquid-form, stomach-coating, over-the-counter product such as Pepto-Bismol, Kaopectate, Gelusil, Mylanta, or Maalox (human products available at drug and grocery stores). Give your small dog a teaspoon of the liquid form; give your medium-sized dog 2 teaspoons, and your large/giant dog a tablespoon, every 6 hours for 24 hours. (For how to give your dog an oral dose of liquid, see page 260.)

Step 3: *Gradually introduce water or clear broth.* After you've withheld food/water ➤

for the prescribed period, give your dog small amounts of room-temperature water or clear broth (several swallows at a time) every 15 minutes. If he keeps the water/broth down for an hour...

Step 4: *Gradually introduce baby food.* Feed him small amounts of chicken-and-rice baby food every hour or so. If he keeps that down...

Step 5: *Gradually introduce his regular food.* Give him about a fourth or less of his regular food amount. (Soak the food in warm water, if it's in kibble form, to soften it, thus making it easier to digest.) Feed him small amounts, about 4 times a day, for 24 hours. Gradually increase the amount/decrease the frequency over the next several days, until you're feeding him on his normal schedule. If your dog continues to vomit during home treatment, call your veterinarian.

HOME TREATMENT #2:

Step 1: *Feed smaller amounts more frequently.* If your puppy or dog bolts his food, and your schedule permits, divide his daily food ration into smaller, more frequent feedings. That way he's less likely to rapidly ingest an amount of food that could cause him to vomit. For instance, if you feed your adult dog a cup of food, two times a day, divide his ration into half-cup portions and feed him four times a day.

Step 2: *Slow down his eating, by using "obstacles."* Put several large, smooth objects (such as smooth rocks or hard plastic balls) in his food bowl, so that he's forced to eat around them. Having to push around the objects in order to eat will slow his rate of ingestion. ***Caution:*** Be sure to only use objects that are too large for him to swallow. Otherwise, you could inadvertantly put him at risk for choking.

Be Strong...

...it's normal to feel guilty for withholding food from your vomiting dog. But you're actually doing him a favor. If you were to feed him to make yourself feel better, you'd risk making him feel worse. Even if he begs you with those big, brown eyes, hang tough. Dogs evolved as hunters, so adult dogs can actually go several days without food between "kills," and not suffer untoward effects. You can generally rest assured that skipping a meal isn't going to hurt your buddy!

What you see: Your dog's abdomen is markedly distended, as though a balloon has inflated within it. (For how to identify distension, see "**Bloat Check**," next page.) You may have noticed the bloating within a few hours of when he was last fed. He may or may not be showing signs of discomfort, such as restlessness or lethargy. He may also be making repeated—yet unsuccessful—attempts to vomit.

What this might mean: His stomach may simply be distended with food, water, and/or gas. Or he may have an acute, life-threatening emergency called gastric dilatation volvulus^G (bloat).

9 - C

BLOAT/ ABDOMINAL DISTENSION

ACTION PLAN:

Has your dog eaten recently? Is he drooling and retching? Dull, lethargic and unresponsive? Is his abdomen tense and painful? Are his gums pale gray or bright red?

 YES Call your veterinarian *NOW* if you answered yes to any query—it could be the first signs of a life-threatening emergency known as bloat^G.

NO

Has there been a gradual onset of the abdominal distension? Does his abdomen seem to be filled with fluid? Does your dog have pale gums, difficulty breathing, or is he coughing?

 YES Call your veterinarian *NOW* if you answered yes to any query—it could be congestive heart failure^G, abdominal cancer, or other such serious problem.

 NO

Has your dog recently eaten a large meal? Is he otherwise normal?

YES It may be normal—or early signs of bloat. Monitor him closely for signs of increasing abdominal distension. (See "**Bloat Check**," next page.)

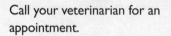 **NO**

Call your veterinarian for an appointment.

➤

YOUR VET MAY NEED TO:

- **Sedate your dog, in order to X-ray his abdomen.**
- **Perform lab work.**
- **Administer IV fluids.**
- **Monitor his heart.**
- **Euthanize the dog, if a case of bloat has progressed beyond repair. (Mortality rates can be as high as 30% to 60%.)**

Canine 9-1-1

Your ability to act fast in a bloat emergency could mean the difference between life and death for your dog. The sooner your get him to a large, full-service emergency clinic or vet hospital with surgical facilities, the better his chances of living. Be sure to call ahead to the facility to alert them of your dog's condition and your anticipated arrival time. That way, the staff can be prepared to tackle the emergency the moment your dog arrives.

Bloat Check

Here's how to measure your dog's abdomen, to monitor for distension:

1. Grab a seamstress tape, or a piece of soft rope or string that's long enough to encircle your dog's abdomen.

2. With your dog standing, loop the tape or string/rope around his abdomen at the point where his last rib meets it. (See page 293.)

3. Carefully note or mark your measurement.

4. Repeat again—in the exact same spot—in 15 minutes.

5. If the measurement is larger, call your vet NOW!

6. If your measurement is the same or smaller—and your dog isn't showing any signs of distress as outlined in the action plan—recheck him in a half-hour. If, at any time, the measurement increases or he begins to shows signs of distress, call your vet NOW!

Bloat Basics

Gastric-dilatation volvulus[G] (GDV), commonly known as "bloat," often occurs after your dog has eaten. His stomach fills with fluid and gas that can't be expelled by burping or vomiting. Once distended, it may twist abruptly. If the twist is less than 180 degrees on the stomach's long axis, it's known as a *torsion*. If the twist is greater than 180 degrees, it's known as a *volvulus*. Researchers don't yet understand the actual cause of this life-threatening condition, but this much is known:

• Bloat generally affects dogs between 4 and 7 years of age. About two-thirds of those affected are males.

• It primarily affects large-breed (over 50 pounds), deep-chested dogs such as Bloodhounds, Boxers, Doberman Pinschers, German Shepherds, Great Danes, Great Pyrenees, Irish Setters, Irish Wolfhounds, Labrador Retrievers, Saint Bernards, Standard Poodles, and Weimaraners, but can affect any size or breed.

• Dogs who bloat tend to eat a diet consisting of large amounts of dry dog food.

• Exercise and large intakes of water immediately after eating can increase the risk for bloat.

• Dogs who bloat may have a history of gastritis[G] (digestive disturbances).

• Bloat is also commonly associated with stress (or any change in routine), such as boarding, surgery, breeding, showing, or travel. It may have something to do with *aerophagia*—swallowing air when nervous or excited.

• Bloat appears to have a hereditary link. In other words, if your dog's relative suffered from bloat, your dog may be at greater risk than a dog without bloat in his heritage.

• For how to reduce your dog's risk for bloat, see page 291.

What you see: Your dog has episodes of diarrhea (frequent, watery, and/or bloody stools), or is passing soft stools with or without mucus and/or blood. These are evident as shapeless, strong-smelling piles of stool, or puddles on the ground (or splattered on walls). You may also see dried stool on your dog's tail, buttocks, and hind legs.

What this might mean: It could be a problem ranging from mild intestinal irritation, to food poisoning or infectious disease, parasites, a tumor, or a foreign body in his gastrointestinal tract.

DIARRHEA
(Soft, Mucoid, or Bloody Stools)

ACTION PLAN:

Is the diarrhea sudden-onset, marked by large amounts of bright-red or dark, bloody, foul-smelling stool that may resemble raspberry jam? Is he depressed?

 Call your veterinarian *NOW* if you answered yes to either query—it could be hemorrhagic gastroenteritisᴳ, parvovirusᴳ, Addison's diseaseᴳ, or a bleeding disorder. See **Before You Leave**, next page.

Is your dog lethargic, feverish, lacking appetite, and/or vomiting? Does he get into garbage, animal carcasses, or chew plastic and other non-food materials?

 Call your veterinarian *NOW* if you answered yes to any query—it could be food poisoning, parvovirusᴳ, distemperᴳ Addison's diseaseᴳ, a foreign body lodged in your dog's gastrointestinal tract, or other such serious condition. See **Before You Leave**.

Is your dog straining to defecate? Does he have soft stools that are the consistency of wet concrete, or thinner? Do they contain mucus (clear, KY-Jelly-looking or thick, yellow, custard-like material) and/or blood?

 Call your veterinarian *TODAY*—it could be colitisᴳ and/or a parasite infestation. See **Before You Leave**.

Does your dog have large-volume, light-colored or greasy/oily-looking stools? Is he unusually thin with a dull, dry hair coat?

 Call your veterinarian *TODAY*—it could be a pancreatic insufficiencyᴳ or other maldigestion or malabsorption problem.

Is his diarrhea a chronic problem (meaning he has frequent bouts)? Does your dog otherwise act normal, meaning he's bright, alert, and interested in food?

 Call your veterinarian *TODAY*—it could be a food allergy or diet problem, inflammatory bowel disease, or a mild bacterial infection. See **Before You Leave, Steps 2** and **3**.

➤

YOUR VET MAY NEED TO:

- **Sedate your dog, in order to take X-rays.**
- **Perform lab work, including blood work, urinalysis, culture/sensitivity.**
- **Perform an endoscopyᴳ.**
- **Take a biopsy, if a mass is found.**
- **Perform a fecal exam for internal parasites.**

Was the diarrhea rapid-onset? Has your dog recently eaten anything unusual? Have you changed food recently, or fed table scraps? Is he bright, alert, and otherwise normal?

YES ▶ See **Home Treatment**.

NO ▼

Call your veterinarian for an appointment.

BEFORE YOU LEAVE:

1. *Isolate your dog from other dogs in case it's contagious.* To prevent spread of possible infectious disease, confine your dog to a warm, dry area, apart from other dogs. Wash your hands and disinfect your shoes (see page 374) after handling your dog and before handling other dogs.

2. *Pick up food and water.* Ingestion of solids and large amounts of liquids could further exacerbate your dog's digestive upset. If he acts thirsty, allow several swallows of water every half-hour, or give him ice cubes. Ask your veterinarian for specific post-appointment feeding/watering instructions.

3. *Take in a fresh stool sample.* Use a tongue depressor or plastic spoon to get a tablespoon-sized sample of fresh stool (less than an hour old). Put the sample in a plastic baggie or clean margarine container. (If you can't leave right away, put the sample in your refrigerator until you do.) Your vet can then test the sample for parasites or other pathogens.

HOME TREATMENT:

*(See **Action Plan** to determine whether home treatment is appropriate for your dog's diarrhea. If at any time during home treatment your answers on the action plan change for the worse, call your veterinarian.)*

Step 1: *Check your dog for dehydration.* Grasp a fold of loose skin over your dog's shoulder blades, and slightly pull it an inch or so away from his body. (This won't hurt him.) Hold it there for about 5 seconds, then release. If the skin immediately returns to its normal position, your dog isn't dehydrated. Move on to Step 2. However, if it remains "standing" (known as "tenting") before slowly falling back into place, your dog is dehydrated. Cease your home treatment and call your veterinarian immediately.

Step 2: *Withhold food.* Pick up food for 24 hours, to give your dog's gastrointestinal system a chance to "rest." Provide plenty of fresh water—the liquid he's passing in his diarrhea could quickly lead to dehydration.

Step 3: *Give him an intestine-soothing product.* Give your dog a liquid-form of intestine-coating, over-the-counter product such as Pepto-Bismol or Kaopectate (human products available at drug and grocery stores). Or a human anti-diarrhea product such as Immodium. As a rule of thumb, administer 1 teaspoon per 20 pounds of body-weight. For instance, give your small dog a teaspoon of the liquid form; give your medium-sized dog 2 teaspoons, and your large/giant dog a tablespoon, every 6 hours for 24 hours. (For how to give your dog an oral dose of liquid, see page 260.)

Step 4: *Gradually introduce baby food.* After 24 hours, feed him small amounts of chicken-and-rice baby food every hour or so. If he shows no signs of diarrhea on the baby-food diet...

Step 5: *Gradually introduce his regular food.* Give him about a fourth or less of his regular food amount. (Soak the food in warm water, if it's in kibble form, to soften it, thus making it easier to digest.) Feed him small amounts, about 4 times a day, for 24 hours. Gradually increase the amount/decrease the frequency over the next several days, until you're feeding him on his normal schedule. If your dog continues to have diarrhea during home treatment, call your veterinarian.

Step 5: *Take in a fresh stool sample to your vet.* Use a tongue depressor or plastic spoon to get a tablespoon-sized sample of fresh stool (less than an hour old. Put the sample in a plastic baggie or clean margarine container. (If you can't leave right away, keep the sample in the refrigerator until you do, to preserve any parasite eggs.) Your vet can then test the sample for parasites.

Did You Know...

...when you see your dog straining to defecate (frequent, urgent squatting and straining), do you automatically assume he's constipated? Take a closer look. Dogs rarely suffer from constipation as a primary problem. Generally, it's due to a colon, anus, or perianal[G] disorder. Colitis[G] frequently causes such straining. This inflammation of the large bowel (colon) can cause your dog discomfort as he defecates, which is what you see as straining.

To help determine if your dog is suffering from constipation or colitis, take a good look at his stools. If he's straining to pass several small, hard balls, he is constipated. (See page 146.) However, if he's passing small amounts of loose stool containing blood and/or mucus, it's likely to be colitis. Call your veterinarian for an appointment.

What you see: Your dog's stool is a color other than its normal medium brown. He may or may not be passing an abnormal amount, and it may be thicker or thinner than normal in consistency.

ABNORMAL STOOL COLOR

What this might mean: It could simply be a reflection of your dog's diet (for instance, that he ate something that affected his stool color). Or, it could indicate a more serious problem.

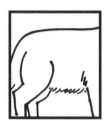

ACTION PLAN:

Is your dog lethargic, feverish, or lacking appetite? Is there bright-red blood in his stool? Is the stool black and "tarry?"

 NO

 YES → Call your veterinarian *NOW* if you answered yes to any query—it could be hemorrhagic gastroenteritis[G], parvovirus[G], Addison's disease[G], or a bleeding disorder. See **Before You Leave**, opposite page.

Is the stool orange, black, or bloody? Is your dog on any medication?

 NO

 YES → Call your veterinarian *NOW*—it may be a secondary effect of medication.

Is the stool gray and clay-like? Is it light-colored and oily/greasy? Does your dog have unusually frequent or large-volume stools? Is he jaundiced[G] (yellow around his eyes/gums)?

 NO

YES → Call your veterinarian *TODAY* if you answered yes to any query—it could be due to a pancreatic insufficiency[G], bile duct obstruction, or some other digestive problem.

Is the stool dry and white? Are there flecks of fresh, red blood in it? Is your dog straining to defecate? Has he recently been fed bones? Is he bright, alert, and otherwise normal?

 NO

YES → Stop feeding him bones that can be chewed up/digested. See **Home Treatment**, opposite page. Call your veterinarian if other symptoms develop.

Call your veterinarian for an appointment.

BEFORE YOU LEAVE:

1. *Isolate your dog from other dogs in case it's contagious.* To prevent spread of possible infectious disease, confine your dog to a warm, dry area, apart from other dogs. Wash your hands and disinfect your shoes (see page 374) after handling your dog and before handling other dogs.

2. *Pick up food and water.* Ingestion of solids and large amounts of liquids could further exacerbate problems in your dog's digestive tract. If he acts thirsty, allow several swallows of water every half-hour, or give him ice cubes. Ask your veterinarian for specific post-appointment feeding/watering instructions.

3. *Take in a fresh stool sample.* Use a tongue depressor or plastic spoon to get a tablespoon-sized sample of fresh stool (less than an hour old). Put the sample in a plastic baggie or clean margarine container. (If you can't leave right away, refrigerate the sample until you can, to preserve any parasite eggs.) Your vet can then test it for parasites or other pathogens.

HOME TREATMENT:

*(See **Action Plan** to determine whether home treatment is appropriate for your dog's off-color stool. If at any time during home treatment your answers on the action plan change for the worse, call your veterinarian.)*

Step 1: *Feed him a fiber supplement.* Adding fiber to your dog's ration will help soften his stools, enabling him to more easily pass the bone fragments. Feed him canned pumpkin (2 tablespoons for a toy dog, eighth a cup for a small dog, one-fourth cup for a medium dog, and a half-cup for a large dog) 2 to 3 times a day. (Most dogs love it.) If your dog turns up his nose at pumpkin, try giving him bran cereal (1 to 3 tablespoons, several times a day).

Step 2: *Take in a fresh stool sample.* Use a tongue depressor or plastic spoon to get a tablespoon-sized sample of fresh stool (less than an hour old—if you can't leave right away, refrigerate the sample, to preserve any parasite eggs). Put the sample in a plastic baggie or clean margarine container. Your vet can then test it for parasites or other pathogens.

Fact or Fiction: When your dog eats grass, it means he has a belly ache.

If you answered "fiction," you get the prize. Dogs will often "graze" on spring grass even when they feel fine. Some veterinarians theorize that this grass-eating behavior is a throw-back to your dog's den-dwelling days. During winter, animals in the wild that are used to fresh meat often must subside on old, dried food or carrion. Ingesting spring grass may act as a "tonic," as it has a cathartic (purging) effect. If it irritates your dog's stomach, it can cause him to vomit. If it travels to his digestive tract, it can cause diarrhea, which also is a way to purge his system. In short, grazing on grass may be nature's way of giving your dog's digestive tract a spring cleaning.

What you see: Your dog is squatting frequently, and straining to pass stool. Or, it takes him an unusually long time to defecate

STRAINING TO DEFECATE

What this might mean: It could signal something as simple as constipation. Or it could mean something more serious, such as colitis^G—or colon cancer.

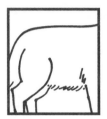

ACTION PLAN:

Is your dog passing bright red blood? Is he unable to pass any stool, or only small amounts of stool with blood and/or mucus?

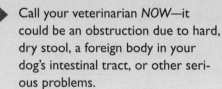 **YES** Call your veterinarian *NOW*—it could be an obstruction due to hard, dry stool, a foreign body in your dog's intestinal tract, or other serious problems.

NO

Is there a pink, donut-shaped tissue mass protruding from his anus?

YES Call your veterinarian *NOW*—it could be rectal prolapse^G.

NO

Can you see a bulge to the side of his rectum? Is it an unaltered male dog?

YES Call your veterinarian *NOW*—it could be a perineal hernia^G, which could require a surgical correction.

NO

Is there visible foreign material protruding from his anus (such as string or panty hose)?

YES Call your veterinarian *NOW*—he or she will need to carefully remove the object, which may require surgery. See "Stop!" box, opposite page.

NO

Is your dog having frequent, soft, mucoid, and/or bloody stools?

YES Call your veterinarian *NOW*—it could be colitis^G, due to any one of many causes (see "Possible Causes of Colitis," page 148, and **Before You Leave**).

NO

Does your dog seem uncomfortable when he defecates, walking around as he squats? Does he lick his anus, and/or scoot or drag it across the floor?

YES Call your veterinarian *NOW*—it could be an anal sac abscess^G.

NO

Is he weak/uncoordinated in his rear end? Is there pain over his pelvis or when you raise his tail?

YES Call your veterinarian *NOW*—it could be lumbosacral instability^G.

NO

ACTION PLAN (CONTINUED):

Is your dog normal other than passing hard, dry stools? **YES** See **Home Treatment**, below. If not improved in 48 hours, call your veterinarian.

NO

Is his stool white, with small pieces of bone and/or flecks of blood. Do you feed your dog bones? **YES** Stop feeding him bones that can be chewed up/digested. See **Home Treatment**, below. Call your veterinarian if other symptoms develop.

NO

Call your veterinarian for an appointment.

BEFORE YOU LEAVE:

1. *Isolate your dog from other dogs in case it's contagious.* To prevent spread of possible infectious disease, confine your dog to a warm, dry area, apart from other dogs. Wash your hands and disinfect your shoes (see page 374) after handling your dog and before handling other dogs.

2. *Pick up food and water.* Ingestion of solids and large amounts of liquids could further exacerbate problems in your dog's digestive tract. If he acts thirsty, allow several swallows of water every half-hour, or give him ice cubes. Ask your veterinarian for specific post-appointment feeding/watering instructions.

3. *Take in a fresh stool sample.* Use a tongue depressor or plastic spoon to get a table-spoon-sized sample of fresh stool (less than an hour old). Put the sample in a plastic baggie or clean margarine container. (If you can't leave right away, refrigerate it until you do, to preserve any parasite eggs.) Your vet can then test the sample for parasites or other pathogens.

HOME TREATMENT:

*(See **Action Plan** to determine whether home treatment is appropriate for your dog's straining. If at any time during home treatment your answers on the action plan change for the worse, call your veterinarian.)*

> **Never attempt to pull a protruding object from your dog's anus. If you see string, panty hose, or other such object hanging from his anus, it's a medical emergency. If you were to attempt to pull it out, you'd risk causing serious—even life-threatening—damage to his anus, rectum, or colon. Leave the object in place and allow your vet to assess the situation. He or she will likely use X-rays to assess the safest route of removal, which could include surgery.**

Step 1: *Feed him a fiber supplement.* Adding fiber to your dog's ration will help soften his stools, enabling him to more easily pass stool and/or bone fragments. Feed him canned pumpkin (2 tablespoons for a toy dog, eighth a cup for a small dog, one-fourth cup for a medium dog, and a half-cup for a large dog) 2 to 3 times a day. (Most dogs love it.) If your dog turns up his nose at pumpkin, try giving him bran cereal (1 to 3 tablespoons, several times a day).

Step 2: *Take in a fresh stool sample.* Use a tongue depressor or plastic spoon to get a table-spoon-sized sample of fresh stool (less than an hour old). Put the sample in a plastic baggie or clean margarine container. (If you can't leave right away, refrigerate it until you do, to preserve the parasite eggs.) Your vet can then test the sample for parasites or other pathogens.

Is It *Really* Constipation?

When you see your dog straining to defecate (frequent, urgent squatting and straining), do you automatically assume he's constipated? Take a closer look. Dogs rarely suffer from constipation as a primary problem. Generally, it's due to a colon, anus, or perianal^G disorder. Colitis^G frequently causes such straining. This inflammation of the large bowel (colon) can cause your dog discomfort as he defecates, which is what you see as straining.

To help determine if your dog is suffering from constipation or colitis, take a good look at his stools. If he's straining to pass several small, hard balls, he is constipated. (See page 147.) However, if he's passing small amounts of loose stool containing blood and/or mucus, it's likely to be colitis. Call your veterinarian for an appointment.

Possible Causes of Colitis

Colitis is a collective term for inflammation of your dog's colon. You may never determine the root cause of your dog's colitis, but here's a sampling of typical culprits:

- Giardia^G
- Ingestion of garbage
- Ingestion of abrasive foreign material (such as plastics and bones)
- Clostridium^G
- Chronic inflammatory bowel disease

- Colon cancer
- Escherichia coli^G (E-coli)
- Salmonella^G
- Parasites, such as hookworms^G and whipworms^G
- Food-induced allergy

What you see: In your dog's stool piles, you notice small, ivory-colored or off-white, rice-like worms moving on the surface. Or, you see off-white, coiled, or spaghetti-like worms threaded through or on top of the piles.

WORMS IN STOOL

What this might mean: Your dog is suffering from an internal parasite[G] infestation. These nasty invaders can affect his digestion and absorption of nutrients, leading to nutritional deficiencies even if his diet is adequate. A dull hair coat is one external sign of under-nourishment.

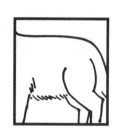

ACTION PLAN:

Are the worms moving, rice-like specs on the surface of your dog's fresh stool?

YES → Call your veterinarian *TODAY*—it sounds like tapeworms[G]. See "How To Get A Stool Sample," below.

 NO

Are they coiled or spaghetti-like worms mixed in the stool?

YES → Call your veterinarian *TODAY*—it sounds like ascarids[G], the common roundworms of dogs. See "How To Get A Stool Sample," below.

 NO

Do you see small, off-white worms in yesterday's stool?

YES → It could be fly larvae (maggots). Observe a fresh pile of stool, and take in fresh stool sample for analysis.

NO

Call your vet for an appointment.

YOUR VET MAY NEED TO:

• Examine a stool sample, to determine the type of parasite.
• Perform lab work.
• Treat any problem secondary to the infestation, such as colitis[G].

How to Get a Stool Sample

Use these tips to give your veterinarian his or her best shot at battling the parasites that are invading your dog.

• *Keep it fresh.* Select a pile that's less than an hour old. Your veterinarian will be looking for eggs in the stool, which can hatch into larvae in stool older than an hour. If he or she finds no eggs in older stool, it could result in a false-negative reading.

• *A little dab will do you.* Use a tongue depressor or plastic spoon to gather about a tablespoon of stool (that's all needed for analysis).

• *Store it.* Place the sample in a clean plastic baggie or clean margarine container.

• *Cool it.* If you won't be leaving for the vet's immediately, store the sample in your refrigerator, to prevent any parasite eggs from hatching into larvae.

• *Take it.* Don't forget to grab the sample before heading to your vet's.

What you hear: Your dog is sitting or lying down, and you hear abdominal sounds emanating from him. It sounds as though his stomach is "growling"—loudly. He may or may not act aware of the noise.

INCREASED ABDOMINAL NOISE

What this might mean: The noise is due to increased intestinal movement (motility). You're hearing the sounds of gas and fluid moving within your dog's intestine. It could simply due to a mild digestive upset—or a sign of a more serious problem.

ACTION PLAN:

Does your dog seem uncomfortable? Is he restless? Vomiting or having diarrhea?

YES Call your veterinarian *NOW*—it could be gastritis^G, gastroenteritis^G, pancreatitis^G, or other such condition. Go to **pages 136** and **141**.

 NO

Is your dog is otherwise normal?

YES See **Home Treatment**, below.

HOME TREATMENT:

*(See **Action Plan** to determine whether home treatment is appropriate for your dog's increased abdominal noise. If at any time during home treatment your answers on the action plan change for the worse, call your veterinarian.)*

Step 1: *Withhold food and water.* Pick up and food and water sources for 4 to 6 hours, to give your dog's gastrointestinal system a chance to "rest." (If he acts thirsty, offer him an occasional ice cube or several swallows of water every half-hour.)

Step 2: *Give him a stomach-soothing product.* Give your dog a liquid-form, stomach-coating, over-the-counter product such as Pepto-Bismol, Kaopectate, Gelusil, Mylanta, or Maalox (human products available at drug and grocery stores). Give your small dog a teaspoon of the liquid form; give your medium-sized dog 2 teaspoons,

and your large/giant dog a tablespoon, every 6 hours for 24 hours. (For how to give your dog an oral dose of liquid, see page 260.)

Step 3: *Gradually introduce water.* After you've withheld food/water for the prescribed period, allow your dog small amounts of room-temperature water.

Step 4: *Gradually introduce food.* Give him about a fourth or less of his regular food amount. (Soak the food in warm water, if it's in kibble form, to soften it, thus making it easier to digest.) Feed him small amounts, about 4 times a day, for 24 hours. Gradually increase the amount/decrease the frequency over the next several days, until you're feeding him on his normal schedule. If your dog becomes lethargic, runs a fever, and/or begins vomiting or having diarrhea any time during home treatment, call your veterinarian.

What you hear/smell: You may hear your dog expelling intestinal gas, and/or smell a gaseous odor.

What this might mean: Though gas is a normal part of digestion, it also could signal that something's awry in your dog's gastrointestinal tract. It may be the result of the bacterial fermentation of incompletely digested food, a sign of illness, or the result of your dog gulping air.

GAS
(Flatulence)

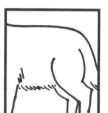

ACTION PLAN:

Does your dog have watery or soft stools? **YES** → He may have a maldigestion or malabsorption problem (such as pancreatitis^G) or he may have gastroenteristis^G. Go to **page 141**.

NO ↓

Have you recently changed dog food or fed unusual foods to your dog? **YES** → See **Home Treatment #1**, below.

NO ↓

Is the gas persistent on the same diet you've always fed? **YES** → See **Home Treatment #2**.

NO ↓

Call your vet for an appointment.

HOME TREATMENT #1:
*(See **Action Plan** to determine whether home treatment is appropriate for your dog's flatulence. If at any time during home treatment your answers on the action plan change for the worse, call your veterinarian.)*

Step 1: Stick to your dog's normal diet. Feed your dog only his regular dog food, to reduce the risk of a digestive upset that could lead to gas. Cut out table scraps or any other "treats."

HOME TREATMENT #2:
Step 1: *Change dog food.* Diets high in meats can cause flatulence. Gradually switch your dog to a different food. For instance, if he's currently eating one whose primary ingredients are beef and corn, make the change to one that's comprised of lamb and rice. When you make the change, start by mixing your old food with the new, to avoid a digestive upset. For instance, if he gets 1 cup of food twice a day, start with 1/4 cup of the new food and 3/4 cup of the old food for the first day. Then graduate to 1/2 cup of each for day 2, and so on, introducing the new food in quarter-cup increments. If he continues to be gassy on the new food, talk to your vet about switching him to a highly digestible diet, such as Hills i/d or k/d. ➤

Flatulence Fighters

Products that help control gas in humans can help your dog, too.
Here are three that you can use to help stem the flow
of your pooch's gas attacks.

• **Plain yogurt.** Many yogurts contain bacteria that can aid in
digestion and help decrease flatulence. Select a brand that contains
lactobacillus (live active cultures—it will say so on the label). Give
a teaspoon to your small dog and a tablespoon to a large dog, once
a day. Most dogs love the taste so you won't need to hide it in your
dog's food. Even pets who are lactose intolerant can usually handle
yogurt without a problem.

• **Simethicone.** Human digestion aids, such as Gas-X, contain
a surfactant that causes small gas bubbles to coalesce (grow
together), making the gas easier to expel. Follow manufacturer's
instructions.

• **Beano.** You've heard of the product Beano for gas problems in
people. Try it for your dog. Follow manufacturer's instructions.

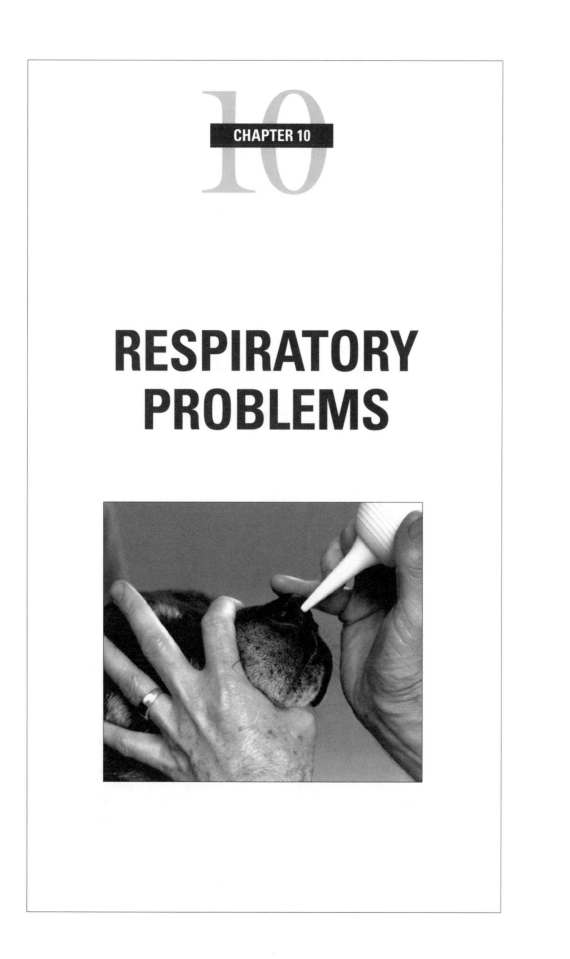

CHAPTER 10

RESPIRATORY PROBLEMS

SNEEZING/ SNORTING

What you see/hear: Your dog is sneezing or snorting, with or without nasal discharge.

What this might mean: He has an irritation in the front part of his nose. This could be due to an infection, foreign body, dust/dirt, or other problem.

ACTION PLAN:

Does your dog have a discharge coming from his nose? Is the sneezing violent? Is he pawing or scratching at his nose?

YES ▶ Go to **page 32.** It could be a foreign body, dust, or other nasal irritant.

NO ▼

Is his nose bleeding?

YES ▶ Go to **page 34.**

NO ▼

Is he sneezing, with no evidence of a discharge?

YES ▶ Call your veterinarian *TODAY*—your dog may have gotten a foreign body up his nose, or may be suffering from a nasal allergy.

NO ▼

Does his breathing sound labored? Is he snorting and sniffling? Are his nostrils constricted? Does he have a clear, foamy nasal discharge? Is he a short-nosed breed, such as a Pug, Boxer, Pekinese, Mastiff, or Bulldog?

YES ▶ Call your veterinarian *TODAY* if you answered yes to two or more of these queries—it could be a collapsed nostril^G, a problem specific to short-nosed breeds. It could ultimately require surgery for repair.

NO ▼

Does it sound like a violent, repeated snorting or snoring sound? As though your dog is trying to forcefully inhale air through his nose?

YES ▶ Call your veterinarian *TODAY*—it sounds like reverse sneezing^G. While these episodes generally go away on their own, surgical treatment may occasionally be required to solve the underlying problem.

NO ▼

Is he snorting after having been digging in the dirt?

YES ▶ He's likely irritated his nasal passages. See **Home Treatment**, opposite page.

NO ▼

Call your veterinarian for an appointment.

YOUR VET MAY NEED TO:

Examine the tissues deep within your dog's nasal passages and throat, using X-ray, ultrasound^G, and/or endoscopy^G. Any of these may require sedation for safety and to facilitate a thorough exam.

HOME TREATMENT:

*(See **Action Plan** to determine whether home treatment is appropriate for your dog's irritated nasal passages. If at any time during home treatment, your answers on the action plan change for the worse, call your vet.)*

Step 1. Gently use a bulb syringe and a gentle stream of warm water to irrigate your dog's nose. This will serve to flush out the irritant (see page 270). (You'll likely need a helper to hold your dog as you do so, and may need to apply a muzzle to avoid a reactive bite. (For how to apply a muzzle, see page 328.)

Step 2. Repeat until irrigation water runs clear, and/or your dog quits snorting.

Step 3. Watch him closely for signs of nasal irritation (sneezing or snorting) and/or discharge. If you see one or both of these signs, call your veterinarian.

Did You Know...

...although your dog can suffer from a nasal allergy, it's rare. So when you hear him sneezing and sniffling, it's most likely a sign of some other type of problem. While people commonly fall prey to such sneezing/sniffing allergies as hay fever, those in dogs tend to present themselves in different ways. One common sign of a canine allergic condition is a skin problem.

What you see/hear: Your dog has developed a cough. It may be harsh and shallow, or deep and moist. It could be self-perpetuating, in that one cough seems to bring on another one—your dog can't seem to stop coughing.

10-B

COUGH

What this might mean: He has an irritation in his airways or lungs. This could be due to an infection (such as pneumonia[G]), allergic reaction, foreign body, or tumor[G]. Or, it could be secondary to congestive heart failure[G] or other such problem.

YOUR VET MAY NEED TO:

• Take blood and/or throat-culture samples to specifically identify invading microorganisms.
• X-ray and/or perform an ultrasound on your dog's chest.

ACTION PLAN:

Is your dog lethargic, feverish, eating less, losing weight, and/or tiring easily? Is he coughing up yellow/green mucus?

 Call your veterinarian *NOW* if you answered yes to any query—it could be pneumonia[G], histoplasmosis[G], lung cancer, congestive heart failure[G], or other such serious problem. See **Before You Leave**, opposite page.

NO ↓

Does your dog cough several times in a row? Does he cough when you apply pressure to his collar? Is the cough harsh and dry? Has he been exposed to strange dogs recently, such as at the groomer's, kennel, or dog park?

 Call your veterinarian *NOW*—it could be kennel cough[G] (infectious tracheal bronchitis). Another possibility could be a tracheal collapse[G] or bronchial foreign body. To be safe, see **Before You Leave**, and **"Kennel Cough Caution,"** opposite page.

NO ↓

Did your dog start coughing immediately after eating, drinking, vomiting, or receiving oral medications?

 Call your veterinarian *NOW*—your dog may have aspirated foreign material into his lungs, putting him at risk for aspiration pneumonia[G].

NO ↓

Is the cough intermittent? Do you live in a mosquito-ridden (heartworm) area? Does your dog otherwise seem normal?

 Call your veterinarian *TODAY*—it could be embolic parasitic pneumonia[G], allergic pneumonitis[G], or other pulmonary problem.

NO ↓

Is your dog an adult? Did his cough initially seem triggered by exercise or excitement? Has it now become chronic[G]?

 Call your veterinarian *TODAY*—it could be allergic or chronic bronchitis[G], emphysema[G], or heart disease.

NO ↓

Call your veterinarian for an appointment.

BEFORE YOU LEAVE:

1. *Isolate your dog from other dogs in case it's contagious.* To prevent spread of possible infectious disease, confine your dog to a warm, dry area with a separate water supply, apart from other dogs. Wash your hands and disinfect your shoes (see page 374) after handling your dog and before handling other dogs.

Kennel Cough Caution

If your dog is diagnosed with kennel cough, please be a responsible owner. While most cases are mild, this is a highly contagious disease that requires forward thinking on your part to prevent inadvertent spread to other dogs:

· **Isolate your dog from other dogs.** Keep him in a warm, dry area with a separate water supply. Wash your hands and disinfect your shoes (see page 374) after you handle him and before handling other dogs. Disinfect his "sick bay" once he's given a clean bill of health.

· **Don't walk him off your property.** To avoid spreading the disease, keep your dog at home, providing moderate, on-leash exercise there, as instructed by your veterinarian.

· **Avoid taking him to public places.** For the sake of other dogs, keep him home from the groomers until he's declared disease-free. If you absolutely must board him, alert the kennel as to his condition. Do the same when you take him to your vet's.

Cough Phonics

The type of cough you hear will give you and your vet insights into its probable origin. Listen carefully as your dog coughs, then provide your vet with the details. Here are some guidelines to help you:

• A harsh, dry (without phlegm), honking-type cough, especially when pulling against leash pressure, is typical of kennel cough[G], tracheal disease, and tracheal collapse[G] (especially in toy dogs).

• A moist, gurgling cough (sounds like "smoker's cough") is a sign of fluid on the lungs.

• Cough spasms immediately following exercise can point to bronchitis[G] or heart disease.

• A cough that starts as dry then changes to productive (your dog coughs up mucus) may indicate a viral infection.

• A weak, gagging cough, with swallowing or lip-licking, can indicate tonsillitis[G] and a sore throat.

What you hear: Your dog makes an unusual noise when he breathes in or out, such as a harsh, moist, restricted squeaking and/or whistling sound.

NOISY BREATHING

What this might mean: There's something interfering with the normal flow of air into your dog's airways or lungs. It could be mucus, fluid, airway constriction, or other serious problem.

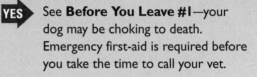

ACTION PLAN:

Is he gagging, gasping, and/or gulping? Pawing at his mouth? Showing agitation and anxiety?

 See **Before You Leave #1**—your dog may be choking to death. Emergency first-aid is required before you take the time to call your vet.

Is your dog in obvious respiratory distress (e.g., is he having trouble breathing)?

 Call your veterinarian *NOW* if you answered yes—it could be a life-threatening problem, such as bronchoconstriction^G due to anaphylaxis or other problem. See **Before You Leave #2**, opposite.

Has your dog been exposed to an insect bite or sting? Has he recently been given injectable or oral medications?

Call your veterinarian *NOW*—it could be an acute (anaphylactic) allergic reaction, or aspiration pneumonia^G. See **Before You Leave #2**.

Are there signs of trauma on your dog? Could he have been kicked by livestock or hit by a car?

 Call your veterinarian *NOW*—it could be due to a penetrating chest wound that's caused your dog's lungs to collapse, or a trauma-induced diaphragmatic hernia^G. See **Before You Leave #3**.

Does he have an increased respiratory effort, meaning you can see him work for each breath? Does your dog tire easily? Does he have a chronic cough, or spasms of coughing after exercise?

Call your veterinarian *NOW*—it could be asthma^G, congestive heart failure^G, pneumonia^G, an elongated soft palate^G, or other serious problem.

ACTION PLAN (CONTINUED):

Does your dog have a short nose and flat face? Is it hot/humid outside, and/or are his nostrils small or obstructed by mucus?

Call your veterinarian for an appointment.

 Call your veterinarian *NOW*—it could be an infection or other cause of nasal discharge. (See **page 32.**) Or, the noise could be due to your short-nosed dog's obstructed airways. See **Before You Leave #2**, Steps 1 and 2.

BEFORE YOU LEAVE #1:

1. *Restrain yourself.* Do NOT attempt to examine your dog's mouth while he's conscious. In his panic and agitation, he'll likely bite you.

2. *Perform a modified Heimlich maneuver.* Position yourself behind your dog. Wrap your arms or hands (depending on his size) around his abdomen. Briskly compress the area several times, or until your dog spits out the object.

3. *Try a chest thump.* If Step 2 didn't work, thump your dog's chest simultaneously on both sides, with cupped hands. Repeat several times. If that, too, fails, head immediately to your veterinarian's.

4. *If your dog is unconscious, examine his throat.* Grab a flashlight. Open your dog's mouth wide, and pull his tongue out and downward, to expose his throat. Look deeply down the throat for a foreign body.

5. *Remove the obstruction.* If you can see the foreign body, grasp it firmly, using tweezers or pliers if necessary, to remove it. **CAUTION:** If you see thread or string in your dog's throat, don't remove it—a hook or needle could be attached, resulting in severe damage to your dog's throat if you were to pull it out. Instead, rush to your vet's or a nearby emergency clinic. Be sure to phone first, to alert them to your arrival so the staff can prepare.

BEFORE YOU LEAVE #2:

1. *Protect yourself.* If your dog is displaying anxious behavior—pacing, whining, eyes open wide, panting—his judgment is impaired and he might inadvertently hurt you. Be especially cautious.

2. *Improve ventilation.* If your dog is having difficulty breathing, make fresh air available. (Much of the anxiety displayed in dogs with anaphylaxis is the result of panic due to difficulty breathing.)

3. *Recall all potential allergens.* Think back: can you think of anything that might have brought on an allergic response? A change in feed sources? A change to a different type of topical flea/tick insecticide? Any medications, vaccinations, or vitamin products given? Any topical cosmetic or therapeutic substances applied to his skin? Any biting or stinging bugs noticed? Be sure to report all suspicions to your veterinarian.

BEFORE YOU LEAVE #3:

1. *See Steps 1 and 2, above.* Take the action outlined in "Before You Leave #2," Steps 1 and 2, above.

2. *Block the escape of air.* If there's a visible penetrating wound on your dog's chest, use your fingers to pinch the chest wound's tissues together, making an airtight seal. Recruit a helper to drive you to the emergency clinic.

➤

Short-Nosed Breed Problems

If you own a short-nosed (brachycephalic[G]) breed, such as a Boston Terrier, Boxer, Bulldog, Lhaso Apso, Pekinese, or Pug, you've probably noticed that his breathing can be noisy, especially in hot weather. Don't take that for "normal." Such breeds are predisposed to respiratory problems that can lead to secondary problems, such as overheating. If your short-nosed dog exhibits breathing noises, have your veterinarian rule out any insidious cause. And be sure to provide the dog with a cool, shady spot in the summer. His nose conformation makes it difficult for him to cool off as effectively as his longer-nosed cousins, which puts him at risk for heat stroke[G]. Here are a few congenital conditions common in short-nosed breeds:

• **Stenotic nares[G]:** a narrowing of the nasal passages that can make for noisy, difficult mouth breathing, snoring, and overheating.

• **Tracheal collapse[G]:** a collapsed windpipe, which can lead to coughing, bronchitis[G], and pneumonia[G].

• **Tracheal hypoplasia[G]:** an underdeveloped windpipe, which can lead to pneumonia[G].

• **Elongated soft palate[G]:** occurs when the soft palate extends into the pharynx (throat) in varying degrees, partially obstructing it and interfering with normal breathing.

Common Foreign Bodies

Sometimes dogs ingest—or try to ingest—the strangest things, in the name of hunger, boredom (chewing), or play. Here's a list of common foreign bodies that vets can run across:

- Chunks of wood
- Pieces of plastic
- Chunks/shards of bone (poultry and pork bones are common offenders)
- Sewing needles
- Straight pins
- Grass seeds
- Awns
- Sticks/twigs
- Small balls
- Splintered cow-hoof chews

What you see: Your dog is taking rapid, shallow breaths. He may be calm—or he may seem anxious.

What this might mean: There could be a normal explanation (such as cooling off on a hot day or after exercise), or it may indicate a serious problem, such as asthma^G.

RAPID, SHALLOW BREATHING

ACTION PLAN:

Is your dog in severe respiratory distress? Has he recently been exposed to an insect bite or sting? Has he recently been given vaccines or medicines via injection?

 YES — Call your veterinarian *NOW* if you answered yes to any query—it could be an acute (anaphylactic^G) allergic reaction with bronchoconstriction^G. See **Before You Leave #1**, next page.

NO

Has your dog been left in a car on a warm day, or had other such heat exposure? Has he been exercised heavily on a hot/humid day?

YES — Call your veterinarian *NOW* if you answered yes to any query—it could be heat stroke^G or heat exhaustion. See **Before You Leave #2**.

NO

Is your dog's abdomen tense and painful?

YES — Call your veterinarian *NOW*—in an effort to protect an acutely painful abdomen, your dog may be breathing in a shallow manner. See **Before You Leave #1**, Steps 1 and 2.

NO

Has your dog had possible exposure to such common household poisons as fertilizer or other nitrite products? Has he had access to acetaminophen (Tylenol), aspirin, amphetamines (diet drugs such as Dexatrim), or hexachlorophene (in soaps such as Dial and Phisohex)?

YES — Call your veterinarian *NOW*—it could be a toxic reaction to something your dog ingested. See **Page 352**.

NO

Has he been drinking and urinating a lot recently? Is he depressed and poorly responsive?

YES — Call your veterinarian *NOW*—it could be diabetic ketoacidosis^G. See **Before You Leave #1**, Steps 1 and 2.

NO

➤

ACTION PLAN (CONTINUED):

Are your dog's mucus membranes pale, bright red, or blue-gray? Is he irritable, dizzy, vomiting, or showing a lack of coordination? Has he been exposed to a running car in an enclosed area, or to smoke from a fire?

 NO

Is your dog currently taking corticosteroids?

 NO

Was your dog recently exercised, is it an unusually warm day, and/or has he recently been frightened or excited?

NO

Call your veterinarian for an appointment.

 YES Call your veterinarian *NOW* if you answered yes to any query—it could a sign of anemia^G or carbon monoxide poisoning^G. See **Before You Leave #1**, Steps 1 and 2.

 YES Panting is a common side effect of these drugs and should cease within a few days of stopping medication. Call your vet for advice.

YES Watch him closely, and keep him in a cool, quiet place. If his breathing isn't back to normal within a half-hour, call your vet.

BEFORE YOU LEAVE #1:

1. *Protect yourself.* If your dog is displaying anxious behavior—pacing, whining, eyes open wide, panting—his judgment is impaired and he might inadvertently hurt you. Be especially cautious.

2. *Improve ventilation.* If your dog is having difficulty breathing, make fresh air available. (Much of the anxiety displayed in dogs with anaphylaxis is the result of panic due to difficulty breathing.)

3. *Recall all potential allergens.* Think back: can you think of anything that might have brought on an allergic response? A change in feed sources? A change to a different type of topical flea/tick insecticide? Any medications, vaccinations, or vitamin products given? Any topical cosmetic or therapeutic substances applied to his skin? Any biting or

stinging bugs noticed? Be sure to report all suspicions to your veterinarian.

BEFORE YOU LEAVE #2:

Use proper cool-down techniques to safely lower your dog's body temperature.

1. *Take your dog's temperature.* Use a rectal thermometer to take and record his temperature. If it's over 105°F, your goal will be to lower it to 103° (but no lower). If it's less than 105°, head straight to your vet's.

2. *Cool him down.* Take him to a cool, shaded spot. Using cool—not cold—water, sponge or hose your dog's body, paying particular attention to his underside. (Major arteries run beneath his neck, arm pits, and hind legs. Cooling those areas will help cool his blood, and thus his body.) If you have rubbing alcohol on hand, use a mix of 50:50 alcohol to water, to sponge his abdomen, arm pits, and the underside of his neck. The alcohol's evaporative cooling effect will speed the cool-down process. Direct a fan toward his body to increase evaporative cooling. Continue for about 5 minutes.

3. *Re-take his temperature.* Check his temperature once more. If it remains above 103°, repeat Step 2.

4. *The instant his temperature reaches 103°, stop!* Carefully monitor his temperature, ceasing your cool-down efforts when it reaches 103°. Your dog has essentially lost the ability to control his body temperature. If you were to continue to cool him, his temperature could drop dangerously low, putting him at risk for shock[G].

5. *Get to the vet's.* Drive carefully to the vet clinic. Be sure to call ahead to alert them.

Your Aging Dog and Panting

Some aging dogs seem to experience spontaneous periods of panting for no apparent reason. If your older dog begins to pant but is otherwise normal, watch him carefully. If he doesn't recover within a half-hour, call your veterinarian. And if the "phantom" panting is recurrent, call your vet. There could be an underlying cause, such as heart disease or systemic illness, that requires medical attention.

10-E

INCREASED RESPIRATORY EFFORT

What you see/hear: Your dog is sitting up or standing with his elbows out. He has his mouth open and neck extended as he expands his chest to the max in an effort to get air. You also may notice his abdomen expand and contract as he uses his abdominal muscles to aid in breathing.

What this might mean: He's having trouble getting enough oxygen. This could be due to congestive heart failure[G], bronchoconstriction[G], pneumonia[G] or other serious problem.

ACTION PLAN:

Is your dog in severe respiratory distress, meaning he's gulping/gasping for air? Are his gums/tongue gray/blue? Is he poorly responsive, lethargic, or lacking interest in food?

 NO

YES Call your veterinarian *NOW*—your dog may need oxygen and other emergency care due to acute congestive heart failure[G], anyphylaxis[G], pneumonia[G], or other condition. See **Before You Leave #1**, opposite page.

Has your dog been left in a car on a warm day, or had other such heat exposure? Has he been exercised heavily on a hot/humid day?

 NO

YES Call your veterinarian *NOW* if you answered yes to any query—it could be heat stroke[G] or heat exhaustion[G]. See **Before You Leave #2**.

Is your dog gagging, pawing at his mouth, drooling, and making increased respiratory sounds?

 NO

YES See **Before You Leave #3**—your dog may be choking to death. Emergency first-aid is needed before you call your veterinarian.

Has your dog been exposed to such common household toxins as paint thinner, or to plants such as Oleander and Yew?

 NO

YES Call your veterinarian *NOW*—your dog could have been exposed to life-threatening toxins. See **page 352**.

Is your dog's breathing noisy? Does he cough or tire easily? But is he otherwise alert and responsive?

 NO

YES Call your veterinarian *NOW*—it could be asthma[G], pneumonia[G], congestive heart failure[G], or other serious problem.

ACTION PLAN (CONTINUED):

Is it an unusually warm day, or has your dog been recently exercised, excited, or frightened? **YES** ➤ Keep your dog quiet and cool for a half-hour. If he fails to recover in that time, call your veterinarian.

NO ⬇

Call your veterinarian for an appointment.

BEFORE YOU LEAVE #1:

1. *Protect yourself.* If your dog is displaying anxious behavior—pacing, whining, eyes open wide, panting—his judgment is impaired and he might inadvertently hurt you. Be especially cautious.

2. *Improve ventilation.* If your dog is having difficulty breathing, make fresh air available. (Much of the anxiety displayed in dogs with anaphylaxis is the result of panic due to difficulty breathing.)

BEFORE YOU LEAVE #2:

Use proper cool-down techniques to safely lower your dog's body temperature.

1. *Take your dog's temperature.* Use a rectal thermometer to take and record his temperature. If it's over 105°F, your goal will be to lower it to 103° (but no lower). If it's less than 105°, head straight to your vet's.

2. *Cool him down.* Take him to a cool, shaded spot. Using cool—not cold—water, sponge or hose your dog's body, paying particular attention to his underside. (Major arteries run beneath his neck, arm pits, and hind legs. Cooling those areas will help cool his blood, and thus his body.) If you have rubbing alcohol on hand, use a mix of 50:50 alcohol to water, to sponge his abdomen, arm pits, and the underside of his neck. The alcohol's evaporative cooling effect will speed the cool-down process.

Direct a fan toward his body to increase evaporative cooling. Continue for about 5 minutes.

3. *Re-take his temperature.* Check his temperature once more. If it remains above 103°, repeat Step 2.

4. *The instant his temperature reaches 103°, stop!* Carefully monitor his temperature, ceasing your cool-down efforts when it reaches 103°. Your dog has essentially lost the ability to control his body temperature. If you were to continue to cool him, his temperature could drop dangerously low, putting him at risk for shock[G].

5. *Get to the vet's.* Now!

BEFORE YOU LEAVE #3:

1. *Restrain yourself.* Do NOT attempt to examine your dog's mouth while he's conscious. In his panic and agitation, he'll likely bite you.

2. *Perform a modified Heimlich maneuver.* Position yourself behind your dog. Wrap your arms or hands (depending on his size) around his abdomen. Briskly compress the area several times, or until your dog spits out the object.

3. *Try a chest thump.* If Step 2 didn't work, thump your dog's chest simultaneously ➤

on both sides, with cupped hands. Repeat several times. If that, too, fails, head immediately to your veterinarian's.

4. *If your dog is unconscious, examine his throat.* Grab a flashlight. Open your dog's mouth wide, and pull his tongue out and downward, using your fingers or a washcloth/towel, to expose his throat. Using the light, look deeply down the throat for a foreign body.

5. *Remove the obstruction.* If you can see the foreign body, grasp it firmly, using tweezers or pliers if necessary, to remove it. **CAUTION:** If you see thread or string in your dog's throat, don't remove it—a hook or needle could be attached, resulting in severe damage to your dog's throat if you were to pull it out. Instead, rush to your vet's or a nearby emergency clinic. (Be sure to phone first, to alert them to your arrival so the staff can prepare.)

THE DEADLY 7 The following items can be the 7 deadliest of toxins for dogs. Remove dangerous plants from your yard and house, and be sure to keep all other products well out of reach of your dog. Be wary of accidental spills–and quick to clean them up.

1. Acetaminophen (non-aspirin pain relievers, such as Tylenol)
2. Antifreeze
3. Cleaning products such as Draino, Ajax, pine oil, toilet bowl cleaners, dishwasher detergents
4. Japanese yew plant
5. Rodenticides (rat, mice, gopher, mole poisons)
6. Insecticides/weed killers/fertilizers
7. Snail poisons

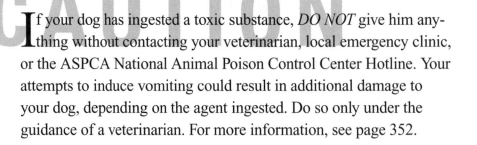

CAUTION

If your dog has ingested a toxic substance, *DO NOT* give him anything without contacting your veterinarian, local emergency clinic, or the ASPCA National Animal Poison Control Center Hotline. Your attempts to induce vomiting could result in additional damage to your dog, depending on the agent ingested. Do so only under the guidance of a veterinarian. For more information, see page 352.

CHAPTER 11

UROGENITAL PROBLEMS

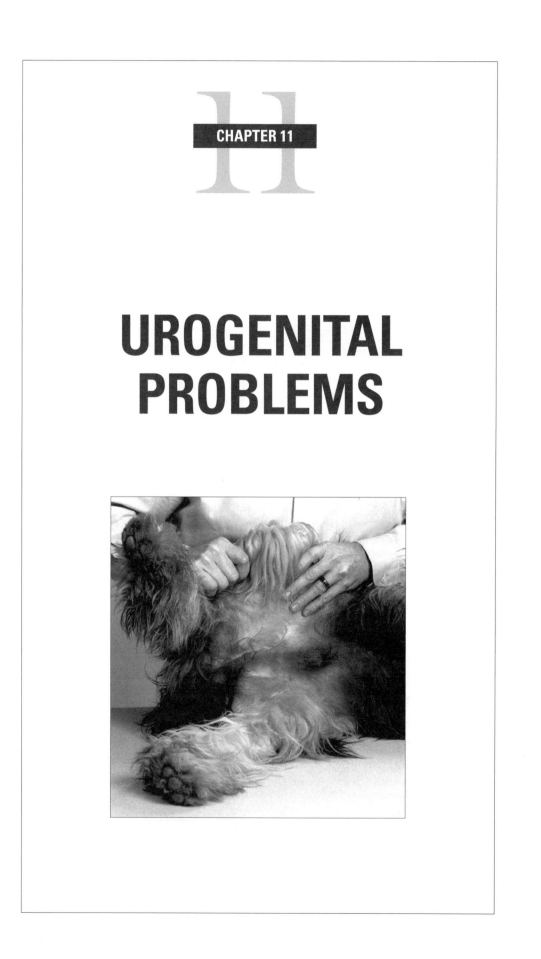

ABNORMAL URINATION

What you see: Your dog is urinating frequently, passing small amounts of urine, and going in abnormal locations. He seems to do so with urgency, with discomfort, and/or is passing urine that's abnormal in color.

What this might mean: He may have a source or irritation within the urinary tract. This could be due to an infection, stones, tumor, or other serious problem.

YOUR VET MAY NEED TO:

- Perform a urinalysis.
- Perform blood work.

ACTION PLAN:

Is your dog straining (standing with his leg up for a long time if he's a male; squatting for extended periods if she's a female), but unable to pass more than a few drops of possibly bloody urine?

YES Call your veterinarian *NOW*—there may be a stone obstructing the urethra. See **Before You Leave**, opposite page.

 NO

Has your dog recently been hit by a car, fallen off a balcony, or had some other serious trauma? Has he failed to urinate effectively since the trauma? Does he seem unusually quiet?

YES Call your veterinarian *NOW*—it could be a ruptured bladder.

 NO

Is he urinating frequently in small amounts, and in unusual places? Is he doing so with discomfort and/or with abnormal colored urine?

YES Call your veterinarian *NOW*—it could be cystitis^G (bladder infection) and/or urethritis^G, with or without bladder stones^G. See **Before You Leave**.

 NO

Is your dog's urine coffee-colored, golden yellow, or orange? Are the whites of his eyes and his gums yellow?

YES Call your veterinarian *NOW*—it could be due to liver disease or hemolytic anemia^G.

 NO

Is the urine bloody? Is your dog also bleeding from his nose and/or mouth, or is there blood in his stool?

YES Call your veterinarian *NOW*—it could be hemorrhage due to ingestion of rodent poison, or it could be due to trauma, hemolytic anemia^G, or other bleeding disorder.

 NO

ACTION PLAN (CONTINUED):

Is your dog drinking large amounts or water and urinating more than usual? Is the urine clear (dilute) with little odor? Is your dog also eating more but not gaining weight?

 Call your veterinarian *TODAY*—it could be diabetes[G].

 NO

Is your dog drinking and urinating more than normal? Eating more than normal? Does he have a thin coat and pendulous abdomen? Has he recently been given cortisone?

 Call your veterinarian *TODAY*—it could be Cushing's disease[G] or it may be a side effect of the cortisone.

 NO

Is your dog drinking more and urinating more, but eating less? Is he losing weight and less active?

 Call your veterinarian *TODAY*—it could be kidney disease.

 NO

Is your spayed female leaking urine when she sleeps? Is your male or female leaking urine after having received cortisone medication?

 Call your veterinarian *TODAY*—your spayed female's incontinence[G] could be the result of an estrogen deficiency. Or, your dog's incontinence could be a side effect of cortisone. See **Before You Leave**.

 NO

Call your veterinarian for an appointment.

BEFORE YOU LEAVE:

1. *Collect a urine sample.* If your dog is a male, grab a clean, large-mouth jar. If she's female, use a clean pie pan. When your dog lifts his leg or squats to urinate, place the container under his penis/her vulva. Collect as much urine as possible, but don't despair if you only nab a small amount. A teaspoon will do, but more is better.

INCONTINENCE TIP:

If your dog is having trouble controlling his or her urine flow, try using diapers (either baby ones or adult sized, such as Depends, depending on the size of your dog). Such a "wet-stopper" can help prevent in-home accidents. Be sure to change/check the diapers every several hours, to help prevent irritation. You may also need to cut a hole in the diaper, to accommodate your dog's tail.

ABNORMAL GENITALIA

What you see: Your dog has an abnormal discharge or swelling associated with his penis or her vulva. He or she may be frequently licking at the area.

What it might mean: It may be normal for your dog, or a sign of infection, tumor, or numerous other problems.

ACTION PLAN:

Are your male dog's testicles swollen, hot, and/or painful?

 NO

YES Call your veterinarian *NOW*—it could be an infection such as epididymitis^G or brucellosis^G. See **Before You Leave** and "Brucellosis Alert," opposite page.

Is there a heavy, cloudy discharge from the vulva? Has your bitch recently been in season? Is she lethargic, eating less, or drinking more?

 NO

YES Call your veterinarian *NOW*—it may be a life-threatening uterine infection known as pyometra^G.

Has your female recently been in season or had a litter of puppies? Do you see a pink mass protruding from her vulva?

 NO

YES Call your veterinarian *NOW*—it could be a uterine prolapse^G or vaginal hyperplasia^G.

Are your male dog's testicles of unequal size? Can you feel a non-painful mass in one or both testicles? Is he attractive to other male dogs? Does he have a pendulous penis? Enlarged mammary glands? A thin hair coat?

 NO

YES Call your veterinarian *TODAY* if you answered yes to any query—it could be a testicular tumor, which may or may not be producing estrogen.

Is there localized swelling in the lips of your female's vulva or on your male's penis?

 NO

YES Call your veterinarian *TODAY*—it could be due to infection, cysts^G, or tumors^G.

Does your male dog have a cloudy discharge at the tip of his penis? Is he licking it excessively?

 NO

YES Call your veterinarian *TODAY*—it could be an infection with or without a foreign body lodged in the dog's penis.

ACTION PLAN (CONTINUED):

Does your young female dog have a scant, clear, watery, or mucus-like discharge coming from her vulva? Is she otherwise normal?

YES → It sounds like juvenile vaginitis^G. If discharge persists for several days, or other symptoms develop, call your vet.

 NO

Is your female dog's vulva swollen? Is there a reddish discharge? Is she attractive to male dogs?

YES → Relax. She's probably in season. If it lasts longer than 3 weeks, call for an appointment. Consider spaying her to prevent unwanted puppies, and to reduce chances of infection or mammary tumors. (See page 363.)

 NO

Are you unable to locate one or both testicles on your young male dog?

YES → It could be normal if he's less then 4 months old. It's a sign that his testicles have not yet descended. However, if he's older than 4 months old, call your vet. Retained testicles in older dogs have a higher incidence of developing tumors, so should be located and surgically removed.

 NO

Does your male dog have a firm, symmetrical, non-painful swelling in the area of his penis, just forward of the base of his scrotum?

YES → That's probably normal enlargement associated with an erection. Call for an appointment if it fails to go away.

 NO

Call your veterinarian for an appointment.

BEFORE YOU LEAVE:

1. *Isolate your dog from other dogs in case it's contagious.* To prevent spread of possible infectious disease, confine your dog to a warm, dry area with a separate water supply, apart from other dogs. Wash your hands and disinfect your shoes (see page 374) after handling your dog and before handling other dogs.

CAUTION

Brucellosis^G has been known on rare occasions to pass from dogs to people. Always wash and disinfect your hands after handling an infected dog, and be sure any family members do the same.

➤

The Mating Dance

You've found a female dog tail to tail with a male dog immediately after they've mated. They move together like awkward Siamese Twins. What's happening—and what can you do about it? The male dog's erect penis is "locked" in the female's vagina by a bulbous glans penis[G], making withdrawal of his penis impossible. This is sometimes referred to as being "tied." It's nature's way of being sure that the dog's sperm has a chance to reach its destination, because he doesn't actually ejaculate sperm until he's dismounted and reached the tie portion of the mating process. There's nothing you can—or should—do. Any attempts to separate the dogs could result in serious injury to one or both dogs (not to mention to you–you'd likely get bitten!). They may stay locked together for as little as a few minutes or for as long as an hour. Just try to keep them as still as possible, and let nature take its course.

CHAPTER 12

Problems of the
MAMMARY
GLANDS

12-A

Mammary Gland

LUMPS/ BUMPS

YOUR VET MAY NEED TO:

Sedate your dog to take a biopsy, to determine whether the mass is cancerous.

What you see/feel: You're rubbing your male or female dog's stomach when you feel something. It's one or more hard or soft lumps beneath his/her nipples. The dog may ignore your manipulation of the bump, or react by flinching or yelping.

What it might mean: Lumps in the mammary gland area can signal an infection, cyst[G], or tumor[G].

ACTION PLAN:

Are your female dog's mammary glands hot and painful? Has she recently been in heat or had a litter of puppies? Is her milk an abnormal color (such as gray, yellow, or reddish brown)?

 YES Call your veterinarian *NOW*—it could be mastitis[G] associated with a false pregnancy[G] or nursing, or a mammary abscess.

NO

Does your female dog have a solitary lump or multiple firm lumps in one or more of her mammary glands?

 YES Call your veterinarian *TODAY*—it could be a mammary cyst[G] or tumor[G].

NO

Has your female dog recently been in heat? Does she have marked mammary development?

 YES Call your veterinarian *THIS WEEK*— the dog could be pregnant, or going through a false pregnancy[G].

NO

Is your female dog in heat? Are her mammary glands slightly enlarged and/or tender?

 YES Don't worry. These are normal changes associated with being in season.

NO

Does your male dog have enlarged mammary glands (nipples)? Does he have a thin hair coat? Pendulous penis? Is he attractive to male dogs? Are his testicles unequal in size?

 YES Call your veterinarian *TODAY*—it could be a Sertoli cell[G] or other type of testicular tumor[G].

NO

Have you seen or felt a firm mass in the area of your male dog's nipples?

 YES This may be normal for the nipples on your male dog, or in rare instances, he may have a mammary tumor[G] or cyst[G]. Call your veterinarian for advice.

NO

Call your veterinarian for an appointment.

Did You Know?...

...male dogs have mammary glands, too. Just as male men can suffer from breast cancer, male dogs can suffer from mammary gland problems, such as cysts and tumors. Normally, both male and female dogs will have 3 to 5 pairs of nipples on their underbelly. The nipples should be small, "tight," and barely noticeable. If you feel any type of lump or bump beneath a nipple—regardless of your dog's sex—use the action plan at left to determine whether veterinary care is needed.

When it doubt, check it out.

Long-term Benefits of
SPAYING & NEUTERING

Do you think you're doing your dog a favor by leaving him or her "intact?" Letting him "be a dog" and allowing her to have a litter of "adorable" puppies? Think again. By leaving your dog intact, you not only are contributing to massive world pet overpopulation (and leaving yourself open for management problems), but you also are putting your dog at risk for health problems, such as mammary tumors. For more information, see page 363.

NOTES

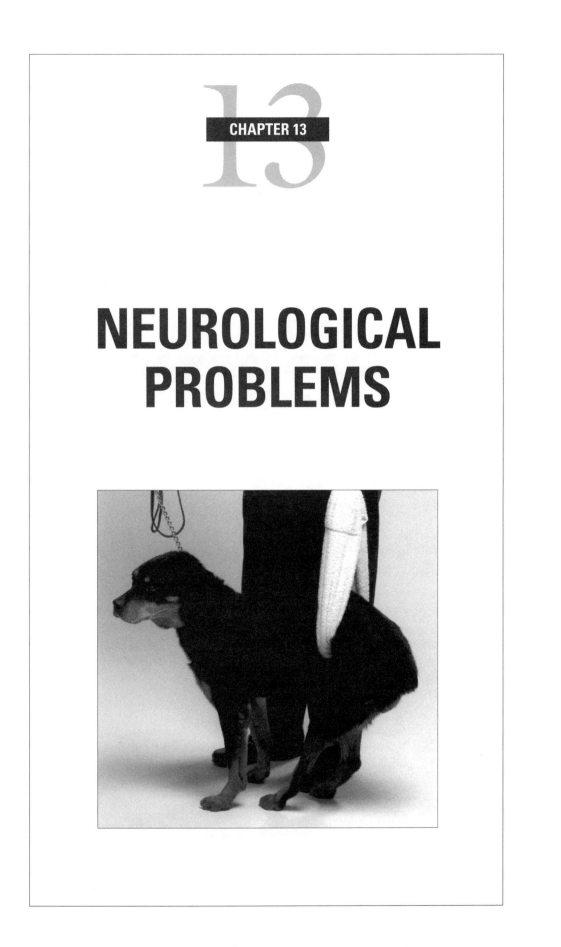

13
CHAPTER 13

NEUROLOGICAL PROBLEMS

What you see: Your dog is having a seizure. It may be as subtle as staring blankly into space, barking or whining at nothing, shaking or extending a leg, or crying out as though in pain. Or, he may have more generalized symptoms, such as chomping his jaws, spastic shaking/tremors, inability to stand, unconsciousness, or being unresponsive, with his legs in rigid extension or pulled tightly against his body with his head pulled back. He may void his bladder and bowels. The episode may last from seconds to minutes.

13-A

SEIZURES

What this might mean: He's had a brief episode of neurological derangement caused by an abnormal burst of electrical activity in his brain. The underlying cause could be congenital, metabolic, inflammatory, poison, trauma, or a tumor[G].

YOUR VET MAY NEED TO:

• **Sedate your dog in order to do a thorough neurological work up, which could include X-raying the skull as well as blood and urine analysis.**

• **Refer you to a specialist, who could perform such neurological tests as a CAT scan[G], MRI[G], myelogram[G], or a cerebral spinal fluid analysis.**

ACTION PLAN:

Has your dog of any age recently suffered a penetrating wound? Is he standing in a "saw-horse" stance, his limbs stiff, his tail held straight out, his ears erect, and the corners of his mouth contracted into a "smile?" Can you see his third eyelid[G]? Are his jaw muscles rigid?

YES ▶ Call your veterinarian *NOW*—it could be tetanus[G] ("lockjaw").

 NO

Has your dog had tremors for longer than 5 minutes, or does he cease the tremors, only to begin again shortly after the initial episode? Is he drooling and/or uncoordinated? Does he exhibit other abnormal signs, such as lethargy, fever, confusion, and/or aggression?

YES ▶ Call your veterinarian *NOW* if you answered yes to any query—it could be rabies[G] (see **Caution**, page 185), epilepsy[G] (go to page 182), poisoning, or other serious neurological problem. See **Before You Leave**, page 180.

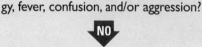 **NO**

Was your dog sick as a puppy? Is only one leg affected? Doe he have short episodes of champing his jaws, or short-duration seizures?

YES ▶ Call your veterinarian *NOW*—it could be rabies[G], epilepsy[G], neuritis[G], or post-distemper encephalitis[G]. See **Before You Leave**.

 NO

Is your dog less than 6 months old, and acting disoriented, confused, uncoordinated, and weak after eating?

YES ▶ Call your veterinarian *NOW*—it could be a congenital liver problem.

 NO

ACTION PLAN (CONTINUED):

Is your dog less than 6 months old? Has he not eaten in over 4 hours? Is he dull and lethargic, or unconscious and/or paddling his legs?

YES ▶ It could be a hypoglycemic^G episode due to lack of ability to store sugar at this young age. Rub Karo syrup or honey on his tongue and gums. (About a tablespoon, rubbed on in small amounts at a time, for a small-breed puppy; up to 2 tablespoons for a large-breed puppy.) Call your vet if the dog fails to regain consciousness within a few minutes. In the future, feed your pup small, multiple meals to reduce the risk of a hypoglycemic episode.

 NO

Is your dog less than 6 months old, a Chihuahua, Poodle, or short-nosed breed puppy (such as a Boxer, Pug, or Pekinese), who has a soft spot on the top of his head? Does his head have a domed appearance? Does he occasionally lose consciousness, or have short periods of muscle twitching or rigidity?

YES ▶ Call your veterinarian *TODAY* if you answered yes to any query—it could be hydrocephalus^G.

NO

Is your dog less than 6 months old, with a thick nasal discharge, cough, fever, and poor appetite? Is he lethargic, and having either generalized muscle tremors or a single leg that twitches uncontrollably?

YES ▶ Call your veterinarian *NOW*—it could be an infectious or inflammatory neurological disease such as distemper^G. See **Before You Leave**, next page.

NO

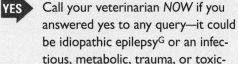 Is your dog aged from 6 months to five years? Is this his first seizure, or has he had previous episodes?

YES ▶ Call your veterinarian *NOW* if you answered yes to any query—it could be idiopathic epilepsy^G or an infectious, metabolic, trauma, or toxic-related condition. See **"Seizure Sources,"** page 182, for specific possibilities.

 NO

Is your dog over 5 years old? Is this his first seizure?

YES ▶ Call your veterinarian *NOW*—it could be cerebral neoplasia^G. See **"Seizure Sources"** for other possibilities.

 NO

 ➤

ACTION PLAN (CONTINUED):

Did your dog suddenly collapse, with no muscle movement, and a rapid, alert recovery? **YES** ▷ Call your veterinarian *NOW*—it may not have been a seizure, but rather a heart-related incident.

 NO

Is your dog between 6 months and 5 years of age? Is he a small, white-coated breed, such as a Maltese, West Highland White Terrier, or a Bichon Frise? Is he suffering disabling tremors on his entire body, with greater involvement in his head and trunk than in his legs? **YES** ▷ Call your veterinarian *TODAY*—it could be White Dog Shaker SyndromeG, a condition more common in, but not limited to, dogs with white hair coats.

 NO

Call your veterinarian for an appointment.

BEFORE YOU LEAVE:

1. *Isolate your dog from other dogs in case it's contagious.* To prevent spread of possible infectious disease, confine your dog to warm, dry area with a separate water supply, apart from other dogs. Wash your hands and disinfect your shoes (see page 374) after handling your dog and before handling other dogs.

2. CAUTION: If your dog is showing any signs that could point to the rare—but dangerous—disease rabies, don't take chances, take precautions. See page 185.

CAUTION

Any seizure lasting longer than 5 minutes is an emergency–your dog is in danger of over-heating (heat strokeG) and permanent brain damage. Also, if your dog appears to recover from the initial seizure, then immediately lapses into another one or does so within 2 hours of the first, he may have a condition called status epilepticusG. He needs immediate veterinary assistance.

Did You Know?...

…before a seizure, some dogs act as though they know something's about to happen. If your dog is one of them, he may suddenly seem agitated for no apparent reason. He may pace or whine, stare off into space, sniff in corners, or snap at the air. Such pre-seizure perception is known as an "aura." It occurs due to pre-seizure neurologic activity.

HOW TO HANDLE YOUR DOG'S SEIZURE

DON'T PANIC!

Seizures can be very dramatic and scary to behold. The good news is that they're rarely life-threatening unless they're recurrent. Episodes generally last less than 5 minutes (with an average of less than 2 minutes; see "Caution," at left.) You can help your dog by taking the following precautions, then carefully observing the seizure and noting its specific characteristics for your vet. Here's what to do:

1. *Do not attempt to quiet your dog.* Make no attempt to move him, or to manually still his body. If you were to do so, you'd put yourself and him at risk of injury. Unless noted otherwise, below, stay away from him until he's fully alert, which could take up to 15 minutes after he's quit convulsing.

2. *Do not attempt to pull out his tongue.* Contrary to popular belief, your dog won't swallow his tongue during a seizure—but he may bite you severely should you try to grab the tongue.

3. *If you can do so safely, wrap him in a blanket.* If you can wrap him in a blanket or sheet without risk of being bitten, do so. Safely securing him in such a way will help avoid inadvertent injury.

4. *Clear the area and keep things quiet.* Move any objects, especially sharp ones, from around your dog, to prevent contact injuries. Block off any steps or stairs. Send away children and pets, to keep noise and distractions to a minimum. (If your dog is over-stimulated by noise or excitement as he emerges from a seizure, he could lapse into another one.)

5. *Watch your dog closely.* If he begins to vomit, act quickly. Grab him and turn him upside down, to reduce the risk that he'll choke on or aspirate his vomit. (If he's of a size that makes this impossible, try to tilt his head and neck downward.) If he's unconscious, try to clean out his mouth and throat, administer CPR (see below), then head for the nearest vet clinic.

6. *If necessary, administer CPR.* If your dog is unconscious, check his gum and tongue color. If it becomes ashen gray or blue, he's suffering oxygen deprivation. Give him mouth-to-mouth breathing. (See page 339.)

NOTE THE SEIZURE CHARACTERISTICS

Use the following list of questions to help describe the seizure to your vet.

• Did you observe a change in your dog's behavior right before the seizure? (See "Did You Know," at left.)

• Did all of your dog's muscles stiffen at the same time, or was there thrashing and/or paddling of his limbs?

• Did just one part of his body twitch, such as his face, a leg, or a whole side)? Or was his entire body stiff, twitching, or convulsing?

• Did he black out? Fail to recognize your voice?

• How long did the seizure last?

• How did your dog emerge from it? Alert? Confused? If the latter, how long did it take him to recover?

KEEP A SEIZURE DIARY

Record the above seizure characteristics every time your dog has an episode. Such detailed tracking can better help your veterinarian narrow down a cause, and devise a treatment plan. Though epilepsy is considered a chronic condition, so isn't curable, it can generally be managed with medication.

➤

Science of Seizures
There are three levels of seizures suffered in dogs.

1. Petit mal. The mildest of the three, petit mal seizures generally are characterized by such signs as a blank stare, the shaking of a single leg, or crying out, as though in pain. Seizure length is usually less than a minute.

2. Grand mal. This is the most common of the three forms, and is characterized by the dog falling to one side, urinating/defecating, paddling his feet as though swimming, frothing at the mouth, and/or crying out. He may be unaware of you or his sur-roundings. Seizure length is usually 2 minutes or less.

3. Status epilepticus. The most severe seizure form, it will mirror the signs of a grand mal episode, but may last for hours or more. As soon as the dog seems to recover, he slips back into another seizure. Such seizures require immediate veterinary attention to prevent heat stroke (due to increased body temperature that results from repeated violent convulsions) and brain damage.

Seizure Sources

Most episodes of seizures in dogs have no detectable cause, and are termed idiopathic epilepsy[G]. (Your vet may simply refer to it as "epilepsy.") While the exact cause may remain unknown, the following may act as triggers:

In Dogs Less Than 6 Months of Age	Congenital conditions, such as hydrocephalus[G] in Chihuahuas, Pekinese, Poodles, and Boston Terriers • Infectious/ inflammatory diseases (such as distemper[G]) • Metabolic disorders, such as hypoglycemia[G] and liver disease • Poison • Trauma • In-utero[G] trauma
In Dogs 6 Months to 5 Years Old	Primary epilepsy[G], in such high-incidence breeds as German Shepherds, Golden Retrievers, Irish Setters, Labrador Retrievers, Miniature Poodles, and Cocker Spaniels; genetic link proven in German Shepherds, Beagles, Keeshonds, Tervuren Shepherds • Infectious/inflammatory diseases • Metabolic disorders, such as hypoglycemia[G] and liver disease • Poison • Trauma • Acquired epilepsy[G]
In Dogs Older Than 5 Years of Age	Cerebral neoplasia[G] • Metabolic disorders, such as hypoglycemia[G] and liver disease • Acquired epilepsy[G] • Neoplasia • Infectious/inflammatory disease • Poison • Trauma

Adapted from: Handbook of Small Animal Practice, edited by Rhea Morgan; Churchill Livingstone

What you see: One or more of your dog's legs is trembling or shaking spasmodically. He may be conscious, but unaware of your presence or his surroundings.

What this might mean: Your dog may be experiencing a seizure (see page 178), he may have been exposed to insecticides or other poisons, or he may have a neurological disease or injury.

TREMORS
(Trembling or Shaking)

ACTION PLAN:

Does your dog appear to be having a seizure of some kind?

 Go to **page 178**.

 NO

Has your dog had tremors for longer than 5 minutes, or does he cease the tremors, only to begin again shortly after the initial episode? Is he drooling and/or uncoordinated? Does he exhibit other abnormal signs, such as lethargy, fever, confusion, and/or aggression?

 Call your veterinarian *NOW* if you answered yes to any query—it could be rabies G (see **Caution,** page 185), epilepsy G (go to **page 181**), poisoning, or other serious neurological problem. See **Before You Leave,** next page.

 NO

Was your dog sick as a puppy? Is only one leg affected? Doe he have short episodes of champing his jaws, or short-duration seizures?

 Call your veterinarian *NOW*—it could be rabies G, epilepsy G, neuritis G or post-distemper encephalitis G. See **Before You Leave.**

 NO

Has your dog of any age recently suffered a penetrating wound? Is he standing in a "saw-horse" stance, his limbs stiff, his tail held straight out, his ears erect, and the corners of his mouth contracted into a "smile?" Can you see his third eyelid G? Are his jaw muscles rigid?

Call your veterinarian *NOW*—it could be tetanus G ("lockjaw").

 NO

➤

YOUR VET MAY NEED TO:

• Sedate your dog in order to do a thorough neurological work up, which could include X-raying the skull as well as blood and urine analysis.

• Refer you to a specialist, who could perform such neurological tests as a CAT scan G, MRI G, myelogram G, or a cerebral spinal fluid analysis.

ACTION PLAN (CONTINUED):

Is your dog between 6 months and 5 years of age? Is he a small, white-coated breed, such as a Maltese, West Highland White Terrier, or a Bichon Frise? Is he suffering disabling tremors on his entire body, with greater involvement in his head and trunk than in his legs?

 YES Call your veterinarian *TODAY*—it could be White Dog Shaker Syndrome^G, a condition more common in, but not limited to, dogs with white hair coats.

 NO

Is your dog asleep? Is he twitching and quietly yelping, his feet moving as though he's running?

YES He may simply be dreaming. If he appears normal when he wakes up, relax. If not, turn to the flow chart appropriate to his symptoms.

 NO

Call your vet for an appointment.

BEFORE YOU LEAVE:

1. *Isolate your dog from other dogs in case it's contagious.* To prevent spread of possible infectious disease, confine your dog to a warm, dry area with a separate water supply, apart from other dogs. Wash your hands and disinfect your shoes (see page 374) after handling your dog and before handling other dogs.

DANGERS OF DISTEMPER

Distemper can be deadly. While modern vaccines have helped control this killer in the U.S., it remains the leading cause of infectious-disease deaths in dogs worldwide. The disease is caused by a virus that's similar to one that causes measles in humans. It's highly contagious. A proper vaccination program is your dog's only means of protection. (See page 237.)

Though most common in unvaccinated puppies between 3 to 8 months of age, it can affect older unvaccinated dogs as well. About half of infected dogs show little or no signs, but remain contagious. In others, signs of illness can be severe, and may include:

Stage I: General illness
- Fever of 103 to 105° F
- Lethargy, lack of appetite
- Watery discharge from eyes and nose that progresses to thick, yellow, and sticky
- Dry cough
- Diarrhea and/or vomiting
- Hard-pad^G of nose and pads, a thick, hornylike skin that forms on your dog's nose and pads.

Stage II: Neurological signs
Some dogs begin to show signs of brain involvement (once neurological signs appear, they may be permanent).
- Brief episodes of slobbering, head shaking, and chewing, as though trying to rid himself of a bad taste in his mouth
- Tremors (rhythmic jerks or twitches), most commonly in the head, when dog is at rest or sleeping; may also cry out
- Seizures
- Circling
- Confusion

CAUTION

Among the possible causes of drooling, an inability to swallow, mental changes, and/or gait abnormalities is a rare but notorious one: **Rabies**[G]. If rabies is a consideration in your dog's case, don't take chances—take precautions.

1. **Call for help!** This is a veterinary 9-1-1. Call your veterinarian and/or animal control. Such professionals can advise you of how to impound the dog. Rabies is always fatal in dogs—your goal now will be to minimize exposure to yourself, your family, and other pets/animals.

2. **Isolate!** Immediately isolate the dog from all other animals and humans in your household. A rabid dog's saliva is teaming with rabies virus, which is highly contagious to humans/animals. Avoid any contact with the dog. If you must handle him, don intact, water-repellant gloves (such as household rubber gloves), and protect all other body parts from contact with his saliva. Shower immediately after exposure to the dog.

3. **Be alert** for unexpected behavior. Rabies can cause aggression and/or a lack of coordination. Stay out of harm's way.

4. **If you or anyone in your family is bitten** or licked by a suspected rabies carrier, immediately wash the area with warm, soapy water—and call your doctor for advice.

5. **Clean up!** Ask your vet and/or animal control official how to properly disinfect any areas the dog has been.

6. **Think back.** Has your dog had any contact/exposure with wildlife, such as skunks, bats, racoons, or foxes? Familiarize yourself with those animals that are known rabies carriers in your area, and protect your pets—and children—from them.

7. **Alert animal control** officials if you see an odd-behaving critter in your area. (For instance, if you see a nocturnal animal such as a skunk or racoon moseying around during daylight, that's a red-alert.)

8. **Save it.** If your dog kills a wild animal, use the above clothing precautions, then bag the carcass and call your vet or the health department. They can test the animal for the rabies virus, so you'll know whether your dog—and family—have been exposed.

What you see: Your dog is acting oddly. He walks in circles, veers to one side when he's walking, and/or falls to the side to which he circles. He may tilt his head to the same side.

13-C

CIRCLING

What this might mean: He may have a problem affecting his middle or inner ear. It could be secondary to infection, an infectious disease, trauma, a tumor, or other serious problem.

ACTION PLAN:

Does your dog tilt his head or fall to one side when walking? Is he drooling, uncoordinated, or showing other abnormal behavior?

 NO

YES Call your veterinarian *NOW*—it could be rabies^G, a middle or inner ear infection^G, encephalitis^G, or other serious condition. See **Caution**, page 185, and **Before You Leave**, below.

Is your dog tilting his head to one side? Is he shaking it, and/or pawing or scratching at it?

 NO

YES Call your veterinarian *NOW*—it could be a foreign body in your dog's ear canal.

Is your dog old? Is he tilting his head? Does he have unequal pupils and/or abnormal eye movement? Did this come on suddenly? Is he otherwise normal?

 NO

Call your veterinarian for an appointment.

YES Call your veterinarian *TODAY* if you answered yes to any query—it could be old-dog vestibular syndrome^G. It could be idiopathic (of unknown origin) and clear up spontaneously, or it could have an insidious cause, such as a tumor^G or infection.

BEFORE YOU LEAVE:

1. *Isolate your dog from other dogs in case it's contagious.* To prevent spread of possible infectious disease, confine your dog to a warm, dry area with a separate water supply, apart from other dogs. Wash your hands and disinfect your shoes (see page 374) after handling your dog and before handling other dogs.

What you see: Your dog's head is tilted to one side, as though he's curious about something. He may be shaking it, and/or pawing or scratching at it. Those may be the only signs you see, or you might observe your dog circling in the direction of his head tilt, veering to that side, falling down, or lacking coordination.

13-D

What it might mean: He could have a problem that's as simple as a foreign body in his ear—or as deadly as rabies[G].

HEAD TILT

ACTION PLAN:

Is your dog circling or veering to the side of his head tilt? Is he drooling, uncoordinated, or showing other abnormal behaviors?

 NO

YES ▶ Call your veterinarian *NOW*—it could be rabies[G], a brain tumor, middle- or inner-ear infection, or other serious neurological inflammation. See **Caution,** page 185, and **Before You Leave,** below.

Is he shaking his head? Does he have a large, fluid-filled swelling on his ear flap?

 NO

YES ▶ Call your veterinarian *NOW*—it could be an ear infection, foreign body in the internal, middle, or external ear canal, or a aural hematoma[G]. See **pages 80** and **86.**

Is your dog old? Does he have unequal pupils and/or abnormal eye movement? Did this come on suddenly? Is he otherwise normal?

 NO

YES ▶ Call your veterinarian *TODAY*—it could be old-dog vestibular syndrome[G]. It could be idiopathic (of unknown origin) and clear up spontaneously, or it could have an insidious cause, such as a tumor[G] or infection.

Call your veterinarian for an appointment.

YOUR VET MAY NEED TO:

• **Sedate your dog in order to do a thorough neurological work up, which could include X-raying the skull as well as blood and urine analysis.**
• **Refer you to a specialist, who could perform such neurological tests as a CAT scan[G], MRI[G], myelogram[G], or a cerebral spinal fluid analysis.**

BEFORE YOU LEAVE:

1. *Isolate your dog from other dogs in case it's contagious.* To prevent spread of possible infectious disease, confine your dog to a warm, dry area with a separate water supply, apart from other dogs. Wash your hands and disinfect your shoes (see page 374) after handling your dog and before handling other dogs.

What you see: Your dog is moving with a strange gait. He may seem uncoordinated or weak in his front or rear end, staggering or moving as though he's drunk. Or, he may move stiffly, with a rigid neck and/or arched back.

WEAK/UN-COORDINATED/ DRAGGING FEET

(Front or Rear Legs)

What this might mean: He may have been injured, he could have an infectious disease that's affected his brain, have spinal disk disease, or cervical or lumbar spinal instability, or he may have arthritis in his elbows or hips.

YOUR VET MAY NEED TO:

• Sedate your dog in order to do a thorough neuro-logical work up, which could include X-raying the affected area and blood/urine analysis.

• Refer you to a specialist, who could perform such neurological tests as a CAT scan^G, MRI^G, myelogram^G, or cerebral spinal fluid analysis.

ACTION PLAN:

Is your dog lethargic and not eating? Is he feverish? Is he uncoordinated on all four legs?

 NO

 YES — Call your veterinarian *NOW*—it could be an inflammatory brain disease such as rabies^G (see **Caution**, page 190), or enchephalitis^G, or it could be a brain tumor. See **Before You Leave #1**, opposite page.

Was the lack of coordination rapid-onset in all four legs? Is your dog vomiting? Does he have diarrhea?

 NO

YES — Call your veterinarian *NOW*—it could be poison. Try to determine the toxin if possible. For more informa-tion, call the ASPCA National Poison Control Center, at (800) 548-2423 and/or see page 352.

Does your dog appear to be paralyzed?

 NO

 YES — Call your veterinarian *NOW*—it could be a ruptured disk^G. See **Before You Leave #2**.

Does your dog have front or rear-leg lameness or uncoordination, with or without pain in his neck or over his pelvis?

 NO

YES — Call your veterinarian *NOW*—it could be cervical or lumbosacral instability^G. See **Before You Leave #2**.

Is your dog showing signs of neck pain/stiffness? Is he reluctant to turn his head to the side, or lower it to eat/drink?

 NO

 YES — Call your veterinarian *NOW*—it could be cervical disk disease or instability. (Help your dog access water by elevating his dish. Phone books work well.) See **Before You Leave #2**.

ACTION PLAN (CONTINUED):

Is there evidence of trauma? Are there open wounds, bruising, or abrasions on his head, limbs, or body?

 YES Call your veterinarian *NOW*—it could be due to serious muscle, bone, brain, and/or nerve injury. See **Before You Leave #2**.

NO

Does one or more leg tremor or jerk uncontrollably?

 YES Call your veterinarian *NOW*—it could be due to poison (such as insecticides) or secondary to systemic illness such distemper^G, or to nerve injury.

NO

Is your dog's back arched or painful? Is he reluctant to jump, or go up/down steps? Does he lose control of his rear legs when he turns corners? Does he have difficulty posturing for elimination?

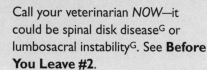 **YES** Call your veterinarian *NOW*—it could be spinal disk disease^G or lumbosacral instability^G. See **Before You Leave #2**.

NO

Is your dog dragging a single leg or legs? Does he seem unaware that he's "knuckling over," or standing on the tops of his feet rather than his pads?

 YES Call your veterinarian *NOW*—it could be due to an injury or tumor, or spinal disk disease or injury. See **Before You Leave #2**.

NO

Is your dog less active than normal? Does he have difficulty going up or down stairs, or getting in and out of your car? Is he having trouble getting up and down? Have you noticed any atrophy^G in his hind leg muscles?

YES Call your veterinarian *TODAY*—it could be elbow or hip dysplasia^G.

NO

Call your veterinarian today for an appointment.

BEFORE YOU LEAVE #1:

1. *Isolate your dog from other dogs in case it's contagious.* To prevent the spread of possible infectious disease, confine your dog to an area with a separate water supply, apart from other dogs. Wash your hands and disinfect your shoes (see page 374) after handling your dog and before handling other dogs.

2. *Protect your dog from further injury.* Remove protruding objects from his area, and keep noise to a minimum to avoid startling him.

BEFORE YOU LEAVE #2:

1. *Keep him quiet.* Place him in a quiet, ➤

confined place (such as a crate or box) until you leave, to limit movement and thus help protect him from further damage. Minimize stress and noise to avoid exciting him.

2. *Take care in transport.* If your dog is small enough to carry, do so in such a way as to keep his spine straight from head to tail. One method is to insert your forearm lengthwise between his hind and front legs, then lift, supporting his chest with your hand. (His legs will straddle your forearm, both left legs on one side, both right legs on the other.) For a medium to large dog, squat with your chest opposite your dog's rib cage. Place one arm under his chest, just behind his front legs; place the other under his abdomen, just in front of his hind legs. Slowly stand to lift him, concentrating on keeping his back perfectly straight as you do so. (For more information on safe emergency transport, see page 335.)

3. *Use car sense.* If he's a small dog, place him/his box on the car floor, so he won't inadvertently fall off the car seat, causing further damage. If he's a medium-sized or larger dog who won't fit on the floor, transport him in a crate or box that can be secured on the seat. If you can, have a helper drive with you to be sure the carrier doesn't move around.

> **If your dog is showing any signs that could point to the rare—but dangerous—disease rabies, don't take chances, take precautions. See page 194.**

What you see: Your dog appears to be paralyzed on a single leg, or is down and unable to move both front and rear legs, or just his rear legs. If you see the latter, you may see your dog trying to pull himself around with his front legs. He may seem agitated or distressed. He may or may not be in severe pain, and may or may not seem to have feeling in his hind feet or tail.

What this might mean: He may have a tumor, or an acute spinal injury, which could include a ruptured intervertebral disk^G or other problem.

PARALYSIS

ACTION PLAN:

Has your dog been a victim of recent trauma, such as being hit by a car or falling a long distance? Does he have neck pain/stiffness (reluctance to turn his head, and/or lower it to eat/drink)? Is he paralyzed on all four legs and his tail?

 Call your veterinarian *NOW*—it could be a fracture or other serious injury to your dog's spine. See **Before You Leave #1** and **#2**, next page.

 NO

Is your dog lethargic and not eating? Is he feverish? Is he paralyzed on all four legs?

 Call your veterinarian *NOW* if you answered yes to either query—it could be an inflammatory brain disease such as rabies^G (see **Caution**, next page), or enchephalitis^G, or it could be a brain tumor. See **Before You Leave #1**.

 NO

Was the paralysis rapid-onset in all four legs? Is your dog vomiting? Does he have diarrhea?

Call your veterinarian *NOW*—it could be poison. Try to determine the toxin if possible. For more information, call the ASPCA National Poison Control Center, at (800) 548-2423, and/or see page 352.

 NO

Is your dog paralyzed in his hindquarters, attempting to drag himself around with his front legs? Was the paralysis rapid-onset?

 Call your veterinarian *NOW*—it could be a ruptured disk. See **Before You Leave #2**.

 NO

Was the paralysis gradual in onset? Is your dog of German Shepherd descent? **NO**

 Call your veterinarian *NOW*—it could be degenerative myelopathy^G.

Call your vet *NOW*. ➤

YOUR VET MAY NEED TO:

• Sedate your dog in order to do a thorough neurological work up, which could include X-raying the affected area and blood/urine analysis.

• Refer you to a specialist, who could perform such neurological tests as a CAT scan^G, MRI^G, myelogram^G, or cerebral spinal fluid analysis.

BEFORE YOU LEAVE #1:

1. *Isolate your dog from other dogs in case it's contagious.* To prevent the spread of possible infectious disease, confine your dog to an area with a separate water supply, apart from other dogs. Wash your hands and disinfect your shoes (see page 374) after handling your dog and before handling other dogs.

If your dog is showing any signs that could point to the rare—but dangerous—disease rabies, don't take chances, take precautions. See page 194.

2. *Protect your dog from further injury.* Remove protruding objects from his area, and keep noise to a minimum to avoid startling him.

BEFORE YOU LEAVE #2:

1. *Keep him quiet.* Place him in a quiet, confined place (such as a crate or box) until you leave, to minimize movement and thus help prevent him from causing further damage. Minimize stress and noise to avoid exciting him.

Before you rush out the door in an emergency situation, stop and call ahead to your veterinarian. Be sure to describe the emergency in detail and estimate how long it will take to get your dog to the clinic. That way, your vet can prepare for your arrival, ensuring the best—and fastest—possible care for your dog.

2. *Take care in transport.* If your dog is small enough to carry, do so in such a way as to keep his spine straight from head to tail. One method is to insert your forearm lengthwise between his hind and front legs, then lift, supporting his chest with your hand. (His legs will straddle your forearm, both left legs on one side, both right legs on the other.) For a medium to large dog, squat with your chest opposite your dog's rib cage. Place one arm under his chest, just behind his front legs; place the other under his abdomen, just in front of his hind legs. Slowly stand to lift him, concentrating on keeping his back perfectly straight as you do so. (For more information on safe emergency transport, see page 335.)

3. *Use car sense.* If he's a small dog, place him/his box on the car floor, so he won't inadvertently fall off the car seat, causing further damage. If he's a medium-sized or larger dog who won't fit on the floor, transport him in a crate or box that can be secured on the seat. If you can, have a helper drive with you to be sure the carrier doesn't move around.

Some Breeds Susceptible to Disk and Spinal Instability

Note: Purebred dogs are not the only susceptible ones. If you have a mutt that physically resembles any breed listed, he, too, could carry that breed's predisposition for problems. Also, many large- and giant-breed dogs are susceptible by virtue of their size, as well as are some toy breeds.

- Afghan Hounds
- Beagles
- Boston Terriers
- Boxers
- Brittany Spaniels
- Bulldogs
- Cocker Spaniels

- Dachshunds
- Doberman Pinschers
- English Pointers
- French Bulldogs
- German Shepherds
- Great Danes
- Jack Russell Terriers

- Miniature Poodles
- Pekinese
- Sheepdogs (and other tail-less or naturally short-tailed breeds)
- Swedish Laplands
- Weimaraners

What you see: Your dog seems confused. He gets lost in the house, is no longer housebroken, and is occasionally startled to see you in the room. If he walks into a corner or behind furniture, he seems unable to find his way out.

What this might mean: It could indicate a serious brain inflammation (infectious disease, trauma, tumor, etc.) or brain changes due to advancing age.

CONFUSION/ DISORIENTATION
(And Senility)

ACTION PLAN:

Is your dog of any age lethargic and not eating? Is he feverish? Is he uncoordinated on all four legs? Is he drooling? Could he have been exposed to wild animals?

 YES → Call your veterinarian *NOW*—it could be an inflammatory brain disease such as rabies^G (see **Caution**, next page), or enchephalitis^G, or it could be a brain tumor. See **Before You Leave,** below.

 NO

Is there any evidence or possibility of head trauma, such as bruising, hair loss, scrapes, or swellings? Are your dog's pupils unequal in size?

 YES → Call your veterinarian *NOW*—it could be a concussive head injury, possibly with intercranial bleeding.

 NO

Is your dog over 10 years old? Has the onset of symptoms been gradual? Does he seem to sleep unusually soundly/deeply? Is he sometimes startled to see you? Does he get lost in house or trapped in small spaces?

 YES → Call your veterinarian *TODAY*—it could be senile brain changes or a brain tumor^G.

 NO

Call your veterinarian for an appointment.

BEFORE YOU LEAVE:

1. *Isolate your dog from other dogs in case it's contagious.* To prevent the spread of possible infectious disease, confine your dog to an area with a separate water supply, apart from other dogs. Wash your hands and disinfect your shoes (see page 374) after handling your dog and before handling other dogs.

2. *Remove loose objects.* To prevent inadvertent injury to your dog, remove any loose and/or sharp objects in the area with which he could intersect.

➤

Senility and Your Aging Dog

If you've noticed some of the changes outlined on page 193 in your aging dog, there's hope. Cognitive dysfunction is the canine equivalent of Alzheimer's disease, and includes a host of signs that your dog has lost touch with such previously learned skills as being housebroken. New drug therapies provide hope for what was once a hopeless downward spiral for some dogs. Ask your vet about Deprenyl for your senile pet. Such drugs can help up to 75 percent of dogs afflicted with cognitive dysfunction to some degree. First, though, your vet will likely rule out any potential underlying causes of the behavior change.

CAUTION

Among the possible causes of drooling, an inability to swallow, mental changes, and/or gait abnormalities is a rare but notorious one: **Rabies**[G]. If rabies is a consideration in your dog's case, don't take chances—take precautions.

1. Call for help! This is a veterinary 9-1-1. Call your veterinarian and/or animal control. Such professionals can advise you of how to impound the dog. Rabies is always fatal in dogs—your goal now will be to minimize exposure to yourself, your family, and other pets/animals.

2. Isolate! Immediately isolate the dog from all other animals and humans in your household. A rabid dog's saliva is teaming with rabies virus, which is highly contagious to humans/animals. Avoid any contact with the dog. If you must handle him, don intact, water-repellant gloves (such as household rubber gloves), and protect all other body parts from contact with his saliva. Shower immediately after exposure to the dog.

3. Be alert for unexpected behavior. Rabies can cause aggression and/or a lack of coordination. Stay out of harm's way.

4. If you or anyone in your family is bitten or licked by a suspected rabies carrier, immediately wash the area with warm, soapy water—and call your doctor for advice.

5. Clean up! Ask your vet and/or animal control official how to properly disinfect any areas the dog has been.

6. Think back. Has your dog had any contact/exposure with wildlife, such as skunks, bats, racoons, or foxes? Familiarize yourself with those animals that are known rabies carriers in your area, and protect your pets—and children—from them.

7. Alert animal control officials if you see an odd-behaving critter in your area. (For instance, if you see a nocturnal animal such as a skunk or racoon moseying around during daylight, that's a red-alert.)

8. Save it. If your dog kills a wild animal, use the above clothing precautions, then bag the carcass and call your vet or the health department. They can test the animal for the rabies virus, so you'll know whether your dog—and family—have been exposed.

What you see: Your dog's pupils are both widely dilated or tightly constricted in normal light, or are unequal in size.

What this might mean: The reason could be as benign as a recent fright or excitement, or your dog's pupil irregularity could indicate problems involving his brain, nervous system, or the eye itself.

ABNORMAL PUPILS

ACTION PLAN:

Is there any evidence/history of head trauma, such as wounds, scrapes, bruising, or swelling?

 Call your veterinarian *NOW*—it could be a serious brain injury.

NO

Is your dog unconscious or having seizures? Is he poorly responsive, uncoordinated, having tremors, and/or drooling? Is he exhibiting any other abnormal behavior?

 Call your veterinarian *NOW*—it could be rabies^G, encephalitis^G, concussive head injury, poison, or other serious neurological problem. See **Caution**, opposite page and **Before You Leave**, next page.

NO

Does one eye have a smaller pupil than the other? Is there redness or cloudiness in the small-pupil eye?

 Call your veterinarian *NOW*—it could be an eye injury or other cause of ocular^G inflammation.

NO

Is one or both pupils dilated (large)? Is the eye(s) inflamed, larger, and more "tense" than normal? Is the cornea(s) cloudy?

 Call your veterinarian *NOW*—it could be glaucoma^G.

NO

Are both pupils dilated and unresponsive to bright light? Does your dog seem blind in normal light? Do his pupils appear to be gray or white instead of black?

 Call your veterinarian *NOW* if you answered yes to any query—it could be cataracts, or retinal, optic nerve, or brain injury/disease.

NO

Are both pupils dilated? Are they sluggishly responsive to bright light? Does your dog seem blind in reduced light but able to see in bright light?

 Call your veterinarian *TODAY* if you answered yes to any query—it could be progressive retinal atrophy^G.

NO

➤

YOUR VET MAY NEED TO:

• **Sedate your dog in order to do a thorough neurological work up, which could include X-raying the affected area and blood/urine analysis.**
• **Refer you to a specialist, who could perform such neurological tests as a CAT scan^G, MRI^G, myelogram^G, or cerebral spinal fluid analysis.**

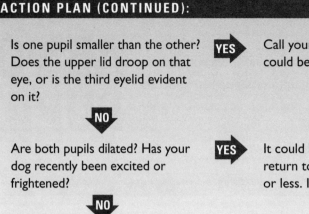

ACTION PLAN (CONTINUED):

Is one pupil smaller than the other? Does the upper lid droop on that eye, or is the third eyelid evident on it? **YES** → Call your veterinarian *TODAY*—it could be Horner's syndrome[G].

NO ↓

Are both pupils dilated? Has your dog recently been excited or frightened? **YES** → It could be normal. His pupils should return to normal within a half hour or less. If they don't, call your vet.

NO ↓

Call your veterinarian for an appointment.

BEFORE YOU LEAVE:

1. *Isolate your dog from other dogs in case it's contagious.* To prevent the spread of possible infectious disease, confine your dog to an area with a separate water supply, apart from other dogs. Wash your hands and disinfect your shoes (see page 374) after handling your dog and before handling other dogs.

2. *Remove loose objects.* To prevent inadvertent injury to your dog, remove any loose and/or sharp objects in the area with which he could intersect.

Breeds Prone to Inherited Cataracts

- Afghan Hounds
- American Cocker Spaniels
- Boston Terriers
- Chesapeake Bay Retrievers
- German Shepherds
- Golden Retrievers
- Labrador Retrievers
- Miniature Schnauzers
- Old English Sheepdogs
- Siberian Huskies
- Staffordshire Bull Terriers
- Standard Poodles
- Welsch Springer Spaniels
- West Highland White Terriers

Breeds Prone to Inherited Progressive Retinal Atrophy (PRA)[G]

- Akitas
- American Cocker Spaniels
- Belgian Sheepdogs
- Border Collies
- Briards
- Collies
- English Cocker Spaniels
- Irish Setters
- Labrador Retrievers
- Longhaired Dachshunds
- Miniature Schnauzers
- Miniature Poodles
- Norwegian Elkhounds
- Samoyeds
- Shetland Sheepdogs
- Tibetan Terriers
- Toy Poodles

What you see: Your dog is down. He may be conscious and unable or unwilling to rise, or he may have collapsed, and is unresponsive to your voice or touch. He may be relaxed or rigid.

What this might mean: It's an emergency situation regardless of the cause.

UNCONSCIOUS
Or Down Dog

ACTION PLAN:

Is your dog unresponsive to your voice or touch?

 YES Call your veterinarian *NOW*—it could be a life-threatening neurological, cardiovascular, or metabolic problem. If he's not breathing, apply CPR. See **page 339**.

 NO

Does your dog seem mentally off—weak, or depressed, and apparently unconcerned about being down?

 YES Call your vet *NOW*—it could be a severe injury or illness causing weakness and an altered mental state. See **Before You Leave #1**, below, and the **Caution**, next page.

NO

Is there evidence that your dog had contact with an electrical source, such as a chewed electric cord, and/or burned/blanched areas on his mouth/tongue?

YES Call your veterinarian *NOW*—your dog could have been electrocuted. Do not touch him until you've shut off the source of electricity (see **page 341**.)

 NO

Is there evidence of severe injury preventing your dog from getting up (obvious wounds, deviated or misshapen legs, joint swellings)? Does he appear to be paralyzed?

YES Call your veterinarian *NOW* if you answered yes to either query—if injury is the cause, additional damage could occur with every attempt your dog makes to rise. See **Before You Leave #2**.

 NO

Call your veterinarian *NOW*.

BEFORE YOU LEAVE #1:

1. *Isolate your dog from other dogs in case it's contagious.* To prevent the spread of possible infectious disease, confine your dog to an area with a separate water supply, apart from other dogs. Wash your hands and disinfect your shoes (see page 374) after handling your dog and before handling other dogs.

2. *Protect your dog from further injury.* Remove protruding objects from his area, and keep noise to a minimum to avoid startling him.

BEFORE YOU LEAVE #2:

1. *Keep him quiet.* Place him in a quiet, ➤

confined place (such as a crate or box) until you leave, to minimize movement and thus help prevent him from causing further damage. Minimize stress and noise to avoid exciting him.

2. *Take care in transport.* If your dog is small enough to carry, do so in such a way as to keep his spine straight from head to tail. One method is to insert your forearm lengthwise between his hind and front legs, then lift, supporting his chest with your hand. (His legs will straddle your forearm, both left legs on one side, both right legs on the other.) For a medium to large dog, squat with your chest opposite your dog's rib cage. Place one arm under his chest, just behind his front legs; place the other under his abdomen, just in front of his hind legs. Slowly stand to lift him, concentrating on keeping his back perfectly straight as you do so. (For more information on safe emergency transport, see page 335.)

3. *Use car sense.* If he's a small dog, place him/his box on the car floor, so he won't inadvertently fall off the car seat, causing further damage. If he's a medium-sized or larger dog who won't fit on the floor, transport him in a crate or box that can be secured on the seat. If you can, have a helper drive with you to be sure the carrier doesn't move around.

> **CAUTION**
>
> Among the possible causes of nervous system disease causing nerve dysfunction is a rare but notorious one: Rabies. Don't take chances—take precautions.
> See page 194.

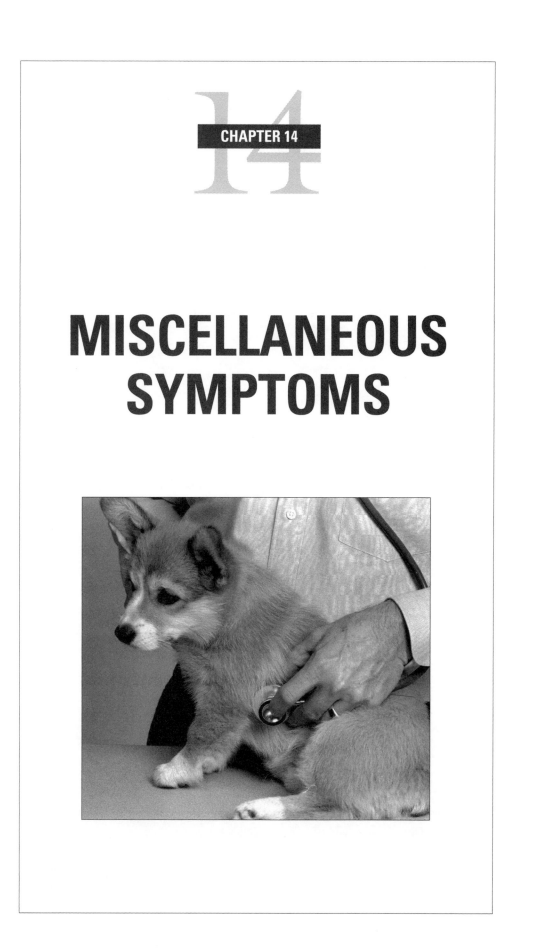

CHAPTER 14

MISCELLANEOUS SYMPTOMS

14-A

What you see: Your dog seems unusually quiet. He's eating less, and may feel excessively warm to your touch. You took his temperature and found it to be higher than his normal range. (See "A Matter of Degrees", at right.)

FEVER

What this might mean: It could be a sign of such problems as infectious disease, drug reaction, cancer, or heat exhaustion/stroke^G.

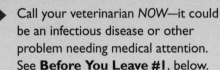

ACTION PLAN:

Shake the thermometer below 100 and take your dog's temperature again. (If it's still elevated? (If it's not, recheck in another 15 minutes.) Is your dog dull, lethargic, and/or lacking interest in food?

 YES → Call your veterinarian *NOW*—it could be an infectious disease or other problem needing medical attention. See **Before You Leave #1**, below.

 NO

Is it an unusually hot or humid day? Is your dog panting and poorly responsive?

YES → Call your veterinarian *NOW*—it could be heat exhaustion^G. See **Before You Leave #2**, opposite page.

 NO

Has your dog been vaccinated or given any medication recently?

YES → Call your veterinarian *NOW*—it could be a mild reaction to a vaccine, or a dangerous reaction known as malignant hyperthermia^G.

 NO

Has your dog been playing or exercising recently?

YES → Allow him to cool down for 30 minutes, then recheck his temperature. If it's still elevated, call your vet.

NO

Call your veterinarian for advice and an appointment. Your dog may have an infectious, inflammatory, or metabolic disease requiring veterinary attention. See **Before You Leave, #1**.

BEFORE YOU LEAVE #1:

1. *Isolate your dog from other dogs in case it's contagious.* To prevent spread of possible infectious disease, confine your dog to a warm, dry area with a separate water supply, apart from other dogs. Wash your hands and disinfect your shoes (see page 374)

after handling your dog and before handling other dogs.

2. *Keep him quiet.* Place him in a quiet, confined place (such as a crate or box) until you leave, to minimize movement and thus help prevent him from further raising his body temperature. Minimize stress and noise to avoid exciting him.

BEFORE YOU LEAVE #2:

Use proper cool-down techniques to safely lower your dog's body temperature.

1. *Take your dog's temperature again.* Record it. If it's 105°F or above, your goal will be to lower it to 103°F (but no lower). If it's less than 105°F, head straight to your veterinarian's.

2. *Cool him down.* Take him to a cool, shaded spot. Using cool—not cold—water, sponge or hose your dog's body, paying particular attention to his underside. (Major arteries run beneath his neck, arm pits, and hind legs. Cooling those areas will help cool his blood, and thus his body.) If you have rubbing alcohol on hand, use a mix of 50:50 alcohol to water, to sponge his abdomen, arm pits, and the underside of his neck. The alcohol's evaporative cooling effect will speed the cool-down process. Direct a fan toward his body to increase evaporative cooling. Continue for about 5 minutes.

3. *Re-take his temperature.* Check his temperature once more. If it remains above 103°, repeat Step 2.

4. *The instant his temperature reaches 103°, stop!* Carefully monitor his temperature, ceasing your cool-down efforts when it reaches 103°. Your dog has essentially lost the ability to control his body temperature. If you were to continue to cool him, his temperature could drop dangerously low, putting him at risk for shock[G].

5. *Go to the vet's.* Now!

A Matter of Degrees...

A fever occurs when your dog's hypothalamus, which regulates his body temperature, adjusts his "thermostat" such that he'll tolerate higher temperatures before cooling mechanisms kick in. This allows his body to battle invading organisms, by creating a hot, unfriendly environment for them—his body is literally trying to burn them out. His temperature also is a good indicator of his health. When you think something's wrong with your dog, one of the first questions your veterinarian is likely to ask is, "What's the dog's temperature?" Here's what those degrees can mean.

Temperature	Possible Causes
105° or higher	Serious viral infection; heat stroke[G]
102.5° to 104.5°	Post-exercise heat; at rest, pain, inflammation, or mild infection
101° to 102.5°	Normal
98.5° to 100°	Mild to moderate shock; hypothermia
98° or below	Severe shock[G]

NO OR POOR APPETITE

What you see: Your dog refuses to eat, or eats very little with no enthusiasm. This is unusual for him—he's normally a chow hound.

What this might mean: If he's alert and playful, it may not be significant. But if his appetite fails to return, or if he's also acting dull, loss of appetite can be an early sign of illness.

ACTION PLAN:

Does your dog have a fever (above 102.5°F)?

 NO

YES Call your veterinarian *NOW*—it could be an early sign of a viral or bacterial disease. See **Before You Leave**, opposite page. Also see **page 200**.

Is your dog less active? Does he have any overt symptoms, such as vomiting, diarrhea, a cough, or pain?

 NO

YES Call your veterinarian *NOW*—it could be a serious illness or condition. See **Before You Leave**.

Is your dog drooling? Does he approach food as though hungry, but fail to eat? Or does he take a mouthful of food, then let it fall out of his mouth? Is he pawing at his mouth?

 NO

YES Call your veterinarian *NOW*—it could be dental pain or other oral or neurological problem.

Was your female dog recently in season? Has she increased her water consumption? Does she have a vulvar discharge?

 NO

YES Call your veterinarian *NOW* if you answered yes to any query—it could be pyometra^G, which can be a life-threatening problem.

Is your dog middle aged or older? Is he less active, but not losing weight?

 NO

YES It may be a normal aging change due to decreased activity and a lower metabolic rate. Keep a close eye on him, and call your veterinarian immediately if he develops any of the other signs outlined in this action plan.

ACTION PLAN (CONTINUED):

Is your dog otherwise acting normal? Is he bright, alert, and happy? Does he seem to prefer "people food" to his own?

 YES Don't worry. He should eat his food when he's hungry enough. Continue to offer him his normal diet—no people treats! If he doesn't eat after 48 hours, or begins to lose weight, consult your veterinarian.

NO

Call your veterinarian for an appointment.

BEFORE YOU LEAVE:

1. *Isolate your dog from other dogs in case it's contagious.* To prevent spread of possible infectious disease, confine your dog to a warm, dry area with a separate water supply, apart from other dogs. Wash your hands and disinfect your shoes (see page 374) after handling your dog and before handling other dogs.

2. *Keep him quiet.* Place your dog in a quiet, confined place (such as a crate or box) until you leave. Doing so will minimize his movement and thus help prevent him from further raising his body temperature. Also, be sure to minimize stress and noise to avoid exciting him. (For, instance, keep kids and pets away from him, and turn off the T.V.).

What you see: Your dog is less active than usual. Perhaps he's moving around less, wagging his tail less, or just plain seems down in the dumps. He may be slow to respond, lack interest in playing with you or his canine pals, or seem reluctant to go for a walk. (This is where knowledge of your dog's baseline behavior is invaluable. See page 229.)

14-C

DULL/ LETHARGIC

What this might mean: It can signify that your dog is ill, or is experiencing mild to moderate physical pain and is distracted by it. Or, it may be exactly what it appears to be: mental dulling, due to a problem in his brain.

ACTION PLAN:

Is he a large-breed dog? Have you fed him recently? Does he have abdominal distension? Is he retching?

 NO

 YES It could be an emergency known as bloat^G! Go to **page 211**.

Is there any history or evidence of trauma? Can you see wounds, swelling, bruising, or signs of discomfort? Is he reluctant to move, with back arched and/or a stiff neck? Or is he favoring a leg?

 NO

YES Call your veterinarian *NOW*—it could be due to pain or a neurological injury from trauma, intervertebral disk disease^G, or spinal instability. See **Before You Leave #1**, opposite page.

Does your dog have a fever?

 NO

YES Call your veterinarian *NOW*—it could be an early sign of a viral or bacterial infection. See **Before You Leave #2**. And see **page 200**.

Is he walking with a shuffling gait? Is he trembling? Staggering, as though drunk?

 NO

 YES Call your veterinarian *NOW* if you answered yes to any query—it could be weakness from injury, disease, or a toxin. See **Before You Leave #1** and **#2**.

Was your female dog recently in season? Does she have a decreased appetite? Increased water consumption? Vulvar discharge?

 NO

YES Call your veterinarian *NOW* if you answered yes to any query—it could be pyometra^G, which can be a life-threatening problem.

ACTION PLAN (CONTINUED):

Check your dog again in 15 minutes. Any improvement? Is he showing an interest in play or food?

YES Re-evaluate him again in 15 minutes. If all seems well, relax. It might have been nothing, or the problem might have resolved itself. Plan to check on him often over the next few hours, to be sure.

NO

If you find anything abnormal, refer to the appropriate chapter, and call your veterinarian.

BEFORE YOU LEAVE #1:

1. *Keep him quiet.* Place him in a quiet, confined place (such as a crate or box) until you leave, to minimize movement and thus help prevent him from causing further damage. Minimize stress and noise to avoid exciting him.

2. *Take care in transport.* If your dog is small enough to carry, do so in such a way as to keep his spine straight from head to tail. One method is to insert your forearm lengthwise between his hind and front legs, then lift, supporting his chest with your hand. (His legs will straddle your forearm, both left legs on one side, both right legs on the other.) For a medium to large dog, squat with your chest opposite your dog's rib cage. Place one arm under his chest, just behind his front legs; place the other under his abdomen, just in front of his hind legs. Slowly stand to lift him, concentrating on keeping his back perfectly straight as you do so. (For more information on safe emergency transport, see page 335.)

> **If your dog is showing any signs that could point to the rare—but dangerous—disease rabies, don't take chances, take precautions. See page 190.**

3. *Use car sense.* If he's a small dog, place him/his box on the car floor, so he won't inadvertently fall off the car seat, causing further damage. If he's a medium-sized or larger dog who won't fit on the floor, transport him in a crate or box that can be secured on the seat. If you can, have a helper drive with you to be sure the carrier doesn't move around.

BEFORE YOU LEAVE #2:

1. *Isolate your dog from other dogs in case it's contagious.* To prevent spread of possible infectious disease, confine your dog to warm, dry area with a separate water supply, apart from other dogs. Wash your hands and disinfect your shoes (see page 374) after handling your dog.

2. *Keep him quiet.* Place him in a quiet, confined place (such as a crate or box) until you leave, to minimize movement and thus help prevent him from further exacerbating his illness or injury. Minimize stress and noise to avoid exciting him.

14-D

WEIGHT LOSS

What you see: Your dog is losing weight to the point that he weighs in about 10 percent or more below what's normal for him. (For how to assess your dog's body condition, see page 296.)

What this might mean: It can mean one of a full spectrum of problems, ranging from something as simple as inadequate quantity/quality of diet for his current needs, to cancer.

ACTION PLAN:

Has your dog's appetite decreased? Does he have a dull attitude and/or fever? Has he been vomiting or having diarrhea? Showing signs of respiratory distress or exercise intolerance?

 YES Call your veterinarian *NOW* if you answered yes to any query—it could be an infectious or metabolic disease, cancer, or heart disease. See **Before You Leave #1**, opposite.

NO ↓

Is your dog drooling? Is he interested in food, but not eating? Or is he picking up bites of food, then allowing them to drop from his mouth? Does he paw at his face?

 YES Call your veterinarian *NOW*—it could be tooth, jaw, or oral pain, a lodged foreign body, or neurological problems.

NO ↓

Is your dog always hungry? Is he drinking and urinating more than usual?

 YES Call your veterinarian *TODAY*—it could be diabetes[G].

NO ↓

Is his appetite normal? Is he less active than normal, but has no fever? Does he have a dull hair coat?

 YES Call your veterinarian *TODAY*—it could be a parasite infestation. See **Before You Leave #2**.

NO ↓

Does your dog have chronic soft stools or diarrhea? Have you noticed an increased volume of stool, or that it's light colored/greasy?

 YES Call your veterinarian *TODAY*—it could be a maldigestion or malabsorption problem.

NO ↓

ACTION PLAN (CONTINUED):

Can you agree to all these statements? **YES** Consult with your vet to have your dog's ration evaluated and adjusted, based on his age, activity level, and condition. Continue this chart.
• Your dog's diet is the same as it was last year at this time, and his weight was fine then.
• His activity level is the same as it was last year at this time, and his weight was fine then.
• Other dogs eating the same diet look fine.
• He has access to all the fresh water he wants.

 NO

Do you feed multiple dogs at the same time, in the same location? **YES** Observe your dog closely at feed time. Other dogs may be eating his food. If that's the case, feed him separately.

 NO

Call your vet for an appointment.

BEFORE YOU LEAVE #1:

1. *Isolate your dog from other dogs in case it's contagious.* To prevent spread of possible infectious disease, confine your dog to a warm, dry area with a separate water supply, apart from other dogs. Wash your hands and disinfect your shoes (see page 374) after handling your dog and before handling other dogs.

2. *Keep him quiet.* Place him in a quiet, confined place (such as a crate or box) until you leave, to minimize movement and thus help prevent him from further exacerbating his illness or injury. Minimize stress and noise.

BEFORE YOU LEAVE #2:

1. *Take in a fresh stool sample to your vet.* Use a tongue depressor or plastic spoon to get a tablespoon-sized sample of a fresh stool pile (one that's less than an hour old). Put the sample in a plastic baggie or clean margarine container. (If you can't leave right away, store the sample in your refrigerator until you do, to preserve any parasite eggs.) Your vet can then test the sample for parasites, and treat your dog if the test is positive.

Maturity Matters...
Especially If You House Multiple Dogs

As your dog enters the realm of senior citizenship, he'll be more prone to injury and illness, due to a decrease in flexibility and a gradual decline in immune system competence. And, he may lose status within his social circle. When age starts encroaching on well-being, a dog's social niche can erode, and lower pack members sense it. This sets the stage for conflict (and injury) as younger dogs increasingly issue challenges in an attempt to improve their social status. If you see your dog becoming involved in such conflicts, separate him from any top-dog wannabes before somebody gets hurt.

WEIGHT GAIN

What you see: Your dog's weight has increased 10 percent or more than his normal range. (For how to assess your dog's condition, see page 296.)

What this might mean: It could be as simple as too many calories for his activity level (meaning too much food and not enough exercise). Or, he may have a metabolic disorder.

ACTION PLAN:

Is your dog lethargic? Does he have a dull, dry hair coat? Have you noticed increased pigmentation on his abdomen? Is he a "heat seeker," meaning he wants to lie down in warm places?

 YES Call your veterinarian *TODAY*—it could be hypothyroid^G.

NO

Is your dog middle-aged or older? Are you feeding the same amount as when he was younger? Is he otherwise normal?

YES See **Home Treatment**, below.

NO

Are you feeding several dogs together at the same time?

YES Observe your fat pooch. Chances are, he's top dog and is eating other dogs' food. If that's the case, feed him separately.

NO

Call your veterinarian for an appointment.

HOME TREATMENT:

*(See **Action Plan** to determine whether home treatment is appropriate for your dog's weight gain. If at any time during home treatment, your answers on the action plan change for the worse, call your vet.)*

Step 1: *Cut calories.* Reduce your dog's daily intake by one-third. (And talk to your vet about gradually switching the dog to a food specially formulated for less active, adult dogs. Such foods are lower in calories than those formulated for young, active dogs.) Avoid free-choice feedings; instead, restrict him to two meals a day. Be strong—

no between-meal treats! If he acts as though he might starve to death, consider giving him the occasional slice of carrot for a snack.

Step 2: *Increase his exercise.* Start a walking program (you'll both benefit!), and play with him more. If you don't already have one, consider getting him a canine companion. Having another dog to play with and follow around will up his activity level.

Step 3: *Weigh your dog weekly.* Keep a record of his weight loss. Call your vet if you record no weight loss after a month of effort.

Did You Know?...

...obesity is the number-one nutritional problem in dogs in America. And it can pose health problems for your dog. Use the condition assessment tips on page 296 to determine whether your dog's weight is over the line. Then use the action plan here to help determine why. If it appears to be a simple proportion problem (too much food; too little activity), use the steps outlined under "Home Treatment" to peel off those pounds!

HOW TO WEIGH YOUR DOG

Note: If your dog is too large for you to pick up, bring him to your vet's to get an accurate weight reading.

STEP 1: First, step on your bathroom scale. Record your weight.

STEP 2: Pick up your dog, and step back on the scale. Record that number.

STEP 3: Subtract your weight from the combined weight of you and your dog. Record your reading as a baseline.

Increased
WATER
INTAKE

What you see: Your dog is sucking up the water, drinking about twice as much as he normally does.

What this might mean: It could be a normal reaction to hot, humid weather, a side effect of medication, or evidence of serious problem, such as diabetes^G, kidney disease^G, or pyometra^G.

ACTION PLAN:

Has your female dog recently been in season? Is her appetite reduced? Is she dull/lethargic, with or without a cloudy vulvar discharge?

 Call your veterinarian *NOW* if you answered yes to any query—it could be pyometra^G, a life-threatening infection.

 NO

Is your dog urinating more than normal? Has his appetite increased, but you notice that he's losing weight?

 Call your veterinarian *NOW*—it could be diabetes^G.

 NO

Is your dog urinating more than normal? Does he have a thin coat and pendulous abdomen? Or is he on cortisone for a condition such as an allergy^G, arthritis^G, chronic inflammatory bowl disease, or meningitis^G?

 Call your veterinarian *NOW*—it could be Cushing's disease^G or a side effect from the cortisone.

 NO

Is he urinating more, with clear (dilute) urine that has no odor? Have you noticed that his appetite is less than normal? Is he vomiting? Does his breath have an ammonia-like odor?

 Call your veterinarian *NOW* if you answered yes to any query—it could be kidney disease.

NO

Do you have a young, active, bored dog that's otherwise normal?

 Call your veterinarian *TODAY*—it could be psychogenic water consumption^G.

 NO

Is the weather unusually warm or humid?

YES Observe your dog closely. It may be a normal reaction to the heat. Call your vet if the dog develops any other signs outlined in this chart.

NO

Call your veterinarian for an appointment.

What you see: Your dog's abdomen is markedly distended, as though a balloon has inflated within it. (See how to determine distension, next page.) You may have noticed the bloating within a few hours of when he was last fed. He may or may not be showing signs of discomfort, such as restlessness or lethargy. He may also be making repeated—yet unsuccessful—attempts to vomit.

What this might mean: His stomach may simply be distended with food, water, and/or gas. Or he may have an acute, life-threatening emergency called Gastric Dilatation VolvulusG (bloat).

ABDOMINAL DISTENSION
(Bloat)

ACTION PLAN:

Has your dog eaten recently? Is he drooling and retching? Dull, lethargic, and unresponsive? Is his abdomen tense and painful? Are his gums pale gray or bright red?

 NO

 YES Call your veterinarian *NOW* if you answered yes to any query—it could be the first signs of a life-threatening emergency known as bloatG.

Has there been a gradual onset of the abdominal distension? Does his abdomen seem to be filled with fluid? Does your dog have pale gums, difficulty breathing, or is he coughing?

 NO

 YES Call your veterinarian *NOW*—it could be congestive heart failureG, abdominal cancer, or other such serious problem.

Has your female dog recently been in season? Is her appetite reduced? Is she dull/lethargic, with or without a cloudy vulvar discharge?

 NO

 YES Call your veterinarian *NOW* if you answered yes to any query—it could be pyometraG, a life-threatening infection.

Has your dog recently eaten a large meal? Is he otherwise normal?

 NO

YES It may be normal—or early signs of bloat. Monitor him closely for signs of increasing abdominal distension. (See **"Bloat Check,"** next page.)

Call your veterinarian for an appointment.

➤

YOUR VET MAY NEED TO:

- Sedate your dog, in order to X-ray his abdomen.
- Perform lab work.
- Administer IV fluids.
- Intubate your dog.
- Monitor his heart.
- Euthanize the dog, if a case of bloat has progressed beyond repair. (Mortality rates can be as high as 30% to 60%.)

Bloat Check

Here's how to measure your dog's abdomen, to monitor for distension:

1. Grab a seamstress tape, or a piece of soft rope or string that's long enough to encircle your dog's abdomen.

2. With your dog standing, loop the tape or string/rope around his abdomen at the point where his last rib meets it. (See page 293.)

3. Carefully note or mark your measurement.

4. Repeat again—in the exact same spot—in 15 minutes.

5. If the measurement is larger, call you vet NOW!

6. If your measurement is the same or smaller—and your dog isn't showing any signs of distress as outlined in the action plan—recheck him in a half-hour. If, at any time, the measurement increases or he begins to show signs of distress, call your vet NOW!

Anatomy of a Bloat

Gastric-Dilatation Volvulus[G] (GDV), commonly known as "bloat," often occurs after your dog has eaten. His stomach fills with fluid and gas that can't be expelled by burping or vomiting. Once distended, it may twist abruptly. If the twist is less than 180 degrees on the stomach's long axis, it's known as a *torsion*. If the twist is greater than 180 degrees, it's known as a *volvulus*. Researchers don't yet understand the actual cause of this life-threatening condition, but this much is known:

• Bloat generally affects dogs between 4 and 7 years of age. About two-thirds of those affected are males.

• It primarily affects large-breed (over 50 pounds), deep-chested dogs such as Bloodhounds, Boxers, Doberman Pinschers, German Shepherds, Great Danes, Great Pyrenees, Irish Setters, Irish Wolfhounds, Labrador Retrievers, Saint Bernards, Standard Poodles, and Weimaraners, but can affect any size or breed.

• Dogs who bloat tend to eat a diet consisting of large amounts of dry dog food.

• Exercise and large intakes of water immediately after eating can increase the risk for bloat.

• Dogs who bloat may have a history of gastritis[G] (digestive disturbances).

• Bloat is also commonly associated with stress (or any change in routine) such as boarding, surgery, breeding, showing, or travel. It may have something to do with *aerophagia*—swallowing air when nervous or excited.

• Bloat appears to have a hereditary link. In other words, if your dog's relative suffered from bloat, your dog may be at greater risk than a dog without bloat in his heritage.

• For how to reduce your dog's risk for bloat, see page 291.

CHAPTER 15

How to handle
WOUNDS

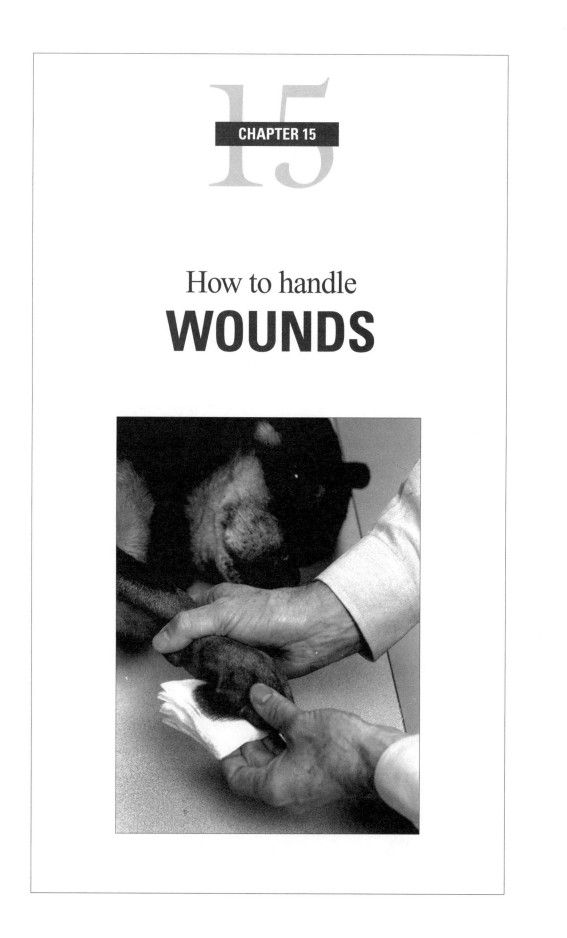

What you see: A torn or jagged cut through your dog's skin. There's dried blood and/or matted hair adhered to its margins, and/or fresh blood spilling from the wound, making it difficult to see if tissues beneath the skin are lacerated too.

What this might mean: Your dog may have been attacked by another animal, or he simply cut himself. If it involves only the skin and the cushion of fat beneath it, without disturbing major blood vessels or vital structures such as tendons, joints, nerves, and ligaments, then your main concern is infection and/or scarring. However, if vital structures are involved, the cut can cause serious—maybe permanent—damage. Proper treatment will help you achieve the best possible outcome.

15-A

BITE WOUND OR CUT
(Laceration)

YOUR VET MAY NEED TO:

Sedate or anesthetize your dog, and/or numb the tissues, in order to fully determine the depth and extent of the injury and to help facilitate the best possible repair.

ACTION PLAN:

Is it bleeding profusely (dripping steadily or spurting)?

YES ▶ Call your veterinarian *NOW*—it might need stitches to stop the bleeding. Go to **Before You Leave,** opposite page.

 NO

Are tissues near the wound drooping? If the wound is on a leg, is the leg buckling or non-weight-bearing?

YES ▶ Call your veterinarian *NOW* if you answer yes to either query—nerves or supporting structures (bone, tendon, or ligament) may be damaged.

 NO

Can you see white tissue in the wound?

YES ▶ Call your veterinarian *NOW*—it could be exposed bone, tendon, or ligament.

 NO

Are the skin edges gaping or easily pulled apart? Is the wound near enough to a joint to gape when the joint moves? Is the wound on a lower leg, below the knee or hock joint? Has it created a flap of tissue?

YES ▶ Call your veterinarian *NOW* if you answered yes to any of these queries— it may require stitches to stabilize edges and minimize scarring.

 NO

Is the wound located over or near a joint? Do you see amber-colored fluid coming from it, or white streaks dried on your dog's coat below the laceration?

YES ▶ Call your veterinarian *NOW* if you answered yes to either query—the wound may have entered a joint or tendon sheath.

 NO

ACTION PLAN (CONTINUED):

Does the wound involve your dog's face and/or eye(s)? **YES** Call your veterinarian *NOW*—the wound may need immediate help to avoid scarring and to help minimize damage to vital tissues.

 NO

Does the wound penetrate all layers of skin, exposing fat and muscle? **YES** Call your veterinarian *TODAY*—your dog may need stitches.

 NO

Is the wound over 24 hours old? And is there sufficient swelling to obscure your view of it? Is there a cloudy, white-yellow or green discharge (pus), or "spoiled" odor? **YES** Go to **page 224.**

 NO

Is the wound less than 4 hours old? Will he allow you to treat the wound? **YES** Apply **Home Treatment,** next page.

 NO

Call your veterinarian *TODAY*.

BEFORE YOU LEAVE

1. *Calm your dog.* If he's excited, his heart will pump harder and his blood will run faster. If possible, have a helper hold him and soothe him as you work. Apply a muzzle if necessary. (For how to apply a homemade muzzle, see page 329.)

2. *Apply direct pressure.* Forget about whether that blood's coming from an artery or a vein—the treatment's the same: Apply pressure over the site with a clean pad of sufficient size to cover the wound and its margins. A folded hand towel, disposable diaper, or a 1-inch thick stack of gauze sponges or paper towels will make a suitable pad. If an ice pack is immediately available, sandwich it between the pad's lay-

> **STOP**
> Unless instructed to do so by your veterinarian, NEVER administer any human or canine medication to your dog. Many medications that are appropriate in one circumstance or species can be harmful in another.

ers to further stem the bleeding. (For how hard to press, see "How Much Pressure," next page.)

IMPORTANT! Resist the temptation to lift the pad again to check the bleeding—you'll only disturb any clots that've formed, undoing the good you've done. If your pad becomes saturated with blood, don't replace it. Keep pressing for a minimum of 5 minutes without moving it.

If there's so much blood you can't tell where it's coming from, press hard for 5 seconds to blanch the site, then briefly lift the pad to find the blood source. If more padding is immediately available, get it now. Center your pressure on the blood source. If you have a helper, have him or her ➤

HOW MUCH PRESSURE?

Try this midway up your own thigh: squeeze or press until you can feel the contours of the bone within. That's the amount of pressure you need to apply to your dog's bleeding wound. Your effectiveness will depend less on the amount of pressure and more on your ability to hold it consistently, without shifting or letting up, for a minimum of 5 minutes.

continue to apply pressure while you drive to your veterinarian's. If you're alone, proceed to Step 3.

3. *Apply a pressure bandage.* After 5 to 10 minutes of pressure, and if the bleeding is coming from a location that lends itself to bandaging, apply a pressure bandage. (See page 315.)

HOME TREATMENT:

*(See **Action Plan,** page 214, to determine whether home treatment is appropriate for your dog's laceration. If at any time during home treatment, your answers on the action plan change for the worse, call your vet.)*

Step 1. *Clip wound margins.* Use scissors or clippers to remove hair from around the wound's edges.

Step 2. *Clean the wound.* (For in-depth instruction, see page 307.) Irrigate the wound with cold hose or tap water or a trigger-type spray bottle filled with homemade saline solution (see page 306). Spray for 1 full minute or until the wound appears visibly clean, whichever takes longer. If necessary, use a gauze pad to remove hair and debris within the wound.

Step 3. *Apply ointment.* Using clean fingers or a fresh gauze pad, gently apply a thin layer of a non-antibiotic dressing, such as povidone iodine ointment (see page 302).

Step 4. *Bandage the wound.*

A. If it's in an area that lends itself to bandaging and if environmental conditions make it likely to get contaminated with dirt, dust, and flies unless covered, press a non-stick pad such as Telfa® or Release® directly over the wound. Choose a pad that's large enough to extend an inch or more past the wound's margins. Secure with bandage materials appropriate for the location. (See page 313.)

B. If the wound is in an area that doesn't lend itself to bandaging, and if environmental conditions make it likely to get contaminated with dirt, dust, and flies unless covered, use a clean gauze pad or your finger to apply a thin layer of a non-antibiotic dressing, such as povidone iodine ointment (see page 302). This will act as a barrier against contamination. If flies are a problem, apply a second layer of Flys-Off®, a canine fly repellant by Farnam, labelled for use on open wounds and available at pet stores.

Avoid using antibiotic powders, sprays, or ointments without consulting your veterinarian. Indiscriminate use of antibiotics in any form can favor the growth of tougher, antibiotic-resistant bacteria.

C. If contamination and flies aren't a problem, leave the wound open to air.

Step 5. *Keep it up.* Repeat steps 2 through 4 once or twice daily, depending on how dirty the wound and bandage become. Begin by changing the bandage twice daily to assess the wound; reduce to once daily if the wound and bandage become only slightly moist. (If the wound becomes swollen, red, angry-looking, or begins to ooze pus and/or smell bad, consult your veterinarian.) Continue until the wound remains clean and uncrusted between cleanings.

What you see: A flesh wound in which layers of your dog's skin and subcutaneous tissue have been scraped away. Droplets of blood and/or clear, amber-colored fluid are oozing from or drying on the wound's surface.

What this might mean: It's potentially serious, depending on the depth and breadth of skin involved and whether the injured tissue is embedded with foreign material, such as dirt or hair. As a rule of thumb, the larger and more contaminated the abrasion, the more vulnerable it will be to infection. Deep abrasions can damage hair follicles and skin cells, which can result in scarring. Hair may fail to regrow because of follicle damage. Attending to these wounds can be dangerous to you, because your dog's skin is packed with pain-sensing nerve endings, making abrasions very painful for him—he may try to bite you.

15 - B

THE SCRAPE
(Abrasion)

ACTION PLAN:

Is your dog lame as a result of the injury? **YES** Go to **page 110.**

NO

Does the abrasion involve more than 15 percent of your dog's skin (roughly enough to cover one entire side of his rump)? **YES** Call your veterinarian *NOW*—your dog may have been hit by a car, and/or might require treatment to prevent excessive fluid loss and infection.

NO

Can you see white tissue in the wound? Is the abrasion over or near a joint? **YES** Call your veterinarian *NOW*—the abrasion may be deep enough to reach bone, tendon, or ligament, or it may have damaged a tendon sheath or joint tissues.

NO

Is there foreign material embedded in the wound that you can't entirely remove (e.g., hair, dirt, splinters)? **YES** Call your veterinarian *NOW*—to avoid infection, all debris must be removed.

NO

Is the wound (or a portion of it) swollen, or hot to the touch (when compared to adjacent tissue)? Is it "spoiled" smelling, blackened, or draining white or yellowish pus? **YES** Call your veterinarian *NOW* if you answered yes to any of these queries—it could be infected.

NO

➤

YOUR VET MAY NEED TO:

Sedate or anesthetize your dog, and/or numb the tissues, in order to fully determine the depth and extent of the injury and help facilitate the best possible treatment.

ACTION PLAN (CONTINUED):

Can you see fat or muscle?

 NO

YES Call your veterinarian *NOW*. The wound might require surgical repair, and/or is likely to become infected.

Will your dog allow you to treat the wound?

NO

YES Apply **Home Treatment,** below.

Call your veterinarian *NOW*. The sooner the wound gets proper treatment, the better the odds of quick, uncomplicated healing.

HOME TREATMENT:

*(See **Action Plan** on previous page to determine whether home treatment is appropriate for your dog's abrasion. If at any time during home treatment, your answers on the action plan change for the worse, call your veterinarian.)*

Step 1. *Ice the wound.* This will numb painful nerve endings and limit swelling. Wet a clean cloth, slip an ice pack (see page 311) between its layers, and lay it over the wound, overlapping the wound's margins. Hold the pack in place, either manually or with a wrap, for 5 minutes.

Step 2. *Clip wound margins.* Use scissors or clippers to remove hair from the wound's edges.

Avoid using antibiotic powders, sprays, or ointments without consulting your veterinarian. Indiscriminate use of antibiotics in any form can favor the growth of tougher, antibiotic-resistant bacteria.

Step 3. *Clean the wound.* Irrigate the wound with cold tap or hose water or a trigger-type spray bottle filled with homemade saline solution (see page 306). Hose or spray for 1 full minute or until the wound appears visibly clean, whichever takes longer. If necessary, use a gauze pad to remove hair and debris within the wound.

Step 4. *Dress the wound.* Apply a thin layer of non-antibiotic first-aid cream, such as povidone iodine ointment (see page 302) to keep exposed tissues moist and to act as a barrier to outside contaminants. If flies are a problem, apply an outer layer of Flys-Off®, a canine fly repellant labelled for use on open wounds and available at pet stores.

Step 5. *Exercise daily.* Daily light exercise at the walk is advised to encourage circulation to the injured area and to speed healing. (If your dog's collar contacts the abraded area, remove it.)

Step 6. *Keep it up.* Repeat Steps 3 and 4 once or twice daily, depending on how dirty the wound becomes. Begin by cleaning it twice daily to assess the wound; reduce to once daily if the area is only slightly crusted or soiled. Continue until the wound remains clean and uncrusted between cleanings.

CAVEAT: If the wound becomes persistently red, swollen, pus-filled, or smelly, call your veterinarian.

What you see: Your dog's haircoat may be singed or gone; his skin's appearance will fit roughly into 1 of the following 3 levels:

  1. Exposed skin is fiery red, moist, smooth (no blisters), and very sensitive to the touch. If you press on it lightly with your fingers, it blanches (turns white). This describes most first-degree burns.

  2. Same as above, but with blisters. This describes most second-degree burns.

  3. The skin can vary in color, from white to red to black. It's generally dry, with either a pliable or leathery texture. It seems non-painful, and when you press on it with your fingers, it doesn't blanch. This describes most third-degree burns.

What this might mean: A burn can be serious, depending on its depth (degree) and on how broad an area is involved. As a rule of thumb, the higher the degree of the burn and the broader the skin damage, the greater the potential for dehydration and infection.

15-C

BURNS:
Thermal, chemical, electrical burns, and/or sunburn

ACTION PLAN:

Does the burn involve more than 15 percent of your dog's skin (roughly enough to cover one entire side of his rump)? Does it contain blisters, and/or is it discolored (white, blackened, bright red) or split?

 Call your veterinarian *NOW* if you answered yes to any of these queries—risk of infection and/or dehydration^G is high.

Is there evidence that your dog had contact with an electrical source, such as a chewed electric cord, and/or a burned/blanched area on his mouth/tongue?

 Call your veterinarian *NOW*—your dog could have been electrocuted. Do not touch him until you've shut off the source of electricity (see **page 341**).

Does the burn involve your dog's face, ears, or lower legs?

 Call your veterinarian *NOW*—treatment might be required to prevent scarring and loss of function.

Is it possible your dog inhaled smoke?

Call your veterinarian *NOW*—lung damage from smoke inhalation might not immediately be evident. Without proper treatment it can be debilitating or fatal.

➤

YOUR VET MAY NEED TO:

Sedate or anesthetize your dog, and numb tissues, in order to treat a burn, which can be exquisitely painful if it's of first- or second-degree severity.

ACTION PLAN (CONTINUED):

Is this a sunburn on white-haired or hairless areas? Does it seem excessive compared to other dogs with the same coloration and level of sun exposure?

 Call your veterinarian *NOW* if you answered yes to any of these queries—it could be an underlying condition that's made your dog overly sensitive to sunlight (photosensitivity^G).

NO

Will your dog allow you to treat the wound?

 Apply **Home Treatment**, below.

NO

Call your veterinarian *TODAY*.

HOME TREATMENT:

*(See **Action Plan** on previous page to determine whether home treatment is appropriate for your dog's burn. If at any time during home treatment, your answers on the action plan change for the worse, call your veterinarian.)*

Step 1. *Remove source of burn.* If whatever has burned your dog is still in contact with his skin, remove it as quickly as possible. For instance, if he was scalded by hot water, quickly irrigate the area with cold water, using a gentle flood to avoid pressure damage to already injured tissues. If he was burned by a chemical agent, dilute/neutralize that agent. If he's sunburned, bring him indoors.

Step 2. *Ice the burn.* Wet a clean cloth, slip an ice pack (see page 311) between its layers, and lay it over the burn, overlapping the burn's margins. Hold the pack in place, either manually or with a wrap, for 5 minutes, to numb painful nerve endings and reduce skin damage from stored heat in tissues. Let tissues rest 15 minutes. Repeat cycle (ice on: 5 minutes, ice off: 15 minutes) for a total of 1 hour.

Step 3. *Clean the burn.* Irrigate the burn with cold water, clean gently with soap and water, and remove any debris. Allow to air dry.

> **DON'T** apply butter or ointments, which contain a greasy/oily base that can hold in heat. Use only water-based creams or gels.

Step 4. *Dress the burn.* Apply a thin layer of oil-free, soothing dressing such as 100 percent aloe vera gel mixed 50-50 with povidone iodine cream (not ointment) or Silvadene cream. (The latter is a prescription item you'll have to get from your veterinarian.) This will keep tissues pliable and prevent cracking, and will disinfect the wound.

Step 5. *Protect against further burning.* Remove/repair whatever caused the burn in the first place. To protect against additional sunburn, keep your dog indoors during the day. Coat the burned area with a non-chemical sunblock such as zinc oxide cream or titanium dioxide. And, ask your vet about tattooing the area, to minimize future sunburns.

Step 6. *Keep it up.* Repeat Steps 3 and 4 once or twice daily, depending on how gooey, dirty, or crusty the burned area becomes. Begin with a twice daily schedule to assess the burn; reduce to once daily if the burn becomes only slightly moist. Continue until it remains clean and uncrusted between cleanings. Be sure to remove all residual dressings before reapplying. If the burn becomes swollen, hot, or angry-looking, and/or begins to ooze pus and/or smell, call your veterinarian.

What you see: A flesh wound with one or more holes that penetrate into your dog's tissues. The area around the hole(s) may be swollen, and there may or may not be a discharge or foul-smelling odor.

What this might mean: A puncture wound is potentially serious, depending on its location and depth. Puncture wounds can cause direct damage to internal structures, and can introduce bacteria deep into tissues where infection can be devastating. Tetanus is less of a problem in dogs than in humans (and horses), so tetanus shots are rarely administered. Puncture wounds might be caused by foxtails[G], stepping on a sharp object, such as a thorn or nail, or due to a gunshot. They also can be the result of a snakebite[G], which is dangerous if the snake produces toxic venom. Holes that look like puncture wounds also can result from an internal problem rather than an external injury. For instance, the puncture might be a drainage hole that formed from the inside to release pressure and debris from an internal infection.

15-D

PUNCTURE WOUNDS

ACTION PLAN:

Is the wound bleeding profusely (dripping steadily or spurting)?

YES ▶ Call your veterinarian *NOW*—stitches might be required to stop the bleeding. Go to **Before You Leave**, next page.

NO ▼

Is there external evidence of tissue damage, such as tearing, missing tissue, tissue flaps, scorching of tissue at the hole's margins, or entry-exit holes?

YES ▶ Call your veterinarian *NOW*—the more tissue is traumatized, whether by gunshot or other cause, the greater the risk of infection and disability.

NO ▼

Are tissues near the wound drooping, or is the involved leg (if applicable) buckling, or severely lame?

YES ▶ Call your veterinarian *NOW*—nerves or supporting structures (bone, tendon, ligament) may be damaged.

NO ▼

Is the wound on or near a joint?

YES ▶ Call your veterinarian *NOW*—the joint and/or tendon sheath may have been penetrated.

NO ▼

Is the wound on the underside of his neck/throat region?

YES ▶ Call your veterinarian *NOW*—vital structures in that area may be damaged or at risk for contamination and infection.

NO ▼

▶

YOUR VET MAY NEED TO:

Sedate your dog in order to probe and/or X-ray the wound site to determine cause, depth, and direction of penetration, look for foreign bodies, and to assess damage to internal structures.

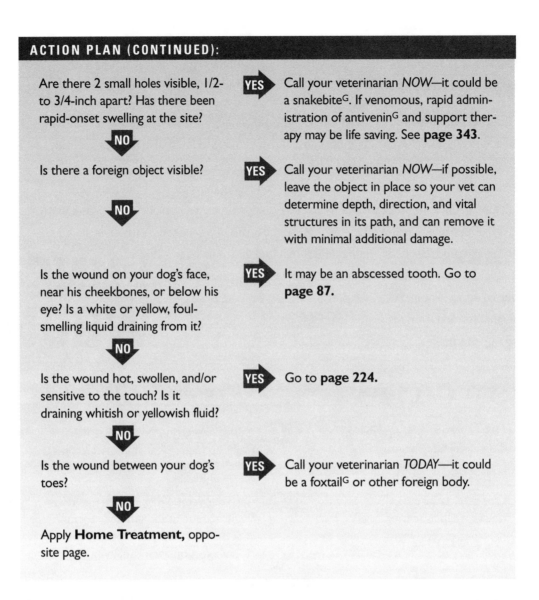

ACTION PLAN (CONTINUED):

Are there 2 small holes visible, 1/2- to 3/4-inch apart? Has there been rapid-onset swelling at the site?

YES → Call your veterinarian *NOW*—it could be a snakebite[G]. If venomous, rapid administration of antivenin[G] and support therapy may be life saving. See **page 343**.

NO ↓

Is there a foreign object visible?

YES → Call your veterinarian *NOW*—if possible, leave the object in place so your vet can determine depth, direction, and vital structures in its path, and can remove it with minimal additional damage.

NO ↓

Is the wound on your dog's face, near his cheekbones, or below his eye? Is a white or yellow, foul-smelling liquid draining from it?

YES → It may be an abscessed tooth. Go to **page 87**.

NO ↓

Is the wound hot, swollen, and/or sensitive to the touch? Is it draining whitish or yellowish fluid?

YES → Go to **page 224**.

NO ↓

Is the wound between your dog's toes?

YES → Call your veterinarian *TODAY*—it could be a foxtail[G] or other foreign body.

NO ↓

Apply **Home Treatment,** opposite page.

BEFORE YOU LEAVE

1. *Calm your dog* If he's excited, his heart will pump harder and his blood will run faster. If possible, have a helper hold him and soothe him as you work. Apply a muzzle if necessary. (For how to apply a home-made muzzle, see page 329.)

2. *Apply direct pressure.* Forget about whether that blood's coming from an artery or a vein—the treatment's the same: Apply pressure over the site with a clean pad of sufficient size to cover the wound and its margins. A folded hand towel, disposable diaper, or a 1-inch thick stack of gauze sponges or paper towels will make a suitable pad. If an ice pack is immediately available, sandwich it between the pad's layers to further stem the bleeding. (For how hard to press, see "How Much Pressure," page 216, this chapter.)

IMPORTANT! Resist the temptation to lift the pad again to check bleeding—you'll only disturb any clots that've formed, undoing the good you've done. If your

> Unless instructed to do so by your veterinarian, NEVER administer any human or canine medication to your dog. Many medications that are appropriate in one circumstance or species can be harmful in another.

pad becomes saturated with blood, don't replace it. Keep pressing for a minimum of 5 minutes without moving it.

If there's so much blood you can't tell where it's coming from, press hard for 5 seconds to blanch the site, then briefly lift the pad to find the blood source. If more padding is immediately available, get it now. Center your pressure on the blood source. If you have a helper, have him or her continue to apply pressure while you drive to your veterinarian's. If you're alone, proceed to Step 3.

3. *Apply a pressure bandage.* After 5 to 10 minutes of pressure, and if the bleeding is coming from a location that lends itself to bandaging, apply a pressure bandage. (See page 315.)

Avoid pressure-spraying water, hydrogen peroxide, saline solution, or any other material directly into a puncture wound. Rather than cleaning it, this might force contaminants deeper, where they can cause infection.

Avoid using antibiotic powders, sprays, or ointments without consulting your veterinarian. Indiscriminate use of antibiotics in any form can favor the growth of tougher, antibiotic-resistant bacteria.

HOME TREATMENT:

*(See **Action Plan,** page 221, to determine whether home treatment is appropriate for your dog's puncture wound. If at any time during home treatment, your answers on the action plan change for the worse, call your vet.)*

Step 1. *Clip wound margins.* Use scissors or clippers to remove hair from the wound's edges.

Step 2. *Clean the wound.* (For in-depth instruction, see page 307.) Irrigate the wound with cold hose or tap water, or a trigger-type spray bottle filled with homemade saline solution (see page 306). Spray for 1 full minute or until the wound appears visibly clean, whichever takes longer. If necessary, use a gauze pad to remove hair and debris within the wound.

Step 3. *Apply ointment.* Using clean fingers or a fresh gauze pad, gently apply a thin layer of a non-antibiotic dressing, such as povidone iodine ointment (see page 302).

Step 4. *Bandage the wound.*

A. If it's in an area that lends itself to bandaging and if environmental conditions make it likely to get contaminated with dirt, dust, and flies unless covered, press a non-stick pad such as Telfa® or Release® directly over the wound. Choose a pad that's large enough to extend an inch or more past the wound's margins. Secure with bandage materials appropriate for the location. (See page 313.)

B. If the wound is in an area that doesn't lend itself to bandaging, and if environmental conditions make it likely to get contaminated with dirt, dust, and flies unless covered, use a clean gauze pad or your finger to apply a thin layer of a non-antibiotic dressing, such as povidone iodine ointment (see page 302). This will act as a barrier against contamination. If flies are a problem, apply a second layer of Flys-Off®, a canine product by Farnam, labelled for use on open wounds and available at pet stores.

C. If contamination and flies aren't a problem, leave the wound open to air.

Step 5. *Keep it up.* Repeat steps 2 through 4 once or twice daily, depending on how dirty the wound and bandage become. Begin by changing the bandage twice daily to assess the wound; reduce to once daily if the wound and bandage become only slightly moist. (If the wound becomes swollen, red, angry-looking, or begins to ooze pus and/or smell bad, consult your veterinarian. Continue until the wound remains clean and uncrusted between cleanings.

What you see: A flesh wound that's become swollen and warm. Your dog may react as though it's painful when you touch it, and there may be a discharge.

What this might mean: These signs can mean the wound's infected, but not necessarily. Heat, swelling, pain, and discharge can be normal components of uncomplicated inflammation, a necessary step in the healing process—it depends on their duration, and on the character and source of the discharge. They also can signal the development of infection, which can delay healing, increase the risk of scarring, and possibly spread to other locations in your dog's body.

Hot, swollen, tender &/or draining
WOUND

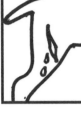

YOUR VET MAY NEED TO:

Clarify the cause and/or extent of the wound with X-rays and/or exploratory surgery.

ACTION PLAN:

Is your dog not eating, dull, or feverish?

YES ▶ Call your veterinarian *NOW*—infection may have spread into the blood (septicemia^G).

NO

Is your dog lame? Is the wound on or near a joint?

YES ▶ Call your veterinarian *NOW* if you answered yes to either query—your dog's muscle, joint, and/or tendon sheath may be involved, injured, or infected.

NO

Are heat, pain, and swelling still escalating the third day after the injury? Is the wound draining a thickened, pus-like, white, yellow, or green substance?

YES ▶ Call your veterinarian *TODAY* if you answered yes to either query—the wound could be infected, and it may require surgery and/or flushing for complete drainage.

NO

Are there tissue flaps? Are portions of the wound cold, hard, or mushy feeling?

YES ▶ Call your veterinarian *TODAY*—dead or dying tissue will have to be removed for healing to proceed.

NO

Is the wound located over a bony area with little soft tissue cushion, such as on the lower legs or skull?

YES ▶ Call your veterinarian *TODAY*—there may be a bone chip interfering with healing (sequestrum^G).

NO

Is it possible there's a splinter, sliver, gravel, or other foreign material in the wound?

YES ▶ Call your veterinarian *TODAY*—the wound won't heal as long as foreign matter is trapped inside.

NO

ACTION PLAN (CONTINUED):

Is the wound located on your dog's face, below his eye? **YES** Call your veterinarian *TODAY*—it may be an abscessed tooth. See page 87.

NO

Will your dog allow you to treat the wound? **YES** Apply **Home Treatment**, below.

NO

Call your veterinarian today for an appointment.

HOME TREATMENT:

*(See **Action Plan** to determine whether home treatment is appropriate for your dog's wound. If at any time during home treatment, your answers on the action plan change for the worse, call your veterinarian.)*

Step 1. *Clean the wound.* (For in-depth how-to information, see page 307.) Gently irrigate (don't pulverize) the wound with cold tap or hose water or a trigger-type spray bottle filled with homemade saline solution. (See page 306). Spray for 1 full minute or until exposed tissues appear visibly clean, whichever takes longer. If necessary, use a clean gauze pad to remove hair and debris.

Step 2. *Apply a stimulating hotpack.* To en-

Unless instructed to do so by your veterinarian, NEVER administer any human or canine medication to your dog. Many medications that are appropriate in one circumstance or species can be harmful in another.

courage your dog's local immune system, prepare a hot (but tolerable on your hand) solution of Epsom salts. (See page 306.) Grab a clean cloth large enough to extend 2 inches beyond the wound's edges when folded into fourths. Fold the cloth, dunk it into the Epsom salt solution to saturate, and lay it over the wound. Hold it there for 15 minutes, re-wetting as needed to keep it warm. Or, simply spray the site with warm tap water for 15 minutes.

Step 3. *Keep it up.* Repeat Steps 1 and 2 three times daily until the wound drainage changes from pus to clear, amber-colored fluid. Then manage according to "Home Treatment," page 216. If the wound continues to drain and/or gets worse, call your vet.

SECTION 2

HANDS-ON DOGKEEPING SKILLS

CHAPTER 1

How to establish your dog's
BASELINE BEHAVIOR

How to establish your dog's
BASELINE BEHAVIOR

Here's a chart of typical behaviors for the average dog—behaviors that can reveal how your dog feels. Fill in his personalized version of baseline behavior, then copy and post the chart in a prominent place. Take a mental inventory every time you see him. If you notice abnormal behavior, turn to "Baseline Vital Signs" (page 232). If your findings convince you there's a problem, refer to your dog's symptoms in Section 1.

BASELINE BEHAVIOR			
Setting	**Average Dog**	**Sample Entries**	**Your Dog**
Back yard	Sniffs and marks his/her "territory"	*Sniffs and marks*	
Back yard	Tries to engage you and/or other pets in play	*Loves to play ball in the morning*	
Back yard	Naps in the shade for several hours at midday	*Naptime: 11:30 a.m.*	
In the house	Seeks a soft spot for his nap	*Prefers cool tile*	
In the house	Cleans up all feed	*Always!*	
In the house	Watches outdoor activity through the window	*Paces by window in an effort to go out*	
Group feeding	Feeds according to social position	*Top dog: first to eat*	
Water source	Usually drinks after eating and exercise	*Drinks after playing and after eating a meal*	
At the dog park	Sniffs first; plays second	*Way more interested in playing than sniffing/marking*	
Back yard	2-4 bowel movements per day	*Goes right after breakfast and dinner, then once more before bedtime*	

CHAPTER 2

Baseline
VITAL SIGNS

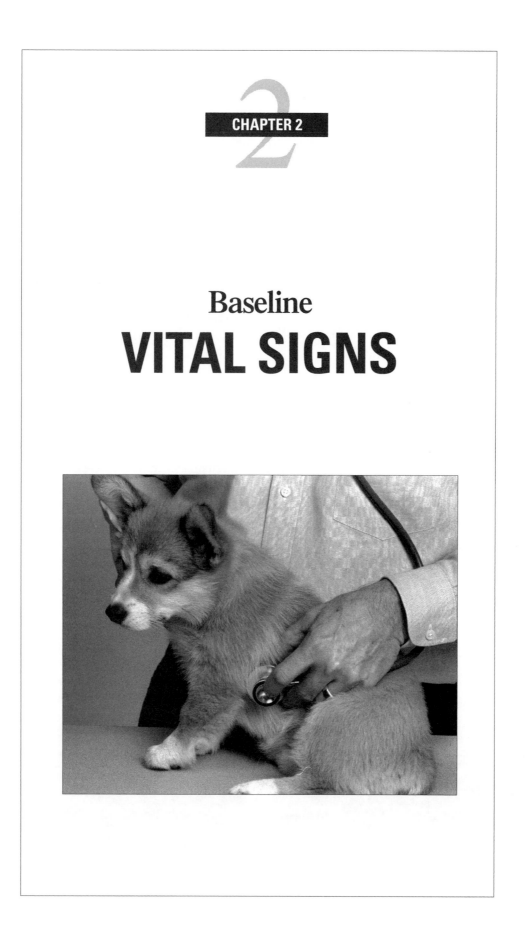

BASELINE VITAL SIGNS

Step-by-step instructions for how to take your dog's vital signs are provided in this section. Compare your findings to the chart on the opposite page. Be ready to relay abnormal readings if you call your veterinarian to report a suspected problem. Your knowledge of both current and baseline readings can help him or her determine how quickly he/she needs to see your dog.

HOW TO TAKE YOUR DOG'S TEMPERATURE

Shake down a glass thermometer or activate an electronic one. Lubricate the tip with a dab of K-Y® or petroleum jelly.

> ### What Kind of Thermometer?
> · **Glass type: about $5 at variety/drug stores.**
> · **Electronic type: about $10 at variety/drug, tack/feed stores, or through vet supply catalogs. Get one that beeps when it's ready to read, and signals when its battery is low.**

> **DON'T leave a rectal thermometer unattended. If your dog should sit down or rub his hindquarters, he might break off the thermometer, injure his rectum, and/or spill poisonous mercury. It takes 2 minutes or less for the temperature to register. Stay with your dog, and hold the end of the thermometer constantly.**

Step 1: Lift your dog's tail and gently insert the thermometer into his anus, to a depth of 1 inch.

Step 2: With the heel of your hand resting against his buttock for stability, hold up your dog, and hold the thermometer in place. Release his tail if he fusses (clamps or swishes it). Some dogs will tolerate a thermometer better if their tails are free. It takes about 2 minutes for a glass thermometer to register; about 30 seconds for an electronic one (listen for the beep).

Step 3: Remove the thermometer. Wipe it with a tissue (for glass thermometers) and read. Swab the tip with alcohol, then rinse. Or, wash well with soap and water.

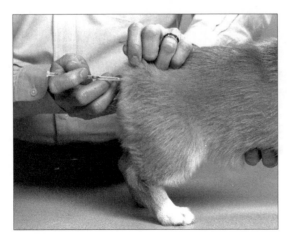

Step 1.

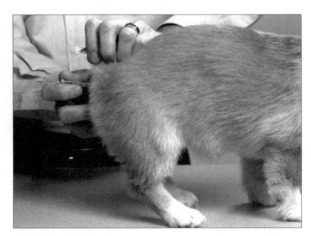

Step 2.

Tip 1: Your dog's normal temperature will be lowest in early morning, and up to 2 degrees F higher in late afternoon. It's unaffected by weather unless he's shivering or has just exercised in hot weather. To establish a baseline, record his morning, midday, and late afternoon temperatures daily for 1 week, then average the readings for each time of day.

Tip 2: Exercise causes a normal rise in your dog's temperature—to as high as around 104 degrees F. It can take up to 2 hours to return to baseline. To determine whether an elevated temperature is due to illness or exercise, check at 15-minute intervals.

Tip 3: Keep an extra thermometer. If you get an abnormal reading, check again with the backup thermometer to confirm the reading and rule out technical error.

BASELINE VITAL SIGNS			
Vital Sign	**Normal Range**	**Abnormals & Possible Cause**	**Your Dog**
Temperature	101-102.5°F	*Below normal:* hypothermia; shock. *Above normal:* infection; heat exhaustion; exercise/muscle exertion.	6 a.m.: Noon: 6 p.m.:
Heart rate	60-160 beats per minute *(slower for a large dog; faster for a small dog)*	*Below normal:* good athletic condition; heart problem; poisoning; hypothermia; shock. *Above normal:* exercise; pain; fever; heat exhaustion; shock; heart problem; anxiety; anemia.	
Respiratory rate	30 - 80 breaths per minute *(slower for a large dog; faster for a small dog)*; no effort; breathing slow/in normal rhythm	*Below normal:* hypothermia; shock; drug effect. *Above normal:* exercise; excitement; fear; pain; fever; heat exhaustion; shock; respiratory infection.	
Gum color	Pale to bubble-gum pink	*Whitish gums:* could indicate anemia or shock. *Bright pink gums:* could indicate illness; poisoning; shock; or could be normal if the dog has just been exercising. *Brick-red, gray/blue, or muddy-colored gums:* could indicate poisoning or shock[G].	
Capillary refill time (CRT)	CRT: 1-2 seconds	*Faster-than-usual CRT:* means your dog's blood pressure is elevated, probably due to recent exercise, excitement, or anxiety. *Slow CRT:* can indicate illness; poisoning; or shock.	

➤

What Kind of Stethoscope?

• **Littman-type:** about $10-$15 at feed stores, medical supply stores, or vet supply catalogs. Usually comes with 2 bells, a wide one and a narrow one. Use the wide one, which makes accurate placement less critical for listening to heart rate.

• **Hewlett-Packard type:** about $25-$50 at medical supply stores and through vet supply catalogs. The bell is narrower and deeper than in a Littman-type, for clearer sounds over a smaller area.

Checking heart rate with a stethoscope.

HOW TO TAKE YOUR DOG'S HEART RATE WITH A STETHOSCOPE

Grab a watch with a second hand or digital timer. Kneel by your dog's left side, facing his left elbow. Or, if he's small enough, you can stand on his right side and reach over, as shown. Place the scope's bell just behind the point of his elbow and press it gently into his armpit. His heart beat should have both a lub and a dub component—count the two together as one beat. Count the number of beats in a 15-second period and multiply by 4 for beats-per-minute.

HOW TO CHECK YOUR DOG'S HEART RATE DIGITALLY

While holding you dog's collar with one hand, place the fingertips of your other hand on the underside of his thigh, where the leg joins his body. Press with your fingers, until you locate the pulse of his femoral artery. Or, use your fingers to feel behind the left elbow, where the stethoscope was placed, above. Once you've found the heart beat or pulse, count the number of beats in 15 seconds. Multiply by 4 for beats-per-minute.

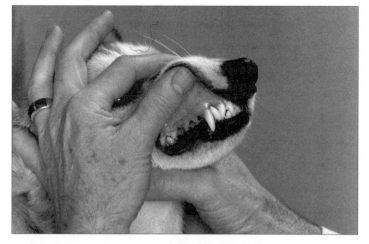

Step 1: Lift upper lip and check gum color...

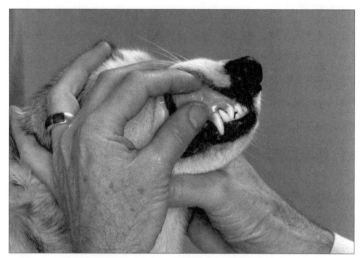

Step 2: ...then press with a finger or thumb...

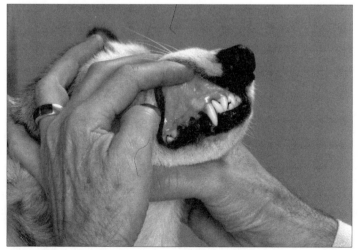

Step 3: ...and count.

HOW TO CHECK YOUR DOG'S MUCOUS MEMBRANE COLOR AND CAPILLARY REFILL TIME (CRT)

Step 1: Lift your dog's upper lip and look at the color of his gums. Are they a normal pale to bubble-gum pink? Or are they whitish, brick-red, blue/gray, or muddy colored? (If it's the latter, call your vet—NOW!)

Step 2: Next, check his capillary refill time. Press on the gums with a finger or thumb to blanch out the color.

Step 3: Then remove your finger and count how many seconds the gum takes to resume its original color. Normal is 1-2 seconds. (See chart, page 233.)

NOTES

CHAPTER 3

The right
VACCINATION
PROGRAM

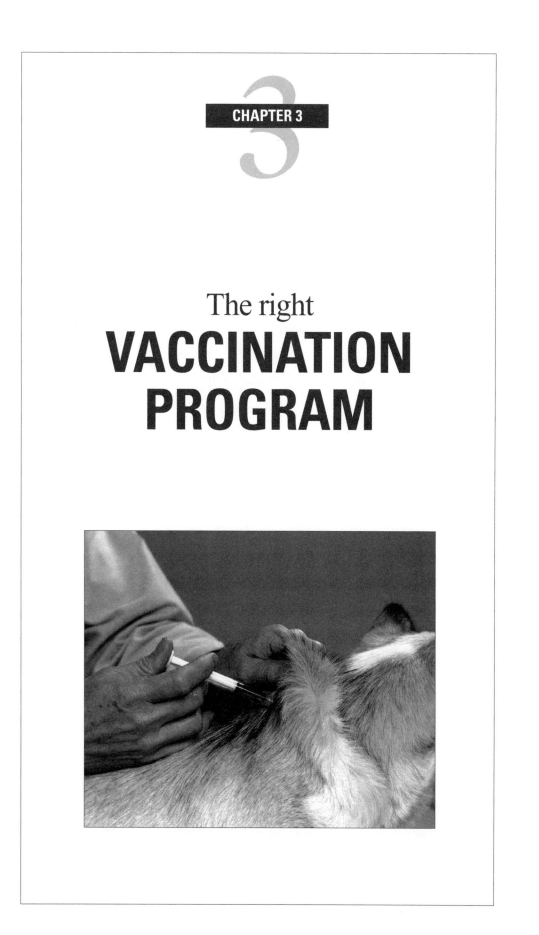

The Right
³VACCINATION PROGRAM

Depending on where you and your dog live, and on your dog's lifestyle, your canine vaccination program is going to entail getting him vaccinated every 1 to 3 years, and maybe more often. Which shots does your dog need? To help you decide, read the following chart and consult with your vet, checking the box in the right-hand column for the optional vaccines your dog should have. (We've checked the column for you, for must-have vaccinations.) Then mark your calendar and make sure proper shots are given.

Disease	What it is	Frequency of vaccination	Mode of administration	Does your dog need it?	
Coronavirus	Viral infection that can cause diarrhea in dogs, which can range from mild to fatal (the latter being uncommon). Death is most likely to occur in puppies under 6 months of age. Spread via contaminated fecal material.	For puppies, initial dose at age 6 - 8 weeks, again at 10 - 12 weeks; annual thereafter.	Injection (subcutaneous or intramuscular).	Optional; consult your vet.	?
Distemper	Viral infection that remains a killer of dogs worldwide. Related to the virus that causes measles in humans. Characterized initially by signs of upper respiratory disease, and later by more severe respiratory disease, vomiting, diarrhea, and neurological signs. Transmitted both through the air, and via body secretions, such as urine.	For puppies, initial dose at age 6 - 8 weeks, then again at 10 - 12 weeks and 14 - 16 weeks; annual thereafter.	Injection (subcutaneous or intramuscular).	Yes	✔

Disease	What it is	Frequency of vaccination	Mode of administration	Does your dog need it?	
Infectious canine hepatitis	Viral infection of dogs and foxes characterized by signs involving the liver, kidneys, eyes ("blue eye"), and cells lining the inner surface of blood vessels. Spread via body fluids, including urine and nasal discharge.	For puppies, initial dose at age 6 - 8 weeks, then again at 10 - 12 weeks and 14 - 16 weeks; annual thereafter.	Injection (subcutaneous or intramuscular).	Yes	✔
Kennel cough (parainfluenza)	A highly contagious viral disease characterized by a honk-like dry cough. Causes inflammation of the trachea, larynx, and bronchi. Rarely fatal. Spread mainly via airborne particles.	For puppies, initial dose at age 6 - 8 weeks, then again at 10 - 12 weeks and 14 - 16 weeks; annual thereafter. Vaccinated dogs should receive booster intranasal immunizations approximately 1 week before potential exposure (boarding, showing, etc.).	Injection (subcutaneous or intramuscular) or intranasal (spray in nose).	Optional; consult your vet.	?
Leptospirosis	A bacterial disease characterized by kidney disease, liver disease, or hemorrhages. Spread in the urine of infected animals; rats appear to be main reservoirs of the bacteria. Can be transmitted to humans in the form of a condition called Weil's disease.	For puppies, initial dose at age 6 - 8 weeks, then again at 10 - 12 weeks and 14 - 16 weeks; annual thereafter.	Injection (subcutaneous or intramuscular).	If leptospirosis is endemic in your area, consult with your vet.	? ➤

Disease	What it is	Frequency of vaccination	Mode of administration	Does your dog need it?	
Lyme disease	A tick-borne illness caused by the bacteria, Borrelia burgdorferi. Characterized by sudden-onset lameness caused by tender, swollen joints that are painful to the touch (infectious arthritis). Regarded as the most common tick-borne disease in the U.S.	For puppies, initial dose at age 6 - 8 weeks, again at 10 - 12 weeks; annual thereafter.	Injection (intramuscular).	If Lyme disease is endemic in your area, consult your vet.	**?**
Parvovirus	A viral infection that's one of the most contagious and fatal diseases in the dog world. Characterized by vomiting and diarrhea. While it's generally thought of as a puppy disease, can affect–and kill–dogs of any age. Diarrhea is usually severe–projectile and bloody. The disease is transmitted via direct and indirect contact with contaminated dogs.	For puppies, initial dose at age 6 - 8 weeks, then again at 10 - 12 weeks and 14 - 16 weeks. An optional fourth vaccination can be given at 18 to 20 weeks (consult your vet); annual thereafter.	Injection (subcutaneous or intramuscular).	Yes!	✔
Rabies	Fatal viral disease spread by the bite or saliva of infected mammals; all other animals (including humans) that come into contact with an affected dog are at risk. Characterized by drooling, incoordination, aggression, confusion.	Initial vaccine at 12 weeks; every 1 to 3 years thereafter, depending on the vaccine used and local/state ordinances.	Injection (subcutaneous or intramuscular).	Yes!	✔

4

NO MORE FLEAS AND TICKS

External Parasite Control

4 EXTERNAL PARASITE CONTROL
(No More Fleas & Ticks)

They're your dog's nemesis, those biting insects that torment him (and you) by feasting on his (and your) blood. No only are they pesky pests whose saliva can cause allergies in your dog (such as flea-bite dermatitis[G]), but they also can be transmitters of parasites and disease. For instance, ticks in certain areas of the country can be carriers of Lyme disease[G] and Rocky Mountain Spotted Fever[G], and fleas are carriers of tapeworms[G] and the bubonic plague.

Flea Factoids

• Fleas are roughly pin-head sized, wingless insects that live off the blood of dogs, cats, pigs, rodents, birds, and humans.

• They're excellent jumpers, leaping vertically up to 7 inches and horizontally 13 inches. (An equivalent hop for a human is said to be 250 vertical feet and 450 horizontal feet.)

• Adult fleas have been known to survive for months, even up to a year, without a blood meal.

• Fleas have a 4-stage life cycle: adult, egg, larvae, pupae. Completion of the life cycle varies from about 2 weeks to 8 months, depending on temperature, humidity, food, and species.

Adult → Egg → Larvae → Pupae → Adult

• They flourish in home environments, where the temperatures range from 70 to 85 degrees F, with 52% to 92% humidity. (70% humidity is optimal for fleas.)

• Females can lay up to 25 eggs per day (up to 600 in a lifetime) in your home or on your dog.

• Eggs loosely laid in your dog's hair coat hatch into larvae within 2 days to 2 weeks.

• These burrow into floor cracks, and crevices, along baseboards, under rug edges, and in furniture and beds. Outside, they seek sandy gravel soils, which is the reason fleas are erroneously called "sand fleas." The larvae stage lasts several weeks.

• The larvae then spin a cocoon and pupate. In this state, they are safe from insecticides and cold temperatures. Pupae can survive up to a year.

• In warm weather, adult fleas emerge from these cocoons in about 5 to 14 days, or when they sense a blood meal is near.

• Fleas don't spend all day on your dog. Rather, they spend only about 10 minutes a day on him, hopping on to eat a blood meal and lay eggs, then hopping off to hang out in your carpet, furniture, yard, or other flea favorites.

DOES YOUR DOG HAVE FLEAS?

Are your home and your dog infested with these pests? Here's how to check.

Your Dog:

Step 1: With your dog lying down or standing, part the hair around the base of his tail and look for:

• Tiny black specs, which could be "flea dirt." (You may also notice them in his bed.) This is actually blood-rich flea feces, which the larvae eat for nourishment.

• Fleas, which you'll see scurrying away through your dog's hairs. Or, use a flea comb (available at pet stores). Run it through your pet's coat, making sure to penetrate its base. When you pull off the comb, look for either flea dirt or fleas. If you find fleas, nab them with your fingers and kill them in a bowl of soapy water, so they don't reinfest your dog.

Step 2: Didn't see any fleas at the base of his tail? Now roll your dog over, and check his belly–a flea favorite, and an easy area in which to spot them, due to the lack of hair.

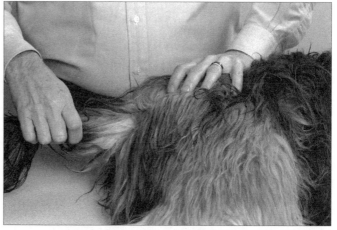

Step 1: Flea check at tail base.

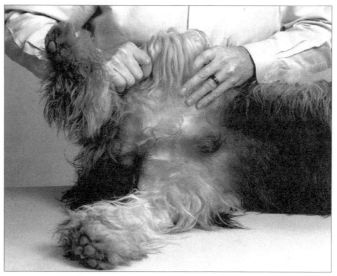

Step 2: Flea check on belly.

Your Home:

Step 1: Place a shallow pan of water with a squirt of dish soap on the floor. Position a lamp about 5 to 6 inches above the liquid surface. At night, adult fleas will leap toward the light, fall into the detergent solution, and drown. (The Happy Jack and Zema flea traps are commercial products based on the same principal.)

FLEA FIGHTERS

To wage a successful war against these pesky enemies, you'll have to use an integrated approach that attacks different life stages, resulting in fewer adult fleas. For best results, perform this 5-step assault all in one day. (*Tip: Many pest-control manufacturers offer a line of integrated products that are designed to work together, to maximize efficiency. Let your location, lifestyle–and safety–drive your selection. When in doubt, consult your veterinarian for his/her advice.*)

Step 1. *Clear the area.* Cover fish tanks, remove bird cages, pet food/water ➤

A sampling of pest-control products.

dishes, and wash or dry clean any pet bedding. Pick up all toys, shoes, etc., to ensure best access for treatment.

Step 2. *Minimize flea larvae in your home.* Vacuum and mop, to get rid of as many eggs, larvae, and pupae as possible. Use a beater-bar-type vacuum, to remove eggs and dried blood feces (larval food). This also will also open up the carpet nap for more effective insecticide treatment. Sprinkle some flea powder on carpets before vacuuming, to kill any fleas that get sucked into the bag. Vacuum especially along baseboards, around carpet edges, on ventilators, around heat registers, in floor cracks, and under and on furniture, where your pet sleeps. Repeat at least weekly, to help prevent re-infestation. After each vacuum session, remove and dispose of the vacuum bag, to avoid having those fleas that survive the assault escape and once again infest your dog and home.

Step 3. *Treat your home.* Contact a commercial pest control company, or choose from several forms that make up the hundreds of commercial products available:

Biological: These contain an insect growth regulator (IGR), which is a hormone to prevent eggs from hatching and larvae from pupating into biting adults. (Such products include Precor, Nylor, and Archer.) IGR's are said to be of negligible hazard to humans, pets, and the environment, and can be found in the form of sprays, foggers, and powders.

Boric acids: Boric acid-based commercial products (Fleabusters, Flea Halt) kill fleas in the larvae stage, via a stomach poison. Borates are said to be environmentally safe, odorless, and can be used in homes with kids and pets.

Botanicals: Pyrethrins, which are derived from chrysanthemum flowers, and rotenone (from the roots of derris, cube, and cracca plants), are good contact insecticides. Linalool (Demize), a citrus-peel extract, is a fast-acting flea killer. Other botanicals include d-Limonene (Flea Stop).

Chemical: There are hundreds of such products on the market, in the form of carpet powders, sprays, and foggers. If you'll be doing the treatment yourself, read the instructions carefully. Get your family and pets out of the house during treatment, and for several hours afterward, to minimize chemical exposure.

Step 4. *Treat your yard.* Use flea-specific premise insecticides in your yard to decrease pest insect populations. Mow the lawn and rake up leaves, brush, or clippings. This will create a drier, less-ideal environment for flea larvae. Then spray the yard, paying special attention to your pet's favorite spots. (**Tip:** If your ground is dry, soak it first, to bring flea larvae to the surface.) Discourage nesting or roosting of rodents/birds on or near your premises. Seal or screen vents, chimneys, crevices, etc., which act as magnets for rats, mice, squirrels, and other flea carriers.

Step 5. *Treat your pet.* Consult your vet about a prescription flea-control medication. Multi-purpose products are available (such as Sentinel) that control not only fleas, but also heartworms, hookworms, whipworms, and roundworms. Consider applying a topical, monthly flea adulticide, such as Advantage, Revolution, or Frontline. A few drops applied between your dog's shoulder blades and at the base of his tail can prove effective against flea infestations for 30 days or more.

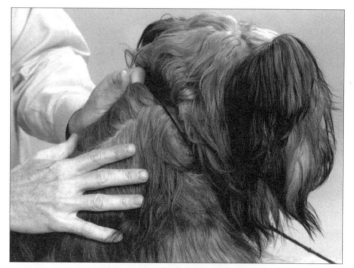

Applying a monthly flea killer: First, part the hair...

To apply , part the hair at between your dog's shoulder blades, as shown, to reveal a clear line of skin.

On a small dog, apply the entire, weight-specific dose there. On a large dog, apply half the container there, then repeat at a spot just in front of the tail base. (***Note:** Always read all manufacturer's instructions and cautions before applying any flea-control product to your dog.*)

If you opt out of the monthly topical insecticides, use commercial flea/tick shampoos, sprays, powders, and dips–as directed–to combat biting insects. ➤

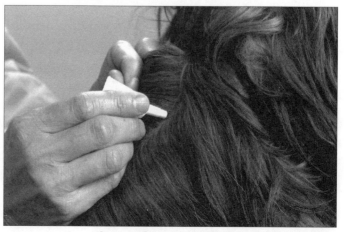

...then apply, per manufacturer's instructions.

*(**Caveat:** Do not mix products without thoroughly reading manufacturer's warnings/instructions. And if your dog wears a flea collar, avoid applying additional flea treatments. Doing so could cause poisoning.)*

Though many home flea remedies exist, consisting of the feeding of garlic, brewer's yeast, vinegar, kelp, and vitamin C, many veterinarians and researchers remain skeptical of their effectiveness in keeping your dog flea-free. Still, the addition of a dash of garlic powder or oil and brewer's yeast is unlikely to hurt your dog, and could make him less appetizing to biting insects.

TICKED OFF

They're the nasty little vampires of the bug world, not true insects, but rather *arachnids*, 8-legged pests that include spiders, mites, and scorpions. Not only can a tick bite cause illness, but a severe infestation can cause anemia[G] in your dog. One serious tick-bite related illness is tick paralysis. When a tick feeds on your dog, he also transmits a toxin into your pet's bloodstream. This toxin can cause paralysis that starts in your dog's hind legs, then migrates to his front legs. Untreated, the toxin can shut down his respiratory system, killing him.

Every time a tick takes a blood meal, there's a chance it's picking up a disease that won't affect it—but may harm its next victim, once the tick transmits the disease. That's because a tick feeds by ingesting blood, retaining solid material from the meal, and returning liquid plasma back into its victim. When it does so, it may also be injecting any disease that it's carrying.

Tick Factoids

• There are two kinds of ticks, hard ticks and soft ones. Soft ticks feed only at night, so are less of a threat to dogs that are kept inside during that time. Hard ticks are by far the most common threat to dogs.

• A tick must drink blood to pass from one life stage to the next. When it's ready to move onto the next life stage, it'll bite its victim, bury its head under the victim's skin, and stay there from hours to days.

• Ticks are attracted to brushy or wooded areas. But that doesn't limit their habitat to such areas. If your back yard has trees and shrubs, you could have ticks.

• Ticks can move from area to area via your pets, or rodents and birds.

• Most ticks lay their eggs in leaf litter, where larvae emerge. They stay there until ready to feed, at which time they climb onto foliage and await a passing blood meal.

• Ticks are tough. They've been shown to live up to 20 years, and to survive years between blood meals.

• They're active in weather above 40 degrees F, so are more likely to be a threat in spring, summer, and early fall months (in most parts of the country) than during winter months.

DOES YOUR DOG HAVE TICKS?

During months when ticks are active (roughly April to November in cold-weather states), check your dog daily for tick infestation. (Ticks generally don't transmit disease the first day they attach, so early removal is critical):

• Thoroughly brush, comb, or pet his coat, stopping whenever you feel a small, hard bump. When you do, carefully examine the area, parting the hair to do so. If you see a tick, remove it immediately. (For how to do so, see "How To Remove A Tick—The Right Way," next page.)

• Next, carefully examine your dog's ears, a common tick hideout.

• Finally, check your dog's feet, between his toes and pads.

TICK FIGHTERS

You'll need a two-fold plan to make your dog and premises unfriendly to ticks.

Step 1. *Control ticks on your dog.*

• Deploy regular use of a tick-killing spray, dip, or powder. Known as "acaricides," such agents are generally only effective for a week or two, so be diligent. (Such agents include pyrethrin, rotenone, and d-Limonene.)

• Or, consider applying a topical, monthly flea and tick insecticide, such as Frontline (which is said to kill 4 types of ticks). A few drops applied between your dog's shoulder blades and at the base of his tail can prove effective against flea and certain type of tick infestations for 30 days or more.

• Flea and tick collars may prevent ticks from attaching, but can take about 72 hours to kill already-attached ticks, which is too late to halt the transmission of disease.

• Try a collar only after you're sure your dog is tick-free. And avoid using other insecticide treatments on your dog while he's wearing a flea/tick collar, as the results could be toxic for him.

Step 2. *Control ticks on your premises.*

Keep your yard mowed and your bushes trimmed, to make them less attractive to ticks (and fleas).

• Avoid piling leaves and brush; such piles are a favorite tick habitat. Plus, the reduced cover raises the ground temperature and lowers the humidity, so ticks can dry out and die. **Bonus:** *Brush removal eliminates areas favored by small rodents (such as mice), which are critical to the tick's life cycle.*

• Limit your dog's and children's access to tick-infested areas, to help prevent ticks from being brought onto your property.

• If your yard is infested, consult a pest-control specialist about having it treated for ticks, or choose a chemical spray labeled specifically for tick control. (Be sure to follow label directions and take any outlined safety precautions.)

➤

HOW TO REMOVE A TICK—THE RIGHT WAY

Tick removal can be a challenge. This is especially true with hard ticks, which secrete a glue-like substance that locks them into place in your dog's skin. By correctly using the technique outlined below, you can successfully remove a tick. However, if you're squeamish or just plain unsure about your tick-removal abilities, have your veterinarian do the honors.

Step 1. *Protect yourself.* Many of the germs ticks carry can also infect you. Shield your fingers with rubber gloves, and use tweezers to avoid contact with the tick.

Step 2. *Be firm, but gentle.* Use the tweezers to grasp the tick as close to your dog's skin as possible. Use steady pressure to pull the tick straight out. If you were to pull too fast, or to twist and jerk, you could leave the head or part of the head imbedded in your dog's skin. Also, take care not to crush the tick as you remove it, which could spread any contaminated body fluids on your dog.

Step 3. *Dispose of the tick.* Drop the tick in a small container of rubbing alcohol, or flush it down the toilet. (***Note:*** *You may be able to have the tick tested for Rocky Mountain Spotted Fever[G] or Lyme disease[G]. If you opt to do so, place the just-removed tick in a small jar or plastic bag, along with a few blades of grass, for moisture. Contact the vector-borne disease program at your state's health department for information on where to take the tick for testing. Store it in a cool place until you can deliver it.)*

Step 4. *Disinfect the bite site.* Swab the site with alcohol, to kill any bacteria that might remain.

Step 5. *Check to be sure you got the head.* If you see a small, dark spot under your dog's skin at the bite site, chances are you left the head, or at least part of it, behind, despite your efforts. You can attempt to tweeze out the head, or use a sterilized needle to remove it like a splinter. Or, you can simply let it be. The area will likely form a small pimple-like bump around the head, then fall off. However, if the bite site gets red, tender, and/or sore, consult with your veterinarian.

Step 6. *Disinfect your hands.* Wash your hands thoroughly with soap and water.

MASSACRE THE MITES AND LICE
Ear Mites

You see your dog scratching at his ears, or shaking his head in agitation. When you peek inside his ear, you see dark, soil-like debris caked inside. While the mites themselves are nearly invisible to the naked eye, what you're seeing is a telltale sign of their presence.

Tick Removal "Dont's"

• Avoid touching a tick with your bare hands. Its secretions could be infectious. For instance, Rocky Mountain Spotted Fever[G] can spread to you when infected tick body fluids come in contact with broken skin, your mouth, or your eyes.

• Don't use heat (in the form of a hot match or cigarette) on a tick in an effort to get it to "let go." Doing so can cause the tick to release pathogens into your dog's skin before losing its grip, and/or can cause it to burst, spreading potentially contaminated body fluids.

Fortunately, many commercial products exist for managing ear mites (such as Mita-Clear and Nolvamite), that are available at your local pet store, or through pet supply catalogs.

Step 1. *Clean and treat your dog's ears.* See page 268 for pictorial instructions on how to clean your dog's ears, and how to properly apply medication. Then carefully follow label directions. Consult your veterinarian if your dog fails to respond to treatment.

Step 2. *Check other pets in your home for ear mites.* These pests are easily passed from dog to dog, or even dog to cat. Check and treat all pets in your household.

Step 3. *Begin a preventive program.* To help keep ear mites at bay, regularly treat your dog with a mite or flea/tick insecticide designed specifically for dogs. Be sure to follow label instructions and precautions.

Skin Mites

Your dog is biting and scratching at his skin. You can't find any fleas or ticks to explain his scratching, and he has no known food allergies. You also spot dandruff in the area, but it's not moving (see "Lice," below). He could have mites.

Step 1. *Eliminate skin parasites from the affected area.* If mites are a problem, use a canine insecticide (such as LymDyp or Paramite Dip) designed to kill mites. Follow label instructions and heed precautions.

Step 2. *Treat other pets in your home for mites.* These pests are easily passed from dog to dog, or even dog to cat. As a precaution, treat all animals in your household, using feline products to treat any cats.

Step 3. *Consult your vet if your efforts fail.* If your dog continues to scratch and bite at himself, and/or his skin appears to worsen, consult your veterinarian.

Lice

Your dog is scratching and biting at his skin. If you spot what looks like moving dandruff, he may have lice. Grab a magnifying glass and take a closer look. If you see small, flat, white, wingless insects, or white/silver eggs attached to his hairs, he has lice.

Step 1. *Kill the lice.* Treat him with a commercial canine preparation designed to kill lice, such as Hilo Dip, to eradicate the pests. Be sure to carefully follow label instructions and heed precautions.

Step 2. *Treat other pets in your home for lice.* These pests are easily passed from dog to dog, or even dog to cat. As a precaution, treat all animals in your household, using feline products to treat any cats.

Step 3. *Consult your vet if your efforts fail.* If your dog continues to scratch and bite at himself, and/or his skin appears to worsen, consult your veterinarian.

NOTES

CHAPTER 5

DECLARE WAR ON WORMS!

Internal Parasite Control

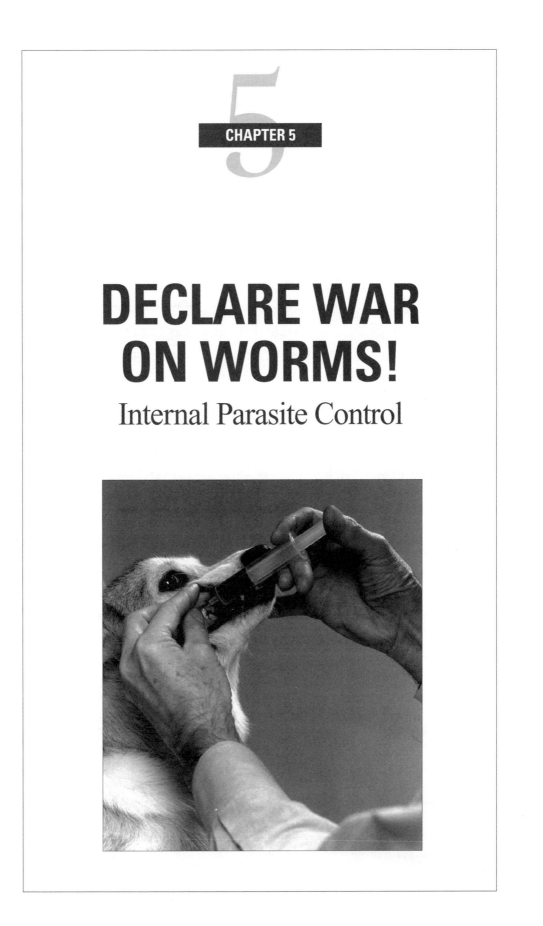

Internal Parasite Control
5 DECLARE WAR ON WORMS

When you declare war on worms, you're not just helping your dog lead a healthy life. You're also preventing the possibility that these nasty internal parasites could infect you or members of your family. Here's just one example of how this can happen: Many puppies are born with roundworms, which are passed to them from their mother through her placenta and/or milk. Dogs also can contract roundworms via contact with contaminated soil or by ingesting contaminated stool.

If roundworm eggs are somehow ingested by someone in your family (typically young children who eat dirt), these eggs can migrate through his or her organs, or to the eyes or central nervous system. This can result in organ damage, blindness, or even death. Though rare (one estimate reveals about 2.8 % of the people in the United States test positive for roundworm infestation), it can happen.

Hookworms are another canine parasite that can be passed to humans, by migrating through your skin. Convinced that your dog needs a regular deworming program? Thought so. First, take a look at the list of common parasitic invaders you'll be fighting, then use the battle plans provided to wage a successful war against them.

Parasite:	How they attack your dog:	Signs of infestation include:	How they're transmitted:	How to detect them:	Can they affect you?
Coccidia Protozoa, which are single-celled organisms.	The organisms multiply in your dog's intestine, causing destruction of its lining.	Diarrhea, with or without dark, tar-like blood. Weight loss is also a byproduct of coccidia infestation.	Contaminated feces.	Your veterinarian must test a stool sample. (For how to collect a stool sample, see box, page 254.)	No.

How to control them: Consult your veterinarian for his/her recommendation on a treatment regimen. To help prevent infestation:
• Keep your yard/kennel clean. Pick up stool at least daily, and dispose of it out of reach of your pets.
• Clean hard surfaces with a strong ammonium hydroxide solution (coccidia are resistant to many common disinfectants).
• Steam-clean kennels weekly (the heat will kill the organism).

Parasite:	How they attack your dog:	Signs of infestation include:	How they're transmitted:	How to detect them:	Can they affect you?
Heartworms A parasitic worm, Dirofilaria immitis, which is long and slender, reaching up to 12 inches in length.	Heartworms live in the heart and adjoining vessels, and are capable of causing significant damage to the heart and lungs of an infected dog.	Coughing, difficulty breathing, lethargy, and weight loss.	Via mosquito. Larval stages of the worm circulate in the blood of infected animals, and are picked up by mosquitoes that bite them. These larvae are then passed on to other animals the mosquito goes on to bite.	Your vet will need to perform a blood test.	No.

How to control them: If your dog is infected, consult your vet—treatment can be risky. However, failure to treat your dog could mean the spread of heartworm disease to other pets.
• If your dog's blood test is negative for heartworms, start him on a monthly heartworm-control regimen, available through your vet in pill or chewable form in such products as Sentinel (which also controls fleas, hookworms, whipworms, and roundworms), Interceptor (which also protects against hookworms), and Heartgard (which also protects against roundworms and hookworms).
• Keep up the treatment throughout mosquito season in your area, and 60 days beyond it, or year-round, if you live in a temperate climate.
• Have your dog tested anually for heartworm infestation.

Parasite:	How they attack your dog:	Signs of infestation include:	How they're transmitted:	How to detect them:	Can they affect you?
Hookworms Small, thin worms about 1/4- to 1/2-inch long.	They fasten to the wall of your dog's small intestine and draw blood from him.	Anemia and diarrhea, with bloody, wine-dark or tarry-black stools. Puppies between the ages of 2 to 8 weeks are most commonly affected, though problems can occasionally be seen in older dogs.	Through contact with contaminated soil or feces (either via ingestion of or skin penetration by infective larvae). Puppies can acquire them before birth (though this is rare), or via their mother's milk.	Your vet will need to check a stool sample.	Yes. Hookworms can be passed to people, via penetration through the skin. The resulting condition is known as "creeping eruption," and presents itself as lumps and streaks beneath the skin, with itching.

How to control them: If your dog has an infestation, consult your veterinarian. He or she will prescribe or recommend a deworming agent that can kill the parasite without harming your dog.
• Prevent/control hookworm infestation, via monthly administration of a heartworm preventative that's also labeled as effective against hookworms, such as Interceptor, Sentinel or Heartgard,
• Keep your yard/kennel clean. Pick up stool daily, and dispose of it out of reach of your pets.
• Apply a 1% solution of bleach to runs and/or hard surfaces frequented by your dogs, to kill the parasites.
• If your dogs live on sand and/or gravel surfaces, spread a thin layer of rock salt or Borax, which will destroy hookworms.
• Always wash your hands with soap and water after handling a dog or puppy, or after working in soil. Instruct your family to do likewise.
• Have a stool sample tested annually.

➤

Parasite:	How they attack your dog:	Signs of infestation include:	How they're transmitted:	How to detect them:	Can they affect you?
Roundworms (Ascarids) The most common of all canine parasites, this spaghetti-like worm can range from 1 to 7 inches in length.	Eggs/intermediate hosts are ingested, then hatch in your dog's intestine. Larvae are carried to your dog's lungs via his bloodstream. From there, they can migrate to the intestine where they hatch into adults. Larvae may become encysted (dormant) in an adult dog's tissues. In a pregnant female, normal hormonal changes can "awaken" these larvae, which then cross her placenta and infect her puppies.	Older dogs rarely show signs, though you may see worms in the infested dog's stool. In puppies, a pot-bellied appearance; a rough haircoat; light musculature; vomiting; and diarrhea.	Contact with soil containing roundworm eggs, and/or by ingesting contaminated stool. In puppies, via their mother before they're born, and/or via her milk afterward.	You may see worms in your puppy's vomit or diarrhea; your vet can check for roundworms in a stool sample.	Yes. If roundworm eggs are ingested (typically by young children who ingest dirt), eggs can migrate to organs, or to the eyes or central nervous system, resulting in organ damage, blindness, or even death.

How to control them: If your dog has an infestation, consult your veterinarian. He or she will prescribe or recommend a deworming agent that can kill the parasite without harming your dog.
• Centers for Disease Control and Prevention (CDC) now recommend that a female dog and her litter be dewormed with a medication that targets roundworms at 2, 4, 6, and 8 weeks after the puppies are born—regardless of whether stool samples were positive for the parasite. (Be sure to use a dewormer labelled safe for these ages; consult your vet.)
• Newly purchased, weaned puppies should be dewormed per your vet's suggestion.
• Prevent/control roundworm infestation, via monthly administration of a heartworm preventative, such as Sentinel or Heartgard, which is also labeled as effective against roundworms.
• Observe your dog's stool and vomit for signs of roundworms. Consult your vet for a proper deworming agent if such signs are evident.
• Keep your yard/kennel clean. Pick up stool at least once a week, and dispose of it out of reach of your pets.
• Have a stool sample tested annually.
• Don't allow your children to play in areas frequented by dogs. (If you do, at least be sure the area has a stringent leash-law and "doggie-bag" law, requiring stool clean-up.)
• Always wash your hands with soap and water after handling a dog or puppy. Instruct your family to do likewise.

HOW TO COLLECT A STOOL SAMPLE
• Grab a tongue depressor or plastic spoon.
• Find a fresh pile (one that's less than an hour old).
• Extract about a tablespoon-sized sample (no less, but your vet doesn't need the whole pile!).
• Put the sample in a plastic baggie or a clean margarine container.
• Refrigerate the sample if you won't be leaving for the clinic right away.

Parasite:	How they attack your dog:	Signs of infestation include:	How they're transmitted:	How to detect them:	Can they affect you?
Tapeworms Segemented flatworms that vary in length from an inch to several feet.	They live in your dog's small intestine, attaching themselves to his gut wall via hooks and suckers. Fortunately, the tapeworm is virtually harmless to its host.	Rice-grain-like tapeworm segments wriggling in your dog's bed, stool, or on his hind end. Irritation can cause him to "scoot" with his hind end. Heavy infestations can cause mild diarrhea, weight loss, and reduced appetite.	Most commonly via fleas; and, less commonly, via lice. Tapeworm eggs are ingested by flea larvae or lice, which in turn are ingested by your dog. Other types are acquired by eating raw meat or raw fish.	Watch for the grain-like segments in your dog's stool, bed, or on the hairs around his anus. (Eggs usually aren't visible in a stool sample.)	Yes. Children can get tapeworms if they accidentally swallow a flea. More serious is the risk of acquiring the tapeworm Echinococcus Granulosus from your dog. Dogs acquire the parasite by eating uncooked meat from infected sheep. The result is Hydatid disease, which is potentially fatal.

How to control them: If your dog is infested, consult with your veterinarian to develop a deworming regimen that will safely rid the dog of the parasites.
• Practice diligent flea control. (See Chapter 4, "External Parasites," page 241.)
• Don't let your dog roam. If he's out of sight, there's no telling what he's eating—including carrion that could contain tapeworms.
• If you live in a rural area, have your dog's stool examined for tapeworms at least twice a year.
• Always wash your hands after handling a dog or puppy. Instruct your family to do likewise.

OTHER CANINE PARASITIC PREDATORS

Ask your vet about these less-common parasites, and how you can detect/prevent them in your dog. Those marked with an asterisk* can also infect humans. Of particular significance recently is Giardia*[G], for which a canine vaccine has recently been developed.

Babesia*	Leishmania*	Physaloptera*	Trematode (Flukes)
Giant Kidney Worm *	Lungworms	Spirocerca Lupi	Trichina spiralis*
Giardia*	Neospora Caninum	Toxoplasma*	Trypanosoma Cruzi*

➤

Parasite:	How they attack your dog:	Signs of infestation include:	How they're transmitted:	How to detect them:	Can they affect you?
Threadworms Small, round worms.	They live in the surface tissues of your dog's small intestine.	Profuse, watery diarrhea, and signs of lung infection. Affects puppies more often than adult dogs.	By ingestion of larvae (such as in contaminated stool), or direct penetration through your dog's skin by larvae in contaminated soil. Threadworms are more common in warm climates than in cold ones, but infestations generally are rare in either climate type.	Your vet will need to check a stool sample.	Yes. Strains vary in their ability to affect humans, with people living in tropical climates most commonly affected.

How to control them: If your dog is infested, consult with your veterinarian to develop a deworming regimen that will safely rid your dog of the parasites.
• Keep your yard/kennel clean. Pick up stool daily, and dispose of it out of reach of your pets.
• Apply a 1% solution of bleach to runs and/or hard surfaces frequented by your dogs, to kill the parasites.
• Always wash your hands after handling a dog or puppy. Instruct your family to do likewise.

Parasite:	How they attack your dog:	Signs of infestation include:	How they're transmitted:	How to detect them:	Can they affect you?
Whipworms Threadlike worms that grow to be 2 to 3 inches long. One end of the parasite is thicker than the other end, hence the name.	The adult whipworm attaches itself to the wall of your dog's large intestine, where it feeds on his blood.	Light infestations generally don't cause signs, but heavy ones can cause diarrhea, anemia, and weight loss.	Via ingestion of eggs, such as from the ingestion of contaminated stool.	Your vet will need to examine a stool sample (although they can be difficult to detect).	No.

How to control them: If your dog is infested, consult with your veterinarian to develop a deworming regimen that will safely rid your dog of the parasites.
• Prevent/control whipworm infestation, via monthly administration of a heartworm preventative, such as Sentinel, which is also labeled as effective against whipworms.
• If you opt out of a monthly control medication, practice diligent stool pick-up, and have your dog checked for whipworms twice a year.

CHAPTER 6

HOW TO GIVE ORAL MEDICATION

(And Still be Your Dog's Best Friend)

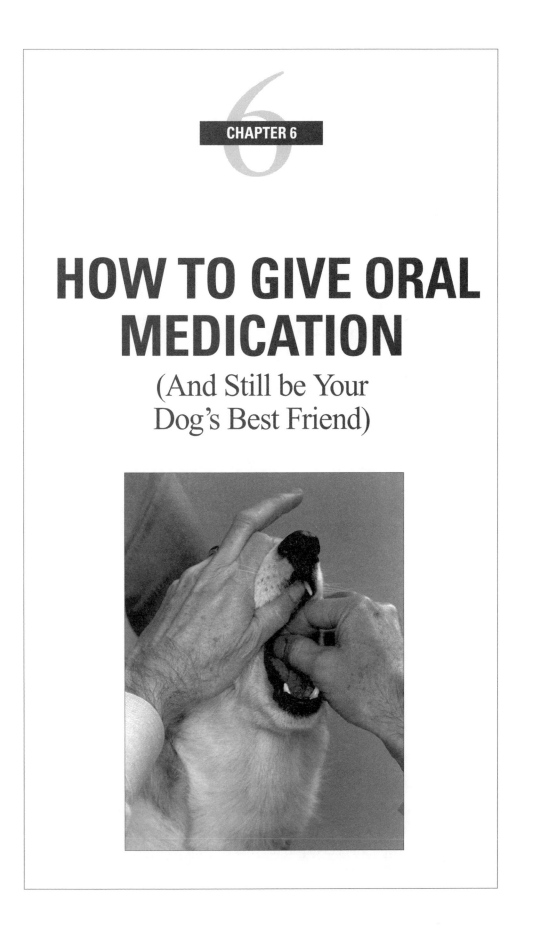

6 HOW TO GIVE ORAL MEDICATION
(And Still Be Your Dog's Best Friend)

From time to time, you'll find it necessary to administer oral medication to your dog. Using the correct technique will minimize stress on both you and him, and ensure that the medicine ends up in his system–and not on the kitchen floor!

Use the following guidelines to dose your dog without a fight, be it medication in pill or liquid form.

Use Finesse, Not Force

When giving oral or liquid doses, ask your vet for (or select) a flavored product that will be palatable to your dog, if one is available. A palatable product will make voluntary ingestion easier, thus lessening the chance of a fight.

• If your dog is eating well, and the medication is in pill form, try burying it in a small ball of canned dog food, cheese, cream cheese, bread, hot dog, or liver sausage (if your dog's diet isn't restricted). Most dogs will readily ingest such a treat. However, be sure yours swallows the pill ball completely, and doesn't slip away and spit out his medicine.

• Avoid hiding the pill in your dog's regular food. If he's not eating well, he might not ingest it. Or, he could take it in his mouth, only to slink away and spit it out later.

• If the pill you're trying to administer is large or in capsule form, try rubbing it with a bit of salad oil or butter to aid its passage down your dog's throat.

• Use a calm, confident approach when dosing your dog. Your positive attitude and confidence will rub off on him, which will make the situation easier for you both.

• To make liquid dosing a positive experience, give him a small dose of dilute broth immediately after the medicine dose.

HOW TO ADMINISTER A PILL OR CAPSULE

Step 1. Stand or kneel in front of your dog. With the pill in one hand, insert the thumb of your other hand in the space behind the upper canine teeth, pressing upward on the roof of his mouth to part his jaws. (***Tip:*** *If your dog is difficult to contain, have a helper hold him, so both of your hands are free.*)

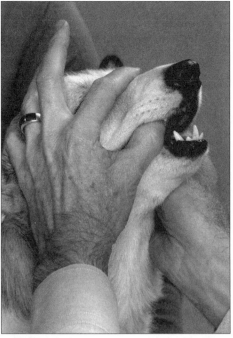

Step 1: Open mouth.

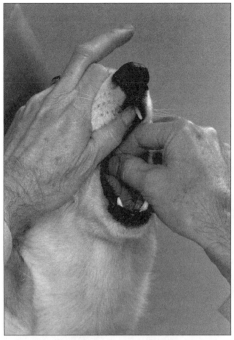

Step 2: Drop pill on back/center of tongue.

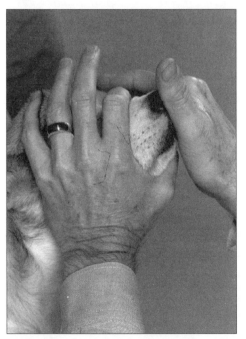

Step 3: Close mouth and rub nose.

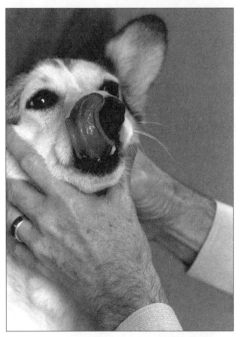

Step 4: Release after he's swallowed.

Step 2. Use the base of your pill-hand thumb to press down on his lower jaw. When his jaws are extended such that you can clearly see the back of his throat, drop the pill in the middle of the farthest back part of his tongue that you can reach. (If you drop it to one side or the other, your dog can work it forward and spit it out.) Keep his head pointed upward so gravity aids the pill's passage down his throat. ➤

Step 3. Immediately withdraw your hands and gently hold your dog's mouth shut, so he can't spit out the pill. Keeping his head tipped up, softly rub your thumb over his nose...

Step 4. ...which will encourage him to lick his nose, which in turn will cause him to swallow, thus ingesting the pill. (***Note:*** *Avoid letting go of your dog's mouth until you're certain he's swallowed the pill. Otherwise, he could spit it out.*)

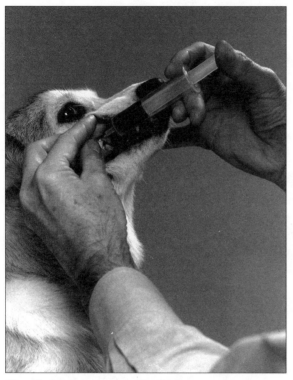

Step 3: Administering a liquid dose.

HOW TO ADMINISTER A LIQUID DOSE

Step 1. Using a needle-less syringe, a turkey baster, or an eye dropper, measure out the appropriate dosage.

Step 2. Holding the syringe or dropper in one hand, use your other hand to slightly tip back your dog's head to about a 45-degree angle. Pull out the lips at the corner of his mouth, exposing the pouch between his molar teeth and his cheeks. (***Tip:*** *If your dog is a squirmer, recruit a helper so you have both hands free.*)

Step 3. Place the syringe or eye-dropper tip into that pocket. Continue to hold the cheek out, so the medicine doesn't spill.

Step 4. Gently depress the plunger part way, releasing a small amount of medication into your dog's mouth.

Step 5. Gently hold your dog's mouth closed, and tip up his nose. Rub your thumb across his nose as you did in Step 3, "How to Administer A Pill or Capsule," until he licks his nose, indicating that he's swallowed that portion of the dose. Repeat until he's swallowed the entire dose.

CHAPTER 7

How to Examine and
TREAT YOUR DOG'S EYES

7 How to examine and
TREAT YOUR DOG'S EYES

Unfortunately, a lot of serious eye problems look exactly the same as minor ones: You see squinting, watering, redness, and/or rubbing. Many times, however, mild to moderate eye discomfort is the result of something simple, such as dust in the eye. This you can resolve quickly and easily with minor first aid—if your dog will allow it. The more serious cases that'll require veterinary intervention reveal themselves by failing to improve within a few minutes of home treatment.

If your dog won't allow you to check an eye problem without a fight, don't engage him. There are eye problems that leave the eyeball weak and vulnerable to rupture. The added pressure of an eyelid tightly clenched against your efforts to force it open could actually damage the globe itself. However, if your dog will allow you to examine and treat his sore eye, there are techniques you can use to help you achieve your goal without doing harm. Following are guidelines for examining an eye, rinsing it, and applying ophthalmic ointment.

EXAMINING AN EYE

TIP: Consider applying a muzzle to your dog if he becomes reactive during the course of his eye treatment. And recruit a helper to restrain him. Even if he doesn't strenuously resist your treatments, any sudden movement on his part could increase the risk of injury to his eye. Proper restraint can decrease the likelihood of such movement. For how to apply a makeshift muzzle, and how to correctly apply a restraint hold, see pages 329 and 331.

Symptoms that say, "Stop! Call your vet now!" are marked with an asterisk.*

Step 1. Stand at a distance (as close as you can get without stimulating an anticipatory increase in squinting). How widely your dog holds the eye open, and whether or not it's watering, are crude but relatively accurate measures of how painful it is. Make your observations, and refer to them later to determine whether your treatments have helped.

Step 2. Put a leash on your dog. Stand to the side of the eye. Without touching his face, take a close look, and make the following observations:

• If there's a discharge, is it watery, thick, or colored? Is his face crusted with it, telling you it's been going on for more than just a few minutes?

• Is there evidence that he's been rubbing at it? (You'll see raw, hairless places on his face, and/or swollen eyelids*.)

• If he holds the eyelids at least partially open, aim a penlight into the eye (don't hold it any closer than 1 foot away) and look for a rough or irregular surface* and/or cloudy spots* on the clear portion of the eyeball.

• Look also at the pupil. Memorize its size, then examine the pupil in your dog's good eye so you can compare the two. Is the pupil in the sore eye a different size from the one in the good eye*?

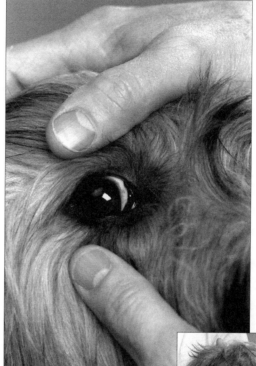

Step 3. If you have a helper, have him or her hold your dog, so that your hands are free. If you're working alone, position your dog in a corner, so that any sideways or backward evasion is blocked. Standing in front of him (which will block any forward escape), place one thumb on his upper eyelid, and one on his lower lid, as shown. If your dog has hair hanging in his eyes (inset photo), part the hair to clearly reveal his eye as you position your hands.)

Step 3: Beginning the exam.

Part hair, if needed.

Step 4. Press and gently lift with the thumb on his upper lid, to raise it and reveal the upper portion of his eyeball. Take a quick survey of all the visible parts: the white part (sclera) above his cornea; cornea (the clear part); pupil; and conjunctiva (the normally pale pink, tissues that connect the eyeball to the skin around it). ➤

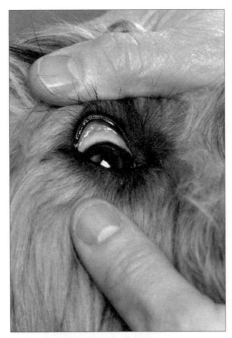

Step 4: Raise the upper lid.

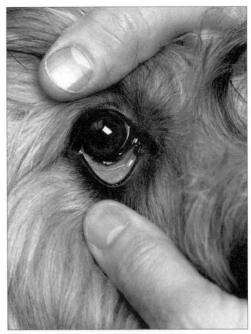

Step 5: Pull down the lower lid.

Is the conjunctiva red or swollen? Is the sclera covered with small red vessels? Do you see a foreign body*? Is the eye very painful*? Is the cornea surface cloudy*, rough*, or irregular*?

Step 5. Release his upper lid, and press down with your lower thumb, to pull down his lower lid. Call your veterinarian immediately if you notice any of the "call the vet now" symptoms marked. Otherwise, rinse your dog's eye as outlined below, to rid it of irritating dust.

RINSING AN EYE

Step 1. Warm a squeeze bottle of human or veterinary sterile eye-wash solution, by holding it under hot tap water until a drop of the solution on the underside of your wrist feels slightly warm (*not* hot).

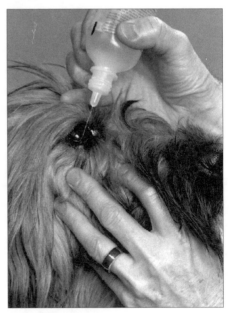

Step 2. If you have a helper, ask him/her to restrain your dog while standing on the good-eye side. Position your dog so solid walls limit any sideways or backward retreat. Stand to the side of his sore eye.

Step 3: Eye rinse.

Step 3. Cup one hand under your dog's chin, using the fingers of that hand to gently pull down on his lower eyelid. With the bottle of rinse solution in your other hand, press the heel of your hand into the skin above your dog's upper lid, to gently pull it open. As you do so, immediately squeeze the solution onto the eyeball, so it runs from the inner corner to the outer corner. Direct the stream upward, then downward on your dog's eye, maintaining it for 5 to 10 seconds, if he'll let you. Open and close his eyelids, to clear the eye's surface.

> **TIP:** When the solution first touches your dog's eye, he'll probably object by lifting his head and pulling back. Most dogs will relax and tolerate this treatment as soon as they realize it doesn't hurt and the treatment has continued despite their reaction.
>
> However, some dogs—particularly if in significant pain—will react more violently, by snapping or biting. Stay alert, stay out of biting range, and be ready to move out of harm's way. Muzzle the dog, if necessary, before continuing treatment. Or, take him to your vet's, for further treatment.

HOW TO APPLY EYE OINTMENT

Step 1. Position your dog as you did for the eye rinse.

Step 2. Cup one hand under your dog's chin, using the fingers of that hand to gently pull down on his lower eyelid. With the open ointment tube in your ➤

TIP: The squeeze bottle's tip should be close to the eye (within an inch or 2) so the stream of eye-wash solution can forcefully wash the eye and inside the eyelids.

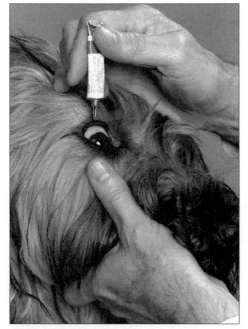

Step 2: Applying ointment.

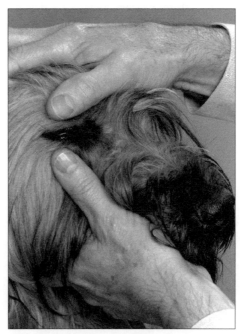

Step 3: Spreading ointment.

other hand, press the heel of your hand into the skin above your dog's upper lid, to gently pull it open. As you do so, immediately squeeze the ointment onto his eyeball.

Step 3. Put down the ointment tube, then gently massage your dog's eyelids together. The warmth of his tissues will melt the ointment, and your gentle massage will help spread it over his eyeball and inside his eyelids.

THE THIRD EYELID

Did you know that your dog has a third eyelid on each of his eyes? It's called the nictitating membrane[G], and is a pink, curtain-like membrane that's usually tucked into the inner corner of the eye, where the upper and lower lids meet. This third eyelid covers your dog's eyeball when his upper eyelid closes. (You may have seen it when he's sound asleep and his eyelids are slightly parted.)

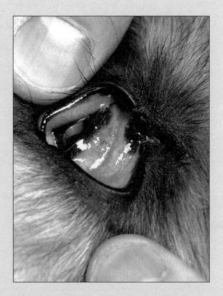

However, if the third eyelid reveals itself when your dog's eye is open, something's wrong. A variety of problems can make it come out of hiding: Some are mild and temporary, such as superficial pain from dust. Others can be severe and permanent, such as serious systemic disease—or brain damage. If your dog's third eyelid is persistently visible, turn to page 73 for an action plan.

8

How to Examine and
TREAT YOUR DOG'S EARS AND NOSE

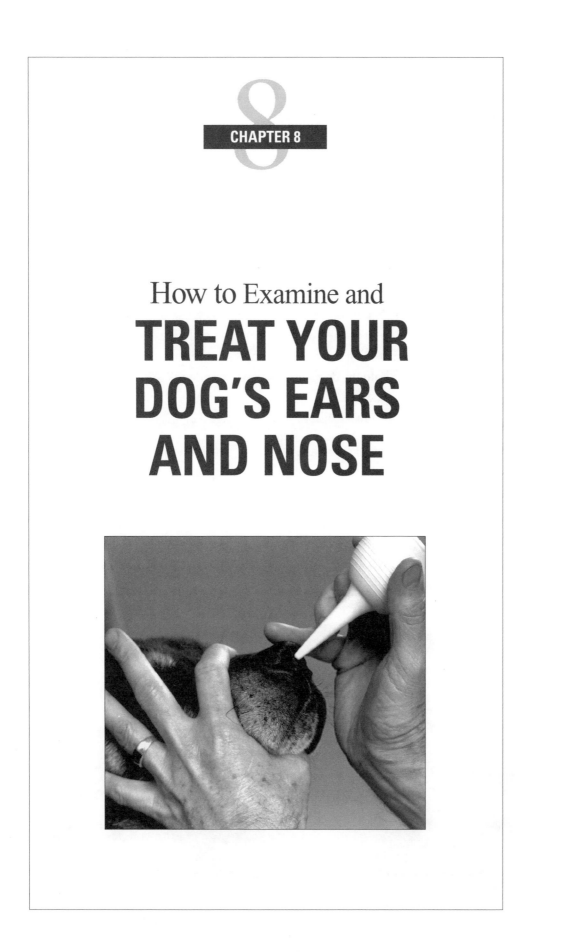

8 How to examine and
TREAT YOUR DOG'S EARS AND NOSE

Your vet has recommended that you clean and medicate your dog's ears, to control ear mites or some other problem. Or perhaps you referred to an action plan, and determined that your dog's nasal passages have been irritated. Here's how to treat his ears and nose with minimal stress for you both.

HOW TO CLEAN AN EAR

Step 1. Ask a helper to hold the dog. If it's a large dog, he or she can squat behind the dog, wrapping his/her arms around the animal, then use one hand over the top of the dog's nose, to stabilize the head. If yours is a small dog, have your helper restrain the dog from moving, by holding him against his or her chest. You can use your free hand to hold the dog's head still. If your dog is reactive, consider applying a muzzle for the safety of all involved. (For more about safe restraint, including how to apply a makeshift muzzle, see page 327.)

Step 2. Expose the external ear canal, by flipping back the ear flap.

Step 3. Use a Q-tip moistened with water or mineral oil to gently clean dirt/wax from the outer ear's crevices, as well as those on the ear flap. (***Note:*** *The ear canal drops vertically a good distance before it takes a turn and heads in a horizontal direction, ending at the ear drum. Avoid inadvertent injury by holding the Q-tip vertically, and directing it downward. Under no circumstances should you insert it horizontally into the ear canal. And, it's critical that your dog remain*

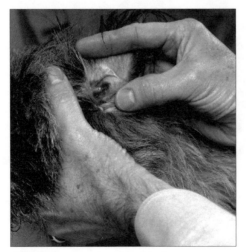

Step 2: Expose the ear canal.

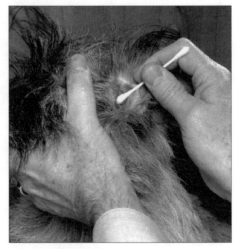

Step 3: Gently clean crevices.

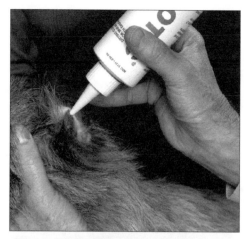
Step 4: Apply cleansing solution.

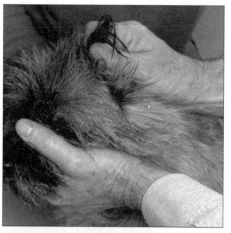
Step 5: Spread the cleanser.

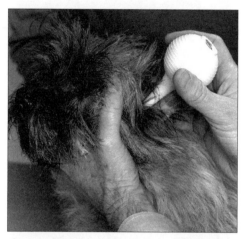
Step 6: Suction out solution and debris.

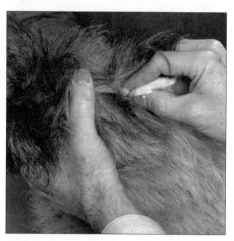
Step 7: Blot remaining moisture/debris.

still, as a sudden jerk on his part could cause you to damage one of the delicate hearing structures.)

Step 4. Using a commercial ear-cleaning solution (such as Epi-Otic or Nolvasan Otic Cleansing Solution), dispense the amount called for on the product label into your dog's ear canal, by gently inserting the dispenser tip into the canal. (If you feel resistance, you've gone too far! Back out the tip.)

Step 5. Remove the dispenser. Fold over your dog's ear flap and gently massage the base of his ear for a minute or two, to spread the cleanser.

Step 6. Use a bulb syringe to remove cleaning solution and debris, via suction.

Step 7. Blot any excess moisture and remaining dirt/wax, using gauze squares, cotton balls, or tissue. ➤

Step 8. Repeat the cleaning steps several times, until debris no longer shows on the wipe.

HOW TO ADMINISTER EAR OINTMENT

Step 1. Restrain your dog and fold back his ear flap, as outlined in Steps 1 and 2, previous page.

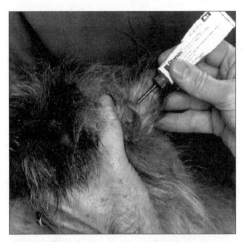

Step 2: Gently insert the tube tip...

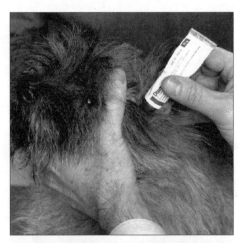

Step 3: ...all the way into the ear.

Step 2. With you or your helper holding the dog's head firmly in place, insert the ointment tube's tip...

Step 3. ...all the way into your dog's ear, as shown. Immediately dispense a small amount. (Do *not* try to fill the canal.)

Step 4. Remove the ointment tube. Massage the base of your dog's ear for a minute or two, to spread the ointment. Clean any excess with cotton or tissue.

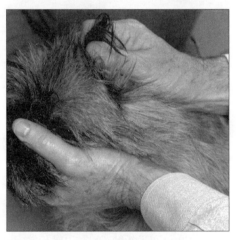

Step 4 : Massage ear to spread.

HOW TO IRRIGATE YOUR DOG'S NOSE

Your dog is snorting or sneezing. You used the action plan on page 36 to determine that he may have a nasal irritant, such as dust or dirt, in his nose. Here's how to safely irrigate the nasal passage to flush out any irritants.

Step 1. Grab a bulb syringe. Fill it with warm water. (You'll likely need a helper to hold your dog as you irrigate the nasal passages, and may need to apply a muzzle to avoid a reactive bite. For how to safely restrain your dog, and how to apply a makeshift muzzle, see page 329.)

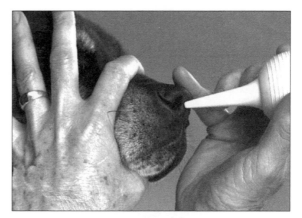

Step 2: Irrigating nasal passages.

Step 2. Use your free hand to hold your dog's head level or tipped slightly downward. As you do so, use that hand to hold your dog's mouth closed, and to block his eyes, as shown. With your other hand, position the bulb syringe's tip at the opening of your dog's nostril, then immediately squeeze the bulb to direct a *gentle* stream of warm water into his nasal passage. Allow water to drain out.

Step 3. Repeat on each nostril, until irrigation water runs clear, and/or your dog quits snorting/sneezing.

Step 4. Watch him closely for signs of nasal irritation (sneezing or snorting) and/or discharge. If you see one or both of these signs, call your veterinarian.

Did You Know...

...Most dogs seldom need to have their ears cleaned. Too much cleaning can do more harm than good, as a certain amount of ear wax is necessary to maintain the ear's health. Work with your veterinarian to develop an ear-care program suitable to your dog's ear type and lifestyle. If you notice excessively dirty and/or smelly ears on your dog, it could be an indication of a problem brewing. Consult with your veterinarian if you notice either sign.

Ear Health Tips

• Avoid getting water in your dog's ear when you bathe him. Not only is it irritating to him, but it also can set up a breeding ground for bacteria or yeast infection. (As with people, dogs can suffer from a condition called "swimmer's ear.") To avoid inadvertent ear wetting, insert a wad of cotton in your dog's ear canals before you bathe him. (Be sure to remove it immediately afterward!)

• Always check your dog's ear flaps after a dog fight. Injury-related serum and blood are a magnet for bacterial growth.

• Never irrigate your dog's ears with alcohol or other such products not specifically labeled for canine ear use. Such liquids are extremely irritating, and could cause pain and tissue swelling. Mineral oil can safely be used as a cleanser without irritating your dog's ear.

• Foreign bodies under your dog's ear flap could cause irritation—and infection. Carefully check your dog's ear canal every time you groom him, and after he's been allowed to run in brush and tall grass. Remove any irritants you find, or have your vet do so.

• If your dog is of a breed that has large amounts of hair growing under his ear flap, clip it away yourself. Hair can interfere with air circulation, increasing the risk of infection. (*Tip: Avoid plucking such hairs in healthy ears, as this can lead to serum release, and thus infection. However, plucking hair from the canal can be helpful in already-infected ears. Check with your vet.*)

NOTES

CHAPTER 9

How to examine and
CLEAN YOUR DOG'S TEETH

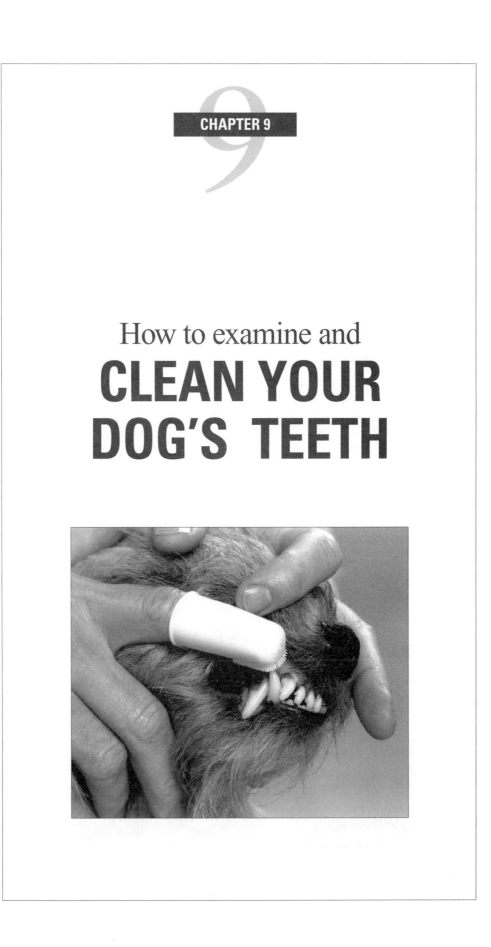

9 How to examine and CLEAN YOUR DOG'S TEETH

If you want to provide your pet with the best possible care, don't ignore his teeth. Doggie dental care should be a key part of your overall canine management routine. Without proper care, your dog's teeth will develop tarter, which could lead to dental disease, and eventually, tooth loss. This is especially true in small-breed dogs, which can develop dental problems as they age. Use this plan to ensure the best possible care for your dog's teeth.

HOW TO EXAMINE YOUR DOG'S GUMS AND TEETH

Step 1. With one hand, hold your dog's head steady while using the fingers of that hand to gently pull back his lower lips. Place your other hand over the top of his nose, then gently peel back his upper lips. Carefully examine his upper and lower front teeth and gums, for signs of trouble. If you see any redness, swelling, or bleeding in his gums, and/or chipped, fractured, broken, or missing teeth, or layers of brown/yellow plaque, consult your veterinarian.

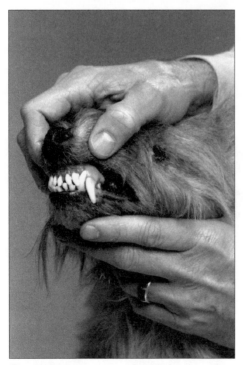

Step 1: Examine upper/lower front teeth and gums.

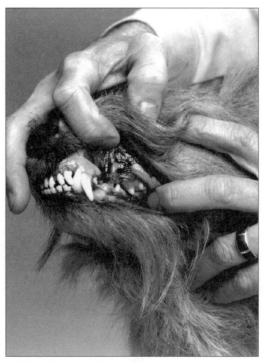

Step 2: Examine his molars.

Step 2. Now examine your dog's molars. With one hand positioned over his nose, and the other under his chin, gently pull back the corner of his mouth on one side of his face, exposing the molars, as shown. Examine the gums and teeth in that area for the signs of trouble outlined earlier.

Step 3. Repeat on the other side.

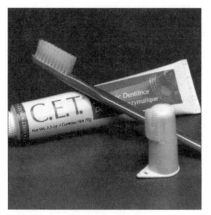

Step 1: Assemble supplies.

HOW TO BRUSH YOUR DOG'S TEETH

Step 1. Assemble your supplies. Use a finger brush, gauze, wash-cloth, or doggie tooth brush, and either doggie tooth paste (available from your vet or pet store) or moistened baking soda. (We'll be demonstrating the use of a finger brush.)

Step 2. With one hand, gently peel back your dog's upper lips, exposing the front portion of his teeth. (Most dogs won't object to this procedure if you don't force their mouths open.) Holding the brush at a 45-degree angle to the gum/tooth surface, gently brush each tooth with a small circular

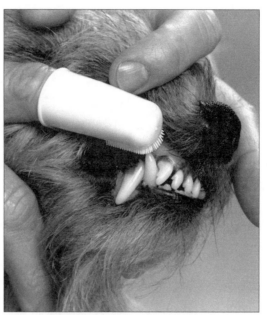

Step 2: Gently brush each front tooth.

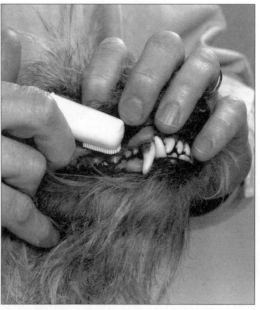

Step 3 : Finally, brush his molars. ➤

Tooth Care Tips

• Brush/clean your dog's teeth once or twice a week, or per your veterinarian's instructions. (*Tip: Initiate your teeth-cleaning regimen when your dog is a puppy. As with most grooming procedures, the earlier your dog becomes familiar with and accepting of teeth cleaning, the easier your job will be.*)

• To acclimate your puppy or dog to tooth care, begin by simply rubbing your fingers across his teeth after slipping them under his lips. If he objects, you may be moving too fast, or pressing too hard. Start over, and be gentle, but persistent. The instant your dog relaxes and allows you to rub your fingers on his teeth, stop, and withdraw your fingers to reward him. Repeat, gradually increasing the amount of time you spend rubbing his teeth as he grows more relaxed with your efforts.

• Once he'll tolerate your fingers rubbing on all his teeth (this could take a few minutes or a few days, depending on your dog's temperament), add a teeth-cleaning tool. Use a finger brush (a flexible rubber tube with a brush-like tip that fits over your index finger and is available in doggie dental kits), or a washcloth or piece of gauze wrapped around your finger. Begin your acclimation process once more. (*Note: Rubbing with gauze or a washcloth is a great way to remove mild tarter buildup at the gum line in your adult dog's mouth.*)

• When your dog will tolerate the teeth-cleaning tool, you can graduate to a soft or medium children's or adult toothbrush (depending on the size of your dog), if you'd like to. Again, take your time about introducing the new gear to your dog.

• Use canine toothpaste, per label directions, that contains chlorhexidine in a palatable base. This will help control plaque/tartar formation. If you don't have canine toothpaste, use slightly moistened baking soda as a cleaning agent. Avoid using human toothpaste—its taste and foaming action may offend your dog. It's also too abrasive and can cause digestive upset.

• If you're not regularly cleaning your dog's teeth, schedule annual or bi-annual dental checks with your veterinarian. He or she will have to anesthetize your dog in order to do a thorough scraping and polishing of the dog's teeth, and in order to thoroughly examine your dog's mouth for any signs of underlying problems.

• Feed dry "kibble" food, if possible. The kibbles' abrasive surfaces act to help clean teeth via friction. Hard dog biscuits fed on a daily basis can accomplish the same cleaning action.

• Provide your dog with hard, nylon chew toys specially designed to help with tarter control, such as Plaque Attacker and Nylabone products. These can be found at pet stores and through pet supply catalogs.

motion, as you do when brushing your own teeth. Pay particular attention to the outside tooth surfaces near the gum line, where stains and tarter deposits will be the worst, and to the plaque-trapping areas between each tooth. Replenish the brush with tooth paste, as needed. Repeat on the lower front teeth.

Step 3. Now peel back the corner of his mouth to expose his molars. Perform a thorough brushing on those teeth. Repeat on the other side, brushing all tooth surfaces in his mouth. (***Note:*** *Your dog's gums may bleed in response to vigorous brushing, indicating gum disease. Continued daily brushing will help "tighten" his gums. Bleeding should disappear in a week or so. If it doesn't, consult your vet.*)

Step 4. If your dog will let you open his mouth and clean his inner tooth surfaces, do so. (Although, there is generally less tartar on inner tooth surfaces, due to his active—and abrasive—tongue.) If not, schedule annual or bi-annual dental exams with your vet, so that your dog's teeth can be thoroughly cleaned.

Tooth Trivia

One cubic millimeter of doggie dental plaque can contain over 300 million bacteria. As bacteria invade your dog's gums and teeth, they can also enter his bloodstream, causing infection in such critical areas as his kidneys and heart. Save yourself some future vet bills by investing in regular dental exams for your dog, and brushing his teeth weekly at home. (See page 275.)

NOTES

CHAPTER 10

How to
CLIP YOUR
DOG'S TOENAILS
(And Stop the Bleeding)

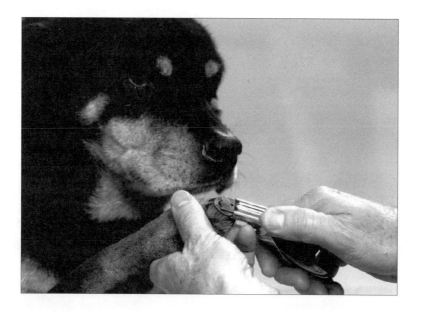

10

How to
CLIP YOUR DOG'S TOENAILS

Your dog's toe nails grow constantly, just like your nails do. When he doesn't naturally wear them down by activity on hard or rough ground, you'll need to clip them regularly to prevent excessive length from leading to problems. Failure to do so can lead to such trouble as in-grown nails, as well as painful nail breakage or even loss.

NAIL CLIP TIPS

• As with all grooming procedures, acclimating your dog to nail trims is best started when he's a puppy. If you'll be starting with an adult dog, take your time introducing the procedure to him, so you avoid a struggle. Start by gently manipulating the nails on all four feet, until he's relaxed while you do so. Then rub the nails with the clippers, until he's once again relaxed. (This could take a moment or two, or several sessions spread over a matter of days.) Only when he shows no anxiety with the clippers against his nails should you try to actually trim his nails.

• Your dog's nails are in need of a trim if you can hear them click-click across a hard floor, or if they extend below his pads.

• If you're squeamish about trimming your dog's nails, or if he objects to the procedure, have your vet or a groomer do so—and demonstrate the technique to you.

You'll need:
• **A pair of canine nail clippers (either the scissor-type or guillotine design)**
• **Cotton balls**
• **A styptic pencil, or other blood-clotting agent, such as Kwik-Stop**
• **A Q-tip**

• Mark a reminder on your calendar to trim your dog's nails once a month—then keep it up.

• If your dog's nails are currently overly long, trim back a sliver every other day, to encourage the "quick," which contains nerves and blood vessels, to retreat back into the nail. When you've reached the desired length, you can resume a once-a-month schedule.

• Remember, you can always cut more. Take off small portions at a time until you reach the desired length. If the nail bleeds, you've cut into live tissue. (For how to stop the bleeding, see opposite page.)

• Pay special attention to your dog's dew claws, the "first toes", which are located on the lower inside area of his legs, above his front feet, and, less commonly, his rear ones. (Often these are removed by breeders when your dog is a puppy.) Since those nails don't contact the ground, they can grow to the point of being ingrown, causing pain and infection.

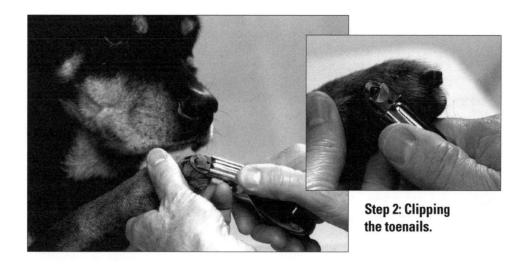

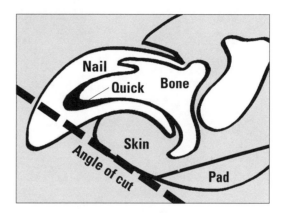

Step 2: Clipping
the toenails.

HOW TO CLIP HIS NAILS

Step 1. If your dog is a squirmer, have a helper restrain him. (For how to properly restrain a dog, see page 327.) Otherwise, have your dog sit or lie down.

Step 2. Hold his paw in one hand, pressing gently on his toe pad to extend the nail. Hold your clippers at an angle to the nail end (see diagram and inset above), such that you'll be taking just the dead nail end, and not cutting into live tissue.

Step 3. Quickly and firmly cut the nail tip. Repeat on all of your dog's other nails. (You may want to file sharp ends.)

HOW TO STOP
ANY BLEEDING

Step 1. If a nail bleeds after you've trimmed it, grab a ball of cotton, and apply direct pressure to the site for 3 - 4 minutes. (Resist the temptation to peek, as doing so would disrupt any clotting.)

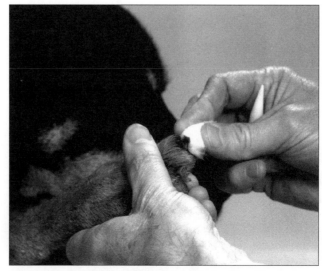

Step 1: Apply direct pressure to stop the bleeding.

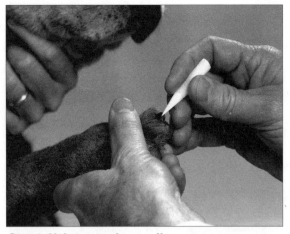

Step 2: Using a stypic pencil...

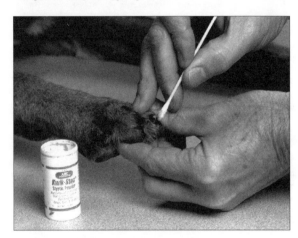

Step 3:...or blood-clotting product.

Step 2. If, after direct pressure, the nail continues to bleed, dampen the tip of a styptic pencil and rub it against the site several times...

Step 3. ...or dip a Q-tip into a blood-clotting product such as Kwik-Stop and rub it against the bleeding nail. Keep your dog quiet until the bleeding stops. Any movement could disrupt your efforts, resulting in additional bleeding.

Step 4. Contact your vet if bleeding persists despite your efforts.

CHAPTER 11

How to give subcutaneous
INJECTIONS

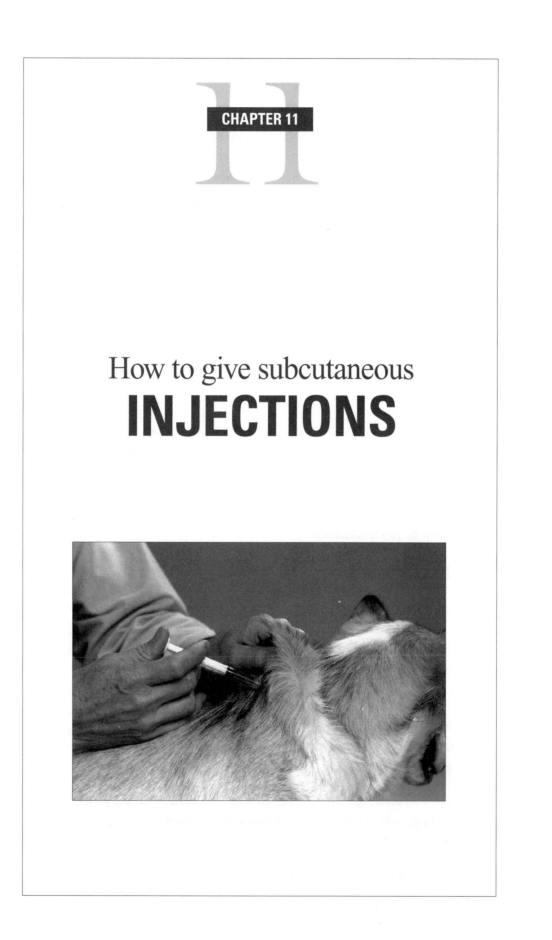

11

How to Give
SUBCUTANEOUS INJECTIONS

If you and your veterinarian feel it's appropriate for you to give subcutaneous (SC, or under the skin) injections to your dog, request a hands-on training session first. This not only will boost your confidence, it'll also help make your technique more comfortable—and therefore safer and more positive—for you and your dog. In addition, it'll give your veterinarian the opportunity to watch your technique and satisfy himself/herself that you understand the important do's and don'ts of safely administering SC injections. After you've passed this hands-on lesson, use the following roadmap when you need a refresher course. Be sure to review the signposts that warn of potential pitfalls.

SC INJECTIONS

It's true that non-veterinarians can give sc injections to their own dogs. It's also true that many of them are taking unnecessary risks in doing so—risks to the health and safety of their dogs. It's not a particularly difficult procedure to follow, but there definitely is a right way to give an sc shot, in order to minimize those risks. If you intend to give sc injections to your dog, there are several things you must do:

1. Understand that even when done properly, there is still a risk of mishaps, including allergic-type medication reactions, accidental injection into a blood vessel (particularly if your dog twitches or moves while you administer the medication), the risk you may inadvertently stick yourself or a helper, infection at the injection site, and the ever-present danger that you'll be bitten while you're giving the shot. Decide whether you accept these risks before proceeding.

2. Learn the proper technique. This will require your veterinarian's cooperation as well as your commitment to refresh your memory before each injection.

3. Avoid administering a drug via injection that has produced any type of reaction in your dog in the past, including hives. Doing so could put your dog at risk for anaphylactic shock[G].

4. Properly dispose of needles and syringes. Your vet can provide guidelines.

STEP 1: GETTING SET UP

• Use only new, sterile, individually packaged, disposable needles and syringes.

• *Needle size:* For most medications given to an adult dog, choose a 22-gauge needle, 1 inch long, so the medication will be deposited deep under the skin. (Accidental placement of the needle in a blood vessel will be easier to detect with this size needle than if you use a smaller gauge. Blood will be more likely to appear in the hub of the larger needle, warning you that it's entered forbidden territory.) For small breeds choose 25-gauge needles that are 5/8-inch long.

• *Syringe size:* Choose a syringe that's at least 30 percent larger than needed for the dose. (Example: For 1 cc of medication, use a 3-cc syringe.) This way, the plunger will be fully seated and it'll be easy to manipulate with one hand.

• *Medication:* Use only fresh, properly stored medications that aren't outdated. (Check the expiration date on the label.)

• When drawing medications from a multiple-dose bottle, clean and disinfect the stopper of the bottle with alcohol and let it air-dry before drawing up the dose.

• If giving vaccinations, avoid multiple-dose vials. Every time a dose is retrieved, what's left in the vial is at risk of contamination, which can cause serious infection.

• With the needle facing upward, tap any bubbles out of the medication into the space at the base of the needle, and press the plunger carefully to bring bubble-free medication to the needle's hub. Be careful not to squirt out a stream of medication, which would lessen the dosage your dog receives. And, aim the needle tip *away* from your face and eyes whenever you depress the plunger.

STEP 2: CHOOSING AN INJECTION SITE

For SC injections, you'll inject the medication beneath the loose skin at the base of your dog's neck, just in front of his shoulder blades. Shots given here are less painful for your dog than those in other locations.

STEP 3: PREPARING THE SITE

• Clean the injection site: Brush and/or bathe the site if it's visibly dirty. Use a clean brush to remove dirt/dust.

• Studies have shown that the risk of causing an infection when a dog is given an injection through undisinfected skin is small. However, it's always best to clean and disinfect the area. Here's an easy, effective way to do so.   ➤

1. Prepare a small, sealable bottle of disinfectant and label it: "Shot Swab." (Choose from one of the following two.)

• Tamed iodine solution: 1 teaspoon Betadine® solution plus enough water to make it look like a weak tea.

• Chlorhexidine solution: 1 teaspoon Nolvasan® solution in 3/4 cup of water.

2. Dampen a clean cotton ball with your disinfectant solution, select your injection site, and swab the site. Repeat, using a fresh cotton ball for every swipe, until the cotton ball comes off clean. (It's important that the cotton ball be damp, but not soaked—you don't want the skin so wet it drips, or it'll take too long to dry.)

3. Wait 1 to 2 minutes for your dog's skin to air-dry.

4. Proceed with your injection.

STEP 4: GIVING AN INJECTION

1. Have a helper hold your dog; apply a muzzle if necessary. (See page 327.)

2. Fill the syringe with the appropriate dose.

3. Grasp the loose skin at the base of your dog's neck, just in front of his shoulder blades. Lift it up about an inch.

4. In a single, smooth motion, insert the needle roughly parallel to your dog's back, advancing it all the way to the hub. Take care not to pierce the skin on the opposite side of the fold, and that you keep the hand holding the fold out of the needle's

RED-ALERT SIGNPOST

What you see: You've barely given the entire dose when your dog begins to breathe heavily, twitch, act excited, or begin backing up. Before you can remove the needle, he collapses.

What's happening: The medication was inadvertently given into a blood vessel. Call your veterinarian NOW.

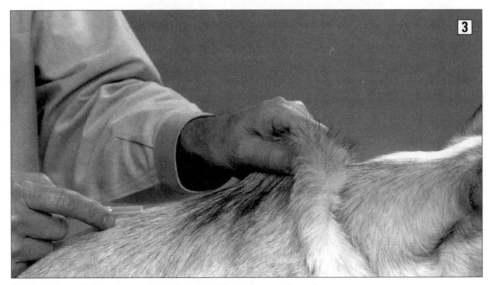

Giving an sc injection—grasp loose skin at base of neck...

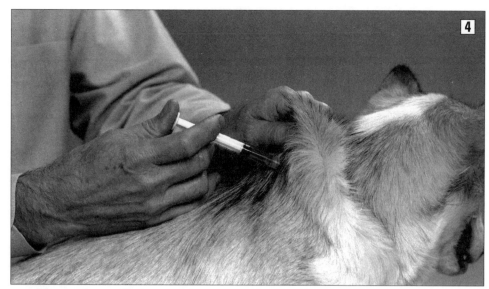

...and insert the needle in a single, smooth motion.

SHOT SAFETY

To be safe, call your veterinarian at the first hint of swelling, heat, or tenderness/soreness at an injection site, regardless of who gave the injection.

path. (Practice first on an orange or grapefruit, if you're unsure as to how much force will be needed.)

5. While steadying the needle hub with one hand, pull back slightly on the plunger to confirm that the needle is not accidentally in a blood vessel. If blood appears in the syringe, pull the needle out, get a fresh needle and a fresh dose of medication, and start over. If no blood appears in the syringe, go on to the next step. (Why get a fresh needle? Because there's blood in this one, which can make it difficult for you to determine whether you've hit another blood vessel on your next attempt.)

6. While continuing to steady the hub of the needle, push the plunger steadily (about 1 to 2 cc per second) until the syringe is empty. Wait for 5 seconds so the medication will have time to dissipate away from the tip of the needle.

7. Pull out the needle in a single, smooth motion and immediately massage the injection site with the balls of your fingertips. This will aid in dispersing the medication and will help close the needle hole.

RED-ALERT SIGNPOST

What you see: Delayed, severe reaction. You've given the entire dose, removed the needle, and up to an hour has gone by when you notice your dog breathing heavily. He has an anxious look, and his skin is riddled with hives.

What's happening: He's having an allergic-type reaction, called anaphylaxis[G], which occurs occasionally when a dog becomes hypersensitized to certain substances, including penicillin and other antibiotics, vaccines, and vitamins. Call your veterinarian NOW.

NOTES

12

LONGEVITY DIET

(And Bloat Prevention)

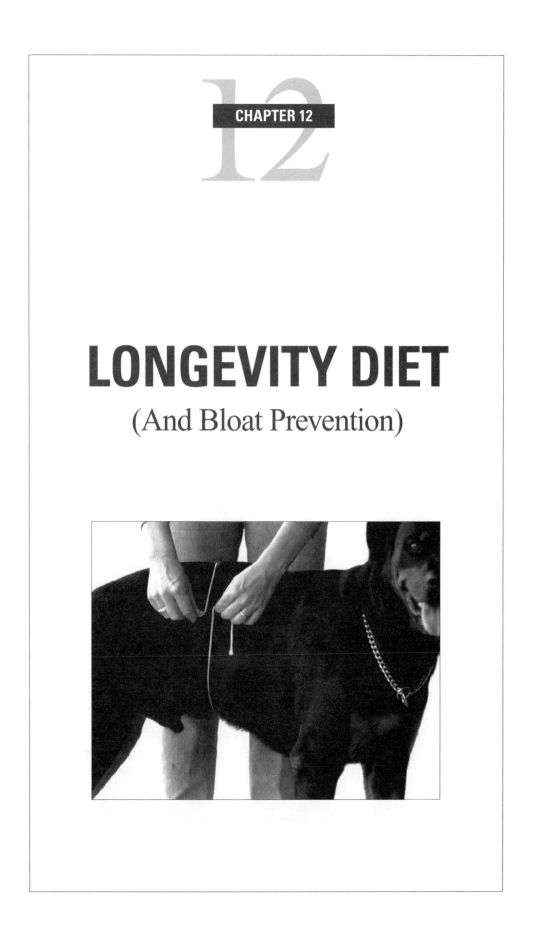

12 LONGEVITY DIET
And Bloat Prevention

You love your dog. And you love to make him happy. One way to do so is with food. But if it's the wrong food, you may be inadvertently harming your pet. Too much of a good thing can lead to obesity and digestive disturbances—some serious or even life-threatening. Sharing certain kinds of "people food" with Fido may make you feel good, but could ultimately harm him.

So what's the right diet for your dog? Use these guidelines to work with your veterinarian to come up with a healthy ration for your pet. Then stick to it. As you'll see, the more willpower you exercise in feeding your dog, the healthier he'll be.

BASIC GRUB DO'S...

· **DO** ask your veterinarian to recommend a high-quality, commercial life-stage ration appropriate to your dog's age and life-style. For instance, if he's a large-breed puppy, specially formulated rations are available through your vet or at pet stores that can help reduce the risk of such growth-related problems as panosteitis[G]. If he's a sedentary, middle-aged dog, reduced-calorie foods may be your best bet. (For more information on assessing your dog's weight and body condition, see page 295.)

· **DO** ask your veterinarian to recommend key ingredients. Perhaps your dog has a skin allergy that may be related to his diet. A switch from, say, a beef-based food to a turkey-and-rice one may be in order. And ask him/her to help you read the labels.

· **DO** buy food that's labeled "complete and balanced" as evaluated by AAFCO, an association of food-control officials. And select a brand that has a stamped expiration date. Out-of-date food could suffer a loss of nutrients, or even go rancid.

· **DO** consider a dry (kibble) or soft-moist product. As a rule, these are generally more nutritionally balanced than canned foods. You can add canned food to Fido's kibble to make it more tasty for him, but limit it to 25% or less of his ration.

· **DO** monitor your dog's stool. High-quality, highly digestible food should result in small, well-shaped stools. Low-quality foods can result in large, loose stools.

· **DO** consult your veterinarian should you decide to switch your dog to a vegetarian diet to reflect your personal beliefs. Although dogs didn't evolve to live a vegetarian lifestyle, they can do well on a complete, balanced vegetarian ration, such

BLOAT PREVENTION TIPS

Here's what you can do to minimize the risk of bloat in your dog. Pay special heed to these tips if he's of a breed prone to bloat (see page 292), or any dog in his immediate family has been a bloat victim. (Your breeder should be able to tell you.)

• Feed multiple, smaller meals per day, rather than one large one. By dividing your dog's ration into smaller portions, you reduce the risk of post-meal stomach distension, which can lead to bloat.

• If you feed dry food, soak it in warm water for 10 minutes before feeding. This will prevent ingested dry food from swelling inside your dog's stomach when he drinks water after eating, thus reducing the risk of distension and bloat.

• Avoid exercising your dog for an hour after a meal. Exercise after eating a full meal has been linked to bloat.

• Keep your dog on a schedule, to avoid stressing him—even when you travel. Stress has been linked to bloat. If you kennel him, advise his handlers to soak dry food before they feed him. And pony up the bucks for playtime and exercise services, if they're offered. The additional attention and activity could help reduce his stress.

• When shopping for a large-breed puppy, ask the breeder about any history of bloat in the sire or mother's lineage. Since bloat may have a hereditary link, you might do well to steer clear of bloodlines that have a history of this condition.

as those available in commercial form. Your vet can help you be sure your dog will get all the nutrients he needs.

· **DO** make any food switch gradual, to avoid upsetting your dog's digestive system. Begin by mixing the old food with a small amount of new food, gradually increasing the amount of new food while decreasing the amount of old. A good rule of thumb is to introduce new food in 25% increments. (For instance, if you feed 1 cup of food twice a day, start with 3/4 cup of old food, and 1/4 cup of new food the first day; 1/2 cup each on day 2; 3/4 new, 1/4 cup old the following day, then all new food on day 4.)

· **DO** offer your dog small amounts of fruits and vegetables (such as a few carrot rounds, a small piece of banana, or a cut-up slice of apple) as snacks. Dogs are omnivores (they evolved to eat both vegetables/fruits and meat), so may enjoy such a nutritious (and low-fat) snack. Grains, such as cooked rice, can also be added to his ration in small amounts, as a special treat.

· **DO** limit other treats to those specially formulated for dogs, such as dog biscuits. Commercial variations of these include low-fat products.

TIP:

Dog biscuits can also help control tartar buildup on your dog's teeth. For more information, see page 276.

· **DO** ask your veterinarian whether your dog needs nutritional supplements in his ration. Many supplements are available, in such forms as vitamin tablets, coat ➤

supplements, and herbal additives. Some may benefit your dog—others may be a waste of money. Your vet can help you determine the right supplements (if any) necessary for your dog's specific needs.

...AND DONT'S

· **DON'T** feed your dog raw meat or raw fish. Uncooked meat/fish can contain pathogens and parasites that can infect your dog. Some of these can then be passed to members of your family. Commercial raw-meat formulas may not be nutritionally balanced to meet all of your dog's needs.

· **DON'T** feed your dog cooked meat/fish containing bones. Splinters of bone could cause him to choke, or even perforate his stomach or intestines. This is especially true of "soft boned" meats, such as pork, chicken, and turkey.

· **DON'T** feed your dog "people food," other than that mentioned earlier under "DO'S". Foods containing onions can be toxic to him. Those high in fats and sugars (pizza, ice cream, anything fried) could lead to obesity at the very least, and pancreatic and other digestive problems at the worst.

· **DON'T** allow your dog to hunt/eat small animals. Not only are parasites, pathogens, and bones a risk, but if he should catch and snack on a rodent that's ingested poison, your dog could be poisoned, too.

· **DON'T** allow your dog to eat from garbage cans. Not only could he ingest bones from tossed carcasses (such as chicken or turkey) and ingest plastic wrap and other foreign bodies, but he also could get severely ill from eating spoiled food.

CANINE 9-1-1

Your ability to act fast in a bloat emergency could mean the difference between life and death for your dog. The sooner you get him to a large, full-service emergency clinic or vet hospital with surgical facilities, the better his chances of living. Be sure to call ahead to the facility to alert them of your dog's condition and your anticipated arrival time. That way, the staff can be prepared to tackle the emergency the moment your dog arrives.

BLOAT: WHAT IT IS

There's a killer condition out there, and it preys mostly on large-breed dogs. It's called **Gastric Dilatation Volvulus**[G] (GDV), commonly known as bloat, and often occurs after your dog has eaten a meal. (For symptoms of bloat and an action plan, see page 211.) When it hits, his stomach fills with fluid and gas that can't be expelled by burping or vomiting. Once distended, it may twist abruptly. If the twist is less than 180 degrees on the stomach's long axis, it's known as a torsion. If the twist is greater than 180 degrees, it's known as a volvulus. Researchers don't yet understand the actual cause of this life-threatening condition, but this much is known:

· Bloat generally affects dogs between 4 and 7 years of age. About two-thirds of those affected are males.

· It primarily affects large-breed (over 50 pounds), deep-chested dogs such as Bloodhounds, Boxers, Doberman Pinschers, German Shepherds, Great Danes, Great Pyrenees, Irish Setters, Irish Wolfhounds, Labrador Retrievers, Saint Bernards, Standard Poodles, and Weimaraners, and but can affect any size or breed.

· Dogs who bloat tend to eat a diet consisting of large amounts of dry dog food.

· Exercise and large intakes of water immediately after eating increase the risk for bloat.

· Dogs who bloat may have a history of gastritis[G] (digestive disturbances).

· Bloat is commonly associated with stress (or any change in routine), such as boarding, surgery, breeding, showing, or travel. It may have something to do with aerophagia—swallowing air when nervous or excited.

· Bloat appears to have a hereditary link. In other words, if your dog's relatives suffered from bloat, your dog may be at greater risk than a dog without bloat in his heritage.

BLOAT CHECK

Here's how to measure your dog's abdomen, to monitor for distension should you suspect bloat (see page 211):

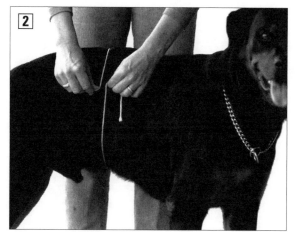

Bloat check.

1. Grab a seamstress tape, or a piece of soft rope or string that's long enough to encircle your dog's abdomen.

2. With your dog standing, loop the tape or string/rope around his abdomen, at the point where his last rib meets his waist.

3. Carefully note or mark your measurement.

4. Repeat again—in the exact same spot—in 15 minutes. If your measurement has increased, call your vet—NOW! If it's the same or smaller—and your dog isn't showing any signs of distress as outlined in the action plan on page 211—recheck him in a half-hour. If, at any time, he begins to show signs of distress or the measurement increases, call your vet *NOW!*

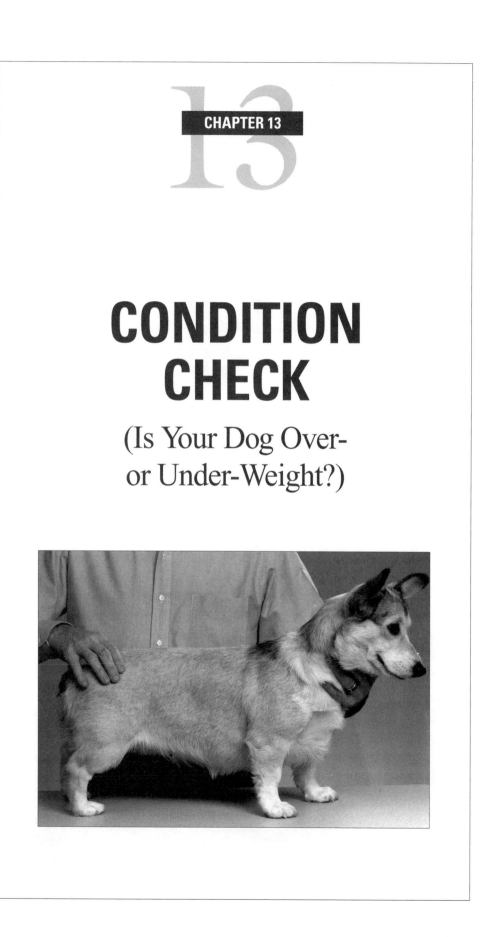

CHAPTER 13

CONDITION CHECK

(Is Your Dog Over- or Under-Weight?)

13 YOUR DOG'S CONDITION

Following are step-by-step guidelines for estimating your dog's condition—is he too fat? Too thin? Or just right? You'll need to know his current weight to calculate the proper dose of medications such as dewormers, and to provide a baseline for future reference as you monitor his condition throughout life. And you'll need an objective assessment of your dog's condition—what a dog owner sees as being "healthy," for example, might be considered obese by veterinary standards. (Obesity can be a significant risk factor for serious, even life-threatening diseases such as heart disease.)

HOW TO WEIGH YOUR DOG

Note: If your dog is too large for you to pick up, bring him to your vet's to get an accurate weight reading. Or, check your local feed store to see if they have a walk-on scale you could use.

Step 1: First, step on your bathroom scale. Record your weight.

Step 2: Pick up your dog, and step back on the scale. Record that number.

Step 3: Subtract your weight from the combined weight of you and your dog. Record your reading as a baseline.

HOW TO ESTIMATE YOUR DOG'S BODY CONDITION

Now that you've got a good assessment of current body weight, determine your dog's body condition by assessing four body-condition checkpoints. For each checkpoint, choose the description that most closely matches your dog's body. Then add up the points and divide the total by 2 to calculate his body condition score, on a scale of 1 to 10 (see opposite page). If your dog scores from 1 to 3, or 8 or above, consult your veterinarian for a safe ration adjustment to address the too-thin or too-fat condition.

THE CHECKPOINTS:

1. Ribs
    a. You have to dig to find them . . . . **5 points**
    b. They're not visible, but easily felt with your fingers . . . . **3 points**
    c. You can see them . . . . **1 point**

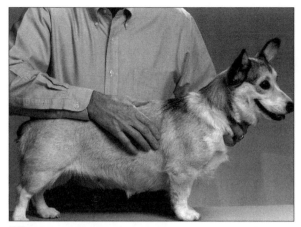

Ribs

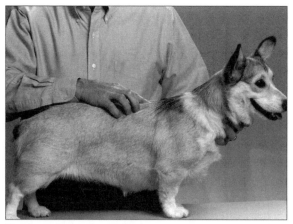

Back

2. SHOULDERS

a. A thick "loaf" of fat behind the shoulders blends them flush with your dog's ribcage . . . . **.5 points**

b. His shoulders are rounded and blend smoothly into his body . . .**3 points**

c. Bone structure of shoulders is easily seen with no fatty covering . . **1 point**

3. BACK

a. You have to dig to feel his spine . . . . **.5 points**

b. His back is level, with no visible ridge; you can easily feel his spine . . . . **3 points**

c. There's a spiny ridge visible along his back . . . . **1 point**

4. HIPS

a. His hip bones are buried under a thick layer of fat . . . . **.5 points**

b. Fat/muscle can be felt around his hipbones, but you can still feel them when you press . . . . **.3 points**

c. His hip bones are prominent . . . . . . **1 point**

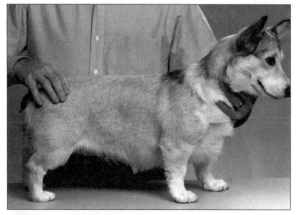

Hips

THE SCALE		
1 = Poor condition	**6** = "Show shape"	
2 = Very thin	**7** = Plump	
3 = Thin	**8** = Fat	
4 = Lean	**9** = Very fat	
5 = Neither fat nor thin	**10** = Dangerously obese	

NOTES

CHAPTER 14

The well-stocked
CANINE
FIRST-AID KIT

14

The well-stocked
CANINE FIRST-AID KIT

Talk to your veterinarian about items appropriate for your home first-aid kit. These will be used for care of your dog's minor illnesses or injuries, or to use on your veterinarian's advice before you leave for his/ her office in more serious cases. Here's a list of medications and devices to consider. Each list has a column marked "E" for items you might want to include in your quick-grab emergency kit. Unless stated otherwise on their labels, perishable items should be replaced every 3 years. Over time, medications can lose their potency or become contaminated.

CAUTION

The "COMMENTS" column, in which common uses are described, is meant to help you decide what items, if any, to stock in your home pharmacy. It is not meant to substitute for the careful, step-wise, conditional advice given in the Action Plan flow charts in Section I.

Do not administer any treatment, topically or internally, to your dog without consulting your veterinarian and the flow chart for your dog's specific symptom(s).

MEDICATIONS

PRODUCT	USE	E	COMMENTS
Stomach coative, such as Pepto Bismol, Maalox, or Kaopectate, liquid form. *Available at human pharmacies.*	To treat minor stomach or intestinal upset.	✔	Be sure to check the appropriate action plan, to be sure veterinary help isn't needed. Rule-of-thumb dosage is 1 teaspoon per 20 lbs. body weight, every 6 hours. When in doubt, consult your vet.
Ivermectin dewormer. *Available from veterinarians.*	For monthly deworming to guard against heartworms and other parasites.		Consult with your veterinarian.
Buffered or enteric coated aspirin (such as Ascriptin). *Available at human pharmacies.*	To treat minor lameness and fever.	✔	Do not dispense without consulting your vet.

EYE PRODUCTS

Eye-wash solution. *Available at human pharmacies, and from veterinarians and veterinary supply catalogs.*	For irrigation of irritated eyes.	✔	If opened, replace within 3 weeks.
Boric acid or Lacri-Lube® eye ointment. *Available at human pharmacies.*	For protection of dry and/or irritated eyes.	✔	If opened, replace within 3 weeks.

CLEANSING AND/OR DEBRIDING AGENTS			
PRODUCT	**USE**	**E**	**COMMENTS**
Saline solution* (homemade or use commercial saline for contact lens rinse).	For irrigating wounds.	✔	Can be used warm or cold.
Double-strength saline solution*.	For wet dressings when drawing is desired.		Can be used warm or cold.
3%-5% benzoyl peroxide acne cleanser. *Available in acne section at most human health and beauty aisles.*	For removing scurf from thickened or scaly skin.		Also available as leave-on gel, for use when rinsing is difficult (e.g., inclement weather).
Medicated scab softener.*	For painless removal of scabs due to infectious skin conditions.		Will keep up to 1 week; store loosely covered.
DRAWING AGENTS			
Homemade poultice.*	For drawing out swellings and festered wounds.		
DISINFECTANTS			
Betadine® (povidone iodine) or Nolvasan® (chlorhexidine) solution. *Available at human pharmacies, or from veterinarians and veterinary supply catalogs.*	To clean certain open wounds.	✔	Water-based; can be daubed, sprayed, or poured on.
Betadine® ointment. *Available at human pharmacies, and from veterinarians, and veterinary supply catalogs.*	To treat certain open wounds.	✔	The petrolatum base makes it an effective protectant.

"Homemade" substances are designated with an asterisk (*); recipes follow.

DISINFECTANTS (CONTINUED)

PRODUCT	USE	E	COMMENTS
Betadine® scrub. *Available at human pharmacies, from veterinarians, pet/feed stores, and veterinary supply catalogs.*	For certain infectious skin conditions.		The lathering base makes it a good cleanser/debrider.
Lysol® Concentrate. *Available in grocery stores.*	For disinfection of premises. (Avoid use around cats; can be toxic.)		For dilution at 2-1/2 T per gallon or 2 drops per cup of water.

EMOLLIENT, ANTI-INFLAMMATORY, ANTI-ITCH, &/OR PROTECTANT AGENTS

PRODUCT	USE	E	COMMENTS
Non-antibiotic first-aid cream, such as zinc oxide, Bactine®, Corona Ointment®, A & D Ointment®, and 100% aloe vera gel. *Available at human pharmacies, grocery stores and from veterinary supply catalogs.*	For soothing and protecting certain open wounds or burns.	✔	On burns, use water-based creams rather than petrolatum-based ointments.
Cortisone ointment. *Available at human pharmacies.*	Human product, used as a topical anti-inflammatory.	✔	Absorption/strength increased if used under waterproof bandage.
Fly repellant labelled for use on open wounds, such as Flys-Off®. *Available from pet/feed stores and veterinary supply catalogs.*	For superficial wounds or over dressings.	✔	Do not use under bandages or waterproof dressings (which would increase absorption of insecticide).
Zinc oxide or titanium dioxide cream. *Available at human pharmacies and grocery stores.*	For use as a sunblock.		
Witch hazel. *Available at human pharmacies and grocery stores.*	Topical anti-itch for certain skin conditions; anti-itch agent.		More effective/longer-lasting if used after bathing.

EMOLLIENT, ANTI-INFLAMMATORY, ANTI-ITCH, &/OR PROTECTANT AGENTS (CONTINUED)			
PRODUCT	**USE**	**E**	**COMMENTS**
Calamine lotion. *Available at human pharmacies and grocery stores.*	To dry, soothe, & protect certain skin conditions.		A good anti-itch agent.
Petroleum jelly. *Available at human pharmacies and grocery stores.*	To moisturize and protect tissues.	✔	Also aids in inserting a thermometer.

USEFUL DEVICES AND GADGETS TO HAVE ON HAND			
ITEM	**USE**	**E**	**COMMENTS**
Instant-read cook's thermometer. *Available at kitchen shops and grocery stores for about $10.*	For adjusting temperature of medicated solutions such as eye washes.		Registers in about 20 seconds.
Stethoscope *Available from drug and medical supply stores, and veterinary supply catalogs for about $6-$50.*	For accurately taking heart rate count.	✔	Choose Littman-type.
Rectal thermometer. *Available at grocery stores, human pharmacies, and from veterinary supply catalogs for $5-$10.*	For taking rectal temperature.	✔	Choose electronic-type with memory and beeper or standard glass type. Have a spare.
Chemical cold pack. *Available at human pharmacies, medical supply stores, and from veterinary supply catalogs, for about $15.*	For chilling wounds when ice is not available.	✔	Follow directions. Can cause frostbite if direct skin contact is prolonged. ➤

USEFUL DEVICES AND GADGETS TO HAVE ON HAND (CONTINUED)			
ITEM	USE	E	COMMENTS
Electric clippers, #40 blade. *Available from tack/feed stores and veterinary supply catalogs for about $100 (clippers) and about $20 for a #40 blade.*	For clipping hair from around wounds and skin conditions.		Clean blade after each use. Have professionally sharpened several times a year.
Latex or rubber examination gloves. *Available at human pharmacies and from medical supply stores or veterinary supply catalogs for about $10 per box of 100 gloves.*	For safe handling of infected body fluids; for use when applying medications; for tick removal.	✔	Choose rubber if you're allergic to latex.
Tongue depressors or plastic spoons. *Available from drug stores.*	For collecting stool samples.	✔	
Nail clippers. *Available from pet stores or through pet supply catalogs for about $7-$15.*	For trimming nails.	✔	Also include a product designed to halt bleeding, such as a stypic pencil or commercial powder such as Kwik-Stop.
Dosing syringe or eye-dropper. *Available from drug stores or veterinary supply catalogs for about $.25/syringe; $1/dropper*	For dispensing liquid medication and/or flushing wounds.	✔	Or choose a 20 cc needle-less syringe for dosing; a turkey baster works in a pinch.
Muzzle. *Available from pet stores and veterinary supply catalogs for about $5-$10.*	To safely restrain your dog during treatment.	✔	See page 329 for how to devise a homemade one.

USEFUL DEVICES AND GADGETS TO HAVE ON HAND (CONTINUED)			
ITEM	**USE**	**E**	**COMMENTS**
Bandage scissors. *Available from drug stores and from veterinary supply catalogs for about $7-$10.*	To remove bandages and dressings.	✔	Use only blunt-edge scissors against your dog's skin.
Trigger-type spray bottle. *Available at grocery and variety stores for about $2 each.*	For pressurized irrigation of wounds with saline solution.		Alternative: 30-60 cc syringe with blunted 18-gauge needle.
Tweezers. *Available at grocery and drug stores for about $2.*	For tick removal.		Choose a style with wide-tipped pinschers, to reduce the risk of rupturing the tick as you remove it.
Q-Tips. *Available at grocery and drug stores for about $2-$5 per package.*	For ear cleaning and to apply medication.		Keep a handful from your family's supply at the ready in a sealed plastic bag.

ITEM	USE/QUANTITY	E	APPROXIMATE PRICES
Bandaging materials. *Available at human pharmacies, grocery stores, and from veterinary supply catalogs.*	(1) 1-lb roll fluffy cotton	✔	$6
	(6) sanitary napkins	✔	$7/box of 30
	(6) disposable diapers	✔	$5/box of 40
	(1) package 4 x 4 gauze sponges	✔	$5 per package of 200
	(12) 4-inch rolls stretch gauze	✔	$1.50 each
	(12) 4-inch rolls Vetrap	✔	$2 each
	(12) 4-inch rolls Elastikon	✔	$3 each
	(Duct tape and electrical tape also work well.)	✔	
	(1) roll 2-inch duct tape	✔	$3 each
	(1) bandage scissors	✔	$6 each

RECIPES

Saline solution
• 1 tsp. table salt
• 1 quart water
Mix in clean container until salt is completely dissolved.

Double-strength saline solution
• 2 tsp. table salt
• 1 quart water
Mix in clean container until salt is completely dissolved.

Scab softener
• 1-16 oz. bottle mineral oil
(baby oil is okay)
• 1-16 oz. bottle 3% USP hydrogen peroxide
• 1 1/2 oz. bottle tincture of iodine
Combine all in large container. Do not close tightly. Mixture will bubble slowly and expand, and can cause a messy explosion.

Epsom salt soaking solution
• 1/2 cup Epsom salts
• 1 gallon warm water (like a hot bath)
Mix until salts are dissolved. Soak affected body part by immersing in a container (such as for a foot), or by applying a wet dressing.

Poultices (All are non-irritating)
1. Mix Epsom salts with enough warm water to make a paste.
2. Mix 1/2 cup Epsom salts + 4 cups miller's bran; mix with enough warm water to make a paste.
3. Kaopectate® mixed with enough flour or miller's bran to make a paste.
4. Sodium bicarbonate (baking soda) mixed with enough witch hazel to make a paste.
5. "Sugardine:" Table sugar mixed with enough Betadine® solution to make a paste.

All recipes by Karen E.N. Hayes, DVM, MS

15

How to
CLEAN A
WOUND

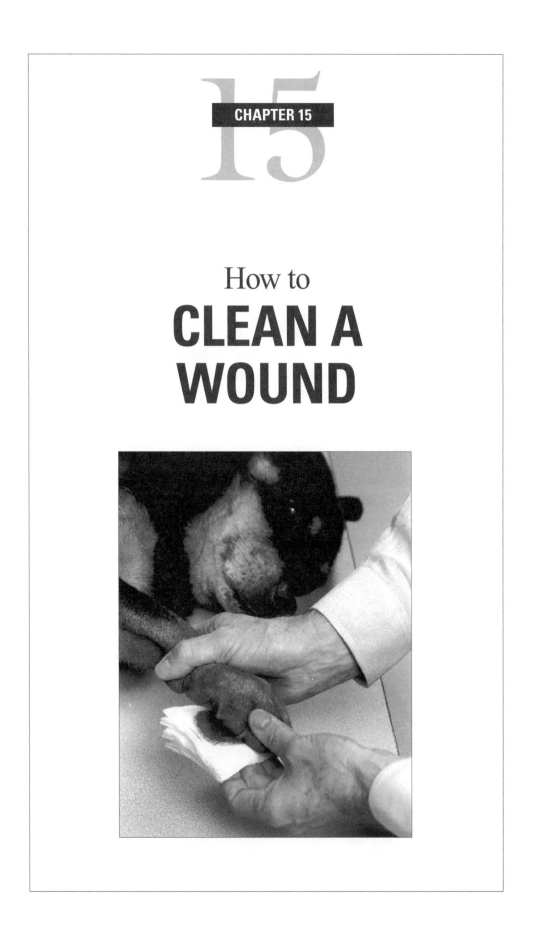

15

How to
CLEAN A WOUND

Every wound has its own special treatment requirements. These are detailed in Section I of this book—find the action plan that best describes your dog's wound, and follow the appropriate instructions. What follows are basic guidelines for removing visible dirt and debris, and invisible (bacterial or fungal) contamination.

1. Hose the wound with a hand-held sink or shower sprayer. Or irrigate it with saline solution (see page 306), using a trigger-type spray bottle or a large syringe with a blunted 18-gauge needle. Start with a gentle stream, aimed below or adjacent to the wound. Gradually move the water stream onto injured tissues, then gradually increase the intensity of the stream until it mimics the force of a Water-Pik on full power. This will help dislodge bacteria sticking to tissues. Continue until the wound appears completely clean, or until 5 minutes have gone by, whichever happens sooner.

2. If after 5 minutes of flushing, portions of the wound still appear dirty, lather it with Betadine® surgical scrub, using your clean fingertips or a brand-new infant's toothbrush. Rinse thoroughly, using saline solution for the final rinse.

3. For wounds that still look visibly dirty after Steps 1 and 2, or when cleaning deep wounds or those in which a joint may be involved, take the following steps before you leave for your veterinarian's office:

• Cover it with a thick stack of gauze pads soaked in double-strength saline solution (see page 306). The solution will moisturize tissues and loosen debris; the salt concentration will kill some bacteria and help to draw out contamination that's penetrated deeper layers.

• If the wound involves your dog's lower leg, anchor the saline-soaked pad with a spiral of stretch gauze and secure it, without excessive pressure, with an outer elastic layer, such as Vetrap®.

16

How to
ICE AN INJURY

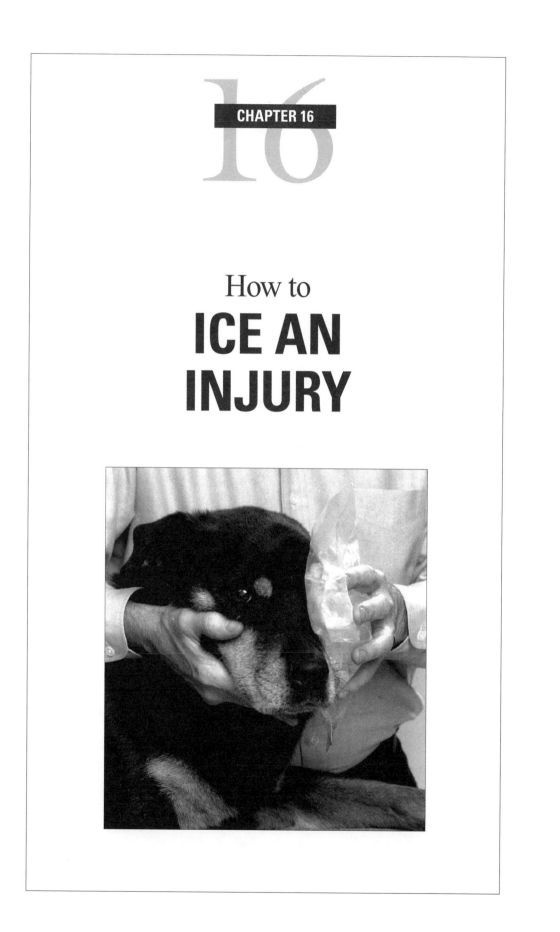

16

How to
ICE AN INJURY

Place a buffer, such as a towel or sheet cotton, between the ice pack and your dog's skin, to protect against tissue damage and help dissipate the cold. The chart at right will tell you which of three types of ice pack would be best to use based on the injury location. It'll also tell you how many layers of buffer to apply, depending on the ice pack and the state of the area being iced. If possible, avoid using chemical cold packs—they can require more protective layers of cloth between pack and skin to prevent frostbite. (However, they're wonderful when you're miles from the nearest freezer and need to ice an injury.) For how long to ice, see Icing Guidelines, below.

TYPES OF ICE PACKS

• **Rigid:** Waterproof packages containing solid slabs of ice, chemical (e.g., for picnic coolers), or frozen wet cloths.

• **Flexible:** Bags of small, frozen fragments, such as crushed ice, frozen peas, or corn kernels.

• **Chemical:** Padded pouches containing separate chambers which, when mixed, create a super-cold chemical reaction.

ICING GUIDELINES

• For injuries over intact skin, the general rule of thumb is: ICE ON 5 minutes; ICE OFF 15 minutes, one time only.

• If the skin is broken, the rule of thumb is: ICE ON 5 minutes; ICE OFF 15 minutes. Repeat 3 times in a row.

• When at least 1 layer of cloth separates the ice pack from your dog's skin, ice can be left on until it melts and is no longer pulling heat from tissues (usually around 1/2 hour). Be sure to remove the pack when it's no longer cooler than the tissue being iced. Otherwise, it might hold heat in.

INJURY LOCATION	BEST ICE PACK TO USE	METHOD
Eye or other fragile area	Flexible	If using a non-chemical ice pack, place a single layer of cotton cloth between ice and skin. If using a chemical ice pack, place a triple layer of cotton cloth between ice and skin.
Muscled area, such as forearm or hip	Rigid (on a small dog, use a flexible type)	If using a non-chemical ice pack, place pack directly against unbroken skin. If skin is broken, place a single layer of cotton cloth between pack and wound. If using a chemical ice pack, place a single layer of cotton cloth between the pack and unbroken skin. If skin is broken, place a double layer of cotton cloth between pack and wound.
Bony (e.g., leg or head)	Flexible	If using a non-chemical ice pack, place pack directly against unbroken skin. If skin is broken, place a single layer of cotton cloth between pack and wound. If using a chemical ice pack, place a single layer of cotton cloth between pack and unbroken skin. If skin is broken, place a double layer of cotton cloth between pack and wound.
Joint	Flexible	If using a non-chemical ice pack, place pack directly against unbroken skin. If skin is broken, place a single layer of cotton cloth between pack and wound. If using a chemical ice pack, place a single layer of cotton cloth between pack and unbroken skin. If skin is broken, place a double layer of cotton cloth between pack and wound.

NOTES

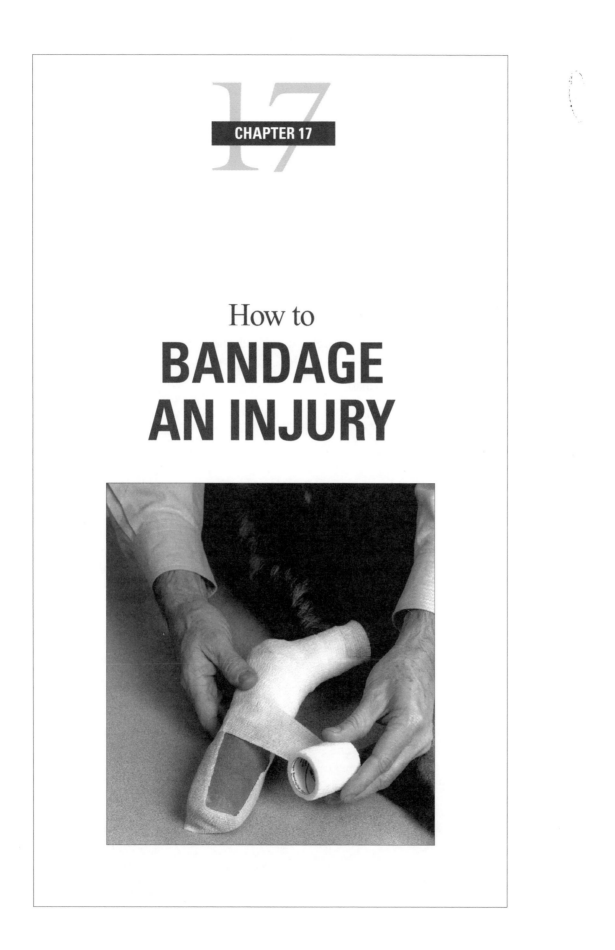

CHAPTER 17

How to
BANDAGE
AN INJURY

17

How to
BANDAGE AN INJURY

When your dog suffers an injury, you may need to bandage the area in order to help stop bleeding, limit swelling, hold tissue edges together until they can be sutured, or to prevent additional damage to a wound or suture site from contamination, insects, or scratching/biting.

Following are step-by-step instructions for common bandages your dog might need. Included are materials needed, tips, and pitfalls to avoid.

BANDAGE #1: PRESSURE BANDAGE

Sample scenario: Your dog deeply cut his pad, and is bleeding extensively. Your task: To stem the bleeding and protect the wound from contamination until you can get him to the veterinarian.

SUPPLIES NEEDED		
IDEALLY	**WHY**	**WHAT TO USE IN A PINCH**
Padding: Several layers of gauze squares.	To press against the source of the bleeding, to spread compressive forces evenly over the leg, and to absorb drainage.	Thick sanitary napkins; disposable diapers; folded washcloths or dish towels.
Security layer: Stretch gauze.	To hold padding in place.	Nylon stocking or cheesecloth cut into a strip, 3 inches wide and 1- to 2-feet long. Or this layer can be omitted.
Elastic bandage: Vetrap®; Elasti-kon®; or something similar.	To compress the bleeding tissues and stop the blood flow so clotting can occur. (Not too tight—you should be able to slip a finger between the bandage and your dog's skin.)	Ace bandage and masking tape.

BANDAGING RULES OF THUMB

1. If your primary goal is to protect the wound from contamination and/or insects:
- Consider applying a chemical barrier, such as petroleum jelly or Flys-Off® (Farnam), instead of a bandage.
- Keep the wound clean and free of insect-attracting serum and crust.

2. If your primary goal is to hold a medicated dressing or ice pack against the wound:
- Choose a light elastic bandage with no adhesive, preferably with 100 percent or greater stretchability (a 4-inch section can be stretched to 8 inches or more). The stretchier the bandage, the better it will conform to the contours of your dressing or ice pack, and the less pressure it will exert on your dog's leg.

3. If your primary goal is to limit swelling and bleeding:
- Use a minimum of 2 layers of padding to help distribute pressure evenly over fragile tissues such as tendons.
- Whenever possible, secure the padding layer in place with stretch gauze or a suitable substitute, such as a rolled-up strip of cheesecloth or nylon stocking. This will help prevent bunching and wrinkling when you compress the padding with an outer elastic layer.
- When in doubt about how much padding to apply, apply more. Extra padding layers help protect blood vessels and tendons from pressure.
- Choose an elastic bandage with 25 percent to 50 percent stretchability (a 4-inch section can be stretched to 5 to 6 inches). The less stretchy a bandaging material is, and the heftier the fabric it's made of, the greater is its ability to compress tissues (to slow or stop bleeding and swelling) and provide mechanical support. For highly moveable and hard-to-bandage areas, choose adhesive-backed elastic bandage materials for greater security and less slippage. (You should always be able to slip a finger between your dog's skin and any compression bandage.)
- If blood soaks through the bandage, don't remove it. (This would disturb any clots that may have formed, and the bleeding would start anew.) Instead, apply additional padding and elastic (compression) layers over the existing bandage. Remember— each additional layer increases compression. Use your "finger check" to be sure the bandage is not too tight.

4. If your primary goal is to hold skin edges in their proper positions:
- Gently press the skin edges in place with your fingertips, then tape a clean, dry wound dressing, such as a 1/2-inch stack of gauze sponges or a sanitary napkin, directly over the wound. Follow with padding and elastic (compression) layers as outlined above for bandaging a swelling/bleeding wound.

PRESSUE BANDAGE HOW-TO:

Step 1. Center the padding material over the wound. Choose a pad that's large enough to completely cover it. Here we used a stack of gauze pads. ➤

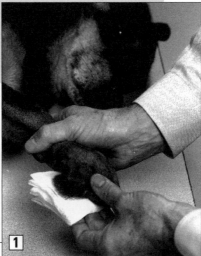

1

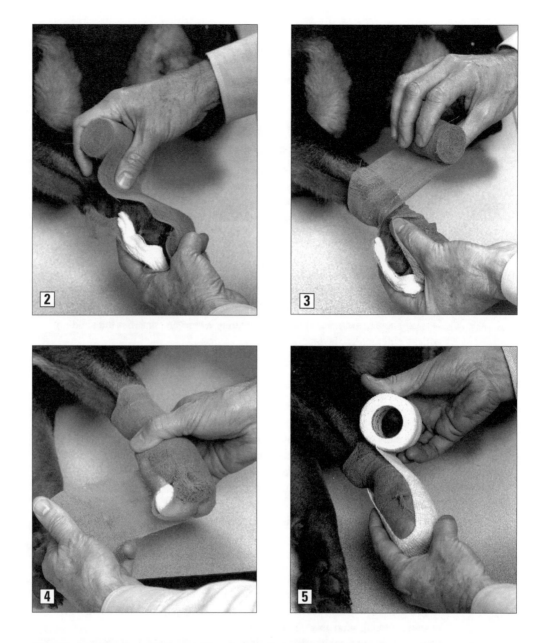

Step 2. Secure the padding with a layer of stretch gauze. To wrap a foot, as shown, unwrap a length of gauze long enough to extend lengthwise over your dog's foot, as shown, extending several inches above his foot on both the bottom and top sides. Hold the gauze's free end in place with one hand...

Step 3. ...using that hand's thumb to hold in place the upper layer as you twist the roll at a 90-degree angle (also see Step 6), so you can being spiraling down the leg. Use enough pressure to firmly secure the padding material, but not so much pressure that you can't insert a finger between your dog's skin and the wrap's upper edge.

Step 4. Continue wrapping down the leg, until you've completely covered the

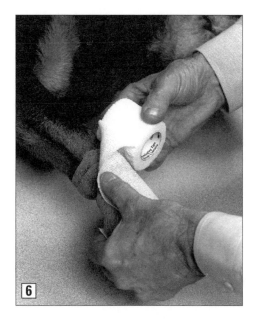

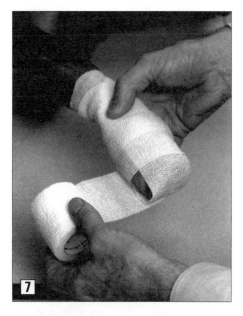

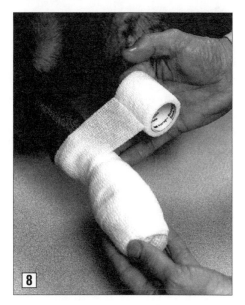

padding material with several layers of gauze. Cut the gauze, holding the free end firmly in place with one hand or loosely anchor the end with adhesive tape.

Step 5. Finish with an elastic bandage layer. Begin by using the lengthwise-wrap technique you used in Step 2.

Step 6. Hold the elastic bandage's free end in place against the bottom of your dog's foot with the fingers of one hand, while the thumb on that hand secures the top length of bandage as you twist the roll at a 90-degree angle.

Step 7. Securely apply several layers of elastic bandage, leaving enough room to admit only your pinky finger between it and your dog's leg. Start with an anchor loop above the wound (or around the top of the foot, if you're wrapping a foot as we are here). Then spiral downward, overlapping each round by half the bandage material's width to secure the padding material in place over the wound.

Step 8. Spiral back upward, finishing where you started. Secure with adhesive tape.

Step 9. If blood should soak through the bandage, repeat Steps 1 to 8 over the existing wrap. If you were to remove it, you'd risk disturbing blood clots that may have formed.

BANDAGE #2: BASIC LEG BANDAGE

Sample Scenario: Your dog's leg has a wound that's hot and swollen. He's licking at it as the flies buzz around it. Your job is to cover the wound and limit swelling until you can get your dog to a vet.

SUPPLIES NEEDED		
IDEALLY	**WHY**	**WHAT TO USE IN A PINCH**
Padding: Several layers of gauze squares.	To press against the source of the bleeding, to spread compressive forces evenly over the leg, and to absorb drainage.	Thick sanitary napkins; disposable diapers; folded washcloths, or dish towels.
Security layer: Stretch gauze.	To hold padding in place.	Nylon stocking or cheese-cloth cut into a strip, 3 inches wide and 1- to 2-feet long. Or this layer can be omitted.
Elastic bandage: Vetrap®; Elasti-kon®; or something similar.	To compress the bleeding tissues and stop the blood flow so clotting can occur.	Ace bandage and masking tape.

BASIC LEG BANDAGE HOW-TO:

Step 1. Apply an absorbent layer of padding, such as sheet cotton, gauze squares, a sanitary pad, or a disposable diaper, cut to fit. Here, we used an initial layer of a sanitary pad over the wound, to absorb any discharge, then...

Step 2. ...applied a second layer of padding by using a cut-in-half disposable diaper, which perfectly fits the length of this dog's lower leg.

Step 3. When using a diaper, securely wrap it around your dog's leg, with the padding side against the wound...

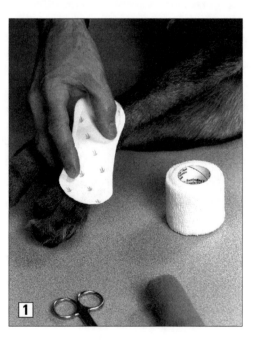

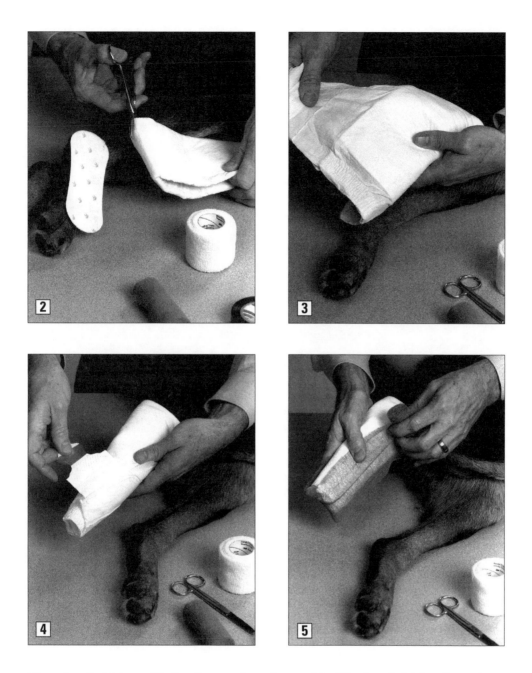

Step 4. ...finishing with the diaper tab to the outside. Use it to hold the diaper in place, as shown, while you reach for the gauze layer.

Step 5. Unwrap a length of gauze long enough to extend lengthwise from above the back of your dog's hock (for a hind leg), around and over his foot, as shown, extending to an equal point on the front side of his leg. (The gauze should extend about 1/2" above the padding material on both sides.) Hold the gauze's free end in place on the bottom side of your dog's leg with one hand...

Step 6. ...while the thumb on that hand secures the top length of gauze as you ➤

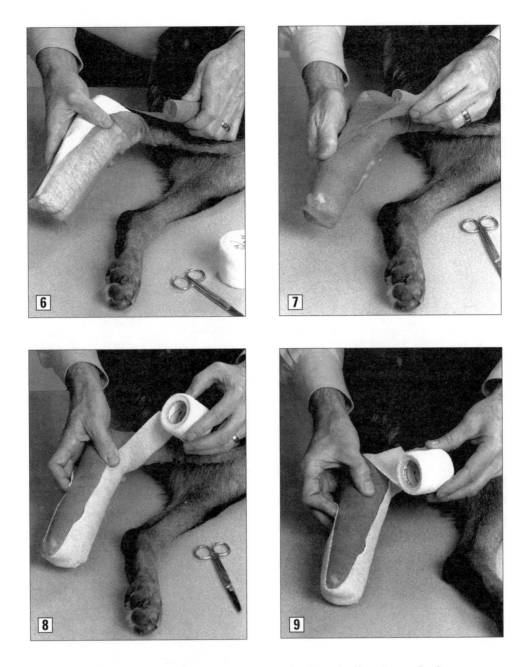

twist the roll at a 90-degree angle so you can begin spiraling down the leg.

Step 7. Spiral down the leg, overlapping each previous round by half the width of the bandage material. Continue down until you've completely wrapped the foot, then spiral back upward, stopping when you've reached your starting point. Secure with a piece of adhesive tape.

Step 8. Apply the elastic bandage, using the same pattern as in Steps 5, 6, and 7, exerting just enough stretch...

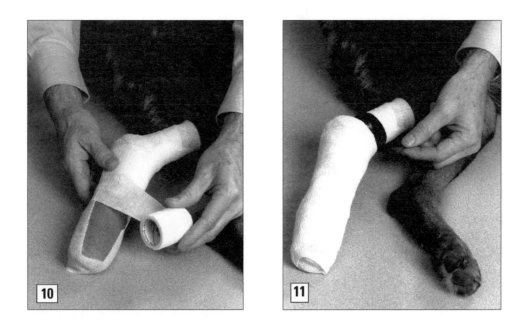

Step 9. ...to make the bandage snug and secure, but not so tight than you're unable to admit your pinkie finger between the leg and bandage at any point around the top.

Step 10. Continue spiraling down, then back up the leg to your starting point.

Step 11. Cut the bandaging material, then secure the free end with a piece of adhesive tape. (We used electrical tape, which is inexpensive, generally found in the garage, and has great adhesive properties.)

BANDAGE #3: THE SIMPLE SOCK WRAP

Sample Scenario: Your dog has a minor abrasion on his pad, hind foot, or leg that's been attracting dirt and insects. Your job is to protect the area from ➤

SUPPLIES NEEDED		
IDEALLY	**WHY**	**WHAT TO USE IN A PINCH**
A child's cotton tube sock (or an infant sock, if your dog is a toy or small breed).	The cotton is breath-able–and washable.	An adult sock cut to fit.
Adhesive tape, such as ban-dage tape and scissors. (We like electrical tape, for it's adhesive properties.)	To hold the sock in place.	Masking or duct tape; Ace bandage and masking tape.

outside contaminants—with a minimum of trouble and expense. (Sock wraps also work well to prevent your dog from licking/chewing a spot.)

SIMPLE SOCK WRAP HOW-TO:

Step 1. Assemble your supplies.

Step 2. Gently pull the tube sock over your dog's leg, as shown.

Step 3. Secure with a strip of adhesive tape above your dog's hock, as shown, which will help prevent slippage. Place enough tension in the tape to hold the sock in place, but not so much that you can't slip a pinkie between it and your dog's leg.

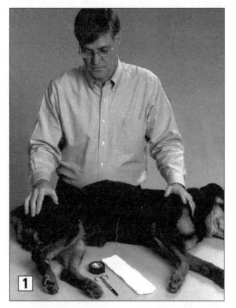

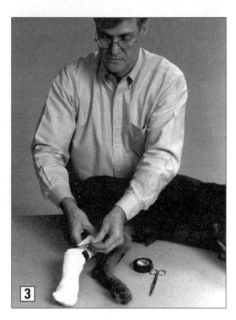

FRONT-LEG SOCK-WRAP TIPS:

While front legs can be fitted with a sock wrap, they're more of a challenge than rear legs, as the sock is more prone to slippage. Try these two stay-up tips:

1. Choose a sock long enough to extend above your dog's elbow. The joint will serve to help anchor the sock, thus helping to block slippage.

2. Fold a length of tape in half lengthwise, sticky side out. Tape it around your dog's leg, above the area to be covered. Pull up the sock and press it to the adhesive surface.

BANDAGE #4: THE BASIC EAR/HEAD WRAP

Sample Scenario: You've discovered an aural hematoma[G] or other injury on your dog's ear. Your task is to prevent further head-shaking/scratching damage by covering the ear and securing it to your dog's head, until you can get to your vet's.

SUPPLIES NEEDED		
IDEALLY	**WHY**	**WHAT TO USE IN A PINCH**
A cotton dish towel or small bath towel (depending on your dog's size), folded lengthwise in thirds.	To act as a padding layer as well as to restrict ear movement.	A similar-sized length of sweat-shirt material, or wide-width ace bandage.
Duct tape.	To hold the wrap in place.	Electrical tape, elastic bandaging material.

BASIC EAR/HEAD WRAP HOW-TO:

Step 1. Holding one free end in place with your hand, securely wrap the towel over the top of your dog's head, as shown.

Step 2. Take the free end under your dog's neck... ➤

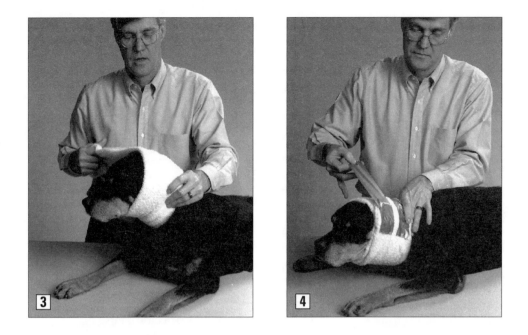

Step 3. ...wrapping until you've reached the towel's end. Apply enough tension to the towel that it stays in place, but not so much that you restrict your dog's throat. (You should be able to slip a pinkie finger between the wrap and your dog's skin. If you can't, the wrap is too tight; if you can slip more than your pinkie in, the wrap is too loose.)

Step 4. Use several lengths of duct tape to secure the towel around your dog's head, as shown, placing the tape 4" - 6" over the free edge, to tape the towel to itself.

BANDAGE #5: THE ABDOMINAL WRAP

Sample Scenario: Your female dog has just been spayed, or your dog has had other abdominal surgery. He or she is chewing at her sutures. Your task is to prevent damage to the area by protecting it from chewing.

SUPPLIES NEEDED		
IDEALLY	**WHY**	**WHAT TO USE IN A PINCH**
A cotton hand towel or bath towel (depending on your dog's size).	To act as protective padding against your dog's chewing efforts.	Any sized towel or towel-like bath mat large enough to encircle your dog's abdomen.
Duct tape.	To hold the wrap in place.	Electrical tape, elastic bandaging material.

ABDOMINAL WRAP HOW-TO:

Step 1. Fold the towel in thirds, lengthwise.

Step 2. With your dog standing or lying down, position the folded towel beneath his belly as shown. Hold one free end of the towel in place over the top of his back.

Step 3. Holding that end firmly in place, grasp the other end of the towel with your free hand and pull it snugly toward you.

Step 4. Continue wrapping the towel around your dog's belly until you reach the end, continuing to apply pressure to the wrap's starting layer, to prevent slippage.

Step 5. Secure with lengths of duct tape.

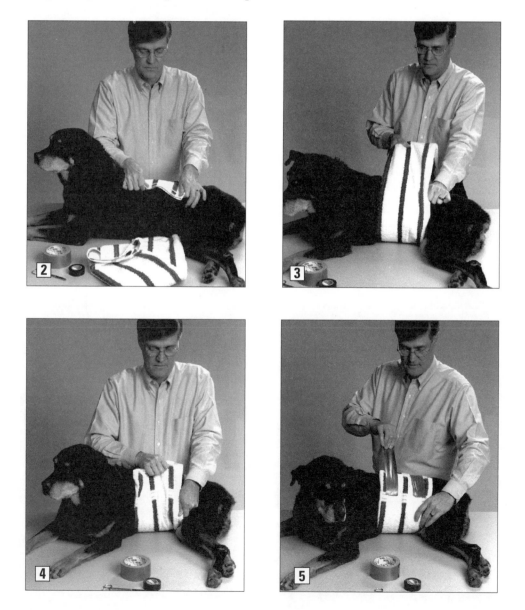

NOTES

18

RESTRAINT

18 RESTRAINT

Fear and/or pain can trigger a snap or bite from even the friendliest of dogs. Knowing how to safely restrain your dog in an emergency—or even when performing unpopular procedures—can help you avoid inadvertent injury and therefore provide the care he needs. Other forms of restraint can help prevent your dog from inflicting harm to a healing wound. Following are four basic forms of restraint that can help you through most common emergencies and/or management situations.

HOW TO APPLY A MUZZLE

There are two kinds of muzzles you can use. You can stock your first-aid kit with a commercial brand of muzzle made to fit your dog's size, or you can improvise with a makeshift version. Muzzles not only work to prevent bites, but also can act as a distraction for your dog, which can help keep him calmer and more accepting than he would be without one. Here's how to apply both types.

HOW TO APPLY A COMMERCIAL MUZZLE

Step 1. Holding the strap end of the muzzle, place it under his chin, as shown.

Step 2. In a smooth, rapid movement, bring the opening over his nose/mouth.

Step 1: Place muzzle under his chin.

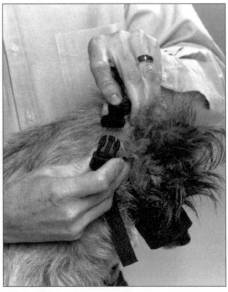

Step 2 & 3: Bring over nose and fasten.

Step 3. Immediately connect the fasteners.

Step 4. Adjust the straps such that you can slip a finger between the straps and your dog's neck. Any tighter, and the muzzle will be too tight, causing your dog to resist. Any looser, and he could slip out of its constraints.

HOW TO APPLY A MAKESHIFT MUZZLE

Step 1. Recruit a helper to hold your dog securely from behind. Grab a bath-robe sash, a neck tie,

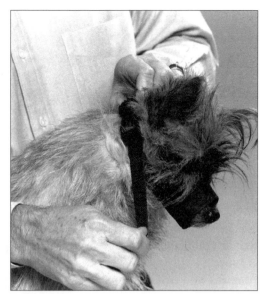

Step 4: Properly adjust straps.

stocking, roll of gauze, or thick, soft cotton rope. Shape a loop in the center of the material by tying it loosely into the first stage of a simple overhand knot, as shown.

Step 2. Quickly slip the loop over your dog's nose/mouth, and tighten so that it's snug enough to stay in place, but not so snug as to restrict breathing. (You should be able to slip a finger between the muzzle and your dog's skin.) ➤

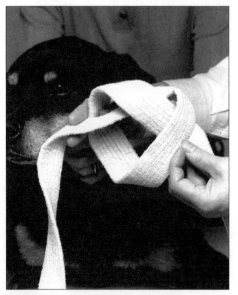

Step 1: Shape a loop, as shown.

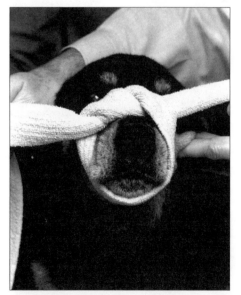

Step 2: Slip over nose and tighten.

Step 3. Crisscross the free ends beneath your dog's chin...

Step 4. ...then bring them back over your dog's neck, behind his ears. Tie a square knot keeping your dog's nose pulled down toward his chest (when he tries to raise his head, the muzzle will tighten). Use enough tension that you can slip a finger between the knot and your dog's neck, but not so loose that he could slip out of the restraint.

Step 5. The finished muzzle.

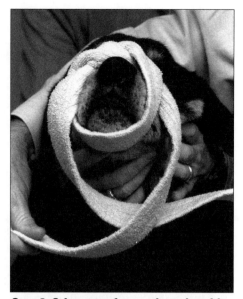

Step 3: Crisscross free ends under chin.

Step 4: Then tie ends over dog's neck.

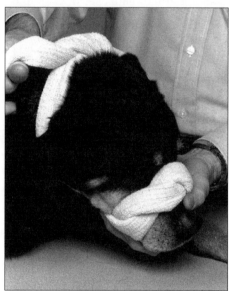

Step 5: Finished muzzle.

NEVER muzzle your dog if he appears to be having trouble breathing, or is vomiting. If you were to do so, you could impede his airflow or cause him to choke on or aspirate his vomit. Consult your veterinarian for advice in either situation.

STOP!

RESTRAINT HOLD

Your ability to safely restrain your dog (or to show a helper how to do so) during emergency or routine treatment can make the situation easier on all involved. Here's the correct way to use a restraint hold on your dog.

Step 1. Muzzle your dog, if necessary. (See page 328.) If you opt not to, keep your face well away from his.

Step 2. For a large dog, have him lie down and position yourself behind him. (We'll give you directions for a dog facing leftward; simply reverse them for a dog lying in the opposite direction.) Wrap your left arm around the dog's neck in a secure "choke hold." (Keep the crook of your elbow against your dog's throat to avoid impeding his airflow.) Use your right hand to grasp your dog's forearm at the elbow, thus restricting his movement with that leg. Use your left forearm and elbow to hold the dog's body next to you. And use only the amount

Step 2, Restraint hold.

of restraint necessary to prevent escape, tightening your grip when your dog struggles, then loosening it when he stays still. If you were to use a constant "death grip" on him when he was compliant, you could invite a battle.

Step 3. For a medium- or small-sized dog, squat down and place one arm under and around the dog's neck, such that your fist points toward your shoulder. (Be sure that the crook of your elbow is under the dog's neck, so his breathing isn't restricted.) Cup your other arm under your dog's belly, just in front of his hind legs, and lift to a standing position. Hold the dog firmly against your body if he should struggle, relaxing your grip when he complies.

LEG HOBBLES

Use these simple masking-tape hobbles on your dog's hind legs to help prevent him from scratching at a wound or sutures on his body, head, or neck.

Step 1. Tear off a length of masking tape long enough to encircle one leg above the hock joint, and to reach a distance of about 4 to 6 inches to the other leg. ➤

(The proper length will depend on the size of your dog. It needs to be long enough to enable your dog to walk, but not so long that he can scratch.) Double over several inches on one end, sticking the two sticky sides together.

Step 2. Place the non-stick side of the doubled-over end around your dog's leg above the hock joint (to prevent slippage), as shown. (The non-stick end will prevent hair pull-out as your dog moves, and when you remove the hobbles.)

Step 3. Forming a cuff-like band around the leg, secure it to the sticky side of the tape with enough tension that it won't slip over the hock, but not so much that you can't slip a finger between the tape cuff and your dog's leg.

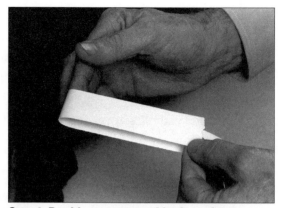

Step 1: Double over several inches of tape.

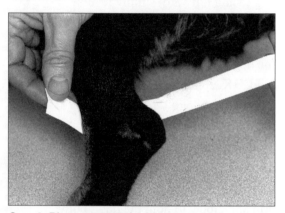

Step 2: Place non-stick side around leg.

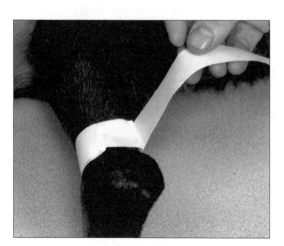

Step 3: Form a cuff-like band.

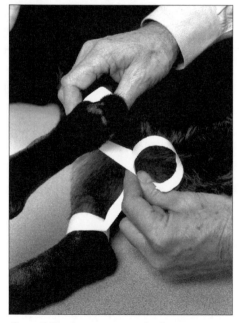

Step 4: Repeat on opposite leg.

Step 4. Repeat on the opposite leg.

Step 5. Connect the hobbles, by affixing the free end of each tape strip to the cuff on the opposite leg.

Step 6. Compress the two tape strips together between your dog's legs, by pressing the sticky sides together.

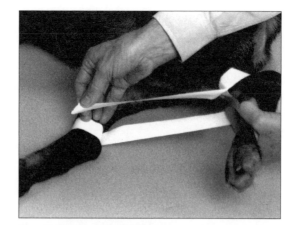

Step 5: Connect hobbles.

Step 7. The finished hobbles. Your dog will be able to stand and walk, but not reach up with his hind legs to scratch at his head, neck, or body. And, should he get into trouble, the tape should snap before he can injure himself.

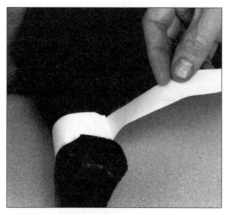

Step 6: Compress tape.

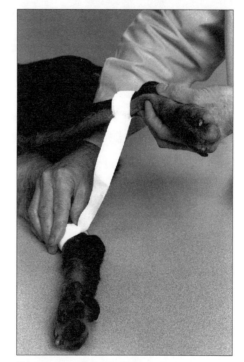

Step 7: Finished hobbles.

CHEW-RESTRICTING CONES/COLLARS

Your dog is worrying a hot spot^G or chewing at a wound or sutures. What do you do? Reach for the cone (also known as an Elizabethan collar). Available through your veterinarian, at pet stores, or through veterinary supply catalogs, such cones enable your dog to drink, but restrict his ability to chew. (***Tip:*** *Before heading out to buy one or placing a phone order, be sure to measure the diameter of your* ➤

dog's neck.) Some cones come equipped with slits that enable them to accommodate your dog's collar. Others are designed to fit without a collar. Some have slit fasteners, others fasten with strips of Velcro® brand hook and loop fasteners. (The latter are a snap to get on and off.) Those made of clear material are less visually restrictive.

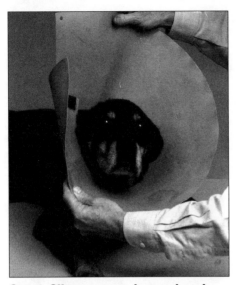

Step 1: Slip narrow end around neck.

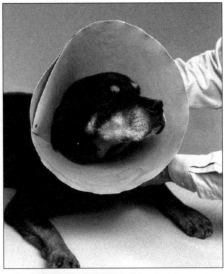

Step 2: Fasten snugly.

Step 1. Slip the narrow end of the cone around your dog's neck, as shown.

Step 2. Fasten it snugly around his neck. You should be able to slip a finger between the cone and your dog's neck, but no more.

CONE HEAD TIPS:

• When you first put on the cone, your dog may paw at his head and/or walk backward (or into walls). Hang in there. Most dogs quickly adapt to the cone's confines and have no problem wearing it.

• For ease of eating, remove it at feed time, replacing it immediately after your dog finishes his meal.

CHAPTER 19

How to safely
TRANSPORT AN INJURED DOG

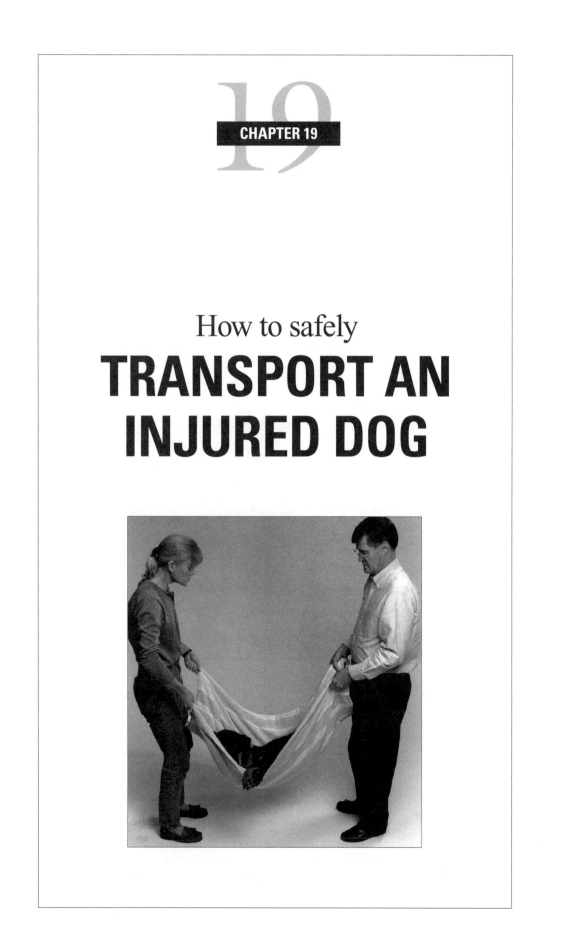

19

How to safely
TRANSPORT AN INJURED DOG

If your dog has suffered a traumatic injury that renders him partially or totally immobile (such as a fall, being hit by a car, or a spinal-disk problem that's left him partially paralyzed), your ability to transport him to an emergency clinic or your veterinarian's–without exacerbating his injury–is key. That means minimal movement of the dog is in order.

Following are two modes of transport, one for small dogs, and one for large dogs, that will help enable you to quickly and safely get your dog to help. (*Note: Call your veterinarian before leaving, so he or she can be prepared for your arrival. Be sure to give him/her a synopsis of the injury, and an estimated arrival time.*)

SMALL DOG TRANSPORT

Small dog transport.

Step 1. Muzzle your dog. (See page 328.) Carefully insert your forearm lengthwise, between your dog's hind legs. Cradle his chest in your hand, between his front legs. Keeping your dog's back as straight as possible, rise to a standing position. Use your free hand to steady him on your arm. (This is not only a good way to transport a dog with a suspected back injury, but also is good for a dog with leg trauma.) Talk soothingly to your dog. Your ability to stay calm in a crisis will help him to do the same, minimizing the risk of a struggle. Have someone drive you to your vet's. (*Note: If you don't have the strength in your arms to support your dog as shown, you can use a small box for transport, taking extreme care to minimize back movement and contact with any wounds.*)

LARGE DOG TRANSPORT

Step 1. Recruit a helper. Muzzle your dog, if he's frightened or in pain. (See page 328.) Grab a blanket (or coat, or poncho). Create a makeshift stretcher out of the blanket by folding it over until it's about 50 percent larger than your dog. (If it's too big, it'll not only be awkward to maneuver, but also will sag deeply under your dog's weight, adding excess movement to any injuries and perhaps causing him to panic.) Lay the blanket beside your dog. Carefully roll him over, onto the stretcher. Position your helper at your dog's tail end, and yourself at your dog's front end. Squat down, then grasp the blanket as close to your dog's body as possible, to minimize sagging.

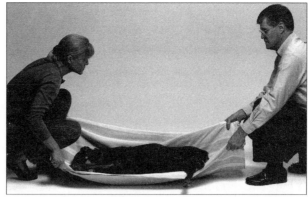
Large dog transport, Step 1: Carefully roll your dog onto the blanket.

Step 2. On the count of three, have your helper slowly rise in synch with you, being careful to push up with your legs and keep your back straight, rather than lifting with your back (which could cause a strain). Carefully walk the dog to a vehicle, place him inside with minimal movement, and seek help. (***Note:*** *If you place him and the blanket on a car seat, be sure to have someone sit with him, so he doesn't slide off the seat onto the floor.*)

Large dog transport, Step 2: Slowly rise on the count of three.

REAR-END SLING

If your dog has a chronic[G] problem that renders him weak or unstable in his hindquarters, you can help him move around with the use of a sling under his abdomen. It acts to support his hind end, while encouraging him to "walk" with his hind legs, which will help keep his joints and muscles more flexible. It's a great way to help a dog recovering from spinal or orthopedic surgery to move around and to go to the bathroom. It's also good for a dog that has advanced hip dysplasia[G] or a neurological problem that's compromised movement in his hindquarters. (***Caveat:*** *Avoid using such a device on a dog that's suffered an acute[G] traumatic injury to his spine or hindquarters. Doing so could* ➤

exacerbate the injury, further damaging your dog. Instead, turn to the other emergency transport suggestions in this chapter.)

What you'll need: A leash and a sheet, bath towel, fleece saddle cinch, or other type of soft, flexible item that can be fashioned into a belly-band-type sling. (It needs to be strong enough to support your dog's weight, and long enough for you to comfortably grasp each end when the dog is standing.)

Step 1: Twist the sheet lengthwise, or fold the bath towel lengthwise, to form a band that's about 4 to 6 inches wide. (Any narrower, and it could make your dog uncomfortable.)

Step 2. Attach a leash to your dog's collar, so you have a way to direct him.

Step 3. Slip the band under your dog's abdomen, behind his rib cage and just in front of his hind legs. Slowly lift him to a standing position. (We sewed nylon handles onto the ends of a folded terry-cloth towel, to make lifting the dog's weight easier—you only need one hand with this design. A fleece, Western-style saddle cinch also works well, as the buckles at either end make good handles.)

Step 4. Use the leash to slowly direct your dog forward as you support his hindquarters with the sling. If his hind legs can bear some weight, keep your support as minimal as possible, to encourage him to use the legs. Just be ready to "catch" him if he should lose his balance.

Step 3: Slip the band under your dog's abdomen.

Step 4: Support his hindquarters as you lead him forward.

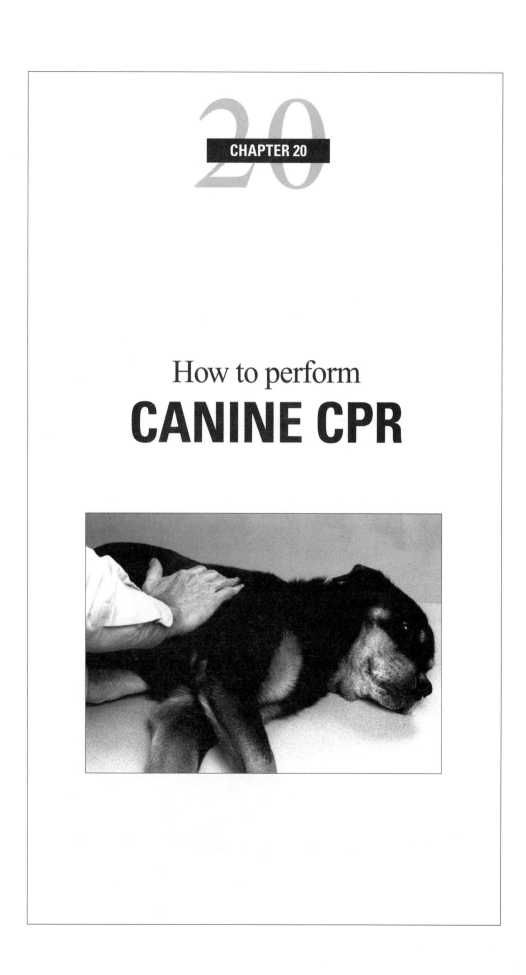

CHAPTER 20

How to perform
CANINE CPR

20

How to perform
CANINE CPR

You find your dog unconscious and unresponsive. Before you call your veterinarian, take these two life-saving steps:

• Check to see if your dog is breathing, by looking for the rise and fall of his chest. If he's not, go immediately to "Artificial Respiration," below.

• Check to see if your dog's heart is beating. Feel just behind his left elbow for the beat. If you can't feel one, press your fingers into his femoral artery to feel for a pulse. (See page 234.) If you still can't feel one, go immediately to "Chest Compression," page 342. (If his heart has stopped, he's likely not breathing, has dilated pupils, and pale gray gums.)

• If your dog's breathing and heartbeat have stopped, he may need a combination of artificial respiration and chest compression, known as CPR.

Once you've completed your resuscitation efforts, immediately call your veterinarian. Then check the area for signs of an obvious cause of your dog's problem.

The Truth about Resuscitation

If your dog is in full-blown cardiac arrest, your efforts may not save him. Even the best-equipped canine emergency centers can have less than 5 percent success rates in such cases. Still, it never hurts to try, and you could beat the odds and save your dog's life.

ARTIFICIAL RESPIRATION

Step 1. Place your dog on his side. With both hands, firmly grasp his muzzle, compressing his lips and mouth to create an air-tight "seal."

Step 2. Pull your dog's head and neck toward you, away from his body, to open his airways. Then form a seal with your lips over his nostrils and blow gently for several seconds,

Step 1: Form a seal with your hands.

CPR SAVVY

• If your dog's lack of breathing and/or heartbeat is due to **electrocution** from biting a plugged-in cord, DO NOT TOUCH THE DOG until you unplug the cord. Otherwise, you could be electrocuted. If you can't unplug it, remove the necessary fuse. If you can't do that, use ropes or a wooden pole *(nothing metallic!)* to move the dog away from the power source before attempting any resuscitation.

• If your dog is a **drowning** victim, remove as much water as possible from him before attempting CPR. If he's a small dog, suspend him by his hind legs for 15 to 20 seconds. If he's too large to lift completely off the ground, raise his hind end such that his head tips down, to facilitate drainage.

• If your dog has vomited, clear his airways using your fingers, and/or by tipping his head down (see above), to help reduce the risk of choking. Maintain a downward head tilt in the event he should vomit again, to help prevent aspiration into his lungs.

watching for his chest to rise. (If his chest doesn't rise, you may not have extended his head and neck far enough, may not be blowing forcefully enough, may need to adjust your hands to better seal your dog's lips, or he may have an obstruction (see page 159). If, despite your efforts you can't inflate your dog's lungs, call your veterinarian.

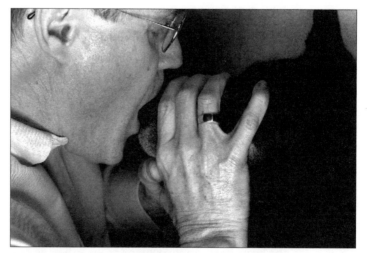

Step 2: Blow gently, watching for his chest to rise.

Step 3. Cease your blowing efforts and listen for your dog to expel the air. Repeat every 5 seconds for 1 minute, then recheck your dog's breathing. Continue until he begins to breathe or until his heart stops beating. (Once he begins to breathe, call your veterinarian.) If he fails to breathe and his heart quits beating, proceed to "Chest Compression." ➤

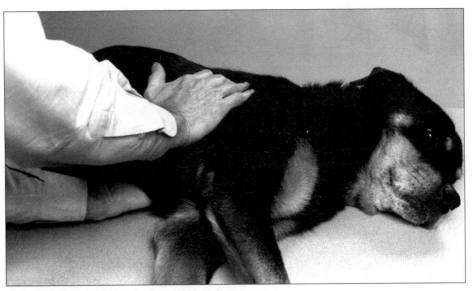

Step 2: Chest compression on a large dog.

CHEST COMPRESSION

Step 1. Complete Steps 1 to 3 of "Artificial Respiration."

Step 2. If your dog's heart is still not beating, place him on his side on a hard, flat surface. (It doesn't matter which side; you'll be compressing both sides of his chest.) Stand or kneel facing his belly. Place the palm of one hand just behind his elbow, as shown. Place your other hand on the opposite side of your dog's chest. Rapidly and firmly compress his chest between the palms of your hands 6 times, immediately releasing after the compression. (Adjust the amount of pressure you use according to your dog's size. For a small dog, use flat-fingered pressure; for a medium-sized dog, keep your fingers extended and closed as you push; and for a large dog, extend and open your fingers, to maximize your compression.)

Step 3. Wait 5 seconds for the chest to expand, then repeat Steps 2 and 3 until the heart beats on its own, or no heartbeat is felt for 5 to 10 minutes.

CHAPTER 21

SNAKEBITE!

Dennis Paulson

21 SNAKEBITE!

You either witnessed your dog have a close encounter with a poisonous snake, or you suspect he may have been bitten, due to rapid swelling in an area, and/or the presence of fang marks. **THIS IS A TRUE EMERGENCY!** Here's what to do.

Step 1. Don't panic. You'll need to act fast, but stay cool in order to give your dog his best shot at survival. Your primary goal will be to get him to help ASAP, but panic and excitement will make your efforts to aid him less successful.

> **CAUTION**
>
> If you opt to kill the snake, bring the whole carcass with you to the veterinarian. But handle with care! Dead snakes can still inflict venomous bites for up to an hour after being killed.

Step 2. Separate your dog from the snake. Without endangering yourself, separate your dog from the snake to minimize the risk of multiple bites.

Step 3. Restrain your dog. With the snake gone, excitement and exercise are now his enemies. In order to help slow down the absorption of venom in his system, your dog must be kept quiet and calm. Put a leash on him and either tie him or have a helper keep him still. Talk to him in soothing tones. If the dog isn't having trouble breathing, and doesn't have a bite wound (or swelling) on his face or head, consider muzzling him (see page 328). Venomous snakebites are extremely painful and could prompt him to bite out of pain and/or fear.

Step 4. Make a visual identification. If you're able to do so without risking a bite, quickly observe the snake, taking a mental picture so you can relay the description to your veterinarian. That way, your vet will know the appropriate antivenin to administer. (He or she will want to know the size and type of snake, if you can provide that information. If not, take note of its color, shape, and size. Any detail will help.)

Step 5. Load your dog. If you have a small dog, carry him to your car, to limit movement that could get his heart pumping harder and thus speed venom through his system. If you have a large dog, either drive your car to him, or slowly walk him to the vehicle.

Step 6. Get to the nearest vet. Drive the speed limit to the nearest vet in your area that has antivenin. (See "Snakebite Do's and Don'ts," page 346.)

SNAKE SAVVY

Two kinds of poisonous snakes are found in the United States: pit vipers and elapines. Familiarize yourself with those living in to your area:

SNAKE	TYPE	DISTINGUISHING CHARACTERISTICS	BITE SYMPTOMS
Copperhead	Pit viper	Adult average of 22" to 36" with copper-colored head and dark-brown cross bands; generally found in the South and Southeast.	Pain and rapid-onset swelling, with tissue discoloration; dark, bloody fluid oozing from fang marks (if not hidden by swelling); restlessness, panting, drooling; weakness; seizures; collapse; shock.
Coral snake	Elapines	Adult average of 20" to 30", with vivid coral-red, yellow, and black bands ("red and yellow, kill a fellow"); small head with black nose; unlike pit vipers, rather than a strike-and-retreat attack, coral snakes must chew on their victims in order to release venom; the burrowing snakes are generally found in the Southern U.S.	Primarily neurological, including incontinence, paralysis, convulsions, and coma; minimal swelling; can include vomiting and diarrhea; no large fang marks are visible.
Moccasin	Pit viper	Adult average of 20" to 48"; thick-bodied, olive-brown with dark crossbars; can be aggressive; generally found near water in the Southeast.	See Copperhead.
Rattlesnake	Pit viper	Various species; can range from 12" to 72" in average adult length; generally brown with mottled markings; distinguished by a series of horny rings at the end of its tail that produce a rattling or buzzing sound; even small rattlers can be deadly.	See Copperhead.

SNAKEBITE DO'S AND DONT'S

• **DO** call your vet to find out if he routinely stocks antivenin before you have a snakebite emergency. That way, you won't waste precious time in a snakebite emergency driving from clinic to clinic in search of one that has antivenin. If your vet doesn't keep it on hand (an many vets don't, due to the drug's high cost and short shelf life), ask him or her to tell you the nearest vet or emergency clinic that does.

• **DON'T** apply a tourniquet above the bite site. Doing so could cause more problems than it solves by restricting circulation to the affected area, exacerbating the toxin's affect.

• **DON'T** cut incisions above the fang marks and attempt to suck out the venom. First, such incisions don't dispel enough venom to make a difference, and thus merely increase the degree of injury to your dog. Second, you could absorb venom through a sore in your mouth, putting yourself at risk of a toxic reaction.

• **DON'T** apply ice or other such cooling agent to the bite site. Doing so could impair circulation already compromised by the venom.

• **DO** stay cool and calm, and get your dog to help–*NOW!*

Snakebite Savvy

• Fatal snakebites are more common in dogs than in other domestic animals. That's because of the relatively small size of a dog compared to the amount of venom injected—the bite of even a small snake can be fatal. Also dogs are naturally curious, and lead with their head and nose, putting them at risk for bites on those areas.

• Still, not all venomous snakebites cause a severe reaction. While some dogs may lapse into shock within minutes of a bite, others may have only slight swelling at the bite site. The amount of venom injected will generally influence the severity of the reaction.

• The amount of venom injected is usually determined by the snake's size and the length of time since its last feeding. (If its venom was recently depleted when killing a meal, the amount of venom injected into your dog could be minimal.)

WAS THE SNAKE POISONOUS?

Not all snakebites are poisonous, though all require veterinary attention due to the risk of serious infection. If you can clearly see the bite pattern on your dog's skin, it can be a guide to the type of snake he fell victim to:

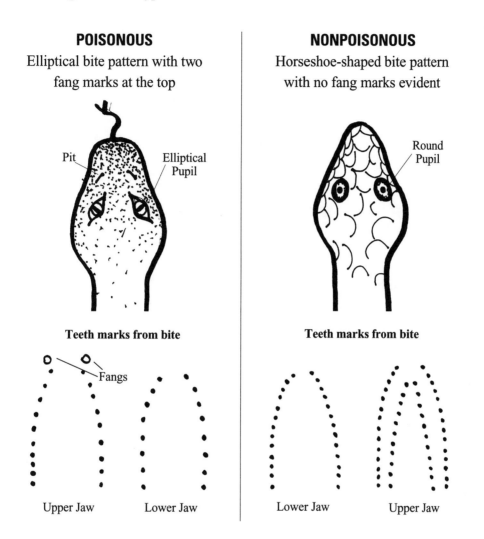

POISONOUS	NONPOISONOUS
Elliptical bite pattern with two fang marks at the top	Horseshoe-shaped bite pattern with no fang marks evident

Poisonous species native to North America are pit vipers, with the exception of the coral snake. Look for elliptical pupils, pits below the eyes, large fangs, and characteristic bite marks.

NOTES

CHAPTER 22

Common
TOXIC PLANTS AND POISONS

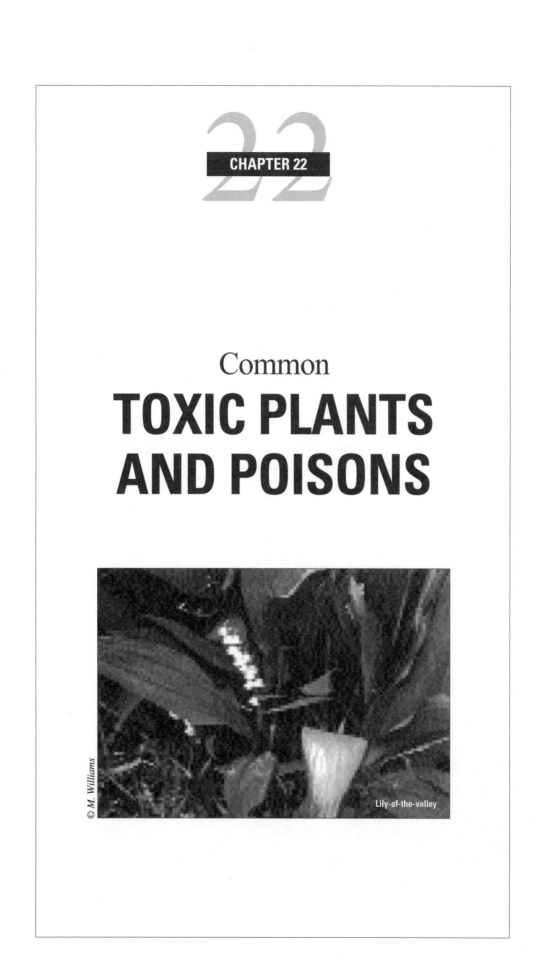

© M. Williams

Lily-of-the-valley

22 Common
TOXIC PLANTS AND POISONS

Your home and yard can be a toxic minefield for your dog. From plants to cleansers, human medicine to staple food items, the list of hazards to him is a long one. Your dog's best line of defense against deadly encounters with household toxins is you. Your knowledge of what dangers lurk around your home–and your ability to keep them away from him–can help you avoid an accidental poisoning.

COMMON HOUSEHOLD TOXINS

Here's a sampling of products that are toxic to your dog. Keep them safely locked away to avoid accidental poisoning. (For a list of toxic agents contained in these and the products listed elsewhere in this section, plus a list of poisoning symptoms, see the chart on page 354.)

Antifreeze
   (Extremely deadly)
Battery acid
Caustic cleansing agents
Creosote
Fertilizer
Glue/Adhesives
Grease solvents
Household cleansers/
   detergents
Dish soap
Hand soap
Laundry detergent
Shampoo
PhisoHex
Disinfectants

Sanitizers
Insecticides/
   pesticides/herbicides
Ant, roach, spider killers
Flea/tick control agents,
   including on-dog and
   premise products
Lawn/yard insecticides
   and weedkillers
Lead
Linoleum
Rug padding
Lead toys
Curtain weights
Lead-based paints
Ceramic glazes

Putty/caulk
Car batteries
Gasoline additives
Oil/grease
Golf balls
Fishing weights
Pellets and gunshot
Lye
Paint, paint thinner
Pine Tar
Plant food
Refrigerants
Snail poisons
Turpentine
Varnish
Wood stains

COMMON TOXIC DRUGS/FOODS

Drugs that help you can be harmful to your dog. So can some foods. Keep these out of his reach, and be sure to administer any kind of human medication to him ONLY under the guidance of your veterinarian.

Acetaminophen *(non-*
   aspirin pain relievers,
   such as Tylenol)

Amphetamines
Diet pills
Mood elevators

Stimulants
Aspirin
   (and Motrin, etc.)

COMMON DRUGS *(CONTINUED)*

Allylproply disulfide
- onions, raw/cooked

Caffeine
- over-the-counter diet pills, mood elevators, fatigue-reduction drugs
- coffee beans
- tea leaves

Chocolate and cocoa

Ibuprofen

Marijuana, hashish

Naproxen

Nicotine
- cigarettes
- cigars
- nicotine patches/gum

Phenylbutazone
- *("bute" in horse barns)*

St.-John's-Wart

For signs of poisoning from common toxins, see page 354.

COMMON TOXIC PLANTS

Beauty is truly in the eye of the beholder. The following sampling of common toxic plants may look good to you, but could be deadly to your dog. (If you have a question about a plant not listed here, consult with your vet or the ASPCA National Animal Poison Control Center. (The number is listed on page 353.) Also see the chart on page 360, under "Toxic Plants."

Aloe vera
Asparagus fern
Autumn crocus
Azalea
Beet tops
Bird of paradise
Black locust
Bracken fern
Buttercup
Caladium
Calla lily
Castor oil or bean
Chinaberry tree
Choke cherry
Christmas rose
Chrysanthemum
Common boxwood
Daffodil
Dumbcane
Easter lily
Elderberry
Elephant ear
English holly

English ivy
Fig *(Ficus)*
Foxglove
Grounsel, ragwort, tansey
Holly *(berries)*
Horsetail
Hyacinth
Hydrangea
Iris or flag
Irish potato *(leaves and sprouts)*
Jessamine
Lady's slipper
Lantana
Laurel
Lily-of-the-valley
Locoweed
Lupine
Machineel
Marijuana *(hemp)*
Milkweed
Mistletoe *(especially berries)*

Morning glory
Mountain laurel
Narcissus
Nettle
Nightshade
Oak
Oleander
Peach *(bark and leaves)*
Peas *(Lathyrus species)*
Philodendron
Poison hemlock
Poison ivy, oak, and sumac
Primrose
Rayless goldenrod
Rhubarb
St.-John's-wart
Tomato *(leaves and stem)*
Water hemlock
Wisteria
Yellow jasmine
Yew

➤

MISCELLANEOUS TOXINS

Some human foods can be hazardous to your dog's health. Avoid allowing him to eat any of the following. Some appeared on other lists because we feel they bear repeating.

Chocolate and cocoa • Coffee beans • Dead animals *(pathogenic toxins)* • Garbage *(food poisoning)* • Marijuana, hashish • Onions • Tea leaves

WHAT TO DO IF YOUR DOG IS POISONED

Your dog could become poisoned despite your best efforts to protect him. Here's what to do:

SKIN/EYE CONTACT:

Step 1. Immediately separate your dog from the toxin.

Step 2. Get your dog into fresh air, to minimize exposure to inhaled toxins.

Step 3. Immediately rinse him with large quantities of water, to remove as much of the residue as possible from his eyes and skin. (For how to rinse his eyes, see page 264.) Muzzle him if necessary (see page 328) and be sure to protect yourself from exposure with non-porous gloves (such as rubber kitchen gloves) and an apron. *DO NOT* attempt to remove the agent with paint thinner or other such solvents, which can cause a toxic reaction.

Step 4. Call your veterinarian, local 24-hour emergency clinic, or the ASPCA/NAPCC (see numbers, opposite page) immediately. Ask him/her to recommend an action plan. Have the following information on hand:
• The agent (or suspected agent) that your dog was exposed to.
• Estimated quantities that your dog came in contact with.
• Your dog's age, weight, sex, breed, and species.
• The amount of time since exposure.
• Symptoms your dog is showing.

Step 5. Take the agent or suspected agent with you to your veterinarian.

INGESTION:

Step 1. Immediately separate your dog from the toxin, if you catch him in the act.

Step 2. If not, try to determine what the dog was exposed to and how much was ingested.

Rule #1:
Stay Calm

If your dog is showing signs of having been poisoned, don't panic. If you're distressed and anxious you'll just add more stress to an emergency situation. Take a deep breath and carefully follow the steps outlined here. Be forewarned: The signs of intoxication are often rapid in onset and can be severe, including tremors, seizures, bleeding, and vomiting. A preplanned course of action is key to you providing your dog his best shot at survival.

Step 3. Call your veterinarian, local 24-hour emergency clinic, or the ASPCA/NAPCC (see numbers below) immediately. *(**Note:** If your dog is suffering seizures or is having trouble breathing, start with your vet or emergency clinic, so he'll get prompt local attention.)* Ask him/her to recommend an action plan. Be sure to have the following information on hand:

• The agent (or suspected agent) that your dog ingested.

• Estimated quantities that your dog ingested.

• Your dog's age, weight, sex, breed, and species.

• The amount of time since ingestion.

• Symptoms your dog is showing.

> If your dog has ingested a toxic substance, *DO NOT* give him anything without contacting your veterinarian, local emergency clinic, or the ASPCA National Animal Poison Control Center Hotline. Your attempts to induce vomiting could result in additional damage to your dog, depending on the agent ingested. Do so only under the guidance of a veterinarian.

Step 4. Scoop up any vomit, or any item your dog may have chewed. Place it in a plastic bag and take it with you to your vet's.

Step 5. Take the agent/suspected agent with you—in its container—to your veterinarian for possible analysis.

POISON EMERGENCY CONTACT NUMBERS:

ASPCA National Animal Poison Control Center Hotline:
(900) 680-0000. $45 per case. If you're unable to access the 900 number, try the 888 number, below.
(888) 426-4435. $45 per case. *(You'll need a credit card. Visa, Mastercard, and American Express accepted.)*

Your veterinarian's number: _____

Back-up veterinarian's number: _____

Nearest emergency clinic number: _____

POISON EMERGENCY KIT

Be sure to have the following at the ready, in the event you're instructed to administer first-aid before leaving for your veterinarian's.

• Syrup of ipecac to induce vomiting. In a pinch, you can use fresh, 3% hydrogen peroxide, table salt, or mustard. *(Do not administer unless directed to do so by a veterinarian.)*

• Turkey baster, bulb syringe, or dosing syringe for administering the vomit-inducer.

➤

- Eye-wash solution, for flushing eyes.
- Rubber gloves, to protect yourself from contact with toxic agents.
- A muzzle, or makeshift muzzle material, such as a bathrobe sash, stocking, gauze wrap, or soft, cotton rope. (Do not use if he's vomiting.)

 **THE DEADLY 7** The following items can be the 7 deadliest of toxins for dogs. Remove dangerous plants from your yard and house, and be sure to keep all other products well out of reach of your dog. Be wary of accidental spills—and quick to clean them up.

1. Acetaminophen (non-aspirin pain relievers, such as Tylenol)
2. Antifreeze
3. Cleaning products such as Draino, Ajax, pine oil, toilet bowl cleaners, dishwasher detergents
4. Japanese yew plant
5. Rodenticides (rat, mice, gopher, mole poisons)
6. Insecticides/weed killers/fertilizers
7. Snail poisons

COMMON TOXIC AGENTS AND SIGNS OF POISONING

RODENT POISONS			
AGENT	**SAMPLE PRODUCT/ FORMS**	**ONSET OF SIGNS AFTER INGESTION**	**SIGNS OF POISONING CAN INCLUDE**
Antu	White or blue-gray powder usually prepared in bread or sausage baits	Usually within hours	Vomiting, salivation; restlessness; increased heart/respiration rates; depression, weakness, coughing; labored breathing
Cholecalciferol	Grain-like products such as Rampage	Usually within 24 hours	Vomiting; lack of appetite; lethargy
Coumarins and related compounds	Warfarin (D Con); usually corn or other grain baits	2 to 5 days	Anemia, weakness; external hemorrhage; bruising under skin; labored breathing; neurological signs due to internal hemorrhage

RODENT POISONS (CONTINUED)

AGENT	SAMPLE PRODUCT/ FORMS	ONSET OF SIGNS AFTER INGESTION	SIGNS OF POISONING CAN INCLUDE
Sodium fluoroacetate (1080 and 1081)	Available only to licensed exterminators; usually mixed with black dye and added to bread, bran, carrots, or cereal	1/2 to 2 hours	Apprehension, irritability, vomiting; repeated urination/defecation; labored breathing; frothing at nostrils & mouth; running fits with abnormal barking/ howling
Strychnine	Sweet pellets or coating on rodent food; usually dyed purple, red, or green	10 minutes to 2 hours	Apprehension, nervousness, overall rigidity/stiffness; seizures
Thallium	USDA banned as a rodenticide in 1965, but still legal for control of wild predators	1 to 4 days	Gastroenteritis^G; hemorrhagic diarrhea; abdominal pain.
Vacor	Quick-kill, single-dose powder	Usually within hours	Vomiting; abdominal pain; trembling and weakness; blindness; collapse
Zinc phosphide	Gray-black powder usually with grain, sugar, or bread bait	15 minutes to 4 hours	Lack of appetite, lethargy; labored breathing; vomiting

PESTICIDES

AGENT	SAMPLE PRODUCT/ FORMS	ONSET OF SIGNS AFTER INGESTION	SIGNS OF POISONING CAN INCLUDE
Arsenic	Ant/roach poisons; Crabgrass killers; wood preservatives	30 minutes to several hours	Restlessness; salivation; vomiting; abdominal pain with watery, bloody diarrhea; weakness, trembling, staggering, incoordination
Borate	Roach and flea control; some toilet bowl cleaners; sanitizers; diaper rinses	Varies with product/ exposure	Local skin irritation; vomiting/diarrhea, often with blood and mucus; weakness, tremors ➤

PESTICIDES (CONTINUED)			
AGENT	**SAMPLE PRODUCT/ FORMS**	**ONSET OF SIGNS AFTER INGESTION**	**SIGNS OF POISONING CAN INCLUDE**
Carbamates	Numerous insecticides, including Carbaryl (Sevin) and Propoxur (Baygon)	Similar to Organophosphates, but shorter duration	See Organophosphates
Chlorinated Hydrocarbons	Veterinary products such as flea/tick powders, sprays, dips, and agricultural pesticides	A few minutes to several days	Apprehension; hypersensitivity; salivation; vomiting; facial twitching; seizures
Metaldehyde	Snail, slug, rat poison in palatable liquid, powder, or pelleted bait	1 to 4 hours	Anxiety; hypersensitivity to touch; incoordination; rapid heart rate; muscle tremors; vomiting; diarrhea
Naphthalene	Coal-tar derivative found in mothballs, moth repellants, and some insect repellents	Minutes to hours after exposure	Vomiting; diarrhea; seizures
Organophosphates	Numerous flea and agricultural products, in the form of Diazinon (Spectracide) and Dichlorvos (Vapona), and Malathion (Cythion) among others	Minutes to hours after exposure	Salivation; watery diarrhea; abdominal pain; tearing; contracted pupils
Pyrethrins and Piperonyl Butoxide	Pyrethrum flower extract (Pyrethrin) and synthetic (PB) insecticides used in insecticides, including veterinary insecticides such as Mycodex Pet Shampoo and some ear mite preparations	Minutes to hours after exposure	Usually seen only in very high doses; contact dermatitis; vomiting and diarrhea, incoordination; seizures
Rotenone	Plant extract used as topical insecticide for lice/mites	Minutes to hours after exposure	Skin irritation; eye irritation; respiratory tract irritation

HERBICIDES			
AGENT	**SAMPLE PRODUCT/ FORMS**	**ONSET OF SIGNS AFTER INGESTION**	**SIGNS OF POISONING CAN INCLUDE**
Algacides	Products for home aquariums; Monuron; Dichlone	Varies with product/ exposure	Skin irritation; depression; lethargy; vomiting; diarrhea; incoordination
Chloro-phenoxy derivatives	Broadleaf and woody plant herbicides/	Varies with product/ exposure	Contact dermatitis; stiffness; weakness; incoordination; paralysis; coma
Dipyridyl compounds	Paraquat and Diquat herbicides	Generally within hours	Excitability; incoordination; seizures; vomiting; diarrhea
Glyphosate	Roundup herbicide	Generally within hours	(Low toxicity when applied properly); skin irritation; vomiting; diarrhea; possible central nervous system (CNS) depression; coma
Triazines	Used on crops, especially corn	Generally within hours	Lack of appetite; lethargy; weakness; salivation; labored breathing; muscle spasms; incoordination

SPOILED FOOD/GARBAGE			
AGENT	**SAMPLE PRODUCT/ FORMS**	**ONSET OF SIGNS AFTER INGESTION**	**SIGNS OF POISONING CAN INCLUDE**
Botulism	Frequently found in feces, food, garbage, or carrion	Within 6 days	Progressive paralysis
E. coli; Salmonella; and other such pathogens	Spoiled food or garbage	15 minutes to 6 hours	Vomiting; abdominal pain; diarrhea (may be hemorrhagic); restlessness, weakness, incoordination

HOUSEHOLD TOXINS

AGENT	SAMPLE PRODUCT/ FORMS	ONSET OF SIGNS AFTER INGESTION	SIGNS OF POISONING CAN INCLUDE
Aromatic hydrocarbons	Creosote and other wood preservatives, solvents, disinfectants, herbicides, fungicides, insecticides, mothballs	Varies according to product; generally minutes to hours	Irritated mouth membranes; depression; vomiting; incoordination; seizures; coma
Corrosives, caustics	Battery acid, lye, cleaning prepartions, refrigerants, grease solvents	Varies according to product; generally minutes to hours	Skin irritation; burned mouth membranes; vomiting; thirst; labored breathing due to swelling from caustic agents in mouth/throat/pharynx
Detergents, soaps	Dishwashing soaps, shampoo, laundry soap, PhisoHex	Varies according to product; generally minutes to hours	Skin irritation; salivation, gagging, respiratory distress; vomiting, diarrhea, abdominal swelling; seizures, incoordination, collapse
Ethylene glycol	Antifreeze, some home dark-room processing solutions	30 minutes to 12 hours	Increased thirst, urination; vomiting; incoordination
Fertilizers, plant food	Those that contain nitrogen, phosphorous, potassium, and in some cases ammonia, metal salts, potash, and sulfur	Varies according to product; generally minutes to hours	Salivation; burned mouth membranes; abdominal pain; fever; weakness, tremors; siezures
Glues, adhesives	Household products	Varies according to product; generally minutes to hours	Skin irritation; ulceration of mouth membranes; listlessness; vomiting; diarrhea
Lead	Lead-based paints, rug padding, glazes, putty/ caulk, batteries, antiknock gasoline additives, oil, grease, golf balls, fishing sinkers, pellets and lead shot	3 to 15 days	Lack of appetite; abdominal pain; vomiting; diarrhea; hysteria; tremors; incoordination; seizures; blindness

HOUSEHOLD TOXINS (CONTINUED)			
AGENT	**SAMPLE PRODUCT/ FORMS**	**ONSET OF SIGNS AFTER INGESTION**	**SIGNS OF POISONING CAN INCLUDE**
Paints, var- nishes	Same, including paint chips from peeling walls/furniture	Varies accord- ing to product; generally min- utes to hours	Skin irritation; lack of appetite; depression; salivation; vomiting; diarrhea; seizures; coma
Paint thinners, turpentine	Same	Varies accord- ing to product; generally min- utes to hours	Skin irritation; burned mouth membranes; vomiting; diarrhea; CNS depression; seizures; tremors; incoordination

HOUSEHOLD DRUGS			
AGENT	**SAMPLE PRODUCT/ FORMS**	**ONSET OF SIGNS AFTER INGESTION**	**SIGNS OF POISONING CAN INCLUDE**
Acetamino- phen, other oxidant drugs	Non-aspirin pain relievers, such as Tylenol; onions, raw and cooked	Varies accord- ing to product/ item	Salivation and facial swelling; depression, weakness, vomiting; rapid breathing/pulse
Amphet- amines	Illegal "uppers," diet pills, mood elevators, stimulants	Varies accord- ing to product	Excitability; sensitivity to touch; rapid heart rate; high temp; panting; dilat- ed pupils; vomiting; diar- rhea; trembling, seizures
Aspirin	Same	4 to 6 hours	Increased respiratory rate, then respiratory depression; high fever; vomiting (may be bloody)
Marijuana, hashish	Same	1 to 2 hours	Drowsiness; depression; low body temp; incoor- dination; poor vision; salivation; vomiting; dilated pupils ➤

HOUSEHOLD DRUGS (CONTINUED)

AGENT	SAMPLE PRODUCT/ FORMS	ONSET OF SIGNS AFTER INGESTION	SIGNS OF POISONING CAN INCLUDE
Nicotine	Cigarettes, cigars some insecticides (Black Leaf 40)	Rapid onset depending on form and amount	Salivation; excitement; increased respiratory and heart rate; vomiting; diarrhea; tremors, inco-ordination, seizures; eventually, slow, shallow respiration, paralysis
Xanthines	Caffeine (over-the-counter diet pills, stimulants), tea leaves, coffee beans, chocolate, cocoa	Varies accord-ing to product	Restlessness; irritability; sensitivity to touch; rapid heart beat; vomit-ing; muscle tension; convulsions

TOXIC PLANTS

AGENT	SAMPLE PLANT(S)	ONSET OF SIGNS AFTER INGESTION	SIGNS OF POISONING CAN INCLUDE
Andro-metoxin	Azalea	Within 6 hours	Depression; weakness; vomiting; diarrhea; incoordination
Blue-green algae endo-toxin	Blooms in lakes ponds in upper Mid-west and Canada dur-ing hot, dry weather	15 to 45 minutes	Vomiting; diarrhea; abdominal pain; trem-bling; incoordination; paralysis; seizures; gener-ally fatal (surviving dogs may have liver damage)
Cardiac gly-cocides	Fox glove, Lilly of the Valley, Oleander	Varies with plant	Depression, dizziness; impaired vision; dilated pupils; vomiting; diarrhea
Contact irri-tants	Asparagus fern, Giant hogweed, Nettles, Poison ivy, oak and sumac, Trumpet creeper or cow itch	Variable; usually 6 to 24 hours	Dermatitis; mouth mem-brane inflammation/irri-tation; vomiting

TOXIC PLANTS			
AGENT	**SAMPLE PLANT(S)**	**ONSET OF SIGNS AFTER INGESTION**	**SIGNS OF POISONING CAN INCLUDE**
Gastro-intestinal irritants	Aloe vera, Mistletoe, Poinsettia	Varies with plant	Irritated mouth membranes; vomiting; diarrhea; abdominal pain; slowed pulse with mistletoe
Insoluble Oxalate-containing plants	Caladium, Dumbcane (Dieffenbachia), Elephant ears (colocasia), Jack-in-the-pulpit (Arisaema), Philodendron, Schefflera	Immediate	Salivation; swelling of tongue/throat; scratching/pawing at lips/face; labored breathing; vomiting; tongue paralysis
Mushrooms	Same	Varies with type	Salivation; vomiting and diarrhea, often with blood/mucus; incoordination; paralysis; coma; neurological signs
Solanceous alkaloids	Jerusalem cherry, Nightshade	Varies with plant	Salivation; vomiting and diarrhea (sometimes bloody); abdominal pain; listlessness, weakness, trembling, paralysis
Soluble oxalates	Beet tops, Devil's Ivy, Dock, Rhubarb	Varies with plant	Vomiting; diarrhea; renal failure
Stimulants	Azalea, Chinaberry tree	Varies with plant	Vomiting; diarrhea; seizures
Taxine alkaloids	Yew plants (European and Japanese)	Immediate	Trembling, weakness, collapse; coma; convulsions; sudden death
Toxalbumins, phyto-toxins	Black locust, Castor bean	Varies with plant	Irritated mouth membranes; vomiting; diarrhea; trembling; incoordination

Source: "Handbook of Small Animal Practice," edited by Rhea V. Morgan; Churchill Livingstone

NOTES

CHAPTER 23

Long Term Benefits of
SPAYING &
NEUTERING

23

Long-term benefits of
SPAYING & NEUTERING

Do you think you're doing your dog a favor by leaving him or her "intact?" Letting him "be a dog" and allowing her have a litter of "adorable" puppies? Think again. By leaving your dog intact, you not only are contributing to massive world pet overpopulation (and leaving yourself open for management problems), but you also are putting your dog at risk for health problems. Here's why:

FEMALE DOGS			
	MANAGEMENT	BEHAVIOR	HEALTH
INTACT	• Can deliver two litters of unwanted puppies per year • Contribute to world pet overpopulation, and thus pet deaths • Come into season every 6 months, leaving a bloody discharge in the house and yard and attracting unwanted male dogs	• Females in season are prone to roam in search of a mate • Females in heat can be restless and irritable	• Risk of mammary (breast) cancer • Risk of life-threatening pyometra (deadly uterine infection) • Risk of ovarian cysts and tumors • Heat-related roaming puts dog at risk for injury, such as getting hit by a car
SPAYED	• No unwanted pregnancies • No contribution to world pet overpopulation • No in-season mess in the house/yard • No unwanted male dogs hanging around	• No heat-related roaming • No heat-related restlessness and irritability	• Statistics show that females spayed prior to their first heat have almost a zero incidence of mammary cancer. *(Each successive heat increases that risk by about 25%; females spayed after the fourth heat can lose the sparing effect.)* • No risk for pyometra–the uterus is removed when spayed. • No risk for ovarian cysts/tumors–ovaries are removed when spayed.

MALE DOGS			
	MANAGEMENT	**BEHAVIOR**	**HEALTH**
INTACT	Driven to mark territory, which can include areas inside your house	• Driven to roam in search of females in heat • Prone to fight other dogs for rights to females/territory	• Increased risk of prostrate problems • Risk of testosterone-related problems such as perineal herniasG, perianal gland tumorsG, and hair loss • Risk of testicular tumors • Risk of acuteG testicular problems, such as epididymitisG • Risk of fight-related injury *(and you're at risk for vet bills)* • Risk of roaming-related injury, such as getting hit by a car
NEUTERED	Reduced urge to mark territory	• No breeding-related roaming • Less prone to fight • Less territorial • Less aggressive • Generally calmer, less of an "edge" • Neutered males are generally considered to be the best companion animals, due to their tractable nature	• Reduced risk of prostrate problems • No risk of testicular tumors–testicles are removed when neutered • No risk of acute testicular problems • Reduced risk of roaming- and fight-related injuries

SPAY/NEUTER SPECIFICS

FEMALES:

What: The procedure's called an ovariohysterectomy (OHE, or spay). It involves removing your dog's ovaries and uterus, so she's unable to have puppies. Though considered a major abdominal operation, it's relatively painless and safe. Your dog may be kept overnight, or sent home the same day. After a day or two of quiet rest, she'll generally be back to normal. (Though her activities may be restricted for up to a week or more, to allow healing.)

➤

When: Spay your female at the age of 5 to 7 months, before her first heat, to reduce the risk of mammary cancer. (Research indicates no adverse affects to spaying as early as 6 weeks of age.)

MALES:

What: The procedure's called castration (neutering, altering). It involves removing your dog's testicles, so he's unable to impregnate a female. Unless your dog has a retained testicle (one that's failed to descend from his abdomen), neutering is a less invasive operation than spaying. Generally, your dog will be sent home the same day or the following one. He'll likely feel like his old self within a day or two, but you'll need to restrict his exercise for about a week, to allow the incision to heal.

When: Around 6 to 10 months of age, when he's sexually mature. (You can neuter an older dog, but testosterone-related behavior will become more ingrained with age, so your greatest behavior-related benefits will come from early-age altering.) You can also ask your vet about neutering your male dog at an earlier age. Many shelters have begun neutering male or female puppies before adoption, to avoid the possibility of having them breed. This practice has proven to be safe. Your vet can discuss the pros and cons with you.

WHAT'S YOUR EXCUSE?

The excuse: "I love my little Muffie and know she'll have the best puppies. My friends all say they want one...."

The reality: If you truly love little Muffie, you'll help ensure a longer, healthier life by spaying her before her first heat. Plus, there aren't enough good homes available for all the puppies and dogs in the U.S. today. (If you don't believe us, take a stroll through any city pound or animal shelter. What makes you think Muffie's puppies will be exempt from that fate?) Suggest that, if your friends want a Muffie of their own, they adopt one of the millions of abandoned puppies and dogs in desperate need of a home. You'd then be saving lives rather than contributing to deaths.

The excuse: "I want my children to witness the miracle of birth. Plus, they promised to help with the puppies, which will teach them responsibility."

The reality: If you were to explain to your kids that, by allowing your dog to have puppies, they'd be contributing to the millions of dogs killed each year, do you think they'd still go for it? We didn't think so. If you want them to see animal births, tapes are available. Ask your vet or humane society for suggestions. And to get a puppy fix, take them on frequent visits to the pound and animal shelters. There are plenty of puppies there that are starved for exercise and attention. Regular visits to needy dogs will also instill that sense of responsibility you're looking for.

The excuse: "My dog's a purebred, so I can sell the puppies. I'm a responsible breeder."

The reality: Hmmmmmmmm. One figure puts the number of purebred pets in shelters today at around 25 percent. That would put the number of purebred pets killed annually at nearly 2 million. Plus, breed rescue programs often have more dogs than they can place in good homes. 'Nuf said.

The excuse: "I can't stand the thought of cutting off Brutus', er, testicles." (This excuse generally comes from men.)

The reality: Look, guys, the dog won't know any difference—trust us. And you really won't miss his, er, testicles, because he'll still be Brutus without them. (Plus, you'll remain intact!) And, you'll be contributing to a longer, healthier life for him. Be a man—help solve the world's pet overpopulation problem. (Women love a sensitive guy!)

The excuse: "I don't want to neuter my dog because it'll change his personality and I love him the way he is!"

The reality: Neutering tends to bring out the best in your dog's personality, and lessen or erase some of the behavior traits you may not have really loved (such as territoriality, aggression, heat-related irritability). You'll have the same personality you loved—only better.

The excuse: "I don't want to put my darling Trudie and Spot through the trauma of surgery. They could die!"

The reality: The safety of today's anesthetics, monitoring, and spay/neuter techniques results in an extremely low incidence of complications. The benefits far outweigh the risks. Just do it!

The excuse: "I can't afford to fix my dog."

The reality: Low-cost—even free—spay/neuter programs are available nationwide. Check with your local humane society or your veterinarian.

So...what's your excuse?

FIX-THEM FACTS

When you allow your dog to breed, you're contributing to these facts and figures (and yes, we mean you!):

• Approximately 12 million or more pets are impounded each year in the U.S. alone.

• Of those pets, up to 60% are killed. That's approximately 7 million animals a year.

• Included in those numbers are purebreds and exotic breeds. (That's right, breeding your purebred dog doesn't exempt you from the overpopulation issue.)

• One figure puts the number of kittens and puppies born each day at about 70,000. That's in the U.S. alone.

NOTES

CHAPTER 24

10 SYMPTOMS
You Should Never Ignore

24 10 SYMPTOMS
You Should Never Ignore

Consider these signs to be 9-1-1 canine emergencies. Your dog needs immediate care in order to have the best chance for recovery. Call your veterinarian *NOW*, then flip to the page mentioned for additional information on what to do before you leave for the vet hospital.

1. ABDOMINAL DISTENSION

What you see: Your dog's belly appears to be bloated. He's lethargic, and may be making repeated unsuccessful attempts to vomit.

What it might mean: The deadly stomach condition called bloat^G. See page 211.

2. RESTLESS POST-INJECTION BEHAVIOR

What you see: You or your vet have just given your dog a shot. Your dog is panting and acting anxious. He may be wheezing and/or gasping for air.

What it might mean: Anaphylactic shock^G. See page 161.

3. RELUCTANCE TO MOVE

What you see: Your dog is down, and fails to rise to greet you. When he attempts to move, it appears that his front and/or hind end isn't working.

What it might mean: Spinal injury, resulting in paralysis. See page 191.

4. STAGGERING

What you see: Your dog is lurching around, as though dizzy or drunk.

What it might mean: He could have a neurological problem affecting his brain or spinal cord, or he could have an inner-ear problem affecting his equilibrium. See pages 186 and 188.

5. CLOSED, TEARING EYE

What you see: One of your dog's eyes is being clamped shut. Tears, a thick discharge, and/or blood is draining from it.

What it might mean: A serious eye injury (such as trauma or a foreign body) or condition (such as uveitis^G) that could permanently affect his vision. See page 60.

6. REPEATED VOMITING

What you see: Your dog is vomiting repeatedly, and now is bringing up nothing, or small amounts of yellow fluid or blood.

What it might mean: Gastritis^G due to infection, poison, a foreign body, or a tumor. See page 136.

7. BLOODY DIARRHEA

What you see: Sudden onset diarrhea marked by large amounts of bright-red or dark, bloody, foul-smelling stool that may resemble raspberry jam. Your dog is lethargic.

What it might mean: Hemorrhagic gastroenteritis^G, parvovirus^G, Addison's disease^G, or a bleeding disorder. See page 141.

8. CHOKING

What you see: Your dog is gagging, gasping, pawing at his mouth, drooling, and making increased respiratory sounds. He's very anxious.

What it might mean: He may be choking to death. This is one case where you need to act first, and call your vet later. See page 159.

9. INCREASED WATER CONSUMPTION AND/OR LETHARGY IN A FEMALE DOG THAT WAS RECENTLY IN HEAT

What you see: Your female dog was recently in season. Now she's lapping up water, turning her nose up at food, and acting dull. She may or may not have a vaginal discharge.

What it might mean: The deadly uterine infection, pyometra^G. See page 210.

10. RAPID, SHALLOW BREATHING WITH BLUISH/GRAY MOUTH MEMBRANES

What you see: Your dog's has played hard on a hot, humid day, has been left in a hot car, or has had some other heat exposure. He's panting and poorly responsive.

What it might mean: Heat exhaustion. See page 161.

NOTES

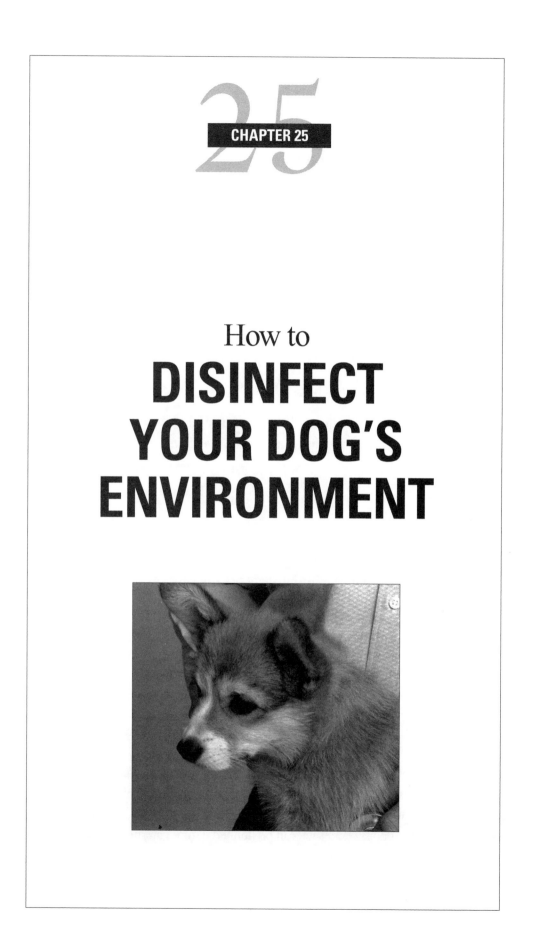

How to
DISINFECT YOUR DOG'S ENVIRONMENT

How to
DISINFECT YOUR DOG'S ENVIRONMENT

HOW TO DISINFECT A ROOM OR KENNEL

To help prevent the spread of contagious disease, you might have to disinfect an area that was inhabited by a sick dog. Here's how.

1. Remove and wash all dog bedding. See next page.

2. Remove all feed/water dishes. Using a mixture of hot water and dish detergent, scrub them free of residue. Rinse thoroughly, then scrub again with a solution of 1 part laundry-type chlorine bleach to 10 parts water. Allow them to air-dry without rinsing. Scrub one more time with hot water and dish detergent. Rinse thoroughly to remove any bleach or detergent residue.

3. Sweep/vacuum the floor, walls, ledges, and door.

4. In a kennel, wash walls and other solid surfaces using a pressure washer (or garden hose), a stiff scrub brush, and dish-washing detergent. In a room, mop any hard-surface floors.

5. For your kennel, mix Lysol® Disinfectant Concentrate (2-1/2 tablespoons per gallon of water) or household bleach solution (2 tablespoons per gallon of water) in a garden-type spray tank. (Avoid using the Lysol® solution in areas with cats.) Wear protective clothing, including long sleeves, long pants, gloves, goggles, and head gear. Spray a soaking mist of disinfectant onto all surfaces and allow to air-dry. Repeat. For a room, sponge the mixture over walls, doors, and hard floors. (If you have carpet, rent a steam cleaner.)

6. Return clean feed/water dishes and clean bedding.

HOW TO DISINFECT YOURSELF

Use these tips to help prevent carrying a contagious disease on your skin or clothing after handling a sick dog.

1. When entering the dog's sick bay: Wear rubber boots and close-weave fabric coveralls with long sleeves. Confine your hair in a hat. Use disposable latex or rubber examination gloves whenever working with/around the sick dog. Leave these garments outside the door, where they can be donned before entering and taken off when you leave.

2. Upon leaving the dog's area: Discard the used disposable gloves in a closed receptacle outside the enclosure. Disinfect your shoes with a plastic scrub brush and Lysol® Disinfectant Concentrate (2-1/2 tablespoons per gallon of water) or household bleach solution (2 tablespoons per gallon of water) in a dishpan or bucket. Leave boots outside the enclosure to dry. Cover or discard the Lysol® or bleach solution for safety. (It's toxic if swallowed.)

3. When tending to more than one dog, take care of the sick one last.

HOW TO DISINFECT GROOMING TOOLS

Clean your brushes and grooming tools at least once a month to help prevent skin problems from developing and spreading, particularly if grooming tools are shared among several dogs.

1. Remove all hair.

2. Soak and scrub your brushes and tools in hot water and dish detergent to loosen and remove all oils, dander, scabs, and other residue.

3. Prepare Lysol® Disinfectant solution (2-1/2 tablespoons per gallon of water) or household bleach solution (2 tablespoons per gallon of water) soak all grooming tools for 30 minutes. Discard solution, allow tools to air-dry, preferably in the sun. (Note: Wooden-handled tools might be damaged by soaking. Use tools that are made of materials that can be soaked safely, such as plastic or metal.)

HOW TO DISINFECT BEDDING

Clean blankets and pads weekly. Doing so will help prevent skin problems from developing and spreading, particularly if these items are shared among several dogs.

1. Remove hair with a plastic brush and/or vacuum cleaner. Discard vacuum cleaner bag.

2. If machine-washable, run pads through the wash cycle with Lysol®. (Use 1 cup in a standard top-loader.) Spin dry, and run through a second wash cycle with Ivory soap flakes. Add vinegar to the rinse water to help remove soap residue. (Use 1 cup in a standard top-loader. Some dogs have a skin sensitivity to detergent residues in bedding. **Tip:** If your washing machine is too small to wash your dog's bedding, inquire at local laundromats for permission to use their machines. Most will allow this but will require that you run the machines once more, empty, after you're finished, to remove hair and other residue.

COMMONLY USED DISINFECTANTS

Category	Example	Uses	Comments
Iodophors 10%	Undiluted Betadine® solution	Skin	Will kill most canine pathogens, even in the presence of organic matter. May stain surfaces permanently.
O-phenylphenol	Lysol® Disinfectant Concentrate, prepared 2-1/2 T per gallon of water	Objects, premises (Avoid using in areas with cats)	Will kill most canine pathogens, even in the presence of organic matter. Should not be used on broken skin. Toxic to cats and humans if ingested or absorbed through open wounds.
Chlorhexidine	Nolvasan®, Virusan	Skin, objects, premises	Effective against most canine pathogens; ineffective against Rotavirus; inactivated in the presence of organic matter.
Hypochlorites	Bleach, mixed 2T per gallon of water	Objects, premises	Effective against many canine pathogens; ineffective against Rotavirus; inactivated in the presence of organic matter.
Pine oil	Pine Sol®	Objects, premises	Ineffective against most canine pathogens.

WHAT'S ORGANIC MATTER?

Anything that is, was, or came from living cells. This includes pollens, molds, cobwebs, fly "tracks," feed, saliva, stool, urine, dirt, hair, blood, scabs, pus....

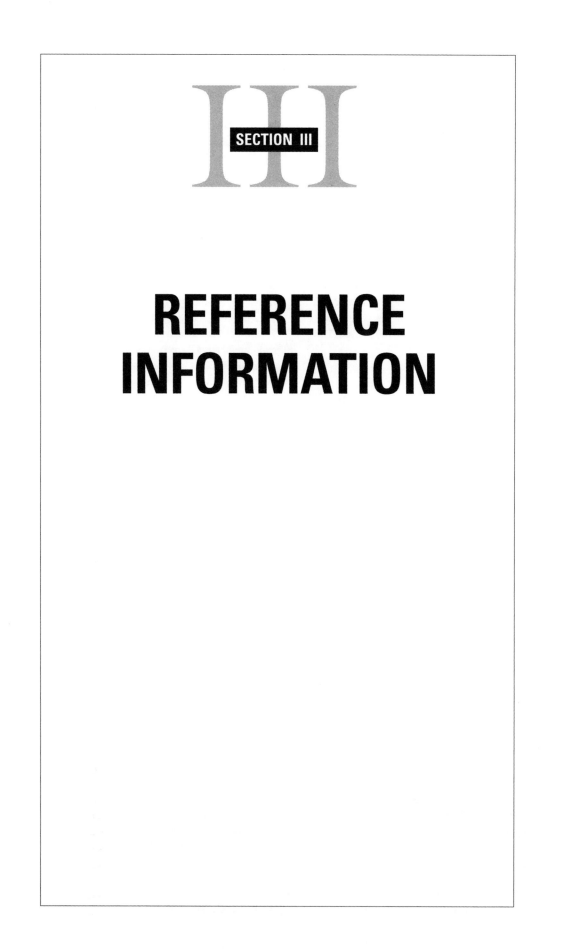

SECTION III

REFERENCE INFORMATION

GLOSSARY

Abscess

An infection around which the body has constructed a wall of fibrous tissue, to isolate it. Treatment with antibiotics is more likely to be effective if drainage of the abscess can be established, eliminating accumulated pus and debris.

Acanthosis nigricans

A rare disease of the Dachshund breed. Signs include hyperpigmentation (abnormal darkening) in the armpit area, which then progresses to hair loss and hardened, leathery skin. The abdomen, groin, anal area, chest, neck, forelimbs, and hind legs may be involved. There is no specific therapy.

Acquired epilepsy

A non-congenital (not inherited) form of epilepsy[G]. Acquired epilepsy can occur following trauma or disease. (See also Idiopathic epilepsy[G].)

Acral lick granuloma

A fairly common, ulcer-like skin condition caused by excessive licking. Generally found on legs or paws. Generally linked to boredom, although it can result from previous trauma to the area. Most common in large, active breeds that crave constant attention. Treatment is generally aimed at alleviating boredom; tranquilizers and other anti-anxiety medications may help during periods of stress.

Acute

Referring to disease or trauma characterized by pain and severity; having a sudden onset, sharp rise, and short course.

Addison's disease

A destructive disease due to deficient secretions from the adrenal glands, which produce steroids such as sex hormones and those hormones concerned with metabolic function. The cause is unknown; signs include lethargy, lack of appetite, and vomiting. Treatment can include cortisone, fluid therapy, and hormone replacement medications. Prognosis for recovery is excellent if the dog is treated promptly and properly, though he may require medication for the remainder of his life.

Allergic hot spot

Self-induced skin condition due to licking/biting of an area made itchy by an allergy, such as that due to fleas.

The dog will generally scratch/chew the affected area, causing an area of raw, inflamed, moist skin. Treatment is generally aimed at reducing inflammation and infection; finding and treating the underlying cause; and keeping the raw area clean and free of additional trauma, to help avoid secondary bacterial infection.

Allergic pneumonitis

Pneumonia produced by an allergic response following the introduction of an antigenic substance (one that stimulates an immune response) into the body.

Allergy

Increased sensitivity to specific substances or agents. Your dog's body develops an allergy after prior exposure, which sensitizes his immune system. Subsequent exposure brings a disproportionate "overreaction," either locally or body-wide. There's disagreement over why an allergy develops: some say it's a genetic predisposition, others say it's cumulative based on chronic exposure.

Anal sac infection/abscess

Typically seen when one or both anal glands become blocked, preventing the excretion of the thick, brown substance that is secreted by glands lining the anal sac, serving as a method of identification and territory marking. Affected dogs may drag their rear ends across the ground, and lick/chew the perianal[G] area, which may be red/swollen and painful. Treatment is generally aimed at "expressing" (squeezing) the anal glands to clear any blockage; antibiotics may be needed to treat infection.

Anaphylaxis, generalized/systemic

An allergic-type hypersensitivity reaction to a substance or agent to which there has been prior exposure. After becoming sensitized (which may follow years of exposure with no evidence of any problem), a particular exposure brings a body-wide overreaction that can include the formation of hives, edema[G] in the respiratory tract, circulatory shock[G], and death.

Anemia

A decrease in red blood cell population due to bleeding, red blood cell destruction, or from decreased production of new red blood cells to replace those that die after their normal life span. This can result from disease of the bone marrow, where red blood cells are manufactured.

Antibiotic sensitivity

A laboratory test to determine what antibiotics, if any,

are effective against bacteria cultured from an infected patient. Small paper discs impregnated with specific antibiotics are placed on a culture plate. Bacteria that are sensitive to the antibiotic won't grow near the disc.

Antivenin
An antitoxin to venom, such as that from a poisonous snake. Used in the treatment of snakebites to help minimize damage from venom.

Arthritis
Joint inflammation due to infectious, metabolic, or other causes (such as age-related wear-and-tear). Characterized by stiffness/lameness, and sometimes, joint swelling. Treatment generally involves identifying an underlying cause, if any, and anti-inflammatory and/or pain-relieving drugs.

Ascarids
The most common type of roundworm in dogs.

Aspiration biopsy
The withdrawal of fluid or tissue from a cyst/tumor via needle and syringe, for the purposes of examination under a microscope.

Aspiration pneumonia
Lung disease resulting from feed, saliva, or regurgitated stomach contents entering the respiratory tract and reaching your dog's lungs, creating inflammation, cell damage, and infection. Common causes of aspiration pneumonia can include: injury or disease interfering with your dog's ability to swallow; and the aspiration of vomit.

Asthma
Condition of an allergic origin that's marked by continued labored breathing, wheezing, and often accompanied by attacks of coughing or gasping.

Atopic allergy
An inherited sensitivity to such environmental allergens as pollens and grass.

Atrophy
Decrease in size, or wasting away of a body part or organ, such as the atrophy of muscle in an afflicted leg.

Aural hematoma
Accumulation of blood in the space between your dog's skin and the cartilage of his ear flap, causing the flap to appear puffy and pillow-like instead of flat. Without proper treatment, an aural hematoma can result in a bunched, misshapen "cauliflower"ear.

Autoimmune disease
An immune response directed against the body's own cells, tissues, and organs. One example of such a disease is discoid lupus erythematosus[G].

Bacterial folliculitis
Infection of the hair follicle, often after the skin has been damaged by injury, insect bites, and/or chronic filth. Most often occurs during warm weather. Signs can include pimples which break open to form hairless, crusted sores. Diagnosis is suggested by the appearance of the lesions, and can be confirmed by biopsy. Treatment usually includes clipping and cleaning the affected area, keeping it clean and dry, and systemic antibiotics.

Benign
Referring to a growth: Not invasive or destructive, and not tending to spread to other areas of the body.

Bladder, infection of, see Cystitis

Bladder stones
Stones formed within your dog's bladder that can irritate the inner bladder lining, causing painful urination. Stone formation may be linked to urine acidity and the way a dog metabolizes salts and other products. Stones can also move into the urethra, causing an obstruction there. And, dogs who form bladder stones may also be at risk for kidney stones. Signs can include frequent attempts to urinate, producing less volume than normal, as well as blood in the urine. Treatment varies, and can range from a diet change to surgery.

Bleeding disorder
Any disorder that interferes with blood clotting in a wound. Causes can include: autoimmune disorders; congenital diseases such as hemophilia[G]; bone marrow diseases that interfere with the formation of blood clotting cells (called platelets); a rare complication after severe infection that causes depletion of platelets (called disseminated intravascular coagulation, or DIC); and poisoning with products containing the chemical warfarin or coumadin.

Bloat, see Gastric-Dilatation Volvulus

Brachycephalic
The flat-faced, short-nosed, bulgy-eyed, wide-headed characteristic of certain breeds, such as Pugs, Pekinese, English Bulldogs, and Boxers.

Bronchitis
Inflammation of the lining of your dog's bronchial

tubes. It can result from infection, allergy, lungworms, or chronic irritation from inhaling dust and molds.

Bronchoconstriction
Constriction of the bronchial air passages, which results in reduced airflow, resulting in difficulty breathing.

Brucellosis
Infection by bacteria of the Brucella family that can invade the reproductive tract and cause infertility and abortions. Because Brucella bacteria can infect several species, including cattle, housepets, and humans, extreme care should be taken when handling a dog suspected of harboring this bacterial strain. Diagnosis is confirmed by laboratory culture of infected tissues and/or blood test; treatment includes antibiotic therapy and the elimination of the infected dog from breeding programs.

Cancer
A malignant tumor of potentially unlimited growth that expands locally by invasion and systemically by metastasis (the spread from original site to other systems/organs).

Canine ichthyosis
A congenital disease characterized by skin that's rough, thick, and scaly, resembling that of a fish.

Carbon monoxide poisoning
Poisoning due to the inhalation of carbon monoxide, a colorless, odorless, highly toxic gas expelled by automobiles as a byproduct of incomplete carbon production. If a dog is in an enclosed area, such as a closed garage, with a running vehicle, carbon monoxide poisoning is a deadly risk.

CAT scan
A sectional view of the body constructed by computed axial tomography, which provides specialized images that are used as a diagnostic tool.

Cataract
An opacity within the eye lens. Once a lens becomes clouded, there is no treatment to restore it. If the cataract is large enough to block vision, the lens may be removed surgically.

Cathartic
A laxative given to quickly purge your dog's bowels of their contents. Examples include Epsom salt solution, mineral oil, or psyllium.

Cerebral neoplasia
A tumor of the brain.

Cervical spinal instability
Excess movement between the vertebrae in your dog's neck, due to such causes as injury or disease. Instability can cause pressure on the spinal cord, resulting in such signs as pain, incoordination, and paralysis.

Cherry eye
Enlargement of the gland on the third eyelid[G], often to the size of a small marble. Can resemble a cherry, hence the name. Generally corrected with surgery aimed at repositioning the gland, rather than removing it.

Chronic
A disease or condition of long duration.

Cicatricial alopecia
A smooth, hairless scar from a healed injury with permanently damaged hair follicles.

Clostridium
Anaerobic bacteria present in soil, animal intestines, and feces that cause such deadly conditions as tetanus[G] and botulism.

Colitis
Inflammation of the colon, usually due to parasite infestation or an infection. Diarrhea, abdominal pain, soft stools, straining to defecate (due to pain), and rapidly progressing dehydration are usually the result. Other causes can include: administration of antibiotics; intestinal lymphosarcoma[G]; and inorganic arsenic poisoning. Treatment focuses on relieving symptoms and preventing dehydration and shock while identifying and treating the underlying cause, if possible.

Collapsed nostrils, see Stenotic nares

Collie eye
An inherited condition of the Collie breed, in which the dog may have a detached retina, optic nerve abnormalities, and/or retinal atrophy. Though loss of vision can result, generally it can only be detected via an ophthalmic exam. There is no treatment to eliminate it; affected dogs should be taken out of breeding programs.

Congestive heart failure
Loss of the heart's efficient pumping ability, commonly due to valve leakage allowing blood to reflux backward, into the lungs. This causes lung congestion and decreases the volume of blood delivered to your dog's extremities. The heart compensates by pumping faster,

which can worsen lung congestion and damage heart muscle. Symptoms can include: weakness; decreased energy; delayed recovery from exercise; and/or cough. Treatment is usually focused on identifying and treating the underlying cause, relieving lung congestion, and improving the heart's efficiency with various medications.

Conjunctivitis

Inflammation of the membrane (conjunctiva) inside the lids and around the eyes. Symptoms can include reddening, itching, watering, and swelling. Causes can include irritants such as dust; trauma; and infection. Treatment usually includes gentle cleaning, addressing the underlying cause, and medicating with ointments containing appropriate antibiotics and/or anti-inflammatory medications.

Contact dermatitis

A skin condition resulting from contact with an irritant, such as acids, alkalis, insecticides, detergents, and soaps. Allergic contact dermatitis results when the dog comes in contact with a substance to which he's developed an allergic sensitivity, such as flea powders, plants, and dyes found in carpets. Treatment for both involves avoidance of the offending irritant or allergen, then symptomatic care.

Cornea

The transparent, domed outer portion of the eyeball.

Corneal abscess

An infection between the onion-like layers of the cornea, most often associated with a penetrating wound. The condition is painful and, if unresolved, can result in blindness. Treatment is challenging because the location of the infection between corneal layers makes it difficult for topical or systemic medications to penetrate to the site. Treatment usually is similar to what is prescribed for corneal ulcer[G]; in non-responsive cases surgery may be needed to remove corneal layers and expose the abscess. (If the infection is resolved, the cornea will generally heal, though usually with a visible area of cloudiness.)

Corneal ulcer

A raw area on the cornea, most often associated with injury and subsequent infection. The condition is painful and, if unresolved, can result in blindness. Treatment usually includes antibiotics and other medications to combat the infection, inflammation, and pain, and facilitate repair of the damaged cornea. In most cases, topical treatment is used, although occasionally surgery may be required.

Cryosurgery

Removal of tissue by freezing with liquid nitrogen or carbon dioxide. This technique is often used to treat certain skin cancers such as squamous cell carcinoma[G].

Culture

The cultivation of a sample of tissue or body fluid in a laboratory growth medium in order to identify infectious bacteria, fungi or viruses present.

Cushing's disease

A hormonal disease due to a pituitary gland tumor (pituitary adenoma[G]). It causes a variety of problems that can include a diabetes-like syndrome and weight loss. There is no cure, but in some cases the signs can be lessened by administration of medications to suppress overproduction of certain hormones, and stimulate production of the neurotransmitter dopamine.

Cyst

An enclosed, smooth lump with a solid or liquid center produced by the cells lining the cyst's wall. A sebaceous cyst contains oil produced by oil glands in the cyst's lining. A serous cyst contains serum. Cysts generally do not cause problems unless their location and size interfere with function of adjacent parts. Treatment options for cysts can include: surgical removal; cryosurgery[G]; cauterization[G]; or obliteration by laser. When a fluid-filled cyst is simply drained, it usually refills within a few days.

Cystitis

A bladder inflammation, generally caused by a bacterial infection. May be accompanied by the formation of bladder stones[G]. Signs can include frequent urination or attempts to urinate, with less-than-normal amounts of urine passed and blood in the urine. Treatment can include anti-inflammatory medications and/or antibiotics.

Cytology

The study of cells on a smear or smudge of tissue placed on a slide and viewed under a microscope.

Debridement

Removal of dead or contaminated tissue and foreign matter from a wound.

Degenerative myelopathy

A global term for a degenerative disease or condition of the spinal cord.

Dehydration

Decrease in the body's normal water content due to

inadequate water intake and/or increased water loss, such as via diarrhea.

Demodectic mange
Mange caused by mites that burrow in your dog's hair follicles, causing pustule formation and patchy hair loss. Treatment is aimed at killing the parasites with topical insecticides specifically targeted toward the mite, then reducing skin irritation until healing is complete. Associated bacterial infections may be treated with antibiotics.

Dermatitis
A global term referring to inflammation of the skin.

Dermoid
A piece of displaced tissue/skin. Commonly seen growing out of or around the eye.

Dermoid cyst
A benign^G cystic mass that generally is covered with hair and located on a dog's back. The cyst results from a rare developmental abnormality, and contains skin and skin derivatives, such as hair or teeth. Boxers and Rhodesian Ridgebacks generally have a higher incidence than other breeds, perhaps suggesting an inherited component. The cysts are generally left untreated, but can be removed surgically.

Dewormer, anthelmintic
Medication given to eliminate intestinal parasites, or "worms."

Diabetes
Any of a variety of chronic conditions characterized by the secretion and excretion of excessive amounts of urine. For instance, diabetes mellitus ("sugar diabetes") is caused either by insufficient production of insulin, or by resistance to the effects of insulin. Without insulin, your dog's body can't utilize sugar in its blood, resulting in an excess that the kidneys must eliminate. This results in excess urination. Diabetes insipidus involves defective synthesis or secretion of an anti-diuretic hormone by your dog's pituitary gland.

Diabetic ketoacidosis
Life-threatening result of poorly or untreated diabetes mellitus, resulting in increased acidity of your dog's blood. The results are lack of appetite, vomiting, weakness, dehydration, breath that has a sweet or ammonia-like odor, and finally, coma.

Diaphragmatic hernia
Rupture of the diaphragm, the muscle that separates your dog's chest cavity from his abdomen. The hernia usually is the result of a traumatic injury, such as a livestock kick or traffic-related impact. Signs include deep, forced breathing. (Breathing depends largely on the diaphragm to enlarge/compress your dog's lungs, causing them to expand/contract.) Once an opening occurs, abdominal contents may move through it, putting pressure on the lungs, thus eliminating their ability to expand. Treatment generally requires surgical repair.

Diarrhea, acute
Abnormally wet stool (semi-solid to watery) passed at least twice as often as normal, for a rapid, short course of less than a week. Treatment usually is aimed at the underlying cause, if known, and at supporting the dog by replacing lost fluids and electrolytes.

Diarrhea, chronic
Abnormally wet stool (semi-solid to watery) passed up to 1-1/2 times more often than normal, for an extended duration of days. Sometimes occurs with longer, intermittent periods of cow-pie or semi-solid stool. Treatment usually is aimed at identifying and correcting the underlying cause.

Diarrhea, infectious causes of
Infections with Ehrlichia, Salmonella, or Clostridium species are common infectious causes of acute or chronic diarrhea in adult dogs. Long-term and/or severe infestation with intestinal parasites also can cause this condition, as can certain poisons.

Discoid lupus erythematosus
An autoimmune skin disease thought to be a milder form of lupus erythematosus^G (systemic). Limited to a dog's face, it results in hair loss, ulceration, and depigmentation along the nose, between the nostrils and eyes, often in a characteristic butterfly shape. Treatment can include steroids and/or vitamin E. Topical sunscreens and avoidance of sunlight might also be recommended.

Distemper
Viral disease that's related to the human measles virus, and is transmitted through the air, and via secretions such as urine. In dogs, it can attack a wide range of organs, including skin, brain, eyes, intestines, and respiratory tract. Puppies are most commonly infected, though dogs of any age can be victims. Signs include eye and nose discharge, lethargy, coughing, diarrhea, vomiting, hardening of nose and pad skin (hard pad^G), and in severe cases, seizures. While there is no specific treatment (therapy is largely supportive), vaccinations exist that can protect your puppy/dog from this disease.

Drainage, surgical
Surgical creation of an opening for accumulated blood, serum, pus, and/or debris to drain from a wound.

Draining tract
An opening formed by your dog's body for accumulated blood, serum, pus, and/or debris to drain from an infection or foreign body. The constant drainage of accumulated liquid along a path between muscle and connective tissue can prevent the tract from healing. Treatment can include resolving the underlying problem that's causing the wound to ooze, such as infection, or the presence of a foreign body[G] or sequestrum[G]. The draining tract is debrided[G] so it can heal.

Dry eye
Inadequate tear production, leading to irritation of the eye's cornea. Treatment usually is aimed at identifying and correcting the underlying cause, if possible, stimulating tear production, and protecting the eye with artificial lubrication.

Dysphagia
Difficulty swallowing, which can be due to pain, obstruction, pharyngitis[G], tonsillitis[G], or a problem with the nerves that govern throat muscles. The most common signs of dysphagia are salivation and obvious difficulty swallowing. Treatment usually is aimed at identifying and resolving the underlying cause, and adjusting feeding methods (e.g., feeding by stomach tube) to avoid aspiration pneumonia[G].

E. coli, see Escherichia coli

Ear canal, infection of; otitis externa
Inflammation of the ear canal outside your dog's ear drum, often secondary to damage from ear ticks, bacteria, and yeast, or foreign matter such as grass awns. Symptoms can include head shaking, ear scratching, and holding the ear drooped to one side. Treatment usually is aimed at the underlying cause, and at cleaning the ear of wax and debris that result from the inflammation. (Sedation may be needed to accomplish this.)

Ear, inner, inflammation of; otitis interna
Inflammation of the nervous portion of the ear, associated with the brain. Causes can include: secondary bacterial infection; infection; or idiopathic vestibular syndrome[G]. Signs may include staggering; holding the head tilted toward the affected side; and rapid sideways, vertical, or rotary movements of the eyeballs (nystagmus). Treatment usually is aimed at identifying and addressing the underlying cause, if possible, and can include systemic antibiotics if bacterial infection is suspected. Anti-inflammatory medications are administered to reduce irritation of the nerves and balancing mechanisms within the inner ear.

Ear-margin seborrhea
Seborrhea[G] of the ear margin, found most commonly in Dachshunds and other pendulous ear breeds, which could suggest an inherited predisposition. Signs include hair loss and a greasy-waxy crust on the ear flap. Treatment can include anti-seborrheic shampoos, and possibly topical antibiotic/steroid medications, to control inflammation.

Ear, middle, inflammation of; otitis media
Inflammation of the middle ear, generally due to a ruptured ear drum and/or bacterial infection. Signs can include a head tilt; ear scratching; fever; and dizziness. The tilt can remain even after the condition has been treated. Treatment can include topical and systemic antibiotics; surgical drainage may be necessary in some cases.

Ear mites
Infestation by parasites that have invaded your dog's ear canal, causing inflammation, itching, and increased wax formation. Signs can include head shaking and holding the ear drooped to one side. Treatment generally is aimed at killing the mites with insecticides, and cleaning the ear of wax and debris that resulted from inflammation. (Sedation may be needed to accomplish this).

Edema
Swelling due to leakage of clear fluid (serum) from the bloodstream into tissues.

Elbow dysplasia
Chronic, developmental joint condition that causes the elbow joint to seat improperly, resulting in abnormal bone/cartilage wear-and-tear that can lead to arthritis. Most commonly found in large-breed dogs, and thought to have a genetic link. Signs include pain; decreased range of motion; elbows held out from the chest; lameness; and, with time, elbow-joint enlargement. Treatment can include anti-inflammatory medications or surgery, though arthritis still might occur in time. Any affected dog should not be bred.

Elongated soft palate
Most often seen in brachycephalic[G] breeds, this occurs when the soft palate extends into the pharynx[G] (throat), partially obstructing it and interfering with normal breathing. When stressed or forced to exercise,

affected dogs find it difficult to inhale sufficient amounts of air through their noses, so must resort to open-mouth panting. Signs include abnormal, noisy breathing when stressed or excited, shortness of breath after exercise, avoidance of exercise, reduced heat tolerance (air exchange is critical to heat dissipation), and snoring. Treatment includes conscientious management; surgery can also be an option.

Embolic parasitic pneumonia
Usually secondary to heartworm infestation in the right side of the heart. Parts of the parasites pass to the lungs via the pulmonary artery—especially after treatment.

Emphysema
A disorder of the lungs characterized by an increase in size and over-expansion of alveoli (air cells in the lungs). Progressive loss of elasticity, and even bursting, of alveoli causes labored breathing, cough, and even heart impairment. Can be caused by second-hand smoke, smoke inhalation, chronic bronchitis, or have an inherited link. It's an irreversible disorder; treatment generally consists of support therapy.

Encephalitis
Inflammation of the brain, usually due to infection.

Endometritis
Inflammation of the uterine lining, usually due to infection.

Endoscopy
Use of an instrument called an endoscope, which is a rigid or flexible fiberoptic device that can be inserted into natural (nostril, urethra, uterus) or man-made (surgical incision) openings to visualize, diagnose, and/or treat internal problems.

Endotoxemia, endotoxic shock
Blood poisoning that occurs when endotoxins, a poisonous substance present in bacteria, are released in your dog's body. As bacteria die, they release a miniscule amount of toxin that has no effect on your dog unless the bacteria are present in larger-than-usual numbers. In such a case, the dose of toxin your dog absorbs can cause endotoxemia, shock^G, and death.

Epididymitis
Painful inflammation of the epididymis, which is an elongated mass of tubes used for storage, maturation, and movement of sperm at the back of an intact male dog's testis. Signs include testicular swelling; heat; pain; and lethargy. Treatment generally involves castration and antibiotoics.

Epilepsy
Any of various disorders marked by disturbed electrical rhythms of the central nervous system generally manifested by convulsive attacks. See also Acquired epilepsy^G, Idiopathic epilepsy^G, and Primary epilepsy^G.

Epiphora
Watery eye; spilling of tears.

Epulis
A common, usually benign mouth tumor that originates in the periodontal ligament, a collection of fibers that attach your dog's tooth roots to his jaw bone. Treatment generally includes surgery, cryosurgery^G, or radiation therapy.

Escherichia coli
An aerobic, gram-negative bacteria that can cause severe gastro-intestinal problems.

False pregnancy
Also called "pseudopregnancy," this syndrome occurs when a female dog shows signs of pregnancy after being in season (estrus), without being pregnant. The bitch may undergo mammary gland development and produce milk, and also show maternal behaviors mirroring those of a truly pregnant female. It may have evolved in wolf ancestors as a way for barren females to act as nursemaids to pups, thus contributing to survival of the pack.

Fatty lipoma, see Lipoma

Fibrosarcoma
A malignant^G tumor derived from fibrous connective tissue.

Flea-bite dermatitis
A skin condition resulting from sensitivity to flea saliva that contacts your dog's skin during flea bites. The skin is becomes inflamed, itchy, and may be scratched/bitten to the point of hair loss and bleeding. Treatment generally consists of an aggressive flea-control program, and may include antihistamines and anti-inflammatory drugs such as corticosteroids.

Folliculitis
Inflammation deep within the hair follicles.

Foreign object, eating of (see also Pica$_G$)
Most commonly the accidental or mischievous ingestion of sticks, rocks, plastics, bones, etc. When any such foreign object is eaten, the intestines may have trouble moving it along, causing obstruction that's likely to require surgery.

Foxtail

A grass awn that has cylindrical spikes featuring spikelets interspersed with stiff bristles. This design encourages migration through skin and tissues.

Frostbite

Tissue damage due to exposure to extreme cold. Mild cases can cause swelling, redness, and pain. Severe cases actually kill tissues, which slough off or become infected with gangrene. The most common site of frostbite injury in dogs is the ear tip, which sloughs off.

Gastric-Dilatation Volvulus

Also known as "bloat," this life-threatening emergency condition generally occurs after a meal. A dog's stomach becomes filled with gas and liquid that can't be expelled by vomiting or burping. The stomach can then twist on its axis, causing a torsion. Signs include dry retching, lethargy, and abdominal distension. Treatment generally is surgical.

Gastric tumors

Tumors that occur in your dog's stomach.

Gastritis

An inflammation of the stomach, especially of the stomach's mucous membrane.

Gastroenteritis

Inflammation of the membrane lining a dog's stomach and intestines.

Giardia

Parasite that can cause mild intestinal inflammation (enteritis) and chronic or intermittent diarrhea in dogs. Puppies are especially susceptible to problems. Also can infect humans.

Glans penis

The tip of your dog's penis.

Glaucoma

An eye disease characterized by increased pressure within the orb, and hardening of the eyeball, which leads to sight impairment that can result in blindness.

Halitosis

Foul-smelling breath, often due to dental/periodontal disease[G].

Hard-pad disease

Another name for distemper[G], so called because that disease can cause hardening of nose and foot-pad skin in affected dogs.

Heat stroke

Increased body temperature due to muscle exertion combined with high environmental temperature and humidity, or by exposure to a super-heated environment, such as a parked car in hot weather. Signs can include: panting; depression; lack of interest in eating or drinking; abdominal pain; elevated rectal temperature (105° and over). Treatment usually focuses on cooling the dog, and bringing body fluid back into balance with massive volumes of intravenous fluids. As soon as body temperature and hydration begin to improve, signs tend to disappear.

Hematoma/seroma

A bruise or contusion, resulting from blunt trauma (e.g., a livestock kick or a car collision). The hematoma is a pocket of blood caused when blood vessels have broken under intact skin; it feels squishy, like a balloon full of thin pancake batter, and it's only minimally tender to touch. A seroma is a hematoma which has matured: instead of a blood-filled center, the seroma is filled with amber-colored serum and a shrinking nugget of clotted red blood cells.

Hemolytic anemia

A decrease in red blood cell count due to increased destruction of red blood cells. Signs increase in severity as anemia worsens, and can include: icterus[G]; brownish discoloration of the urine; fatigue; and weakness. Treatment usually focuses on the underlying problem, such as bacterial infection or exposure to certain poisons. Transfusions are given if the blood count is dangerously low.

Hemophilia

A sex-linked inherited condition almost exclusively in males, in which one of the blood's clotting factors is absent, causing prolonged bleeding from even minor injuries. Signs include bruising, bleeding into joints, and internal hemorrhage. While females are rarely affected, those that inherit the condition can perpetuate the disease if bred.

Hemorrhagic gastroenteritis

Inflammatory disease of the stomach and intestinal tract leading to bloody diarrhea. Treatment generally consist of supportive therapy. An exact cause may not be identified.

Hepatitis

Any disease or condition marked by inflammation of the liver, including chronic hepatitis and infectious hepatitis.

Hepatitis blue eye
Clouding of the cornea^G that results from a viral infection that also usually affects the liver, hence the name.

Herniated disk
Rupture of a spinal disk, the tough, elastic cushion sandwiched between adjoining vertebrae. This often puts pressure on the spinal cord or nerves.

Hip dysplasia
Chronic, hereditary developmental joint condition that causes the hip ball to seat improperly in its socket, resulting in abnormal bone/cartilage wear-and-tear that can lead to arthritis. Most commonly found in large-breed dogs. Signs include rear end weakness/stiffness, lameness, and, with time, difficulty rising from a sitting or lying position. Treatment can include anti-inflammatory medications and joint protectants. Surgery may be an option though arthritis still might occur in time. Any affected dog should not be bred.

Histoplasmosis
Disease caused by a soil fungus common in the midwest and eastern U.S. Once inhaled, it can cause mild respiratory problems before being walled off in a dog's lungs by his immune system. In rare cases, the organism can evade the immune system and spread throughout a dog's body, causing pneumonia and gastrointestinal problems. It can then spread to other organs, including the liver, spleen, and bone marrow. Treatment generally consists of anti-fungal agents and supportive therapy.

Hookworms
Small, thin worms about 1/4- to 1/2-inch long that fasten to your dog's small intestine and feed on his blood. Signs in affected dogs (most commonly puppies) include anemia and bloody diarrhea. Can affect humans, usually via a mild skin condition.

Horner's syndrome
A collection of facial symptoms due to damage to the sympathetic^G portion of the involuntary nerve supply to your dog's face. Symptoms can occur on one or both sides of his face, depending on the location of the nerve damage. These can include: upper eyelid droop; pupil contraction; and protrusion of the third eyelid^G. Treatment usually is focused on addressing the underlying nerve damage problem, and applying protective eye ointment to the eye to keep it from drying.

Hydrocephalus
A congenital condition in which excessive fluid is found within or around a dog's brain, causing the head to appear dome-shaped. Toy breeds are most commonly affected. Generally is fatal, with few hydrocephalic dogs living beyond the age of 2.

Hyperparathyroidism
Hyperactivity of one of the four parathyroid glands located in a dog's neck. These secrete hormones important for calcium and bone metabolism. Too much parathyroid hormone can impair bone formation in young dogs, and weaken the bones of older dogs. Hyperparathyroidism can result from a tumor in one of the glands, secondary to kidney disease, or due to a nutritional deficiency of calcium or vitamin D in the diet.

Hypersensitivity to sunlight, photosensitization
A skin disorder due to a photoactivating substance in the skin that produces skin-damaging chemicals when triggered by the absorption of ultraviolet light. Signs can include: redness; blistering; ulceration; and crusting of exposed skin that's pale colored and not protected by hair, such as muzzle and eye tissues. An effort to determine the type and source of the photoactivating substance must be made so treatment can address the underlying cause. Other preventative steps may include sunblocks or keeping the dog indoors until dusk. Skin lesions are treated as any other superficial ulceration, generally with debridement^G of damaged tissue, disinfection, and protection against further irritation.

Hypertrophic osteodystrophy
A bone disease characterized by painful, firm swellings on the limbs, due to new bone formation along the shafts of affected bones. Such new bone formation can be triggered by a mass elsewhere in the dog's body, including lung or abdominal tumors. Treatment is generally targeted at the underlying mass. HO may or may not regress after removal of the inciting cause.

Hypertrophy
Abnormal development of an organ or part, such as a thickening of muscle fibers.

Hypoglycemia
An abnormal decrease in blood sugar.

Hypoproteinemia
Low protein in your dog's blood, due to abnormally low protein intake in his diet, poor digestion and/or absorption of dietary protein in his intestines, or excessive loss of protein in his stool and/or urine. Signs can include: loss of muscle mass; weakness; fatigue; edema^G (swelling) in the legs and/or lower abdominal

wall; and depression. Treatment usually is focused on identifying and addressing the underlying cause.

Hypothyroidism

Diminished production of thyroid hormones. Signs of hypothyroidism can include general weakness; fatigue; dullness; and obesity. Treatment usually focuses on relieving signs with oral supplementation with a thyroid hormone.

Icterus

Yellow discoloration of skin and mucus membranes (gums, eyelid rims, inner surface of vulva) due to accumulation of pigments normally metabolized by your dog's liver. Causes can include: liver disease; hemolytic anemia[G]; snakebite[G]; and ingestion of certain toxins, such as onions[G] or phenothiazine drugs. Treatment usually is focused on addressing the underlying problem.

Idiopathic epilepsy

Epilepsy that's unexplained, or from an unknown or obscure cause. Generally a dog that reveals no abnormality upon examination is considered to have inherited the condition, since the cause is not apparent. The term idiopathic epilepsy is therefore often interchanged with that of inherited epilepsy.

Idiopathic vestibular syndrome

Inflammation of your dog's inner ear, where balance is regulated, with no discernible underlying cause. (Viral infection is suspected by some researchers.) Signs usually are the same as with other inner ear infections[G].

Impetigo

A skin condition also known as "puppy pyoderma" or "puppy acne" for the fact that it generally affects puppies less than a year old. Characterized by white pustules on the chin and abdomen. It seldom creates more than a localized infection and generally responds well to application of benzoyl peroxide (human acne medication) and topical antibiotics.

Incontinence

Inability to control urination or bowel movements.

Infection, in blood; septicemia

Disease caused by the spread of infectious organisms and their toxins in your dog's bloodstream. See Septicemia[G].

Infection, in wound

A wound becomes infected when bacteria and/or fungi contaminating it begin reproducing in an organized fashion, causing a disproportionate increase in one species over the others. Effective treatment usually focuses on improving the dog's own defenses (e.g., providing drainage, removing dead tissue), and directly attacking the infection with an antibiotic to which the bacteria are sensitive.

Injection, local reaction to

Inflammation in tissues where an intramuscular injection was given, due to caustic or irritating characteristics of the injected substance. Symptoms can include swelling, heat, tenderness, and stiffness of the affected muscle tissue, and reluctance to use or stretch it. Treatment may include: application of warm, moist compresses; massage of affected muscle; administration of anti-inflammatory medication; and (if the injection was given in the neck) adjustment of feed and water sources so your dog can eat and drink without stretching his neck.

Insect sting

Bee, wasp, and ant stings can be toxic, due to nerve-poisons and caustic chemicals in their venom, causing painful skin lesions and occasionally generalized reactions. If your dog is especially sensitive to a toxin, or if multiple stings occurred, hemolysis (see Hemolytic anemia[G]), difficulty breathing (due to swelling within the respiratory tract), collapse, and even death can occur. For local reactions, treatment may include application of ice and a poultice[G] to soothe and draw out swelling and venom. (For how-to information, see pages 309 and 306.) For generalized reactions, treatment usually is focused on halting and reversing respiratory distress and neutralizing the body's reaction to the toxin with such medications as antihistamines and corticosteroids.

Intervertebral disk disease

Any disease affecting the tough, elastic disks located between the vertebrae in your dog's spine.

In-utero

In the uterus, before birth.

Iris cyst

Cyst[G] located on the colored portion of your dog's eye, characterized by small, round dark spots that aren't firmly attached. The cause is unknown and treatment is generally unnecessary as they usually don't affect iris funciton.

Ivermectin

A class of dewormer products. The canine product HeartGard is a member of this class.

Jaundice
See Icterus[G].

Joint capsule
The thick tissue encasing joints in your dog. Joint capsules are richly endowed with blood vessels and sensory nerves, so any inflammation there can cause significant pain.

Juvenile vaginitis
Inflammation of the vagina seen in puppies 6 to 12 weeks of age, and characterized by vulvar discharge. Generally requires no treatment as it will usually clear up on its own.

Kennel cough (Infectious trachobronchitis)
A highly infectious inflammation of the respiratory tract that can be caused by several different infectious agents, which alone or in combination cause nearly identical symptoms. It results in a high-pitched, honking cough. Some dogs will recover within two weeks, others can contract secondary bacterial infections. Treatment can include cough suppressants, antibiotics, bronchodilators (which widen airways), and support therapy. Vaccines are available that can help protect your dog against the various pathogens that cause the condition.

Keratitis
Inflammation of the cornea[G] characterized by pain, cloudy cornea, and sensitivity to light. Can result from infectious agents or trauma.

Kidney disease
Includes several syndromes, including the formation of kidney stones, kidney infection, and a number of disorders that can impair the kidney's ability to function as a filter of toxins and conserver of proteins, minerals, and water. Causes can include: infection; kidney stones; impaired blood circulation to the kidneys; and/or over-medication with drugs such as certain antibiotics and non-steroidal anti-inflammatory medications. Treatment usually includes identifying and addressing the underlying cause and administering intravenous fluids and medications to affect urine output, plus a low-protein diet.

Laryngeal hemiplegia
Paralysis of one side of your dog's larynx, due to malfunction of the nerve that supplies the vocal folds on that side. This causes the cartilage to open, blocking his windpipe, thus reducing that opening. Symptoms result from the reduction in airflow, and can include a change in the quality of bark, fatigue, and sensitivity to heat. Treatment usually is one of several surgical techniques to open that drape and affix it in the open position.

Lead poisoning
Poisoning by ingestion of lead. Sources include used motor oil, being fed from ceramic dishes originating in third-world countries, lead-based paint, or soil or water contaminated by lead from automobile exhaust or from silver mine tailings. The classic sign of lead poisoning is a roaring or snoring sound when breathing, due to laryngeal hemiplegia[G]. Other signs can include: weakness; incoordination; joint enlargement; and stiffness. Treatment usually includes: removal of your dog from the lead source; intravenous administration of specific medication to bind the lead and render it inactive; and general support as needed.

Lens luxation (dislocation)
Altered lens position in the eye, or total lens displacement due to hereditary factors, trauma, glaucoma, or inflammation. Characterized by pain and redness, with corneal cloudiness. Generally requires surgical removal of the lens.

Lenticular sclerosis, see Nuclear sclerosis

Leptospirosis
Infection by bacteria of the Leptospira family, which can infect your dog's kidneys and reproductive tract, and also can invade tissues of the eye. Because Leptospira bacteria can be carried by several species, including mice, rats, pigs, cattle, and wild deer, and can be spread in common water sources, dogs at facilities with confirmed Leptospirosis cases should be kept isolated from other species and provided separate water. Vaccines are available for use in dogs which can be effective in reducing the occurrence and severity of leptospiral disease—but not infection. Leptospiroisis is a potential—and serious—health threat to humans, so infected dogs present a potential health hazard and should be handled with strict hygienic precautions.

Lice
Infestation by biting or blood-sucking lice. Signs can include itching and scratching, patchy hair loss, skin reddening, abrasions, and scaling. Treatment options may include applications of insecticide (spray, dip, or powder).

Lick granuloma
A fairly common, ulcer-like skin condition caused by excessive licking. Generally found on legs or paws. Generally linked to boredom, although it can result from previous trauma to the area. Most common in large, active breeds that crave constant attention. Treatment generally includes topical and systemic

antibiotics, and anti-inflammatories. Alleviating boredom may also help; tranquilizers and other anti-anxiety medications may help during periods of stress.

Lip-fold dermatitis

Bacterial infection of the lip folds on such breeds as Cocker Spaniels, Springer Spaniels, Irish Setters, Newfoundlands, and St. Bernards. One common sign is bad breath. Treatment can include cleansing with an anti-bacterial or benzoyl peroxide shampoo, application of a drying agent, and topical antibiotic and corticosteroid creams.

Lipoma

A benign[G] tumor composed of fat cells.

Liver disease (hepatitis)

The liver is the body's toxic waste dump. Its main job is to detoxify and package toxins for elimination. When liver disease progresses to the point that the organ's function is impaired, a variety of problems can appear, which can include weight loss; dermatitis of unpigmented skin (see Hypersensitivity to sunlight[G]) and icterus[G].

Lumbosacral arthritis

Arthritis[G] at the junction of the lower back and pelvis.

Lumbosacral instability

Instability of the spine at the junction of the lower back and pelvis of a dog, which can lead to pressure on the spinal cord (and thus such neurologic signs as incoordination of the rear end, or paralysis) or arthritis[G].

Lungworms

Nematodes that infect a dog's lungs, causing bronchitis characterized by episodes of harsh, dry coughing. Treatment is administration of a deworming agent labeled effective against the parasite.

Lupus erythematosus (systemic)

A chronic, autoimmune[G] disease that results in anemia[G], arthritis[G], and impaired kidney function. Your dog's immune system attacks his own red blood cells, leading to anemia. It views his joint lining as foreign and attacks it, leading to arthritis. The immune system also attacks part of his kidneys, limiting their function, and even leading to kidney failure. Signs include weakness, jaundice[G], joint stiffness, and excessive drinking/urination. Treatment can include steroids and medications to accommodate kidney malfunction.

Luxating patella

Dislocation of the patella (a dog's "kneecap," which is located just in front of and above the knee) from its

normal position. Generally occurs in small-breed dogs. May require surgical repair.

Luxation

Dislocation of a joint or other body part (such as an eye lens), away from its normal position.

Lyme disease

Infection with the spiral-shaped bacteria Borrelia burgdorferi, spread by the bite of an infected tick. Signs vary widely and can include: recurrent lameness that shifts from one leg to another and for which no other cause can be found; arthritis; stiffness; and reluctance to move. Treatment usually is administration of antibiotics from the penicillin or tetracycline family. Can affect humans.

Lymphosarcoma (also Lymphoma, or Malignant lymphoma

Generally a term that includes various abnormally proliferative, probably tumerous diseases of the lymphoid system.

Magnetic resonance imaging (MRI)

A diagnostic tool that provides a more complete view of the body and organs than do CAT scans[G] and X-rays.

Malignant

Referring to a cancerous growth: Locally invasive and destructive, and/or tending to spread to other areas of the body.

Malignant hyperthermia

Sudden onset of high fever and rigid muscles due to drug reaction or to abnormally low blood calcium levels.

Malignant lymphoma (also see Lymphoma)

One of the most common internal forms of cancer. A variety of tissues can be affected, but the one common site is the lymph nodes along the intestinal tract, resulting in impaired digestion. The lymph nodes adjacent to the heart and lungs also can be affected. Signs may include: weight loss; fever; swollen lymph nodes; impaired vision; signs of respiratory disease; diarrhea; loss of appetite; edema; and depression. Cures are rare; chemotherapy may help.

Mammary cyst

Cyst[G] of the mammary gland, those glands in females that secrete milk. Male dogs also have mammary glands, and also can suffer from mammary cysts.

Mammary tumor

Tumor[G] of the mammary gland, those glands in

females that secrete milk. Male dogs also have mammary glands, and also can suffer from mammary tumors. One way to reduce the risk of mammary tumors is to spay a female dog before her first heat.

Mastitis
Inflammation of the mammary gland, usually caused by infection.

Melanoma
A tumor of pigment cells. Some can grow aggressively, causing erosions and spreading to adjacent lymph nodes and lungs. Can be malignant[G].

Meningitis
Inflammation of the meninges, the membranes surrounding the spinal cord and brain. Can be the result of viral, fungal, or bacterial infection. Signs include fever, lethargy, and reluctance to move, especially the neck and head. Treatment generally includes high doses of steroid medication.

Mites
Any of numerous small to minute arachnids (same family as ticks and spiders), which include the parasitic mites responsible for demodectic[G] and sarcoptic[G] mange in dogs.

MRI, see Magnetic resonance imaging

Myelogram
Diagnostic procedure of the spinal cord that involves the injection of a substance that will show contrast on the developed X-ray, thus helping to highlight problem areas.

Myositis
Inflammation of a muscle.

Nail bed
The point from which a dog's toenail emerges from his skin.

Nasal-fold dermatitis
Bacterial infection of the skin folds on the face of brachycephalic[G] breeds. Common signs include redness, discharge, odor, and ulceration due to scratching. Treatment can include cleansing with an anti-bacterial or benzoyl peroxide shampoo, application of a drying agent, and topical antibiotic and steroid creams.

Nasal mites
Microscopic mites that invade a dog's nose and can also migrate to his sinuses. Signs generally include sneezing (which can transmit the mites to other dogs). A bloody nose may result from irritated nasal membranes. Treatment generally includes medication that kills the parasites.

Nasal septal disease
Any of a number of conditions affecting the nasal septum, including thickening or inflammation due to trauma, infection, or cancerous growth. The result is abnormal air movement through the nostrils, nasal discharge, and/or respiratory noise. Treatment generally focuses on resolving the underlying cause.

Nasal-solar dermatitis
Also known as "collie nose," this genetic condition generally occurs in breeds with little or no facial pigment, and is due to a hypersensitivity to sunlight. Lesions generally develop on the nose, eyelids, and lips. Treatment generally includes reducing exposure to sunlight, application of topical sun block, and/or tattooing the unpigmented areas to protect them against the sun's rays.

Nasolacrimal duct
A duct that transmits tears from the medial corner of the eye to the nose.

Needle aspiration biopsy
A sampling of fluid and suspended bits of soft tissue from a lesion, abscess, or tumor by inserting a needle and pulling back on the syringe's plunger to obtain contents for laboratory examination.

Nephritis
Acute[G] or chronic[G] inflammation of the kidneys that results in scarring. Can be caused by infection, toxic chemicals, such as antifreeze, autoimmune disease[G], or vascular disease.

Neuritis
Inflammation of a nerve.

Nictitating membrane (third eyelid)
The "third eyelid," a pink membrane normally folded out of sight in the inner corner of your dog's eye, covering the eyeball when the upper eyelid closes. If the nictitating membrane is visible while the eye is open, your dog needs medical attention.

Nuclear sclerosis (also Lenticular sclerosis)
The normal change in appearance of an older dog's eye lens. Onset generally occurs around the age of 6 or 7, and is evident by a blue-gray appearance in the pupil that results from a hardening of the lens from

compression of central lens fibers. NS does not impair vision, and should be differentiated from cataracts by a veterinarian.

Obsessive-compulsive disorder

A condition in which a dog is psychologically driven to repeat the same behavior, over and over again. Licking is a typical sign in dogs. The dog will constantly lick the same spot, usually on his leg or paw, often injuring the skin. (See Acral lick granuloma[G].)

OCD, see Osteochondrosis dissecans

Ocular

Having to do with the eye.

Old-dog vestibular syndrome

A syndrome in geriatric dogs characterized by the sudden onset of circling, abnormal eye movements, loss of balance, and/or abnormal position. It generally resolves itself within a few weeks.

Onions

Both wild and cultivated onions are toxic to dogs, causing hemolytic anemia[G]. Signs can include icterus[G], brownish-colored urine, and weakness and loss of stamina as the anemia progresses. Treatment usually is supportive. Prevention of further ingestion of onions is key. If the anemia is severe, a transfusion may be needed.

Optic nerve, injury to

Injury to the optic nerve—the large nerve that connects your dog's eye to his brain—can cause temporary or permanent blindness, depending on the severity of the injury.

Oral dosing

A means of administering a liquid medication, by squirting or pouring it into the side of your dog's mouth with a dosing syringe, eye-dropper, or turkey baster.

Organophosphates

A phosphorus-containing organic pesticide. Malathion is one example. Poisonous to both insects and mammals, including dogs and humans.

Oro-nasal fistula

The result of an opening between the hard palate and nasal cavity. Water and food can enter the cavity and are regurgitated through the dog's nose. Sneezing and a nasal discharge may be evident. Usually due to loss of an infected tooth; surgical repair is generally required.

Osteochondrosis dissecans

A common congenital joint problem in young, growing dogs (especially large-breed, rapidly growing ones). In dogs, it usually affects the shoulder joints, but can affect those of the stifle and hock. Cartilage on the joint surface of developing bones (especially long bones) degenerates or suffers a mechanical injury (such as from trauma), resulting in a painful lesion. The lesion can eventually break off, resulting in a bone or cartilage chip in the joint. Treatment may require strict rest or surgery.

Pancreatic insufficiency

The pancreas serves two functions: to provide digestive enzymes; and to make insulin for sugar metabolism. Failure to make insulin can result in diabetes[G]. Failure to provide digestive enzymes causes incomplete digestion of foods in the small intestine which may lead to "malabsorption syndrome." Signs include voracious appetite; large, cow-pie like stools; weight loss; and/or oily hair around the anus from undigested fat. Treatment generally includes a special, highly digestible diet and oral enzymes and vitamins.

Pancreatitis

Inflammation of the pancreas. Signs can be mild and include loss of appetite, vomiting, and diarrhea. Serious cases can cause acute[G] abdominal pain. An acute case can permanently impair pancreas function, resulting in diabetes[G] or pancreatic insufficiency[G]. Chronic or recurrent cases can be fatal.

Pannus

A corneal[G] inflammation involving one or both eyes and characterized by the growth of a bluish/gray membrane across the dog's cornea. Most commonly affects German Shepherds and their cross-breds. Treatment can include steroid eye ointments and/or injections, and in some cases, surgery. Generally a total cure can't be obtained, but progression can be slowed.

Panosteitis

Also called "growing pains," as it's generally a condition of fast-growing, large-breed young dogs (generally between the ages of 6 and 18 months). Characterized by a "wandering" lameness that moves from leg to leg over the course of several weeks or months. Some cases have a single-leg lameness that comes and goes. The condition usually is self-limiting. Treatment can involve rest; a diet change (from puppy to adult dog food); administration of vitamin C; and analgesics and anti-inflammatory drugs, to relieve pain.

Papilloma
A benign tumor (wart) that results from an overgrowth of skin cells.

Parasite
An organism living in or on another organism, such as a parasitic worm living in your dog's intestines or fleas living on his back.

Parasitic diarrhea
Intestinal parasites cause tiny sores in your dog's intestinal tract as they attach themselves. With heavy and/or long-standing parasite infestation, the amount of tissue damage and inflammation can affect intestinal function and cause chronic diarrhea. Treatment may include: killing the parasites with an appropriate dewormer[G]; soothing the inflamed intestines with medications given systemically; and feeding a bland but nutritious diet. Management changes focus on reducing exposure to parasite eggs and larvae.

Parvovirus
A highly contagious, virulent disease that can be spread via contact with infected feces and is characterized by loss of appetite, lethargy, and bloody diarrhea and vomiting. Can be fatal. Treatment includes supportive therapy; vaccines exist that can help protect your dog from this deadly virus.

Pemphigus foliaceus
A skin disorder caused by the body's immune system mistakenly attacking some of its own cells involved in skin production. Signs tend to wax and wane, and include the formation of blisters and pustules that break open and form crusted sores. Lesions generally start on a dog's face and limbs, eventually spreading to the rest of his body. There's no cure, but treatment can control the lesions and cause the disorder to go into remission. Some reports indicate that the younger a dog is, the greater the chance that the condition will go into long-term remission. Treatment may involve suppression of the immune system by administration of systemic corticosteroids.

Perianal
Of or relating to the tissue surrounding your dog's anus.

Perianal adenoma
A generally benign tumor arising from the glands located around the anus. It often bleeds and resembles a small bunch of grapes. Treatment generally includes surgical removal.

Perineal hernia
Rupture in the abdominal wall near the anal opening.

This allows such abdominal organs as the intestines and bladder to protrude outward, held in only by a skin barrier. The abdominal wall weakness can be genetic in nature; most such hernias involve older male dogs and require surgical repair.

Periodontal disease
Disease of the gums, bone, and connective tissue around your dog's teeth. Common signs of periodontal disease include foul-smelling breath (halitosis[G]), brownish/yellowish tartar collecting on your dog's teeth, and red/inflamed gums.

Peripheral nervous system
Part of the nervous system that's outside the central nervous system. It comprises the cranial nerves (except the optic nerve), the spinal nerves, and the autonomic nervous system, which controls involuntary movements, such as reflexes.

Peritonitis
Inflammation of the membrane that lines the abdominal cavity.

Pharyngitis
Inflammation of the pharynx (throat), where the nasal and mouth cavities converge.

Photosensitivity, see Hypersensitivity to sunlight

Pica
A depraved appetite; a hunger for substances that are not fit for food, such as rocks and feces. It's rarely a nutrition-driven condition as was once thought, but rather a psychological abnormality that becomes a habit. Ingestion of some foreign materials can lead to health problems, requiring surgical removal.

Pigmentary keratitis
Deposit of pigment on the cornea, which is usually secondary to chronic irritation and corneal exposure in brachycephalic[G] breeds.

Pituitary adenoma
The pituitary gland, located at the base of your dog's brain, has the vital role of secreting hormones that regulate a multitude of body functions. A portion of the pituitary gland may become tumorous and begin releasing overdoses of hormones. The result: a condition called Cushing's disease[G], generally characterized by signs including: muscle wasting; excessive water drinking; and excessive urinating. A series of blood tests yield the diagnosis; treatment is mainly symptomatic.

Plastic-dish dermatitis

Skin irritation characterized by depigementation of the nose/lips in dogs fed and watered from plastic dishes. Generally resolves when the dog is switched to a glass or stainless-steel bowl. Also known as a form of contact dermatitis[G].

Pneumonia

Infection in the lungs, sometimes occurring after a viral upper-respiratory infection, or due to bacteria that take advantage of your dog's weakened resistance. Other contributing factors can include: stress; aspiration; shipping/showing, causing exposure to powerful bacteria that can cause pneumonia even in dogs that are otherwise healthy and unstressed. Signs may include fever; lack of appetite, cough; discharge of pus from nostrils; depression; and rapid and/or labored breathing. Treatment usually includes support and administration of appropriate antibiotics.

Pneumothorax

The presence of air or gas in the pleural cavity (the space between your dog's lungs and his chest wall), usually the result of a penetrating wound. Because his lungs can't expand properly, it's difficult for the dog to get enough oxygen. Signs usually include rapid, shallow respiration; anxiety; and preoccupation with breathing. Treatment generally is surgical repair.

Polyarthropothy

Inflammation in multiple joints, characterized by swelling, heat, pain and a reluctance to move or be touched.

Primary epilepsy

A chronic nervous disorder characterized by attacks of unconsciousness and/or convulsions.

Progressive retinal atrophy (PRA)

An inherited condition in which a dog's retinas degenerate. Initial signs can include night blindness, as indicated by a dog's reluctance to leave a lighted area at night to relieve himself in the yard; clinging to the owner; reluctance to mount stairs; missing targets when jumping up, such as on a chair or bed. This can then progress to daytime blindness. There is no effective therapy.

Proptosis

Displacement of the eyeball from its socket, generally due to trauma, and most commonly in bulgy-eyed, flat-faced types of dogs, such as Pugs, Pekinese, and Bulldogs. An emergency—quick veterinary attention is required to replace the eye and minimize swelling and damage.

Psychogenic water consumption

Act of drinking water without thirst, such as out of stress or boredom.

Pulpitis

Inflammation of the pulp of a dog's tooth.

Pus

Yellowish white or pale green, malodorous and cloudy discharge that results from infection, and is made up of tissue debris, white blood cells, and microorganisms.

Pyoderma

Any skin inflammation characterized by pus-filled lesions.

Pyometra

Life-threatening infection of the uterus that generally happens to females that were recently in season. Signs can include loss of appetite, lethargy, vaginal discharge, and increased water intake. A medical emergency–treatment can include support therapy and generally includes spaying the dog.

Rabies

A fatal viral infection of the central nervous system spread by the saliva of an infected animal. Signs can vary widely and can include lameness; bizarre gait; slobbering due to difficulty swallowing; depression or excitability; convulsions; and death within days of onset of signs. There's no treatment. Suspected cases should be quarantined. Euthanasia and definitive diagnosis using laboratory test of brain tissue should be considered in all cases of suspected rabies, so any other animals (human or otherwise) that were exposed can be treated and/or quarantined.

Rectal prolapse

Protrusion of a portion of the anal canal lining through the rectum, due to forceful and prolonged straining. Treatment involves identifying and solving the underlying cause of the straining, and either manually or surgically replacing the prolapse.

Retinal atrophy

Gradual, progressive deterioration of the retina (the neuroreceptive tissues of the eyeball). (See also Progressive retinal atrophy[G].)

Retinal detachment

A condition in which the retinal layer of cells separates from underlying tissue, due to trauma, cysts[G], tumor[G], or eye inflammation. May reattach without treatment, or require medications such as diuretics and steroids. Some cases can result in blindness.

Reverse sneezing

Forced, severe inhalation through the nose thought to be the result of mucus, food, or a foreign body on top of the soft palate. Generally spells of reverse sneezing resolve by themselves. Persistent cases require further examination.

Ringworm

A fungal infection of your dog's skin, contagious to other dogs and to other animals (possibly including humans). The main sign of ringworm is patchy hair loss without itching. Treatment can include: clipping hair from affected areas; daily bathing with iodine-based shampoo; possible application of topical anti-fungal preparations after each bath; strict maintenance of dry shelter; and exposure to sunlight whenever possible. For severe cases, oral administration of anti-fungal medications may be necessary.

Rocky Mountain Spotted Fever

A tick-borne disease that can leave a dog a carrier, without making him ill. However, some dogs do get sick from the disease, showing such signs as lethargy, loss of appetite, vomiting, diarrhea, nose/eye discharge, joint pain, fever, and depression. In severe cases, dogs can have swollen legs, lips, jaws, ears, and genitals. Kidney failure can result, leading to death. Treatment generally consists of supportive care and antibiotic therapy. There currently is no canine vaccine.

Roundworms, see Ascarids

Ruptured cervical disk

Herniated disk[G] in the neck region of the spine.

Ruptured disk, see Herniated disk

Ruptured intervertebral disk, see Herniated disk

Salivary cyst

Cysts[G] that occur when salivary ducts become blocked by secretions or foreign bodies, such as stones or grass awns. Fluid backs up, which can rupture the duct and form a fluid-filled cyst. Surgery is required to treat the condition.

Salivary duct stone

The formation of a stone in your dog's salivary duct, causing a hard lump on the side of his head behind his jawbone, below his ear, or just behind the corner of his mouth. If the duct is completely blocked by a stone, there generally will be heat, swelling, and pain along the side of his head below the ear, due to inflammation in the salivary gland. Treatment usually is surgical removal of the stone.

Salmonellosis, Salmonella infection, Salmonella enteritis

A contagious intestinal infection by Salmonella bacteria, causing severe acute[G] diarrhea or chronic[G] diarrhea. Acute diarrhea is usually accompanied by fever and abdominal pain. Treatment usually requires aggressive intensive care; quarantine; pain management; stress management, and may include antibiotics. Can affect humans.

Sarcoma

A malignant[G] tumor[G] arising in connective tissue, bone, cartilage, or muscle, that spreads via extension into neighboring tissue, or through the bloodstream.

Sarcoptic mange

Also known as "scabies." Skin disease (mange) caused by microscopic, spider-like mites of the genus Sarcoptes that burrow into the skin, especially around the face, ears, elbows, and hocks, causing an intense itch. Can be transferred to humans. Treatment generally involves clipping the effected area and treating with insecticide products effective against sarcoptic mites.

Scrotal dermatitis

Dermatitis[G] of a male dog's scrotum, characterized by scaly, red, and/or oozing skin that itches, causing the dog to chew/lick at the area.

Sebaceous cyst

Cysts[G] arising from a dog's sebaceous glands, which provide oils (called sebum[G]) for the coat and skin. When a gland becomes blocked, it can swell in size, forming a lump known as a sebaceous cyst. Treatment may include surgical removal.

Seborrhea

Abnormally increased secretion of sebum[G] (skin oils), which results in a scaly, oily appearance to the skin. Usually secondary to an allergy, bacterial infection, etc.

Seborrhea, ear-margin, see Ear-margin Seborrhea

Sebum

Oil secreted by the skin's sebaceous glands, to lubricate the coat and skin.

Septicemia

Blood poisoning due to bacteria and their toxins in your dog's bloodstream. Symptoms usually include:

loss of appetite; fever; and depression. Treatment generally includes support and administration of antibiotics to which the causative bacteria are sensitive.

Sequestrum
A loose, dead fragment of broken bone, often associated with a local infection.

Seroma
The result of blunt trauma causing bleeding under the skin. A seroma is a hematoma^G in which accumulated blood has separated into serum and clotted red blood cells.

Sertoli cell tumor
Tumor^G of the Sertoli cells, which are important for the development of sperm in a male dog's testicles. Such tumors can lead to excessive production of the female sex hormone estrogen, and development of female sex characteristics, such as swollen mammary glands, swollen penile sheath, and being attractive to male dogs. Other signs include symmetrical hair loss or coat-color change on the flanks, expanding to include the abdomen, groin, chest, and back. Treatment generally involves castration. Most treatments are successful, as most Sertoli cell tumors are benign.

Serum
A watery portion of blood remaining after clot formation or the normal, watery discharge such as that from a blister.

Shock
A serious—and potentially fatal—state of profound physical and mental depression, secondary to an injury/trauma or emotional disturbance, that causes a shift in the flow of blood, causing it to pool in your dog's veins rather than flow to his heart and lungs. Generally characterized by rapid, weak pulse; rapid, shallow respiration; anxiety or mental dullness; nausea and vomiting due to reduced blood volume; low blood pressure; and below-normal temperature. Treatment usually focuses on trying to increase blood volume/ pressure by administering intravenous fluids and giving medications that can alter blood distribution.

Skin cancer
The most common type of skin cancers causing external tumors in dogs are melanoma^G, lymphoma^G, and squamous cell carcinoma^G.

Snakebite
The bite of certain venomous snakes can cause illness in dogs, including swelling and bruising at the bite site, and potentially dangerous swelling of the respiratory tract. Treatment generally is: administration of anti-inflammatory medications to minimize swelling; tracheotomy^G and/or supplemental oxygen if necessary to aid in breathing; antibiotics; and administration of specific antivenin if the type of snake is known and diagnosis is made very soon after the bite.

Snow nose
A condition in which the nose's black pigment lightens during winter and darkens as summer approaches. Primarily a cosmetic problem in white-coated breeds; may be hereditary. Cause is unknown.

Spinal disk disease, see Intervertebral disk disease

Sprain, tendon or ligament
Stretching and/or tearing of tendon or ligament fibers due to excessive strain. The injury is worsened by swelling and bleeding within the torn tendon or ligament, and by additional strain. Treatment may include ice and pressure bandaging; prevention of further stress by limiting movement of the affected limb with a splint or cast; administration of anti-inflammatory medications; and physical therapy to prevent adhesions that would limit future range of motion.

Squamous cell carcinoma
Cancer of a specific type of cells present in skin and mucus membranes lining internal organs such as the bladder, intestines, and uterus. Squamous cell carcinoma of the skin is commonly associated with ultraviolet rays on unpigmented, hairless skin adjacent to a white-coated area (which reflects sun onto the vulnerable skin for a double dose of ultraviolet rays). When lesions are few and accessible, treatment generally is removal and/or obliteration by surgery, cryosurgery,^{G} radiation therapy, and/or photodynamic therapy. When too extensive or inaccessible, often the only treatment option is chemotherapy.

Staphylococcus
A bacteria of the family Micrococcaceae that include a number of pathogenic spherical organisms common to the skin and mucous membranes.

Status epilepticus
The most severe form of epilepsy^G, in which a seizure can last for hours or more, or the dog will emerge from one only to dissolve back into another.

Stenotic nares
A birth defect that generally occurs in brachycephalic^G breeds, such as Pugs, Pekinese, and Bulldogs. Because

the cartilage of the nostrils is too soft, the nostrils collapse whenever the puppy breathes in, cutting off his air. Signs can include a watery, foamy nasal discharge, and mouth breathing when stressed, excited, or after exercise. Treatment generally is surgery to enlarge the nasal openings.

Streptococcus

A spherical pathogenic bacteria that includes important pathogens in canine disease, generally involved in pus^G-forming infections. Streptococcal infections can cause mastitis^G and polyarthropothy^G.

Stroke

A brain disorder that occurs when a blood clot travels through your dog's bloodstream and becomes lodged in a blood vessel in his brain. This can result in loss of blood supply, leakage of loose blood (which is inflammatory) into the brain tissue, and/or brain swelling. Signs depend on the area of the brain affected. Treatment generally is supportive and aggressive administration of anti-inflammatory medications.

Sympathetic system

The portion of your dog's involuntary nervous system involved primarily with enhancing bodily functions that support "flight or fight," such as dilating the pupils, widening his eyes, raising the blood pressure, and increasing his heart rate.

Synovial cells, synovial membrane

Thin, flexible tissue lining most joints in your dog. The synovial membrane is comprised of synovial cells, which manufacture a viscous fluid (synovial fluid) that fills and lubricates the joints.

Synovitis

Inflammation of the soft, pliable membrane lining a joint. Often the first in a series of events that can lead to degenerative joint disease.

Tapeworms

Segmented, flatworm parasites that can invade dogs and humans, adhering to the host's intestine via suckers, hooks, or grooves. Dogs generally become infested after ingesting fleas. Signs of infestation include rice-like worm segments in feces. Treatment includes a dewormer designed to kill tapeworms.

Testicular tumor

Tumor^G of the testicles.

Tetanus

A disease resulting from toxins produced by bacteria of the Clostridium family, usually resulting when they infect a wound, particularly (but not exclusively) a deep puncture wound, where oxygen is scarce. Clostridium species are natural soil inhabitants. Rare in dogs, as compared to the risk of this disease in horses and humans. (So rare that dogs are not routinely vaccinated.) Signs of tetanus may include: elevation of both nictitating membranes^G when the dog's face is tapped gently below the eye; spasms of the muscles in his jaw, making it difficult or impossible to eat or drink (hence the name "lockjaw"); a "sawhorse" stance with rigid legs; convulsions triggered by noise or other stimuli; and death. Treatment usually is aggressive debridement of the infected wound to prevent further toxin absorption; intravenous administration of tetanus antitoxin; administration of anti-seizure medications, antibiotics, sedatives, and muscle relaxants; and intensive supportive care.

Third eyelid, see Nictitating membrane^G

Tonsillitis

Inflammation of the tonsils.

Toxoplasmosis

Infection with a member of the Toxoplasma family, a protozoal organism.

Tracheal collapse

A condition in which the tracheal rings are weakened, making the trachea easily collapse in response to external or internal pressure. Most common in small or toy breeds. Signs can range from a chronic^G, honking cough in mild cases to coughing fits, retching, vomiting, and even collapse in severe ones. Treatment can involve bronchodilators, corticosteroids, antibiotics, cough suppressants and management changes (to keep the dog quiet), or surgery, for severe cases.

Tracheal hypoplasia

A condition that occurs when a dog is born with an underdeveloped trachea, causing insufficient airflow even at rest. Occurs most often in brachycephalic^G dogs, such as Pugs, Pekinese, and Bulldogs. Signs can include stress and exercise intolerance, and even collapse. No treatment is currently available; management to reduce stress and forced exercise is recommended.

Tracheotomy

An artificial opening made in the windpipe (trachea) when a problem in your dog's nasal cavity or throat has blocked the passage of air, making it impossible to breathe. Usually an emergency procedure.

Trigeminal neuritis

Inflammation of the trigeminal nerve, which supplies motor and sensory "power" to parts of your dog's face and head, causing such neurolgical signs as paralysis (such as of the jaw or lip) or a "droopy" eye. Inflammation can result from such causes as trauma, a cyst[G], tumor[G], or infection.

Tumor

An abnormal mass of tissue that's not inflammatory in origin, that arises from cells or tissue, and serves no useful purpose.

Ultrasonography (ultrasound)

A diagnostic imaging technique used to image soft, deep tissues by sending ultrasonic sound waves to and/or through them, and forming a live image with the sound waves that bounce back. Ultrasound examinations are used commonly in reproduction; and in detecting tumors/cysts in the liver, spleen, kidney, heart, umbilicus, and eye.

Urethra, blockage of

A blocked urethra stops the flow of urine from your dog's bladder to the outside and is, therefore, an emergency situation. Urethral blockage can be caused by passage of a bladder stone or blood clot, or by pressure on the urethra from an adjacent mass. Symptoms generally include frequent posturing and straining to urinate with sporadic or minimal output. Treatment usually is identifying and treating the underlying cause.

Urethritis

Inflammation of the urethra, the canal that carries urine from the bladder.

Uterine prolapse

A condition that occurs when a dog's uterus everts and is passed through the vaginal opening, generally within several days after the dog gave birth. Surgery generally is required to resolve the problem.

Uveitis

Inflammation and/or infection of the uvea, the colored iris of your dog's eye. Several potential causes exist, including trauma to the eye and abnormal immune activity within the eye. However, the cause of most cases of uveitis is never determined. Signs can include: a cloudy cornea; constricted pupil; watery eye; squinting; and rubbing. If allowed to progress, uveitis can lead to breakdown of the eye's internal structures; detachment of the retina; and blindness. Treatment includes frequent application of pupil-dilating ophthalmic medications as well as anti-inflammatory preparations such as dexamethasone or prednisone on the eye and/or systemically; systemic administration of nonsteroidal anti-inflammatory medications; and detection and treatment of the underlying problem, if possible.

Vaginal hyperplasia

A condition that occurs when a female dog's vaginal lining has an abnormal response to the hormone estrogen, resulting in a mass of tissue that protrudes through the vaginal opening. It's usually especially visible during the early stages of a heat cycle, when estrogen levels are on the increase. After the heat cycle, the mass may shrink or disappear until the next cycle. Spaying is generally the treatment of choice.

Vitiligo

A skin condition characterized by smooth areas of pigment loss on various parts of the dog's body, generally around the nose, lips, and muzzle. The pads can also be involved. Can be congenital or acquired.

von Willebrand's Disease

A genetic bleeding disorder in which the blood doesn't clot normally, resulting in excessive bleeding upon injury. It's similar to hemophilia in humans. A blood test is available to determine if a dog has vWD, and support treatment is available though there is no long-term treatment. Affected dogs should be eliminated from breeding programs. Commonly affected breeds include Scottish Terriers, Chesapeake Bay Retrievers, German Shorthaired Pointers, Doberman Pinschers, Shetland Sheepdogs, Standard Poodles, and Golden Retrievers.

Whipworms

Small whip-shaped parasitic worms that attach to the wall of your dog's large intestine, where they feed on his blood. Signs of heavy infestation can include diarrhea, anemia, and weight loss. Treatment includes stool pickup and a dewormer effective against whipworms.

White dog shaker syndrome

Sudden onset of head and body tremors in adult dogs of small, white-coated breeds, such as Maltese and West Highland White Terriers. There is no known cause; treatment usually isn't necessary in mild cases.

Yeast infection

An infection that results from budding, single-celled fungal organisms that often infect moist areas, such as the ears and skin.

REFERENCES

Aiello, S.E., Mays, A., *The Merck Veterinary Manual*, 8th edition (1998); New Jersey, Merck & Co.

Bonagura, J. D., *Kirk's Current Veterinary Therapy, Small Animal Practice,* XII & XIII, (1995, 2000); Philadelphia, W.B. Saunders.

Bordwell, S., *The AAHA Encyclopedia of Dog Health & Care* (1994); New York, William Morrow.

Braund, K.G., *Clinical Syndromes in Veterinary Neurology* (1986); Baltimore, Williams & Wilkins.

Fenner, W. R., *Quick Reference To Veterinary Medicine* (1991); New York, Lippincott Co.

Ford, R.B., *Clinical Signs & Diagnosis In Small Animal Practice* (1988); New York, Churchill Livingstone, Inc.

Georgi, J.R., Georgi, M.E., *Parasitology For Veterinarians,* 5th edition (1990); Philadelphia, W.B. Saunders.

Gfeller, R.W., Messonier, S.P., *Handbook of Small Animal Toxicology & Poisonings* (1998); St. Louis, Mosby.

Kirk, R.W., Bistner, S.I., *Handbook Of Veterinary Procedures & Emergency Treatment* (1985); Philadelphia, W. B. Saunders.

Leib, M.S., Monroe, W.E., *Practical Small Animal Internal Medicine* (1997); Philadelphia, W.B. Saunders.

Morgan, R.V., *Handbook Of Small Animal Practice* (1988); New York, Churchill Livingstone.

Plunket, S.J., *Emergency Procedures For The Small Animal Veterinarian* (1993); Philadelphia, W.B. Saunders.

INDEX